AUSTRALIAN PRIVATE INTERNATIONAL LAW FOR THE 21ST CENTURY

A nation's prosperity depends not only on the willingness of its businesses to export goods and services, and of its citizens and residents to travel to take advantage of opportunities overseas, but also on the willingness of the businesses and citizens of other nations to cross the nation's borders to do business.

Economic expansion, and parallel increases in tourism and immigration have brought Australians more frequently into contact with the laws and legal systems of other nations. In particular, in recent years, trade with partners in the Asia-Pacific Region has become increasingly important to the nation's future. At the same time, Australian courts are faced with a growing number of disputes involving foreign facts and parties. In recognition of these developments, and the need to ensure that the applicable rules meet the needs both of transacting parties and society, the Attorney-General's Department launched in 2012 a full review of Australian rules of private international law.

This collection examines the state and future of Australian private international law against the background of the Attorney-General's review. The contributors approach the topic from a variety of perspectives (judge, policy-maker, practitioner, academic) and with practical and theoretical insights as to operation of private international law rules in Australia and other legal systems.

Volume 16 in the series Studies in Private International Law

Studies in Private International Law
Recent titles in the series

Volume 4: Cases and Materials on EU Private International Law
Stefania Bariatti

Volume 5: International Commercial Disputes: Commercial Conflict of Laws in English Courts
Jonathan Hill and Adeline Chong

Volume 6: International Child Abduction: The Inadequacies of the Law
Thalia Kruger

Volume 7: Mediating International Child Abduction Cases
Sarah Vigers

Volume 8: International Antitrust Litigation: Conflict of Laws and Coordination
Edited by Jürgen Basedow, Stéphanie Francq and Laurence Idot

Volume 9: The Governing Law of Companies in EU Law
Justin Borg-Barthet

Volume 10: Intellectual Property and Private International Law: Comparative Perspectives
Edited by Toshiyuki Kono

Volume 11: Child Abduction within the European Union
Katarina Trimmings

Volume 12: International Surrogacy Arrangements: Legal Regulation at the International Level
Edited by Katarina Trimmings and Paul Beaumont

Volume 13: The Hague Child Abduction Convention: A Critical Analysis
Rhona Schuz

Volume 14: Interregional Recognition and Enforcement of Civil and Commercial Judgments: Lessons for China from the US and EU Law
Jie Huang

Volume 15: The Recovery of Maintenance in the EU and Worldwide
Edited by Paul Beaumont, Burkhard Hess, Lara Walker and Stefanie Spancken

Australian Private International Law for the 21st Century

Facing Outwards

Edited by

Andrew Dickinson
Mary Keyes
and
Thomas John

·HART·
PUBLISHING
OXFORD AND PORTLAND, OREGON
2017

Hart Publishing
An imprint of Bloomsbury Publishing Plc

Hart Publishing Ltd
Kemp House
Chawley Park
Cumnor Hill
Oxford OX2 9PH
UK

Bloomsbury Publishing Plc
50 Bedford Square
London
WC1B 3DP
UK

www.hartpub.co.uk
www.bloomsbury.com

Published in North America (US and Canada) by
Hart Publishing
c/o International Specialized Book Services
920 NE 58th Avenue, Suite 300
Portland, OR 97213-3786
USA

www.isbs.com

First published in hardback, 2014
Paperback edition, 2017

British Library Cataloguing-in-Publication Data
A catalogue record for this book is available from the British Library.

ISBN: HB: 978-1-84946-625-7
PB: 978-1-50991-306-0

Typeset by Compuscript Ltd, Shannon
Printed and bound in Great Britain by
Lightning Source UK Ltd

FOREWORD

The chapters in this volume, and the Conference at which they were first presented as papers, are part of a process of wide-ranging reform of Australian private international law instituted under the auspices of the Standing Council on Law and Justice, the national body on which all Attorneys-General of our federation are represented. The authors are amongst Australia's foremost private international law scholars and the scope and depth of their learning is on full display.

The broad range of issues discussed reflects the breadth of the discipline which knows no boundary, provided there is a cross-border element—whether a transaction or relationship. The chapters discuss the coherence, consistency, clarity and appropriateness of private international law rules in each Australian jurisdiction, as well as New Zealand. They cover such matters as the scope of personal jurisdiction, the exercise of jurisdiction, choice of court, choice of law, enforcement of foreign judgments and proof of foreign law. They encompass the processes and principles applicable within the Australian federation and between the jurisdictions of that federation and international jurisdictions.

The principal focus of the chapters is on the dispute resolution mechanisms in courts, although many of the proposals have implications beyond that. The complexities and contradictions revealed in these chapters with respect to litigation in Australian courts stand in marked contrast to the coherence and simplicity of the regime for commercial arbitration, both domestic and international, where many of the problems are either irrelevant or have been satisfactorily resolved.

I have been an advocate of reform in this sphere of discourse for about a decade.[1] The issues raised in this volume offer numerous suggestions for improvement, within the context of a healthy divergence of views on some matters.

The resolution of the Standing Council on Law and Justice that initiated this reform process focuses on the micro-economic benefits that could flow from clarifying and simplifying the process of cross-border litigation. The chapters in this volume identify a range of changes which fit neatly into a micro-economic reform agenda. However, they go further and consider changes that improve

[1] See the papers listed in JJ Spigelman, 'Between the Parochial and the Cosmopolitan' in Justin T Gleeson and Ruth CA Higgins (eds), *Constituting Law: Legal Argument and Social Values* (Sydney, The Federation Press, 2011) 235, fn 2.

the efficacy and fairness of the processes involved and remedies available in cross-border dispute resolution.

Some reforms serve both purposes. For example, the incoherence of the rules for the assertion of personal jurisdiction amongst the different components of our federation adds an unnecessary level of complexity, which both increases costs and creates risks of injustice. Similarly, the insistence on proof of foreign law as a fact, on the basis of expensive expert evidence, is inappropriate in the case of jurisdictions about which Australian judges are perfectly capable of determining the law, with the assistance of counsel and English language publications.

On the other hand, the rule for the exercise of jurisdiction—the 'clearly inappropriate forum' *Voth* test[2]—can be criticised as being excessively parochial, as I have done in the past. However, the simplicity of its application, in contrast with the process, familiar in other common law jurisdictions, of determining 'the more appropriate forum', suggests that it will discourage venue disputation and is, therefore, more efficient from a micro-economic perspective. There are so few jurisdictions which adopt a cosmopolitan approach that this may be a context in which it is appropriate to maintain the present rule, with an exception where there is genuine reciprocity from the alternative forum, as has been done in the Trans-Tasman Agreement.[3]

Within the Australian federation and in relations with New Zealand the scope for significant economic benefits is present, but limited. Much of the low-hanging fruit has been picked. The greatest benefits are to be found in the international context. The costs and uncertainties associated with international litigation constitute a significant barrier to mutually beneficial exchange in trade and investment. International litigation imposes additional burdens on both trade and investment, including increased complexity, uncertainty about the ability to enforce contractual rights, additional costs of enforcement of judgments (where available at all), risks of unfamiliarity with foreign legal process and unpredictable legal exposure.

These burdens are more significant than many of the other non-tariff barriers to trade and investment which have been the focus of so much international negotiation over recent decades. As I have been emphasising for almost a decade, this barrier has never received the attention it deserves in international trade and investment negotiations.[4] So many opportunities have been lost because Attorney-General's Departments have been excluded from such negotiations.

Reform at international, regional or bilateral levels has been patchy and slow, and, when contrasted with the international commercial arbitration regime, progress borders on the pathetic. Where there are internationally accepted models, they should be embraced with alacrity. Australia's record in doing so is undistinguished. For those treaties and model laws which remain unenacted—such as

[2] *Voth v Manildra Flour Mills Pty Ltd* (1990) 171 CLR 538.

[3] Agreement between the Government of Australia and the Government of New Zealand on Trans-Tasman Court Proceedings and Regulatory Enforcement [2013] ATS 32.

[4] JJ Spigelman, 'Transaction costs and international litigation' (2006) 80 *Australian Law Journal* 438.

the Hague Convention on Choice of Court Agreements—there is no reason for further delay.

Perhaps the principal economic benefit that could flow from an activist reform programme in this area is the development of Australian legal services as a significant export industry. Given the skill and sophistication of our legal profession and judiciary, I have no doubt that this is an objective capable of achievement. However, it will require a wide-ranging commitment to abandoning numerous parochial rules and practices and overcoming the jurisdictional jealousies endemic in a federal system. The chapters in this volume identify many specific reforms which would enhance Australia's international reputation in this regard.

Our substantive laws, as well as our processes and institutions, have many strengths which could appeal to major multinational corporations. For example, our law of contractual interpretation provides a higher degree of certainty than that of many other jurisdictions. However, choosing Australian law as the law of the contract is unlikely when so much of our legislation—in consumer law and insurance contracts—treats multi-billion-dollar corporations as if they were consumers or small businesses. Choice of law is a major determinative factor in choice of professional advisers and of location, whether in litigation or arbitration.

The Conference at which these chapters were presented as papers was not the occasion on which to attempt to quantify the economic benefits of reform. This is, however, a task that must be undertaken if this process is to lead to real change. A focus on micro-economic reform, as distinct from many of the matters that concern scholars, is the only hope. The history of law reform on these matters is a cautionary tale.

Two excellent, innovative and detailed reports of the Australian Law Reform Commission on *Choice of Law*[5] and *Legal Risk in International Transactions*[6] sat on the shelf for decades, without effect. In an analogous context, a similarly innovative report on *Australia as a Financial Centre*[7] has remained un-implemented for a number of years, despite the compelling economic case which it set out. It seems that political attention is difficult to retain for any project that does not involve a hard-hat and a fluoro jacket, or at least a plaque.

This volume of excellent papers is just a start.

James Spigelman
May 2014

[5] Australian Law Reform Commission, *Choice of Law*, Report No 58 (Sydney, Commonwealth of Australia, 1992).

[6] Australian Law Reform Commission, *Legal Risk in International Transactions*, Report No 80 (Sydney, Commonwealth of Australia, 1996).

[7] Australian Financial Centre Forum, *Australia as a Financial Centre: Building on our Strengths* (Canberra, Commonwealth of Australia, 2009).

SERIES EDITORS' PREFACE

This is an edited book that helps Australia carry out its Government's desire to review private international law by reducing the legal complexity of cross-border transactions and relationships. Annex 1 to this book helpfully sets out the Australian Consultation Paper on the comprehensive review of the commercial aspects of private international law. The first chapter of the book by the government insiders responsible for the Consultation Paper (Wilkins and John) helpfully highlights the aspiration to become at least an Asia-Pacific equivalent of London for litigation services. They highlight that London's strength is as an integrated centre for commercial litigation due to its high reputation in dealing with international arbitration and court adjudication as 'complementary mechanisms'. Arbitration and court litigation in London are properly aligned and integrated in their view. They quote a figure showing that international litigation and arbitration in London was worth £20.9 billion to the UK economy in 2011. Wilkins and John see the inability to choose 'Australian' law to govern a contract (because contract law varies between the states and the territories) as a barrier to Australia being at least the regional equivalent of London. They consider the interesting possibility of creating a new federal 'Australian' law just for international transactions. The possibility is enticing but, as in the EU with the common sales law proposal, it is a very difficult task to legislate for the content of a brand new substantive contract law that the parties can select. What Australia can do much more easily is become a party to the Hague Choice of Court Agreements Convention 2005, as suggested by former Chief Justice Spigelman in the foreword to this book. This will give Australia a lead over its main regional competitors in Hong Kong, Singapore and Tokyo and give it first mover advantage in the region. It will also remove doubts about the Australian courts' commitment to party autonomy highlighted by Keyes in her previous work (see Mary Keyes, 'Jurisdiction Under the Hague Choice of Courts Convention: Its Likely Impact on Australian Practice' (2009) 5 *Journal of Private International Law* 181) although her chapter in this book is more optimistic about the Australian courts' commitment to party autonomy based on recent cases. Furthermore ratification of the Hague Convention will take advantage of the forthcoming EU adoption of the Convention (see http://www.hcch.net/index_en.php?act=events.details&year=2014&varevent=380) to secure respect in the EU courts for Australian choice of court clauses (something not likely to happen under the Brussels I Recast for choice of court clauses selecting countries that are not party to the Hague Convention).

Most of the chapters of the book give a helpful analysis of Australian private international law with a range of views emerging as to how it should be reformed. There seems to be a consensus that the very varied provisions on direct jurisdiction in the states and territories of Australia are in need of reform to provide greater legal certainty and to reduce or eliminate exorbitant fora. The work by Schoeman on New Zealand's jurisdictional reforms that entered into force in 2009 highlights how this could be done consistent with maintaining the approach of the traditional English and Welsh rules on direct jurisdiction in a sophisticated modern form. Another solution offered by Dickinson is to follow an adapted version of the EU model seen in the Brussels I Recast. Given the rather narrow nature of Australian *forum non conveniens* there are attractions to arguing for uniform Australian jurisdiction rules in non-family civil and commercial matters based on a modified EU model. Such an approach could have the following hierarchy of jurisdiction rules: a few exclusive jurisdictions (rights *in rem* in immovable property, validity of public registers and of patents, trade marks and other registered intellectual property rights), submission, protective jurisdictions for employment and consumer contracts including limited options for choice of court clauses (but not for insurance contracts in order to be a more successful legal centre for commercial as opposed to consumer insurance contracts than anywhere in the EU), choice of court, and then for all remaining cases the claimant could have a choice between the defendant's residence (rather than the existing presence test) and special jurisdictions based on the cause of action for contract, tort, trusts, branches and restitution and for closely related actions involving multiple defendants. Australia can take some inspiration from the special jurisdiction rules in the Brussels I Recast but it can also be inspired by the best of the common law rules. As Australia is not part of a regional integration system (apart from with New Zealand which is ably described in two chapters in this book) it seems highly unlikely that it would abandon *forum non conveniens* in favour of a non-discretionary *lis pendens*. To keep litigation costs down it might be very wise to retain the current restrictive approach to *forum non conveniens* and thereby attract claimants to choose to litigate in Australia knowing that they are unlikely to be sent away if they meet one of the jurisdiction tests.

The book is obviously a must for people interested in Australian private international law but there is much for all of us to ponder about how to reform the system of private international law in a common law country and how to make a legal system competitive for international legal business in the twenty-first century.

Paul Beaumont, University of Aberdeen
Jonathan Harris, King's College, London

PREFACE

In October 2012, acting on the collective initiative of the justice ministers of Australia, her States and Territories and New Zealand as members of the Standing Council on Law and Justice, the Commonwealth Attorney-General's Department launched a public consultation on the possibility of major reforms to the rules of private international law applied by Australian courts. Its consultation paper (reproduced in Annex I below) reflected a growing consensus that the current rules applied by State and Territory courts, and particularly the differences between them, were unsuited to the modernised globalised economy and damaging to Australia's reputation as a centre of legal excellence.

Prompted by the consultation, Sydney and Griffith Law Schools organised a well-received two day conference, held in Sydney in April 2013, focusing on the state and future shape of private international law in Australia and the wider Asia-Pacific Region in the 21st century. This collection represents the fruits of that event.

The first day of the conference brought together experts in the field from Australia, Asia and Europe taking part in four speaker panels, bookended by two keynote addresses. In his opening address, Roger Wilkins AO, Secretary to the Attorney-General's Department, outlined an ambitious vision for the future development of the Australian legal infrastructure for handling cross-border disputes and transactions, highlighting among possible policy options a major overhaul of substantive and/or private international law rules, changes to the judicial system and reform of the legal profession (see Chapter 1). In his concluding address, the Hon James Allsop AO, Chief Justice of the Federal Court of Australia, offered a biting critique of the current state of Australian private international law, focusing on the shortcomings in the personal jurisdiction regime, and urging swift action to reconcile the currently divergent approaches among the states and territories (see Chapter 3).

The remaining papers in this collection present different perspectives on the reform process. Professor Mary Keyes (Chapter 2) presents a broad overview of the key topics, identifying improvements that she considers as matters of priority. Dr Andrew Bell SC (Chapter 4) focuses on the rules of personal jurisdiction, decrying the current fragmentation and offering a way forward based on the best features of the existing rules. Professor Richard Garnett (Chapter 5) examines the role of the objective of securing a uniform outcome in litigation in the development of Australian choice of law rules. The focus then turns to the Agreement Between the Government of Australia and the Government of New Zealand on

Trans-Tasman Court Proceedings and Regulatory Enforcement, only recently in force, with Professor Reid Mortensen (Chapter 7) and David Goddard QC (Chapter 8) offering perspectives from opposite sides of the Tasman Sea. The final section offers a comparative perspective. Professor Andrew Dickinson (Chapter 9) gives a European perspective on the issues raised by the Attorney-General's Consultation Paper, and Elsabe Schoeman and Adeline Chong (Chapter 10) use recent developments in New Zealand and Singapore to cast a light on the reform process.

The Attorney-General's project having reached the end of its first stage, the next steps in the process are eagerly awaited by many. Although the authors within this collection do not agree on every aspect of the treatment, they do agree that reform is essential. This is particularly the case in the area of personal jurisdiction, where the lack of uniformity in the approach taken by Australian courts, and occasional parochiality in their judgments, have often been criticised. From the editors' perspective, it is hoped that the time and resources of the Australian Governments and Parliaments will be devoted to progressing the reforms necessary to make Australia a jurisdiction of choice for parties entering into commercial transactions in the region.

Andrew Dickinson and Mary Keyes, as organisers of the conference, are grateful to the Attorney-General's Department for its generous sponsorship and to members of the Sydney Law School Events team, in particular to Ariane Wicks, for their excellent work in ensuring that the event ran smoothly. All three of us would like to acknowledge the assistance that we have received in putting together this publication. Our contributors have given generously of their time and expertise. In addition, we have been ably supported by colleagues and by the publishing team at Hart, with particular mention to Rishi Gulati at the Attorney-General's Department.

Chapter 5 and part of chapter 9 are based on articles first published in the *Australian Bar Review* and *New Zealand Law Review* respectively, and material in those chapters is reproduced with the kind permission of the journal editors.

Andrew Dickinson
Oxford

Mary Keyes
Brisbane

Thomas John
The Hague

August 2014

CONTENTS

Part IV—Drawing from Overseas Perspectives

LIST OF CONTRIBUTORS

The Honourable James Allsop AO
Chief Justice of the Federal Court of Australia

Andrew Bell SC
Barrister, Eleven Wentworth Chambers; Adjunct Professor of Law, University of Sydney

Adeline Chong
Associate Professor of Law, Singapore Management University

Andrew Dickinson
Fellow and Tutor, St Catherine's College and Professor of Law, University of Oxford

Richard Garnett
Professor of Law, University Of Melbourne; Consultant, Herbert Smith Freehills

David Goddard QC
Barrister, New Zealand

Thomas John
ACIArb, former Principal Legal Officer, Private International Law and Commercial Arbitration Section, Australian Attorney-General's Department

Mary Keyes
Professor, Griffith University

Reid Mortensen
Professor of Law, University of Southern Queensland, Toowoomba, Australia

Elsabe Schoeman
Associate Professor, Faculty of Law, University of Auckland

Daniel Ward
Associate to the Hon Chief Justice James Allsop AO

Roger Wilkins AO
Secretary, Australian Attorney-General's Department

TABLE OF CASES

Australia

Canada

Court of Justice of the European Union (formerly European Court of Justice)

France

Ireland

New Zealand

Singapore

United Kingdom (including decisions of the Privy Council)

United States of America

TABLE OF LEGISLATION

Australia

Barbados

Canada

European Union

Treaties

Decisions

Directives

Regulations

France

Germany

Japan

Netherlands

New Zealand

Republic of China

Republic of Korea

Singapore

Switzerland

United Kingdom

Statutory Instruments

United States of America

Agreements, Conventions and other Instruments

I

The Agenda for Change

1

Facing Outwards: Australian Private International Law in the 21st Century

ROGER WILKINS AO AND THOMAS JOHN

I. Introduction

In an ever more globalised world, with the markets of many economies interconnected by international free trade agreements, the concept of borders defining the nation state as we know it loses its significance as a barrier to the movement of goods, services, capital and people. Modern information technologies, especially the internet, sophisticated global transport networks and world-wide banking systems, all have contributed to this development. The multi-national corporation, the traditional player in the international arena, is now joined by the 'multinational consumer'.

As a result, businesses and individuals alike increasingly require fresh policy and legal approaches that meet the challenges posed by these cross-border commercial activities. The countries which understand the imperative to accommodate the needs of those engaged in cross-border commercial activities have embraced this development. They see it as an opportunity to expand markets, to attract new business and skills, and to boost their economies.

Establishing and maintaining a regulatory environment conducive to cross-border commercial activities can be seen as a locational advantage for individual states. Astute parties consider which regulatory regimes benefit their commercial activity most when deciding on entering into a cross-border business deal. The ability of businesses to make informed choices between different jurisdictions based on economic considerations can lead to the so-called phenomena of 'regulatory arbitrage' and 'regulatory competition'.[1] This commoditisation of legal systems has also resulted in the emergence of a global market for legal services.[2]

[1] S Vogenauer, 'Regulatory Competition through Choice of Contract Law and Choice of Forum in Europe: Theory and Evidence' (2013) 1 *European Review of Private Law* 13.

[2] H Eidenmüller, 'Regulatory Competition in Contract Law and Dispute Resolution' in H Eidenmüller, *Regulatory Competition in Contract Law and Dispute Resolution* (Oxford, Hart Publishing, 2013) ch 1. See also the brochure 'Law made in Germany', issued by the Alliance for German

For policy-makers, the question is how to approach the differences between different states' legal systems. Do we see difference as a problem, or an opportunity?

A. The Task

The question highlights the nature of the puzzle policy-makers have to solve. On the one hand, the differences between legal systems can pose significant problems. They act as barriers to cross-border commercial and investment activities by increasing a range of risks for participants, including transactional risks, dispute resolution risks, and litigation and enforcement risks. These risks can lead to high transactional and dispute resolution costs. In extreme circumstances, they can prevent parties from transacting altogether. Left unaddressed, the differences between legal systems can have a chilling effect on cross-border trade and investment.

At the same time, the challenge for policy-makers is not necessarily to eliminate all difference. The right sort of difference can give a country like Australia a valuable comparative advantage. Crafting a distinct legal regime in such a fashion that it becomes an attractive choice for parties can draw transactions and prospective litigants to Australia's shores, opening new opportunities. With 'quasi-entrepreneurial' thinking,[3] policy-makers can unlock these opportunities, turning a legal system into an important engine-room for the economy. It can also provide fertile ground for a thriving legal profession that looks after the legal needs of domestic and international businesses and for a strong judiciary, experienced in resolving international commercial disputes.

To take advantage of such opportunities, Australia will need to take a fresh look at its laws dealing with international commercial transactions and disputes. It will be necessary to identify those areas that require reform to offer those trading and investing across borders modernised and internationalised approaches and solutions. To do this requires that we analyse other jurisdictions that are recognised leaders in successfully attracting commercial activities to their shores.

II. What Makes a Successful Market for International Commercial Transactions?

Accepting that the architecture of the domestic legal system can stimulate the economy, including through regulatory competition, we need to ask how a modern system must look for it to be chosen by parties and thus to emerge as a player in

Law and supported by the German Federal Minister for Justice, available at: www.lawmadeingermany.de/, last accessed 16 May 2014.

[3] W Schön, 'Playing Different Games? Regulatory Competition in Tax and Company Law Compared' (2005) 42 *Common Market Law Review* 331, 332–34.

the global transactional market. Plainly, this is a difficult task for policy-makers. The task is characterised by the need to juggle several dichotomies. To name only a few, the legal system of the twenty-first century remains domestic in nature, but it must have a global outlook. It has to provide a high degree of certainty for parties, while being flexible enough to accommodate choices and allow context-driven, commercial solutions. The proceedings must be transparent, while providing parties with sufficient confidentiality, and the jurisdiction needs to champion efficient and early resolution of disputes while ensuring that courts maintain high levels of skills and expertise.

In early 2013, the Australian Attorney-General's Department took steps to gain a better understanding of why certain jurisdictions are more successful than others in attracting commercial activities as preferred jurisdictions for cross-border transactions and dispute resolution. The aims were (1) to identify possible characteristics that make a jurisdiction an attractive commercial destination, and (2) to determine whether there are any such characteristics common to all of those jurisdictions. The Department's Private International Law Section conducted the research. It selected four jurisdictions which are well-known centres of commercial activities and disputes: New York, London, Hong Kong and Singapore.

After reviewing a number of detailed analyses and surveys, the Private International Law Section found that these jurisdictions feature a distinctive, established and well-developed substantive commercial law that is international in outlook and that is characterised by clear, stable and predictable rules and principles that reflect accepted international commercial standards and usages. These rules and principles enshrine a commitment to contractual freedom and party autonomy. These principles are central to those jurisdictions' appeal; interference with them is limited.

In addition, the legal professions in all four jurisdictions are renowned for being experienced in handling complex international commercial transactions and disputes and for being well versed in the business practices of many industries. Also, in all four jurisdictions, arbitration and litigation processes are well integrated. Litigation regimes are strong and efficient, with reliable civil procedure rules to ensure that disputes can be resolved quickly and cheaply. Strong, highly-qualified, professional and independent judiciaries anchor arbitration and preside over litigation. The presence in these jurisdictions of internationally recognised and renowned legal institutions ensures a constant drive towards optimising these jurisdictions' commercial law regimes.

The Private International Law Section also found that the reviewed jurisdictions have a cohesive and holistic approach to the design of laws governing international commercial transactions. Private international law rules and principles, aimed at coordinating different legal systems, are an integral part of this approach. The resolution of disputes arising from international commercial transactions is based on an integrated regime: the reviewed jurisdictions do not focus on dispute settlement through arbitration alone, but understand their domestic courts system as being central to ensuring their strength as arbitration centres, including by providing foreign parties with easy access to the courts. London may serve as an example here: dispute settlement by arbitration and by litigation, the latter taking place in specialised commercial courts, are not understood as competing with one another. Rather, they are viewed as complementary mechanisms that, if properly aligned and integrated, can provide parties with fast, efficient and cost-effective solutions to their problems. The efficiency of both litigation and arbitration is ensured through regimes that allow for the prompt and cost-efficient recognition and enforcement of foreign judgments and arbitral awards.

A. A Matrix to Review Australia's International Commercial Transactions Law

These characteristics and approaches identified in New York, London, Hong Kong and Singapore provide a useful matrix against which Australia can review its international commercial legal system. They can provide a baseline against which it is possible to improve the current system's credentials. Done properly, this exercise can establish Australia as a successful player in the regional and global market for commercial transactions and, thus, as a prime choice for businesses.

The following section will describe some of the areas that could become, at some stage in the future, part of a larger reform package that aims at developing an Australian 'International Commercial Law'. However, the section is subject to two important caveats. First, any reform effort in this area needs to appreciate that what may be labelled 'International Commercial Law', is a complex bundle of closely related and interwoven subject-matters—including contract, private international, civil procedure and arbitration law, and related subject-matters such as financial, insurance, banking, company and corporations law, to name only a few. Secondly, this chapter is not aimed at foreshadowing any specific reforms—rather, what follows is a consideration of possible issues that may be worth exploring further. While plainly, other areas will also need to be considered if the maximum effect of reforms is to be realised, the following section focuses on four central building blocks that may warrant closer examination in the future or which are already subject to reform efforts: a reform of the private international law regime; the development of an international contract law; the strengthening of the Australian court system; and ongoing improvements to Australia's arbitration regime.

III. Private International Law Reform

Many will recall Professor Prosser's famous description of private international law as: 'a dismal swamp, filled with quaking quagmires, and inhabited by learned but eccentric professors who theorize about mysterious matters in a strange and incomprehensible jargon'.[4] Today, this description regularly serves as an entertaining quip, rather than as an illuminating observation. Private international law has come of age.

A. The Increasing Importance of Private International Law

The transformation of private international law from a dismal swamp to a blooming, cultivated landscape can be highlighted by three recent examples. First, regarding the public/private international law divide, Professor McLachlan QC suggested the development of a 'foreign relations law', using private international law as a 'technique' that allocates 'competence and applicable law in cases involving the external exercise of the public power of states'.[5] Secondly, also dealing with the interface between public and private international law, the US Supreme Court recently looked at the interaction between private international law and human rights in relation to commercial activities of multi-national corporations.[6] And, thirdly, a considerable number of legal scholars have observed the constitutionalisation of private law through private international law, and the increasing use of private international law as a global governance and accountability tool. They recognise that: 'a large part of the accounting, quality, safety, social and environmental standards that regulate the global economy is set and monitored by private or hybrid associations and networks'.[7]

Australia's private international law rules and principles have developed under the common law, augmented by the implementation of international instruments and occasional legislative intervention.[8] This development of new, and the reform of existing, rules and principles has been ad hoc. In many cases, the rules and principles have not evolved and have not been adapted so that they would be able to respond to accelerated cross-border trade and investment, to the new digital environment and globalisation in general.

Identifying this incoherent and uncoordinated development as a problem, while demonstrating an appreciation for the increasing importance of private international law, the Australian Standing Council on Law and Justice (SCLJ) agreed that a consultation should determine whether the harmonisation of Australia's private international law principles and rules, such as those governing jurisdiction, choice of forum and choice of law, would deliver worthwhile micro-

[4] WL Prosser, 'Interstate Publication' (1953) 51 *Michigan Law Review* 959, 971.

[5] C McLachlan QC, 'The Allocative Function of Foreign Relations Law' (2011) 82 *British Yearbook of Internationl Law* 349.

[6] *Kiobel v Royal Dutch Petroleum Co*, 569 US ___; 133 S Ct 1659 (2013).

[7] H Schepel, 'Rules of Recognition: A Legal Constructivist Approach to Transnational Private Regulation' in P Jurcys et al, *Regulatory Hybridization in the Transnational Sphere: Developments in International Law* (Leiden, Martinus Nijhoff, 2013) 189.

[8] See generally Australian Law Reform Commission, *Choice of Law*, Report No 58 (Sydney, Commonwealth of Australia, 1992) and Australian Law Reform Commission, *Legal Risk in International Transactions*, Report No 80 (Sydney, Commonwealth of Australia, 1996).

economic benefits for the community. The Australian Standing Council on Law and Justice also mandated that any such reform should take account of solutions adopted by other legal systems and international developments.[9] The results of consultation undertaken through this SCLJ reform project were at the time of writing this chapter in May 2014 under consideration by the Australian Attorney-General's Department. The SCLJ reform project precedes, yet fits neatly into, the Department's broader efforts regarding Australia's international commercial transactions law.[10]

B. Reforming Australia's Private International Law

There are two particularly important aspects that make private international law rules and principles important for policy developers. First, although it is called private 'international' law, the subject-matter itself is inherently domestic law. Thus, policy-makers can adjust private international law and fine-tune the way the rules and principles operate. Secondly, rather than focusing on important, yet time- and resource-intensive unification and harmonisation efforts, policy-makers can utilise private international law to coordinate outcomes between different legal systems. Effective private international law regimes provide clear and certain answers to questions such as which law applies to a transaction and in what forum is a dispute to be resolved. They can also ensure that parties are able to predict with greater clarity and certainty whether the rulings of domestic courts can be enforced in foreign fora. Therefore, a well-designed private international regime can be a fast and cost-effective alternative to unification and harmonisation efforts that are traditionally used to effectively reduce, or even eliminate, existing barriers to trade and investment.

Apart from supplying the rules and principles that provide these answers and allow parties to make these predictions, private international law can also provide clarity, certainty and cost-effectiveness by giving primacy to the parties' choices expressed in their international commercial transactions. The efficacy of such choices is paramount. There is sound evidence to suggest that choice in international commercial transactions, especially in the form of a choice of the applicable law, is of great importance to most parties.[11] Even though parties are

[9] For more information, see Attorney-General's Department Consultation Paper, *Reducing legal complexity of cross-border transactions and relationships: Driving micro-economic reform through the establishment of more cohesive and clearer jurisdictional, applicable law and choice of court rules*, Annex 1 to this volume, pp 1 and 2.

[10] See the comments concerning a possible larger reform package that aims at developing an Australian 'International Commercial Law' referred to under 'A matrix to review Australia's international commercial transactions law', above Section II.A.

[11] Queen Mary University of London, School of International Arbitration, *2010 International Arbitration: Choices in International Arbitration*, available at: www.arbitration.qmul.ac.uk/research/2010/index.html, last accessed 16 May 2014.

likely to favour their domestic law, and lawyers tend to advise clients to choose their domestic law as it is their field of expertise,[12] research also suggests that many businesses conclude contracts containing a choice of a foreign law.[13] For example, a review of standard contractual terms under German law suggested that they discourage parties from choosing German law and encourage them to choose a foreign law instead.[14]

C. Challenges for Policy-makers

For policy-makers, the question then arises: what are the reasons that govern parties' choices? The analysis of data collected in a range of different surveys conducted in Europe suggests that parties are primarily keen to exploit their 'home advantage': parties choose their domestic law and courts with which they are familiar.[15] Alternatively, provided that both parties have equal bargaining power, parties will resort to their 'second best strategy', selecting a jurisdiction they consider 'neutral'. This neutral jurisdiction is often one that most closely resemblances the jurisdiction with which the parties are familiar. It is also one that is known to be frequently chosen by other 'users' of the system—the so-called 'network effect'.[16] Other recent research concludes that the parties' choices are governed by primary factors such as 'familiarity, neutrality and linguistic accessibility', followed by a subsidiary set of more subjective factors such as 'sophistication, fairness and accuracy'.[17]

These factors are important indicators. They reflect characteristics that underpin legal systems. Importantly, they are characteristics over which policy-makers have influence. Of course, the factors are amorphous and their manipulation presents challenges. But carefully considered, appropriate policies can increase the attractiveness of a legal system and induce parties to choose one legal system over others. This choice can result in healthy competition between legal systems with considerable economic benefits, especially for the legal industry. For example, in 2011, the UK Government announced that domestic legal services generated

[12] G Rühl, 'Regulatory Competition in Contract Law: Empirical Evidence and Normative Implications' (2013) 9 *European Review of Contract Law* 61, 67, 89.

[13] S Vogenauer and C Hodges, 'Civil Justice Systems in Europe: Implications for Choice of Law and Choice of Forum—A Business Survey' (Oxford, University of Oxford, 2008) 13. This survey is available at: denning.law.ox.ac.uk/iecl/ocjsurvey.shtml, last accessed 16 May 2014.

[14] H Eidenmüller, 'The Transnational Law Market, Regulatory Competition, and Transnational Corporations' (2011) 18 *Indiana Journal of Global Legal Studies* 707, 747. This research also shows that Swiss and English law have the reputation of granting parties greater autonomy and are therefore chosen more frequently, including by foreign parties.

[15] Similar observations were made by C Fountoulakis, 'The Parties' Choice of "Neutral Law" in International Sales Contracts' (2005) 7 *European Journal of Law Reform* 303, 304.

[16] Vogenauer, above n 1, 25.

[17] ibid, 26.

£20.9 billion for the British economy.[18] There are further, ancillary effects of choice that are positive for an economy. For example, jurisdictions of choice for commercial transactions report a strengthening of their judiciary's expertise and experience in dealing with commercial disputes, a result of regular exposure to frequently complex commercial litigation. Judges carry the benefit of this experience into their dealings with domestic commercial disputes.

Reforming Australia's private international law should be the first step in any effort to capitalise on the opportunities discussed at the beginning of this paper. Any reform in this space must be undertaken with one key aim in mind: to enhance the predictability of outcomes for parties in cross-border relationships and transactions by providing for clear, certain, simple, predictable and accessible law. If reform is conducted in line with this imperative, then private international law can play a crucial rôle in attracting parties to Australia and transforming our jurisdiction into an important part of the global market.

D. Further Opportunities for Australia

Reforming private international law is necessary, but on its own not sufficient, if we wish to create a legal system that can attract transactions and prospective litigants to Australia's shores. As noted above, the jurisdictions that are currently successful in attracting international commercial activities take a cohesive and holistic approach to the design of laws governing such transactions. Only if we adopt a similarly coordinated approach will it be possible to fully realise the available benefits.

Therefore, the following will consider briefly three further areas in which reform may be useful: the development of an international contract law, the strengthening of the Australian court system and ongoing improvements to Australia's arbitration regime.

E. An International Commercial Contract Law

Undoubtedly, contracts are at the heart of international commercial law. They are the very basis for international commercial transactions and the starting point for dispute resolution. However, as the result of Australia's constitutional settings, there is currently no 'Australian Contract Law' as such. Rather, due to Australia's federal structure, parties are not able to simply select Australian law to govern their dealings. Instead, parties must specify which State or Territory law will govern their contract. Also, none of Australia's domestic contract laws are especially

[18] Ministry of Justice, 'UK Legal Services on the International Stage: Underpinning growth and stability', strategy paper, published 14 March 2013, 2, available at: www.gov.uk/government/uploads/system/uploads/attachment_data/file/219802/legal-services-action-plan-0313.pdf, last accessed 16 May 2014.

well adapted to the international context in which many commercial transactions nowadays unfold.

Rather than seeking to replace, augment or harmonise existing domestic contract laws, it may be worth considering the development of an international contract law that would govern a more limited species of contracts: those that are transnational, perhaps concerning only certain transactions and which may be entered into only by defined categories of corporations. Such a law could be designed to apply only by consent, with the choice to opt-in exercisable by domestic or international parties—for the latter irrespective of their connection with the jurisdiction. It may be designed to factor in the fact that many of our regional partners do not share our common law traditions, but rather are steeped in the civil law tradition. A confluence of those traditions, while in parts perhaps contentious, could address existing differences between legal systems and remove some of the barriers that still have dilatory effects on cross-border trade, commerce and investment.

The creation of such a law could have significant advantages, including its simplicity and the potential attractiveness to foreign contracting parties. But because there is clear evidence that a choice of law often goes hand in hand with the corresponding choice of forum, the ability to choose an Australian Contract Law could also be an essential building block for establishing Australia as a prime location for commercial dispute resolution.

F. Strengthening the Role of the Courts

In his seminal work on international commercial litigation, Professor Fentiman noted succinctly that 'the purpose of litigation is settlement'.[19] Indeed, one does not need to be a soothsayer to predict that the trend toward international commercial disputes being resolved either by negotiation and compromise, or by more formal alternative dispute resolution mechanisms such as arbitration, will continue. However, as noted above, despite its private, consensual nature, arbitration does not occur in an unregulated vacuum—the role of the domestic courts at the place of arbitration is relevant to the quality of the arbitration regime itself. Therefore, the role of courts in resolving international commercial disputes will continue to be very important.

This is a particularly challenging area for Australia, given the number of different superior courts we have. Innovative means to make the most of our expertise across different courts merit consideration. These encompass the respective roles of different courts, and the liaison arrangements between them.

Another measure we are studying closely is the advent of so-called 'solicitor-advocates', ie foreign legal practitioners, who, in relation to certain specific matters, are granted special rights of appearance before Australian courts. This

[19] R Fentiman, *International Commercial Litigation* (Oxford, Oxford University Press, 2010) xi.

exclusive grant would be based on the practitioner's significant experience in resolving commercial disputes. Of particular interest could be to permit experienced foreign arbitration lawyers to appear before Australian courts, for example, 'to deal directly with urgent court applications and court enforcement issues relating to arbitration without the need to instruct a new [Australian] party'.[20] This could be beneficial to Australian courts, including through increasing procedural efficiencies; but such a measure could also generate certain economic benefits for clients, including a reduction in the costs associated with briefing counsel. Solicitor-advocates already practise in London, and in March 2013, Hong Kong followed with the appointment of 15 solicitor-advocates.

G. International Commercial Arbitration

Arbitration offers a flexible, neutral and private mechanism to resolve international commercial disputes. Importantly, agreements to arbitrate and resulting foreign arbitral awards can be enforced around much of the world under the New York Convention.[21] In recent years, there has been significant work to promote Australia as a regional centre for international arbitration. A number of further initiatives have been identified that can contribute to the ongoing promotion of Australia as a hub for international commercial dispute resolution, including arbitration. However, policy-makers also need to remember that inward-looking, 'domestic' approaches, which ignore the broader regional and global context in which trade, commerce and investment occur, are likely to isolate Australia. A good understanding of other legal systems, combined with an appreciation that common law legal systems are a minority within the region,[22] is essential to good policy-making in this area of law. As with contract law, in relation to arbitration it will be essential to work towards alleviating key differences between systems so that existing legal barriers are reduced or eliminated altogether.

IV. Conclusion

Australia is part of global, as well as significant regional, markets for commercial transactions. It needs to position itself well in relation to other jurisdictions in order to boost the capacity of our legal and judicial system and to enhance its attractiveness to domestic and foreign parties. A programme of international

[20] Y Kriegler, 'Battlegrounds', *The Lawyer*, 25 March 2013, available at: www.thelawyer.com/battlegrounds/3002574.article, last accessed 16 May 2014.

[21] United Nations Convention on the Recognition and Enforcement of Foreign Arbitral Awards 1958.

[22] D Jones, 'Tapping Asia's Growth: Harmonising Arbitral Procedure across the Asia Region' (2013) 79 *Arbitration* 413, 413.

commercial law reform that takes a coherent and holistic approach, with modern, clear and certain private international law rules and principles, would provide clearer and more certain transactional settings. This would allow parties to choose and better control the shape of their own agreements. This would not only avoid the frustration of parties' expectations, but would also reduce transaction costs and increase the economic efficiency of commercial transactions.

The challenges in this area are large, but the opportunities are even larger.

2

Improving Australian Private International Law

MARY KEYES

I. Introduction

Much attention has been devoted in the last 10 years to reforming private international law at the multilateral and regional levels as well as in many different countries. While these efforts have been concentrated in Europe,[1] there have also been important reforms in several Asian countries. Three of Australia's major trading partners in the region[2] have recently introduced legislation dealing with various aspects of private international law.[3] Australian private international law is mainly derived from case law, much of which is based on the English common law.[4] There have been some significant recent changes to the Australian law, particularly

[1] In this chapter, I refer in particular to Regulation (EC) No 593/2008 of the European Parliament and of the Council of 17 June 2008 on the law applicable to contractual obligations [2008] OJ L177/6 (Rome I Regulation) and Regulation (EC) No 864/2007 of the European Parliament and of the Council of 11 July 2007 on the law applicable to non-contractual obligations [2007] OJ L199/40 (Rome II Regulation). As to the implications for future reform of Australian principles of jurisdiction of Council Regulation (EC) No 44/2001 of 22 December 2000 on jurisdiction and the recognition of judgments in civil and commercial matters [2001] OJ L12/1 (Brussels I Regulation, now recast as Council Regulation (EU) No 1215/2012 [2012] OJ L351/1), see M Keyes, *Jurisdiction in International Litigation* (Sydney, Federation Press, 2005) 229–36 (Keyes, *Jurisdiction in International Litigation*). See also A Dickinson, 'What, if anything, can Australia learn from the EU experience?', Chapter eight in this volume.

[2] China, Japan and the Republic of Korea are Australia's top three export markets. In 2012 they accounted for 50.1% of Australia's total exports: Department of Foreign Affairs and Trade, *Composition of Trade Australia 2012* (Canberra, Commonwealth of Australia, 2013) 19. In 2012, they were Australia's first, second and fourth two-way trading partners, accounting for 37% of total two-way trade: ibid.

[3] The Law of the People's Republic of China on the Laws Applicable to Foreign-Related Civil Relations 2010; the Japanese Act on the General Rules of Application of Laws, Law No 10 of 1898 (as newly titled and amended 21 June 2006) and the Japanese Law to Amend Certain Parts of the Code of Civil Procedure and the Civil Provisional Penalties Act 2011; and the Korean Conflict of Laws Act 2001.

[4] As late as 1991, Sykes and Pryles noted that 'Until recently there were few reported Australian cases and English cases were largely followed': *Australian Private International Law*, 3rd edn (Sydney, Law Book Co, 1991) 2.

affecting the rules of jurisdiction and choice of law in tort claims, but there has never been a systematic review of all three areas of jurisdiction, judgments and choice of law. The Australian Standing Council on Law and Justice[5] project[6] invites critical reflection as to the form as well as the substance of Australian private international law, including what might be learnt from recent international developments.[7] The Australian law would benefit from such a study, in terms of refining the law, improving its internal coherence and ensuring its currency.

This chapter is presented in five sections. Section II describes the existing Australian law of jurisdiction and the treatment of foreign and sister-State judgments. Section III critically analyses the contract, tort and family choice of law rules and considers the inter-relationship between choice of law, jurisdiction and judgments in each of those three areas. Section IV proposes possible reforms to the Australian law and considers the advantages of codifying the Australian law. Section V is a conclusion.

II. Jurisdiction and Judgments

A. Jurisdiction

In Australia, as in other common law countries, jurisdictional competency is addressed separately from the courts' discretion whether to exercise its jurisdiction. Most of the recent legislative changes to Australian private international law have been in the area of jurisdiction. Many of these changes are problematic, as appears below.

The scheme of the Australian law is now effectively largely or totally to dispense with jurisdictional limitations at the stage of competency, and to expect that the courts will prevent inappropriate assertions of jurisdiction if and when the defendant raises an objection to jurisdiction.[8]

[5] This is a forum for the Australian federal, State and Territory Attorneys-General, which is also attended by the Minister of Justice of New Zealand. It has been involved in developing uniform and model laws in a range of areas, including defamation and evidence.

[6] In April 2012, the Standing Council on Law and Justice determined to establish a working group to consider whether 'harmonisation of jurisdictional, choice of court and choice of law rules would deliver worthwhile micro-economic benefits for the community': *Communiqué*, 12–13 April 2012. As at February 2014, this project was in progress: consult.govspace.gov.au/pil/, last accessed 12 February 2014.

[7] In this chapter, I focus on recent legislation in China, the European Union, Japan and the Republic of Korea.

[8] It is possible for the court to review its jurisdiction on its own motion if it considers that the proceedings are an abuse of its process. See also Jurisdiction of Courts (Cross-vesting) Act 1987 (Cth) s 5(7) (recognising that the court may transfer proceedings on its own motion).

(i) *Personal Jurisdiction*

The courts' competency principally depends on its personal jurisdiction over the parties. The common law rules establishing the courts' competency are unchanged from the nineteenth-century English rules, requiring either that the defendant has submitted to the court's jurisdiction or that service of initiating process has been made while the defendant was within the territorial jurisdiction of the court.[9] The common law default rule requiring the defendant's presence is no longer significant in most cases because of the legislation which has substantially expanded the courts' jurisdiction.[10] Different legislation is relevant in international, intranational and New Zealand cases, which are next addressed, in turn.

(a) **Jurisdiction in International Cases**

In most international cases,[11] personal jurisdiction is established by service out of the jurisdiction pursuant to the rules of court, a form of delegated legislation which is made by Rules Committees of the courts.[12] The rules of court permit service *ex iuris* on many bases, several of which are extremely broad. In every jurisdiction except Western Australia, the court is competent to deal with tort claims[13] where the claimant claims to have suffered some loss or injury within the forum, irrespective of where the tort occurred.[14] Other rules require merely trivial connections: in two jurisdictions, service out of the jurisdiction is permitted in contract cases if *either* party is resident in or carries on business within the jurisdiction.[15] In the majority of jurisdictions, the rules have been amended

[9] *Laurie v Carroll* (1958) 98 CLR 310.

[10] This rule remains significant for the purposes of the recognition of foreign judgments, as discussed further below at II.B.

[11] Different regimes apply for international cases involving New Zealand (below at II.A.(i).(c)) and family cases (below at text to n 18).

[12] The relevant rules are of the Federal Court of Australia (which apply also to the High Court of Australia, which exercises only a very limited original jurisdiction: High Court Rules 2004, r 9.07.1) and of the six State and two Territory Supreme Courts. In this chapter, by way of example I refer to provisions of the Federal Court Rules 2011 (Cth) and the Uniform Civil Procedure Rules 2005 (NSW). There are some significant differences between the nine different sets of rules. For detailed references see M Davies, AS Bell and PLG Brereton, *Nygh's Conflict of Laws in Australia*, 9th edn (Sydney, LexisNexis Butterworths, 2014) 50–73, Reid Mortensen et al, *Private International Law in Australia*, 2nd edn (Sydney, LexisNexis Butterworths, 2011) 52–76.

[13] The most common statutory claim, for misleading or deceptive conduct under the Australian Consumer Law 2010 s 18(1) (which replaced the Trade Practices Act 1974 (Cth) s 52(1)), is usually analogised to tort, for the purposes of jurisdiction: *Commonwealth Bank v White* [1999] 2 VR 681, 697–99.

[14] The rules of court in all Australian jurisdictions except Western Australia permit service of process out of the jurisdiction in such cases: eg Federal Court Rules 2011 (Cth) r 10.42(5); Court Procedures Rules 2006 (ACT) r 6501(1)(l); Uniform Civil Procedure Rules 2005 (NSW) r 11.2(1), Sch 6(e). The requirement of local loss or damage is liberally interpreted: *Flaherty v Girgis* (1985) 4 NSWLR 248, *Colosseum Investment Holdings Pty Ltd v Vanguard Logistics Services Pty Ltd* [2005] NSWSC 803.

[15] Court Procedures Rules 2006 (ACT) r 6501(1)(g)(ii); Uniform Civil Procedure Rules 1999 (Qld) r 124(1)(g)(ii).

to dispense with the requirement that the claimant seek prior leave to serve out of the jurisdiction.[16] This requirement was recently reinstated in the Northern Territory rules,[17] which is a promising reversal of the earlier trend.

The rules relevant to the jurisdictional competency of the courts exercising family jurisdiction are even broader than the rules applicable in other civil matters. The courts' jurisdiction depends solely on the personal connections of either party,[18] and for all matters aside from divorce applications, the mere presence of the applicant at the time proceedings are initiated is sufficient to establish jurisdiction. On the other hand, submission has not been accepted as a basis of jurisdiction in the family jurisdiction.[19]

(b) Jurisdiction in Intra-national Cases

The rules relating to personal jurisdiction of the courts in intra-Australian litigation are even broader. The federal Service and Execution of Process Act of 1992 replaced legislation of the same name enacted in 1901, on the recommendation of the Australian Law Reform Commission.[20] The 1901 legislation resembled the rules applicable in international litigation, in that it limited the jurisdiction of Australian courts to cases in which there was a connection between the forum and the parties or the subject-matter of the dispute.[21] The 1992 legislation is quite different. It allows service of the process of any Australian court anywhere within Australia, with no requirement of nexus between the forum and the parties or the subject-matter of the dispute, and no requirement of leave to serve out or of leave to proceed in the absence of an appearance.[22] This scheme assumes that inappropriate assertions of jurisdiction will be deterred or remedied by the transfer or stay of proceedings.[23]

[16] Leave to serve out is required in the Federal Court, the Northern Territory and Western Australia: Federal Court Rules 2011 (Cth) r 10.43; Supreme Court Rules 2012 (NT) r 7.02(1); Rules of the Supreme Court 1971 (WA) r 10(1A)(2). In the Federal Court and the Northern Territory, if service is made out of the jurisdiction without leave, the court can subsequently confirm the leave if there is a satisfactory explanation for the claimant's failure to apply for leave: Federal Court Rules 2011 (Cth) r 10.43(6)–(7); Supreme Court Rules 2012 (NT) r 7.02(5).

[17] Supreme Court Rules 2012 (NT) r 7.02(1).

[18] For most applications, the presence, ordinary residence or citizenship of either party is sufficient to establish the courts' jurisdiction: Family Law Act 1975 (Cth) ss 39(4), 69E(1). In applications for divorce orders, the domicile, ordinary residence or citizenship of either party is required to establish the courts' jurisdiction: Family Law Act 1975 (Cth) s 39(3).

[19] *In the Marriage of Woodhead* (1997) 23 Fam LR 559.

[20] Australian Law Reform Commission, *Service and Execution of Process*, Report No 40 (Canberra, Australian Government Printing Service, 1987) (Australian Law Reform Commission, *Service and Execution of Process* Report).

[21] Service and Execution of Process Act 1901 (Cth) s 11(1).

[22] Service and Execution of Process Act 1992 (Cth) s 15(1). This was justified on the basis that leave requirements waste judicial resources and increase costs: Australian Law Reform Commission, *Service and Execution of Process* Report No 40, above n 20, [168].

[23] Australian Law Reform Commission, *Service and Execution of Process* Report No 40, above n 20, [178]. The law relating to staying and transferring proceedings is discussed below at II.A.(iii).

(c) Service in New Zealand

The Service and Execution of Process Act was the model for the Trans-Tasman Proceedings Act. The Expert Group which recommended adoption of this model expressed the view that it was 'simple, streamlined and cost-effective',[24] and consistent with the current rules of court, which do not require leave to serve out in 'many cases'.[25] Accordingly, the Trans-Tasman Proceedings Act permits the service of initiating process of any Australian court in New Zealand, without requirements of nexus, of leave to serve out or of leave to continue in the absence of appearance.[26] As in the Service and Execution of Process Act scheme, inappropriate assertions of jurisdiction are expected to be resolved by the stay provisions,[27] and deterred by the courts' ability to award costs.[28]

(ii) Subject-matter Jurisdiction

Subject-matter jurisdiction is not often in issue, although it is becoming more significant. At common law, and prior to the establishment of the federal courts,[29] jurisdictional competency related almost exclusively to personal jurisdiction.[30] The High Court stated in 1958 that the jurisdiction of the court 'depends *not in the least* on subject matter but upon the amenability of the defendant to the writ expressing the sovereign's command' (emphasis added).[31] It is now generally

[24] Trans-Tasman Working Group, *Trans-Tasman Court Proceedings and Regulatory Enforcement* (Canberra and Wellington, Commonwealth of Australia and Government of New Zealand, 2006) 12.

[25] ibid, 11. At the time this report was published, leave was required in the Federal Court and in the Supreme Court of Western Australia, in each of which there is a significant amount of international litigation.

[26] Trans-Tasman Proceedings Act 2010 (Cth) s 9(1). The Trans-Tasman Proceedings Act 2010 (Cth) gives effect to the Agreement between the Government of Australia and the Government of New Zealand on Trans-Tasman Court Proceedings and Regulatory Enforcement 2008 (referred to as 'the Trans-Tasman Treaty'). Reciprocal provisions of the New Zealand legislation of the same name permit service of the process of New Zealand courts in Australia without any requirements of leave or nexus: Trans-Tasman Proceedings Act 2010 (NZ) s 13(1), (3).

[27] Trans-Tasman Proceedings Act 2010 (Cth) ss 17–20. These provisions are discussed further below at text to nn 56–59 and 98–99.

[28] Trans-Tasman Working Group, above n 24, 12.

[29] The Family Court of Australia was established by the Family Law Act 1975 (Cth), and the Federal Court of Australia by the Federal Court of Australia Act 1976 (Cth). The State and Territory Supreme Courts are superior courts of record with unlimited general jurisdiction to deal with all common law and equitable matters: eg Constitution of Queensland 2001 (Qld), s 58(2) (the Supreme Court of Queensland has 'subject to the Commonwealth Constitution, unlimited jurisdiction at law, in equity and otherwise'). The federal courts (the Family Court of Australia and the Federal Court of Australia) are courts of limited jurisdiction.

[30] The courts' lack of jurisdiction to deal with claims that enforce foreign governmental interests, and claims concerning title to and possession of foreign immovables (the '*Moçambique*' rule) are well-established limitations to the courts' subject-matter jurisdiction: *Attorney-General for the United Kingdom v Heinemann Publishers Australia Pty Ltd* (1988) 165 CLR 30; *Potter v BHP Co Ltd* (1906) 3 CLR 479. In two jurisdictions, the common law restriction on jurisdiction to deal with foreign land has been repealed in part or in whole: Civil Law (Wrongs) Act 2002 (ACT) s 220; Jurisdiction (Foreign Land) Act 1989 (NSW) s 3.

[31] *Laurie v Carroll* (1958) 98 CLR 310, 322.

accepted that subject-matter jurisdiction may also be relevant.[32] The main area in which this may arise is in the context of intra-Australian litigation.

The cross-vesting legislation is a cooperative scheme between the Commonwealth, States and Territories, the primary objective of which was to overcome uncertainties as to the limits of federal and State jurisdiction.[33] The means of achieving this objective was to considerably expand the subject-matter jurisdiction of all the Australian superior courts.[34] Following a successful constitutional challenge to the part of the scheme that cross-invested State jurisdiction in the federal superior courts,[35] the legislation now only enlarges the subject-matter jurisdiction of the State and Territory superior courts.[36] The cross-vesting legislation uses a similar method of controlling inappropriate assertions of subject-matter jurisdiction to that used in the Service and Execution of Process Act,[37] but rather than requiring the seised court to stay proceedings, the relevant relief is for a transfer of proceedings to another Australian court.[38] The transfer procedure in the cross-vesting legislation is also the method used in superior courts for controlling assertions of jurisdiction under the Service and Execution of Process Act.[39]

The treatment of forum legislation in international litigation is closely related to the limitations of subject-matter jurisdiction. Australian courts, like those of other common law countries, have a tendency to apply forum legislation without

[32] *Lipohar v The Queen* (1999) 200 CLR 485, 517; *PT Garuda Indonesia Ltd v Australian Competition and Consumer Commission* [2012] HCA 33, (2012) 247 CLR 240, [16]–[19] French CJ, Gummow, Hayne and Crennan JJ.

[33] Explanatory Memorandum, Jurisdiction of Courts (Cross-vesting) Bill 1986 (Cth) pp 2–3.

[34] The Commonwealth, the States and the Territories all have legislation of the same name, enacted in all jurisdictions except the ACT in 1987. The ACT enacted legislation of the same name in 1993. The provisions that are referred to in this chapter are identically numbered in all jurisdictions. For simplicity the references to the legislation will be to the Jurisdiction of Courts (Cross-vesting) Act 1987 (Cth), except where it is the State and Territory legislation that is referred to, in which case references are to the NSW legislation.

[35] *Re Wakim; ex parte McNally* (1999) 198 CLR 511.

[36] The State and Territory legislation cross-invests the subject-matter jurisdiction of the superior courts of all the States and Territories in the superior courts of the other States and Territories: see eg Jurisdiction of Courts (Cross-vesting) Act 1987 (NSW) s 4(3). The federal legislation invests most of the subject-matter jurisdiction of federal superior courts in the superior courts of the States and Territories: Jurisdiction of Courts (Cross-vesting) Act 1987 (Cth), s 4(1). The Commonwealth legislation reserves certain matters that cannot be dealt with in State and Territory courts (ibid, s 4(4)), and in most cases 'special federal matters' also cannot be dealt with in State and Territory courts (ibid, ss 3(1) (definition of 'special federal matter', and 6(1) (requiring State and Territory courts to transfer special federal matters to the federal courts).

[37] Before the Service and Execution of Process Act permitted service of Australian courts nationally, service outside of the jurisdiction but within Australia had to come within the rules of court permitting service out of the jurisdiction, and in cross-vesting cases, the rules 'generally require[d] that the forum be an appropriate one for the determination of the proceedings': Sykes and Pryles, above n 4, 97 (citing the rules of court of Victoria, South Australia, Queensland, Western Australia and Tasmania).

[38] Jurisdiction of Courts (Cross-vesting) Act 1987 (Cth) s 5 (discussed below at text to nn 81–91).

[39] Service and Execution of Process Act 1992 (Cth) s 20(1), (10). In inferior courts, the application is for a stay of proceedings under the Service and Execution of Process Act 1992 (Cth) s 20 (discussed below at text to nn 93–96).

regard to the otherwise applicable jurisdictional and choice of law rules.[40] If judges take the view that foreign courts lack subject-matter jurisdiction to deal with forum legislation, they may insist on retaining jurisdiction.

(iii) The Exercise of Jurisdiction

As just explained, the legislative expansion of jurisdictional competence places great stress on the rules relating to the exercise of jurisdiction in order to control unacceptable assertions of jurisdiction, and assumes that this is an effective and appropriate method for allocating jurisdiction. In international cases, most of the principles regarding exercise of jurisdiction are derived from case law,[41] whereas in intra-national cases, most of the principles are statutory.[42] Different rules apply depending on whether the parties have made an effective agreement about forum.

(a) **Choice of Court Agreements**

The case law which is relevant in most international matters distinguishes situations in which there is an effective foreign exclusive jurisdiction clause from those in which there is not.[43] If the parties have incorporated a foreign exclusive jurisdiction clause in their contract, the court should enforce the agreement by staying local proceedings, unless there are strong reasons for non-enforcement.[44] Strong reasons include the court's responsibility to ensure the application of Australian remedial legislation,[45] which a majority of the High Court justified by reference to

[40] In *Lawson v Serco*, the application of the UK Employment Rights Act 1996 was determined by interpretation of the legislation: [2006] 1 All ER 823, [6], [23]. Lord Hoffmann stated that the *forum non conveniens* principle could not be applied because the claims were made under UK legislation and so 'no other tribunal has jurisdiction to hear a claim under' the relevant provision: [2006] 1 All ER 823, [24]. This proposition may need to be reconsidered in the United Kingdom, as a matter of EU law, in light of the Rome I and Rome II Regulations. See, similarly, *John Pfeiffer Pty Ltd v Rogerson* (2000) 203 CLR 503, 548–49 (*Pfeiffer v Rogerson*); and *Faxtech Pty Ltd v ITL Optronics Ltd* [2011] FCA 1320, [18].

[41] There are two main exceptions. First, rules of court in three jurisdictions are relevant in applications to set aside service and stay proceedings (below at text to nn 100–105). Secondly, the Trans-Tasman Proceedings Act 2010 (Cth) exclusively governs applications for a stay of proceedings 'on forum grounds' where the alternative forum is a New Zealand court (s 21(1)), including specific rules applicable to exclusive jurisdiction clauses in commercial cases (s 20) (below at text to nn 98–99).

[42] In intra-Australian cases, the relevant application in the superior courts is for a transfer of proceedings under the cross-vesting legislation; in the inferior courts the application is for a stay under the Service and Execution of Process Act 1992 (Cth). These provisions are discussed below at text to nn 82–97.

[43] *FAI General Insurance Co Ltd v Ocean Marine Mutual Protection & Indemnity Association Ltd* (1997) 41 NSWLR 559, 569; *Global Partners Fund Ltd v Babcock & Brown Ltd (in liq)* (2010) 79 ACSR 383, [91]. This is also the case under the Trans-Tasman Proceedings Act 2010 (Cth) s 20(1).

[44] *Akai Pty Ltd v The People's Insurance Company Ltd* (1996) 188 CLR 418, 445, 447.

[45] *Akai Pty Ltd v The People's Insurance Company Ltd* (1996) 188 CLR 418 (referring to the Insurance Contracts Act 1984 (Cth)). There are a number of lower court decisions in which the courts have held that the foreign jurisdiction clause should not be enforced by a stay of Australian proceedings. Mostly, these cases include claims for breach of s 52(1) of the Trade Practices Act 1974 (Cth) (which has been replaced by s 18(1) of the Australian Consumer Law 2010, with effect from 1 January 2011). See eg *Commonwealth Bank of Australia v White* [1999] 2 VR 681, 704–5; *Faxtech Pty Ltd v Optronics Ltd* [2011] FCA 1320.

public policy.[46] A provision prohibiting misleading or deceptive conduct in trade or commerce, which some courts regard as embodying mandatory public policy, is often pleaded in international commercial litigation in the Australian courts.[47] A number of other arguments are often employed to resist the enforcement of foreign jurisdiction clauses, including that the clause was not validly incorporated into the agreement,[48] that the parties had merely submitted to the non-exclusive jurisdiction of the foreign court,[49] that relevant claims are beyond the scope of the agreement,[50] and that the agreement did not bind non-parties to the contract.[51] While these arguments used to be quite effective in resisting the enforcement of foreign jurisdiction agreements, since 2009, most courts have taken a stricter approach to the enforcement of such agreements.[52]

The Australian principles relating to the effect of jurisdiction agreements make no specific allowance for the position of weaker parties, such as consumers, franchisees and employees. Litigation involving consumers is rare, but the courts are less likely to enforce foreign jurisdictional clauses in those cases.[53] In *Quinlan v SAFE International Försäkrings AB*, Nicholson J stated that

> in a consumer situation the court should not place as much weight on an exclusive jurisdiction clause in determining a stay application as would be placed on such a clause where there was negotiation between business people.[54]

On the other hand, jurisdiction and arbitration clauses tend to be enforced against franchisees. In *Nicola v Ideal Image Development Corporation*, Perram J noted that the claimants were franchisees but apparently did not give that factor any consideration in deciding to enforce the jurisdiction agreement.[55]

The Trans-Tasman Proceedings Act, relevant only to international proceedings involving the New Zealand courts, expressly gives commercial choice of court

[46] *Akai Pty Ltd v The People's Insurance Company Pty Ltd* (1996) 188 CLR 418, 445.

[47] Australian Consumer Law 2010 s 18(1), which replaced the Trade Practices Act 1974 (Cth) s 52(1).

[48] An issue which in Australia is determined according to the law of the forum: *Oceanic Sun Line Special Shipping Co Inc v Fay* (1988) 165 CLR 197, 225 260–61, applied in *Ventner v Ilona MY Ltd* [2012] NSWSC 1029, [27]. Clearly, the issue ought to be determined according to the putative proper law of the contract: Keyes, *Jurisdiction in International Litigation*, above n 1, 95. The decision in *Oceanic* should only be applied in cases where there are protective interests (in that case, the claimant was a consumer and the claim was for damages for personal injuries): Keyes, ibid. The same protection might be extended for the benefit of other vulnerable parties, such as employees.

[49] *Faxtech Pty Ltd v ITL Optronics Ltd* [2011] FCA 1320, [11].

[50] *Reinsurance Australia Corp v HIH Casualty and General Insurance (in liq)* (2003) 254 ALR 29.

[51] *Incitec Ltd v Alkimos Shipping Corporation* (2004) 138 FCR 496.

[52] *Global Partners Fund Ltd v Babcock & Brown Ltd (in liq)* (2010) 79 ACSR 383; *Nicola v Ideal Image Development Corporation Inc* (2009) 261 ALR 1; *Venter v Ilona MY Ltd* [2012] NSWSC 1029; *Yperion Technology SAS v Luminex Pty Ltd* [2012] FCA 554.

[53] *Oceanic Sun Line Special Shipping Co Inc v Fay* (1988) 165 CLR 197 and *Quinlan v SAFE International Försäkrings AB* (2006) 14 ANZ Ins Cas ¶61-693 were both cases involving consumers, in which the Australian courts did not enforce the foreign jurisdiction clause.

[54] *Quinlan v SAFE International Försäkrings AB* (2006) 14 ANZ Ins Cas ¶61-693, [46].

[55] *Nicola v Ideal Image Development Corporation* (2009) 261 ALR 1. See likewise *Timic v Hammock* [2001] FCA 74, in which a foreign arbitration clause was enforced against a franchisee.

agreements the highest priority.[56] It requires Australian courts to stay proceedings brought in breach of an agreement to litigate in New Zealand, with very limited exceptions.[57] These provisions are modelled on the Hague Convention on Choice of Court Agreements,[58] which in turn is based on the United Nations Convention on the Recognition and Enforcement of Foreign Arbitral Awards. The Trans-Tasman Proceedings Act provisions relating to choice of court agreements do not apply to consumer and employment contracts.[59]

The status of forum agreements in international family cases is unexplored in Australia. There is no published Australian case about the effect that should be given to such an agreement. As noted above, it is not possible for the parties to submit to the jurisdiction of the Australian courts, so it seems likely that a forum agreement would not be regarded as enforceable per se, although it may be taken into account in deciding whether to exercise jurisdiction.

Legislation which is applicable in intra-national litigation is far more obscure than the case law and the Trans-Tasman Proceedings Act about the effect to be given to jurisdiction clauses. Exclusive jurisdiction clauses are treated as merely one factor relevant to the court's decision whether to transfer proceedings under the cross-vesting legislation,[60] which is the relevant application in the superior courts. Chief Justice de Jersey of the Queensland Supreme Court stated that an exclusive jurisdiction clause was 'relevant, but subject to other considerations bearing on the comparative convenience of litigating in the competing jurisdictions', and suggested that in 'the cross-vesting context, there is no "bias" (in terms of the common law test) in favour of the contractually agreed jurisdiction where considerations of convenience and efficiency militate in favour of another jurisdiction'.[61]

[56] It does not apply to choice of court agreements where one party is a consumer (s 20(3)(b)) or an employee (s 20(3)(c)).

[57] Trans-Tasman Proceedings Act 2010 (Cth), s 20. The exceptions are based on the relevant provisions of the Hague Convention on Choice of Court Agreements 2005 and are similar to those in the United Nations Convention on the Recognition and Enforcement of Foreign Arbitral Awards 1958. They are deliberately narrow in scope: s 20(2) (if the agreement is null and void under New Zealand law; if either party lacked capacity; if giving effect to the agreement would lead to manifest injustice or be contrary to Australian public policy; if for exceptional reasons the agreement cannot reasonably be performed; if the chosen court has decided not to exercise its jurisdiction).

[58] Trans-Tasman Working Group, above n 24, 18.

[59] Trans-Tasman Proceedings Act 2010 (Cth) s 20(3)(b), (c).

[60] As discussed below, the transfer provisions of the cross-vesting legislation are in general terms and do not identify any factors relevant to the court's decision whether to order a transfer: below at text to nn 81–89.

[61] *River Gum Homes Pty Ltd v Meridian Pty Ltd* [2010] QCA 293, [20] (Muir JA and Philippides J agreeing, at [26] and [27]). The reference to 'bias' is to the judgment of Dixon J in *Huddart Parker Ltd v The Ship 'Mill Hill'*, in which his Honour stated that the court should 'begin with the fact that there is a special contract between the parties to refer, and therefore in the language of Lord Moulton in *Bristol Corporation and John Aird & Co*, consider the circumstances of a case with a strong bias in favour of maintaining the special bargain': (1950) 81 CLR 502, 508–9. See likewise *World Firefighters Games Brisbane v World Firefighters Games Western Australia Inc* (2001) 161 FLR 355, 364–65.

The stay provisions of the Service and Execution of Process Act apply to intranational litigation in the inferior courts. The Act explicitly identifies choice of court agreements as one factor relevant to determining whether proceedings should be stayed, but gives it no particular priority.[62]

(b) *Forum Non Conveniens*

The Australian principle of *forum non conveniens*, applicable to determine whether a stay should be granted if there is no effective jurisdiction agreement, is extremely problematic. The common law version of the principle, which is relevant in international cases,[63] requires the defendant to persuade the court that it is *clearly* inappropriate. This test 'focuses on the advantages and disadvantages arising from a continuation of the proceedings in the selected forum rather than on the need to make a comparative judgment between the two forums'.[64] The Australian principle—referred to as the *Voth* test—consciously retains the traditional common law foundation, which is the court's obligation to prevent abuse of its processes and vexation and oppression of the defendant.[65] This foundation is too narrow, given the extraordinary breadth of the rules of competency and the nature and increasing frequency of international litigation. The relevant factors in determining whether proceedings should be stayed are the same as those that are used in England to determine whether another forum is more appropriate than the English courts.[66] The Australian test therefore is really one of relative appropriateness, rather than one concerned with vexation or oppression, but with the standard set far too high. This gives claimants a significant and unjustified advantage. It is predictably difficult for defendants to succeed in an application to have proceedings stayed, and is often difficult accurately to anticipate how a challenge to jurisdiction will be resolved.

The *Voth* test is much in need of reform. Notwithstanding widespread and cogent criticism,[67] in 2008 all members of the High Court affirmed it in the

[62] Service and Execution of Process Act 1992 (Cth) s 20(4)(d). This reflects the legal position in 1987, when the Australian Law Reform Commission's report on *Service and Execution of Process* was published. The report states that a forum clause is a ground for staying proceedings but is 'not necessarily decisive': Australian Law Reform Commission, *Service and Execution of Process* Report, above n 20, [182]. Although the report noted that in a standard form document used in a consumer contract, a jurisdiction clause should not necessarily be enforced (ibid), this is not explicitly reflected in the legislation.

[63] The Trans-Tasman Proceedings Act provisions exclusively apply to litigation in which a New Zealand court is the available alternative forum: Trans-Tasman Proceedings Act 2010 (Cth) ss 17–19. The relevant provisions are discussed below at text to nn 98–99 below.

[64] *Voth v Manildra Flour Mills Pty Ltd* (1990) 171 CLR 538, 558; *Regie Nationale des Usines Renault SA v Zhang* (2002) 210 CLR 491, 520 (*Renault v Zhang*); *Puttick v Tenon Ltd* (2008) 238 CLR 265, 277.

[65] *Voth v Manildra Flour Mills Pty Ltd* (1990) 171 CLR 538, 554; *Puttick v Tenon Ltd* (2008) 238 CLR 265, 277; *BHP Billiton Ltd v Schultz* (2004) 221 CLR 400, 420.

[66] *Voth v Manildra Flour Mills Pty Ltd* (1990) 171 CLR 538, 564–65.

[67] The detractors on the High Court from the *Voth* test, Wilson, Toohey, Kirby and Callinan JJ, were always in dissent: see, particularly, *Renault v Zhang* (2002) 210 CLR 491,524–25 Kirby J. *Voth* has

only direct challenge that has been brought to it.[68] The judgment of French CJ, Gummow, Hayne and Kiefel JJ did not give reasons for declining to review the *Voth* test. Justices Heydon and Crennan stated that '*Voth*'s case should simply be followed until the time comes, if it ever comes, for full argument to be developed about its correctness'.[69] Most of the *forum non conveniens* cases that have been taken to the High Court, including *Puttick v Tenon Ltd*, involve personal injuries claims, in which Australian courts appear to be sympathetic to claimants. The High Court has held that the Australian court was a clearly inappropriate forum in the commercial cases brought before it.[70]

The *Voth* test is also used in the family jurisdiction.[71] In *Henry v Henry*, the majority of the High Court added further detail to the *Voth* test, by identifying considerations relevant to determining whether parallel proceedings 'between husband and wife with respect to their marital relationship' should be stayed.[72] Most of the factors identified in *Henry v Henry* entail a comparison of the foreign and local proceedings, including 'which forum can provide more effectively for complete resolution' of the dispute, 'the connection of the parties and the marriage with each of the jurisdictions', and whether, 'with regard to their resources and their understanding of language, the parties are able to participate in the respective proceedings on an equal footing'.[73] This is the only situation in which the High Court has tailored the *Voth* test to the subject-matter of the dispute. This was a desirable development,[74] the relevant parts of which have recently been applied in several non-family cases.[75]

The law on *forum non conveniens* is further complicated and confused by the related legislative provisions. There are more than five legislative versions of the *forum non conveniens* principle, each of which uses slightly different words to express the same concept. Each of the statutory versions uses terms which are more consistent with the English *forum non conveniens* test, requiring the court

also been the target of sustained academic criticism. See eg Richard Garnett, 'Stay of Proceedings in Australia: A "Clearly Inappropriate" Test?' (1999) 23 *Melbourne University Law Review* 30.

[68] *Puttick v Tenon Ltd* (2008) 238 CLR 265.

[69] *Puttick v Tenon Ltd* (2008) 238 CLR 265, 280.

[70] *Voth v Manildra Flour Mills Pty Ltd* (1990) 171 CLR 538 and *CSR Ltd v Cigna Insurance Australia Ltd* (1997) 189 CLR 345.

[71] *Henry v Henry* (1996) 185 CLR 571. The test does not apply in cases involving children in which the best interests of the child are relevant: *Pascarl & Oxley* (2014) 49 Fam LR 364.

[72] *Henry v Henry* (1996) 185 CLR 571, 592.

[73] *Henry v Henry* (1996) 185 CLR 571, 592–93. The other considerations identified were whether the orders of each court were enforceable in the other forum and the ease of doing so; the order in which proceedings were commenced, the stage they had reached in each forum, and the costs incurred.

[74] All of the considerations identified involve a comparison between the forum and the foreign court. In *Renault v Zhang* the joint judgment emphasised that the *Voth* test 'is not a question of striking a balance between competing considerations': (2002) 210 CLR 491, 521. The considerations identified in *Henry* should probably therefore be read down so as to only refer to the local proceedings.

[75] *Re Point of Pay Pty Ltd* [2012] VSC 380, [31]; *Centrebet Pty Ltd v Baasland* [2012] NTSC 100, [38]; *Bogart Lingerie Ltd v Steadmark Pty Ltd* [2013] VSC 212, [61].

to stay proceedings in favour of a 'more appropriate forum',[76] than the *Voth* test. Three of these statutory versions occur in primary legislation,[77] and two are found in the rules of court of three different jurisdictions.[78] These provisions are a critical component of the schemes that extend the Australian courts' personal and subject-matter jurisdiction,[79] discussed above. The Explanatory Memorandum for the federal cross-vesting legislation stated that 'Courts will need to be *ruthless* in the exercise of their transferral powers to ensure that litigants do not engage in "forum shopping" by commencing proceedings in inappropriate courts' (emphasis added).[80]

The transfer provisions of the cross-vesting legislation are relevant for proceedings in the superior courts,[81] whether or not the court is exercising cross-vested jurisdiction.[82] They require superior courts to transfer proceedings to other superior courts in three situations. The first is where related proceedings have already been commenced in the other court, in which case the court must transfer proceedings if it is 'more appropriate' that the proceedings be determined in the other court.[83]

Secondly, if the court's subject-matter jurisdiction is largely created by the cross-vesting scheme, the court must transfer proceedings to the court which would have been competent without the cross-vesting scheme if it is 'more appropriate' that proceedings be determined in the other court, by reference to 'the interests of justice'.[84] Thirdly, the court must transfer proceedings if 'it is otherwise in the interests of justice that the relevant proceedings' be determined in the other court.[85] The legislation provides no guidance as to when it will be 'more appropriate' for proceedings to be determined by one court rather than another, nor as to when a transfer would be in the 'interests of justice'.

[76] *Spiliada Maritime Corporation v Cansulex Ltd* [1987] 1 AC 460. However, the legislative versions in Australia lack the subtlety of the English rule, which allows the court to retain jurisdiction if the claimant can show that there are 'special circumstances by reason of which justice requires that the trial should … take place' in the forum: ibid, 476.

[77] Jurisdiction of Courts (Cross-vesting) Act 1987 (Cth) s 5; Service and Execution of Process Act 1992 (Cth) s 20(3); Trans-Tasman Proceedings Act 2010 (Cth) s 19. The States and Territories all have cross-vesting legislation of the same name, which is identical to the Commonwealth legislation on this particular point: eg Jurisdiction of Courts (Cross-vesting) Act 1993 (ACT) s 5; Jurisdiction of Courts (Cross-vesting) Act 1987 (NSW) s 5.

[78] Court Procedures Rules 2006 (ACT) r 6503(3)(b); Uniform Civil Procedure Rules 2005 (NSW) r 11.7(2)(b); Supreme Court (General Civil Procedure) Rules 2005 (Vic) r 7.05(2)(b).

[79] Explanatory Memorandum, Jurisdiction of Courts (Cross-vesting) Bill 1986 (Cth) 3.

[80] ibid.

[81] Jurisdiction of Courts (Cross-vesting) Act 1987 (Cth) s 5; Jurisdiction of Courts (Cross-vesting) Act 1987 (NSW) s 5.

[82] Service and Execution of Process Act 1992 (Cth) s 20(1).

[83] Eg Jurisdiction of Courts (Cross-vesting) Act 1987 (Cth) s 5(1)(b)(i). The legislation laboriously refers to the specific courts which are required to transfer provisions; for simplicity I refer only to the first instance in the Commonwealth legislation. The other instances in the Commonwealth, State and Territory legislation are worded identically, but for the names of the specific courts required to transfer proceedings.

[84] Eg Jurisdiction of Courts (Cross-vesting) Act 1987 (Cth) s 5(1)(b)(ii).

[85] Eg Jurisdiction of Courts (Cross-vesting) Act 1987 (Cth) s 5(1)(b)(iii).

The terms 'more appropriate' and 'the interests of justice' have been interpreted in a way that is consistent with the English version of the *forum non conveniens* principle, under which proceedings are stayed if another court is a 'more appropriate forum',[86] rather than by reference to the *Voth* test. In the leading cases interpreting the cross-vesting transfer provisions, these two terms are treated as being identical.[87]

Most applications for transfer are on the basis that the interests of justice require it. The courts sometimes refer to a judicially created list of factors to be considered in deciding whether it is in the interests of justice to transfer proceedings.[88] These are similar to the factors relevant to the case law principle of *forum non conveniens*, but in addition the court may also have regard to 'convenience to the court system',[89] which cannot be considered under the common law principle.[90] The legislation prohibits appeals from a primary judge's decision whether to transfer proceedings,[91] which has severely hampered authoritative judicial interpretation of the legislation. Several other Commonwealth statutes also contain provisions requiring proceedings under those statutes to be transferred in certain circumstances, which are similar but not all identical to the terms of the cross-vesting legislation. [92]

The test in the Service and Execution of Process Act uses a different form of words again. It requires inferior courts to stay proceedings if there is another competent Australian court which is 'the appropriate court'.[93] This has been interpreted as meaning the court 'with which the action has the most real and substantial connection, and which can therefore be regarded as the natural forum'.[94] Although these terms are clearly derived from the English *forum non conveniens* principle, the Queensland Court of Appeal stated that this test was 'not inconsistent' with the decision in *Renault v Zhang*, a High Court *forum non*

[86] *BHP Billiton Ltd v Schultz* (2004) 221 CLR 400, 421, 422–23; *Bankinvest AG v Seabrook* (1988) 14 NSWLR 711, 728.

[87] *BHP Billiton Ltd v Schultz* (2004) 221 CLR 400, 421, 439; *Bankinvest AG v Seabrook* (1988) 14 NSWLR 711, 728.

[88] The leading case is *Dawson v Baker*, in which Higgins J identified a number of factors that could guide the court in determining whether the interests of justice required a transfer: (1994) 120 ACTR 11, 25.

[89] *Dawson v Baker* (1994) 120 ACTR 11, 25.

[90] *Oceanic Sun Line Special Shipping Co Inc v Fay* (1988) 165 CLR 197, 253–55 Deane J. See also *James Hardie v Grigor* (1998) 45 NSWLR 20, 41 Spigelman CJ.

[91] Jurisdiction of Courts (Cross-vesting) Act 1987 (Cth) s 13(a).

[92] Australian Securities and Investment Commission Act 2001 (Cth) s 12GK; Competition and Consumer Act 2010 (Cth), ss 86A, 138C, 138D; Corporations Act 2001 (Cth) s 1337H–1337K.

[93] Service and Execution of Process Act 1992 (Cth), s 20(3). As noted above, this term is also used in the preamble to the Jurisdiction of Courts (Cross-vesting) Act 1987 (Cth). In the Australian Law Reform Commission report which led to the enactment of the Service and Execution of Process Act, the terms 'appropriate' and 'more appropriate' courts are used interchangeably: Australian Law Reform Commission, *Service and Execution of Process* Report, above n 20, [182] and [187] (referring to the 'appropriate' court), [186] (referring to the 'more appropriate' court).

[94] *Valkama v Jamieson* (1994) 11 SR (WA) 246, 250, approved and applied in *St George Bank Ltd v McTaggart* [2003] 2 Qd R 568 (QCA), [10].

conveniens case in an international case which took a restrictive approach to the exercise of the power to stay.[95] The Service and Execution of Process Act identifies a non-exhaustive list of factors that are relevant to determining whether proceedings should be stayed.[96] The Australian Law Reform Commission recommended that such factors should be identified in the legislation, rather than simply relying on a general form of words, such as where the interests of justice required a stay, in order to minimise the expense of litigation.[97]

The Trans-Tasman Proceedings Act permits an Australian court to stay proceedings if a New Zealand court is 'the more appropriate court' to determine all the matters in dispute between the parties.[98] Like the Service and Execution of Process Act, this statute identifies factors that may be taken into account in determining whether the New Zealand court is more appropriate,[99] which are broadly similar to those listed in the Service and Execution of Process Act. It is unclear why the Commonwealth did not ensure the same verbal formulations were used for the stay test in these two statutes,[100] or why the formulations in these two statutes differ from the formula used in the cross-vesting legislation.

Another two versions of *forum non conveniens* are found in the rules of court of three jurisdictions. These differ from the three versions set out in the primary legislation just discussed. In two jurisdictions, the rules of court permit the court to set aside service *ex iuris* if the court is 'an inappropriate forum'.[101] Despite the apparently significant omission of the word 'clearly' before the word 'inappropriate' in the NSW rules, a majority of the High Court in *Renault v Zhang* held that the provision had the same meaning as the *Voth* test.[102] Justices Kirby and

[95] *St George Bank Ltd v McTaggart* [2003] 2 Qd R 568 (QCA), [10]. In *Rick Cobby Pty Ltd v Podesta Transport Pty Ltd*, Olsson J took a different view, holding that subsection 20(4) exhaustively identified the issues which were relevant in determining whether a stay should be granted, and that the case law on *forum non conveniens* was completely irrelevant to that determination: (1997) 139 FLR 54. This view has not been accepted in other cases.

[96] Service and Execution of Process Act 1992 (Cth) s 20(4). The factors listed in s 20(4) are similar to those used in *forum non conveniens* cases. Several additional factors are also listed, including the financial situation of the parties: s 20(4)(c).

[97] Australian Law Reform Commission, *Service and Execution of Process* Report, above n 20, [180].

[98] Trans-Tasman Proceedings Act 2010 (Cth) s 19(1).

[99] Trans-Tasman Proceedings Act 2010 (Cth) s 19(2). These factors are very similar to those listed in the Service and Execution of Process Act 1992 (Cth) s 20(4).

[100] The term 'more appropriate court' is used in the Trans-Tasman Treaty, to which the Trans-Tasman Proceedings Act gives effect: Agreement between the Government of Australia and the Government of New Zealand on Trans-Tasman Court Proceedings and Regulatory Enforcement 2008 [2013] Australian Treaty Series 32, arts 4.4, 8.1, 8.2.

[101] Court Procedures Rules 2006 (ACT) r 6503(3)(b); Uniform Civil Procedure Rules 2005 (NSW) r 11.7(2)(b).

[102] *Renault v Zhang* (2002) 210 CLR 491, 503. cf *Studorp Ltd v Robinson* [2012] NSWCA 382, [5] (Allsop P noting that 'There seems to me to be a difference in quality and emphasis with the addition of the adverb' clearly), [62] (Hoeben JA, stating that 'The significance of the absence of the word "clearly" [in Uniform Civil Procedure Rules 2005 (NSW) r 11.7] is not obvious, although as a matter of simple English, the phrase "an inappropriate forum" is not as emphatic as "a clearly inappropriate forum"', but concluding that nothing turned on the distinction on the facts of the case).

Callinan, in dissent, strenuously objected to this interpretation.[103] The Victorian rules of court permit the court to grant a stay and to set aside service if 'Victoria is not a convenient forum'.[104] In *Dow Jones v Gutnick*[105] the application for a stay was under this provision. The High Court simply affirmed the trial judge's decision not to stay proceedings, and Kirby J was the only member of the court who referred to the difference between the terminology of the Victorian rules and the *Voth* test.[106]

B. Judgments

The relationship between rules of jurisdiction and of judgments is opaque in the Australian law. At best, these rules are indirectly linked.[107] The substantial changes to jurisdiction described above have not led to corresponding changes to the rules about recognition of foreign judgments. The common law rules of recognition and enforcement, essentially unchanged over the last century, must be used for the judgments of many foreign countries. These rules continue to depend on the common law grounds of international jurisdiction established in the nineteenth century,[108] even though these rules are based on the common law grounds of jurisdiction, presence and submission that have been, in practice, overtaken by the statutory developments described above. Although the common law rules of international jurisdiction are clearly based on reciprocity, reciprocity has not been accepted as a permissible basis for the recognition of foreign court competency,[109] by reference to statutory extensions of the courts' jurisdiction.[110] Accordingly, the link between jurisdiction and judgments that was created by the common law's use of the concepts of presence and submission in both contexts has been severely diluted. The concept of international jurisdiction also has not evolved to incorporate consideration of whether the foreign court ought, by forum standards, to

[103] *Renault v Zhang* (2002) 210 CLR 491, 543 (Kirby J), 562–63 (Callinan J).

[104] Supreme Court (General Civil Procedure) Rules 2005 (Vic) r 7.05(2)(b). Prior to the recent changes to the Northern Territory rules of court, those rules contained a similar provision.

[105] *Dow Jones v Gutnick* (2002) 210 CLR 575.

[106] *Dow Jones & Co Inc v Gutnick* (2002) 210 CLR 575, [158].

[107] The Service and Execution of Process Act 1992 (Cth) and the cross-vesting legislation contain provisions relevant both to jurisdiction in intra-Australian litigation, and to the enforcement of the judgments of other Australian courts. The Trans-Tasman Proceedings Act 2010 (Cth) contains provisions relevant both to jurisdiction in international litigation between Australia and New Zealand, and to the registration of New Zealand judgments within Australia. In neither case are the provisions clearly linked.

[108] Only rarely has it been suggested that there may be additional bases of international jurisdiction. In *Independent Trustee Services Ltd v Morris*, Bryson AJ held that citizenship was a ground of international jurisdiction: [2010] NSWSC 1218, [28].

[109] *Crick v Hennessy* [1973] WAR 74.

[110] The exception is in the family jurisdiction, in which reciprocity is accepted as an additional basis of international jurisdiction at common law: below at text to n 123.

have exercised its jurisdiction, notwithstanding its competence, even though that has become a crucial component of the jurisdictional enquiry.[111]

The federal Foreign Judgments Act allows the registration of certified judgments of specified foreign courts.[112] It is based on UK legislation of the 1930s.[113] The Foreign Judgments Act improves on the common law by providing a simple registration procedure and recognising a few more grounds of international jurisdiction than are recognised at common law.[114] Although the Act makes provision for the recognition of non-money judgments by delegated legislation[115] that possibility still has not been exercised. The main limitation of the legislation is that it does not apply to half of Australia's major trading partners, including China and the United States, which are, respectively, Australia's first and third largest trading partners by two-way trade.[116] Therefore, the common law rules remain very important in practice.

The Family Law Act contains provisions relating to the recognition of foreign determinations. Most of these provisions give effect to various Hague Conventions. For the analysis in this chapter, I refer by way of example to the rules relating to the recognition of foreign decrees of annulment, divorce and judicial separation. These rules, like the common law rules of recognition, depend on the existence of personal connections of the parties to the foreign forum, but have expanded beyond the traditional connection of domicile. The rules of international jurisdiction, derived from a Hague Convention,[117] are narrower than the rules of forum jurisdictional competency contained in the very same Act.[118] They are superior to the jurisdictional rules in that they differentiate the connections of the applicant and the respondent,[119] they do not rely on trivial connections,[120] and they recognise the types of difficulties that litigants can be expected to face in family law.[121]

[111] A Briggs, 'Which Foreign Judgments Should We Recognise Today?' (1987) 36 *International and Comparative Law Quarterly* 240, 248–49.

[112] Foreign Judgments Act 1991 (Cth). The courts to which the scheme applies are listed in the Foreign Judgments Regulation 1992 (Cth) sch 2.

[113] Foreign Judgments (Reciprocal Enforcement) Act 1933 (UK).

[114] Foreign Judgments Act 1991 (Cth) s 7(3), listing other bases of international jurisdiction, including where the judgment debtor was resident in or had its principal place of business in the foreign jurisdiction, where the subject-matter of the judgment is immovable property within the foreign court's jurisdiction, and in actions *in rem* in which the subject-matter of the judgment is movable property within the foreign court's jurisdiction.

[115] Foreign Judgments Act 1991 (Cth) s 5(6).

[116] In 2012, China accounted for 20.3% and the US for 9.1% of Australia's total two-way trade: Department of Foreign Affairs and Trade, above n 2, 19. The scheme does not apply to China (1st), the US (3rd), Thailand (8th), Malaysia (9th) or India (10th). These rankings refer to Australia's top 10 two-way trading partners, derived from 2012 data: ibid.

[117] The Hague Convention on the Recognition of Divorces and Legal Separations 1970.

[118] These are described above at text to n 18.

[119] Compare, eg, the Family Law Act 1975 (Cth) s 104(3)(a) with (b).

[120] Mere presence is not a sufficient connection.

[121] Family Law Act 1975 (Cth) s 104(3)(f).

The Family Law Act also preserves the common law rules of recognition of foreign decrees, if they would not be recognised under the statutory rules.[122] In this context alone, the common law rules relating to recognition of judgments have adapted, following English case law, so that a foreign judgment may be recognised on the basis of reciprocity[123] or of a real and substantial connection.[124] These grounds of international jurisdiction have not been accepted in other areas of private law.[125]

The Service and Execution of Process Act facilitates the enforcement of judgments within Australia. It requires courts to register judgments of other Australian courts,[126] and renders common law rules inapplicable.[127] This is required by section 118 of the Commonwealth Constitution, which relevantly directs that full faith and credit shall be given to 'the judicial proceedings of every State'. The treatment of judgments in the Service and Execution of Process Act is not related, explicitly or implicitly, to the jurisdictional provisions of that Act.[128]

The strict constitutional requirement for the recognition of intra-national judgments has no analogy in international situations. It is curious, then, that the Service and Execution of Process Act's provisions on judgments were used as the model for the Trans-Tasman Proceedings Act. This legislation requires Australian courts to register certain judgments of New Zealand courts on application by the person entitled to enforce the judgment.[129] After registration, the defendant can apply to have registration set aside only in very limited circumstances, which are narrower than at common law or under the Foreign Judgments Act.[130]

122 Family Law Act 1975 (Cth) s 104(5).

123 *In the Marriage of Barriga (No 2)* (1981) 7 Fam LR 909, 917.

124 *In the Marriage of Dornom* (1984) FLC 91-556; *In the Marriage of Barriga (No 2)* (1981) 7 Fam LR 909, 916.

125 *Crick v Hennessy* [1973] WAR 74; *Re Word Publishing Co Ltd* [1992] 2 Qd R 336.

126 Service and Execution of Process Act 1992 (Cth) s 105. Upon registration, the judgment has the same effect as a judgment of the enforcing court. Likewise, the cross-vesting legislation requires courts to enforce judgments rendered in the exercise of cross-vested jurisdiction: eg the Jurisdiction of Courts (Cross-vesting) Act 1987 (NSW) s 14(2). As for the Service and Execution of Process Act, the provisions are contained in the same legislation but are not substantively linked. Because of the strict requirement to enforce judgments, the jurisdictional rules should be sound.

127 Service and Execution of Process Act 1992 (Cth) s 109.

128 Aside from being contained in the same legislation, there is no relationship between the provisions. They do not refer to each other, and the Australian Law Reform Commission Report on the Service and Execution of Process Act does not refer to the relationship between the provisions on jurisdiction and those on judgments: Australian Law Reform Commission, *Service and Execution of Process* Report, above n 20.

129 Trans-Tasman Proceedings Act 2010 (Cth) s 68(1). This only applies to 'registrable' judgments, as broadly defined in s 66(1).

130 Trans-Tasman Proceedings Act 2010 (Cth) s 72(1) (where enforcement would be contrary to Australian public policy; where the judgment was registered in contravention of the Act; or where the judgment was for foreign immovable property, or in a matter *in rem* involving foreign movable property).

III. Different Areas of Private Law

A. Contract

While the Australian courts' treatment of foreign jurisdiction agreements has recently improved significantly, the default jurisdiction rules for contract are unsatisfactory. Some of the rules establishing the courts' jurisdiction in contract cases, which could be invoked even if the parties had agreed to litigate exclusively in a foreign court, are too broad.[131] The *Voth* test of *forum non conveniens*,[132] which will be applied if there is no effective jurisdictional agreement, is an unsuitable control of broad assertions of jurisdiction including in contract disputes.

The rules of jurisdiction and recognition of judgments relevant to contract are integrated to some extent, in that the defendant's submission to the jurisdiction of a foreign court is a basis of international jurisdiction both at common law and under statute.[133]

The contract choice of law rule has remained unchanged since the 1930s when the High Court accepted the principle of party autonomy.[134] The choice of law rule requires enforcement of the parties' actual choices of law, whether expressed or not. If there is no effective choice, then the law of the legal system with the closest and most real connection to the contract—the objective proper law—is applied.[135]

The contract choice of law rule, while superficially satisfactory, suffers from four major problems. The first is that the Australian courts too often subject it to the application of forum legislation, and the choice of law rule does not make it clear in what circumstances this may be done. In the leading recent case on contract choice of law, in which a commercial party relied on forum legislation to avoid the effect of an express and negotiated choice of English courts and law, the majority of the High Court held that the courts must first determine whether forum legislation applies, explicitly or implicitly, to the contract, without direct reference to choice of law rules.[136] The Australian courts, like those of some other

[131] In particular, the rule in the Australian Capital Territory and Queensland which permits service *ex iuris* if either contracting party is resident in or carrying on business in the jurisdiction: above n 15. In every jurisdiction, service out of the jurisdiction is permitted in contract cases if the contract was made in the jurisdiction: eg Federal Court Rules 2011 (Cth) r 10.42(3)(a); Uniform Civil Procedure Rules 2005 (NSW) r 11.2(1), Sch 6(c)(i).

[132] See above text to nn 64–66.

[133] Foreign Judgments Act 1991 (Cth) s 7(3)(a)(i), (iii).

[134] *Barcelo v Electrolytic Zinc Co of Australasia* (1932) 48 CLR 391; *Merwin Pastoral Co Pty Ltd v Moolpa Pastoral Co Pty Ltd* (1933) 48 CLR 565; *Wanganui-Rangitikei Electric Power Board v Australian Mutual Provident Society* (1934) 50 CLR 581. In an earlier decision, also about the scope of application of state legislation within the federation, Isaacs J stated that the governing law for contract was the law of the place of contracting: *Delaney v Great Western Milling Co Ltd* (1916) 22 CLR 150, 167.

[135] *Akai Pty Ltd v The People's Insurance Company Ltd* (1996) 188 CLR 418.

[136] *Akai Pty Ltd v The People's Insurance Company Ltd* (1996) 188 CLR 418, 443. See similarly *Kay's Leasing Corporation Pty Ltd v Fletcher* (1964) 116 CLR 124, 135. In an earlier line of cases, the High

countries, tend to interpret forum legislation as applicable even if foreign law is the law of the cause. This is related to the Australian courts' regrettable record of scepticism regarding the parties' motives for choices of law. In several cases, the courts have been awkwardly intent on the prevention of choices of law which have been characterised as evasive,[137] a mission which is directly incompatible with the general principle that no connection to the chosen legal system is required.

The cases in which expressed choices are not enforced demonstrate an unattractively parochial attitude to safeguarding forum policy, which is often expressed in legislation that does not specify its intended scope of application.[138] This discrimination in favour of local policy is another reason why the jurisdictional rules must be robust, in order to prevent the inappropriate application of forum legislation.

Secondly, the status of inferred choices of law is uncertain. The High Court recently insisted that if there is no effective expressed choice, it is necessary to consider whether the parties' mutual but unexpressed intention can be determined as a matter of contractual construction.[139] This instruction is infrequently observed. In most cases in which there is no expressed choice of law, the court does not refer to the possibility of discerning an actual, though unexpressed, choice of law, instead proceeding directly to identify the legal system with the closest and most real connection.[140] Even if an attempt is made to determine the parties' unexpressed intention, this is done by reference to the same factors as are relevant to determining the objective proper law,[141] suggesting that the requirement to search for an unexpressed (subjective) intention is redundant.

Thirdly, the default rule, requiring identification of the objective proper law, is seriously flawed. The objective proper law test has been repeatedly rejected by the High Court in the context of multistate torts as being unacceptably uncertain and unpredictable.[142] The objective proper law test is highly discretionary, and is likely to lead to litigation. Judges may be persuaded to conclude that the forum is the legal system with the closest connection. The proper law is more likely to lead to

Court held that the application of legislation was determined by reference to contract choice of law rules: *Barcelo v Electrolytic Zinc Co of Australasia* (1932) 48 CLR 391; *Merwin Pastoral Co Pty Ltd v Moolpa Pastoral Co Pty Ltd* (1933) 48 CLR 565; *Wanganui-Rangitikei Electric Power Board v Australian Mutual Provident Society* (1934) 50 CLR 581; *McLelland v Trustees Executors and Agency Company Ltd* (1936) 55 CLR 483. In *Old UGC Inc v Industrial Relations Commission of New South Wales* the court determined the application of forum legislation by statutory interpretation, independently of the choice of law process (2006) 225 CLR 274.

[137] *Akai Pty Ltd v The People's Insurance Co Ltd* (1996) 188 CLR 418, 433, 443.

[138] *Golden Acres Ltd v Queensland Estates Pty Ltd* [1969] Qd R 378.

[139] *Akai Pty Ltd v The People's Insurance Company* (1996) 188 CLR 418, 442–43.

[140] Eg *Attorney-General (Botswana) v Aussie Diamond Products Pty Ltd (No 3)* [2010] WASC 141; *Fleming v Marshall* [2011] NSWCA 86; *Thomson Aviation Pty Ltd v Dufresne* [2011] NSWSC 864.

[141] With the exception that a choice of court clause is relevant to determining the parties' implied choice, but not the objective proper law.

[142] *Pfeiffer v Rogerson* (2000) 203 CLR 503, 538 (referring only to intra-national torts); *Renault v Zhang* (2002) 210 CLR 491, 520; *Neilson v Overseas Projects Corporation of Victoria Ltd* (2005) 223 CLR 331, [34] McHugh J; [64], [91], [93] Gummow and Hayne JJ (*Neilson v OPCV*).

the application of the law of the seller than of the buyer,[143] which may be acceptable in commercial contracts but is at odds with consumer protection concerns.[144]

Finally, although a number of High Court cases concerning contract choice of law have involved the application of legislation in cases involving presumptively weaker parties,[145] the choice of law rule itself makes no explicit allowance for contracts in which there are protective concerns.

The rules of jurisdiction and choice of law relevant to contract are to some extent consistent. In both, the parties' choices are to be enforced unless there are strong grounds for non-enforcement, and several connecting factors are common to rules of jurisdiction and choice of law.[146]

B. Tort

The main rule of jurisdictional competency for tort requires only that the claimant has suffered in the forum some loss or damage as a result of the tort, wherever occurring.[147] This is often applied to the statutory claim for misleading or deceptive conduct,[148] which is commonly raised in commercial litigation.[149] Most of the High Court *forum non conveniens* cases have concerned personal injuries claims. The Australian courts are extremely unlikely to stay personal injuries proceedings on the basis that the court is clearly inappropriate,[150] and an unspoken concern

[143] *Mendelson-Zeller Co Inc v T & C Providores Pty Ltd* [1981] 1 NSWLR 366.

[144] The objective proper law test is used in some Australian legislation as a unilateral choice of law rule: eg Insurance Contracts Act 1984 (Cth) s 8(1). It is also used as the criterion of application of the consumer guarantees provisions in the Australian Consumer Law: s 67(a). This provision is one of the few clear indications of the intended scope of application of the Australian Consumer Law. It appears to misfire, in that the proper law will probably indicate the law of the seller whereas the intention was probably to ensure that the consumer guarantees could not be excluded if the consumer was Australian.

[145] *Mynott v Barnard* (1939) 62 CLR 68 (choice of law rules were not relevant to determine the application of Victorian workers' compensation legislation; the effect was that the employee's dependants were unable to recover any compensation following the employee's death); *Old UGC Inc v Industrial Relations Commission of New South Wales* (2006) 225 CLR 274 (the application of NSW legislation regulating employment contracts was to be determined by reference to statutory interpretation rather than the express choice of foreign law, with the effect that the employee who was a former managing director was protected by NSW legislation).

[146] Namely, the places of contracting and of performance. See eg Federal Court Rules 2011 (Cth) r 10.42(2), (3)(a), (3)(c); Uniform Civil Procedure Rules 2005 (NSW) r 11.2(1), Sch 6(b), (c)(i), (iii) and (iv); *Akai v The People's Insurance Co Ltd* (1996) 188 CLR 418, 437; *John Kaldor Fabricmaker Pty Ltd v Mitchell Cotts Freight (Australia) Pty Ltd* (1989) 18 NSWLR 172, 190.

[147] Eg Federal Court Rules 2011 (Cth) r 10.42(5); Uniform Civil Procedure Rules 2005 (NSW) r 11.2(1), Sch 6(e).

[148] Australian Consumer Law, s 18(1), replacing Trade Practices Act 1974 (Cth) s 52(1).

[149] *Commonwealth Bank v White* [1999] 2 VR 681, 697–99.

[150] *Puttick v Tenon Ltd* (2008) 238 CLR 265. In the decisions of the Australian courts from 1991–2001, stays were not granted in any personal injuries case: Keyes, *Jurisdiction in International Litigation*, above n 1, 173. Since then, the courts continue to retain jurisdiction in most personal injuries cases, with rare exceptions (for one such exception, see *McGregor v Potts* (2005) 68 NSWLR 109).

for injured claimants seems likely to have influenced the peculiarly pro-claimant version of the Australian *forum non conveniens* test.

The legislative provisions on staying and transferring proceedings give no weight to the claimant's unilateral choice of forum.[151] While this appears to be an improvement on the common law principle of *forum non conveniens*, which de facto prioritises the claimant's choice of forum, it may be insufficiently attuned to protective concerns in personal injuries litigation, even if those are less significant in intra-Australian than in international disputes. Their relevance in the trans-Tasman context is another question again.[152]

In three cases decided between 2000 to 2005, the High Court substantially reformed the choice of law rule for tort. The governing law for almost all multi-state torts[153] is now the law of the place of the tort, with no flexible (proper law) exception.[154] In *Neilson v Overseas Projects Corporation of Victoria*, the High Court held that a reference by the forum's choice of law rules to foreign law meant a reference to the whole of the foreign law including its choice of law rules, effectively incorporating *renvoi* into the Australian tort choice of law rule.[155]

It is not uncommon in multistate tort cases that there is a concurrence of liability, which gives the claimant the ability to invoke different choices of law[156] or substantive legislative principles.[157] The interaction between tort and contract law, and between statute and case law, remains unclear and unsettled. In the jurisdictional context, a claim of misleading or deceptive conduct is often analogised to tort,[158] whereas at the choice of law stage, it is usually not.[159] Like other statutory claims, this provision may be applied without regard to choice of law considerations. The application of the State and Territory civil liability legislation

[151] Service and Execution of Process Act 1992 (Cth) s 20(4); Trans-Tasman Proceedings Act 2010 (Cth) s 19(2). The cross-vesting legislation does not explicitly state this but the High Court has interpreted it to this effect: *BHP Billiton Ltd v Schultz* (2004) 221 CLR 400.

[152] This is because of the very restrictive scheme applicable in New Zealand to accident compensation, discussed in detail by Mortensen, Chapter six in this volume.

[153] The main exception is intra-national defamation, which is regulated by a cooperative legislative scheme including a choice of law rule for intra-national defamation: see eg the Defamation Act 2005 (NSW) s 11(2).

[154] *Pfeiffer v Rogerson* (2000) 203 CLR 503, 540; *Renault v Zhang* (2002) 210 CLR 491, 520.

[155] *Neilson v Overseas Projects Corporation of Victoria* (2005) 223 CLR 331.

[156] In *Busst v Lotsirb Nominees*, a case involving a workplace injury that the claimant suffered in New South Wales, the Queensland Court of Appeal found that whereas the governing law of the tort claim was that of New South Wales, the contract was governed by Queensland law: [2003] 1 Qd R 477. See likewise *Garstang v Cedenco JV Australia Ltd* [2002] NSWSC 144.

[157] In *Insight Vacations Ltd v Young*, a NSW resident suffered a personal injury while on a package tour in Europe: (2011) 243 CLR 149. The principal claim advanced was for breach of a term implied by statute in contracts for the provision of services that those services would be rendered with due care and skill: Trade Practices Act 1974 (Cth) s 74(1). This term was presumed to be applicable, even though the tort occurred in Slovakia and the contract contained an express choice of NSW law.

[158] Above n 13.

[159] Although in *Pfeiffer v Rogerson* the joint judgment stated that 'the term "tort" is used … to denote not merely civil wrongs known to the common law but also acts and omissions which by statute are rendered wrongful in the sense that a civil action lies to recover damages occasioned thereby': (2000) 203 CLR 503, 519.

and the Australian Consumer Law in multistate cases is highly uncertain.[160] This is an area which is much in need of attention and clarification.[161]

In the leading tort choice of law decisions, the High Court stated that jurisdiction and choice of law are properly distinguished.[162] It is no great surprise then to find that the rules of jurisdiction and choice of law for international torts are directly inconsistent. The jurisdictional rules facilitate forum shopping; whereas one of the dominant justifications for recent reforms to the choice of law rule was the prevention of that practice.[163] The Australian courts' use of escape devices, which allow reference to forum law rather than the foreign law indicated by the choice of law rules, also undermines the objectives of the choice of law rule.[164] The High Court's repeated rejection of the proper law exception for tort is directly inconsistent with its recent endorsement of the objective proper law as the default contract choice of law rule, which is particularly ironic given that accumulation of actions is permitted in Australia. Therefore, in a case in which there is a concurrence of liability, the proper law may be applied to a contract claim, but not to the identical claim framed in tort. Whether the proper law was applied or not might depend on the accident of whether the claimant's lawyers appreciated that there was a possibility of an alternative claim, and its significance in choice of law terms. [165]

[160] M Davies, 'Choice of Law After the Civil Liability Legislation' (2008) 16 *Torts Law Journal* 104. Most provisions of the Australian Consumer Law and of the civil liability legislation enacted in all the States and Territories contain no indication of their intended application in international cases. The issue arose in *Insight Vacations Ltd v Young*, in which the High Court unconvincingly limited the application of a provision of the NSW civil liability legislation, which is silent as to its intended territorial application, to accidents occurring in the forum: (2011) 243 CLR 149. On the other hand, the court simply assumed that the provision of the Trade Practices Act 1974 (Cth) on which the claimant relied was applicable without any justification for that assumption.

[161] The Australian Law Reform Commission's report on *Choice of Law* made detailed recommendations for the treatment of statutory claims: Australian Law Reform Commission, *Choice of Law*, Report no 58 (Canberra, Australian Government Printing Service, 1992), ch 5 (dealing with statutes generally) and ch 7 (specially dealing with statutory compensation schemes).

[162] In the leading tort choice of law case, the joint judgment stated that 'Questions of jurisdiction (in the sense of authority to decide) are better kept separate from questions of the applicable law … The assumption of jurisdiction raises no question as to the law to be applied in deciding the rights and duties of the parties': *Pfeiffer v Rogerson* (2000) 203 CLR 503, 521. The joint judgment in *Renault v Zhang* referred to this statement twice without disapproval: (2002) 210 CLR 491, 498–99. The joint judgment in *Renault v Zhang* went on to note that 'the distinction between jurisdiction as a "threshold requirement" and choice of law' should be appreciated: ibid, 517. Justice Kirby agreed that 'the issues of jurisdiction and choice of law are separate and distinct' but also noted that 'the two concepts are closely related': ibid, 528. Although the governing law is one of the factors which is relevant to deciding whether the court is a clearly inappropriate forum, in two important High Court cases the court has evidently given this factor little weight: *Renault v Zhang* (2002) 210 CLR 491, 521; *Puttick v Tenon Ltd* (2008) 238 CLR 265.

[163] *Pfeiffer v Rogerson* (2000) 203 CLR 503, 528, 534, 551–53, 570–71; *Neilson v OPCV* (2005) 223 CLR 331, 342, 363, 382–83, 394, 395, 419.

[164] M Keyes, 'Substance and Procedure in Multistate Tort Litigation' (2010) 18 *Torts Law Journal* 201, 205–11.

[165] In *Pfeiffer v Rogerson* the claimant's claim for damages for personal injuries suffered in the course of his employment was pleaded in tort. On the third appeal, the claimant sought leave to amend his pleadings, to claim alternatively in contract. The High Court refused this application: (2000) 203 CLR 503, 515.

C. Family Law

The federal Family Law Act governs most private international law issues that arise in family litigation.[166] Most of the provisions of that statute are domestic rules of family law. The Family Law Act is not quite comprehensive in its treatment of private international law, but it contains all the principles relevant to the courts' competence,[167] the recognition and enforcement of foreign determinations,[168] and the main choice of law rule.[169] It is the closest thing Australian law has to a code of private international law. The inclusion of private international law rules in the same statute that contains the domestic rules is unconventional in common law systems and unique for Australia.

The choice of law rules for family law are undeveloped. For almost all issues, the law of the forum is applied. This is taken to be the effect of subsection 42(1) of the Family Law Act, which relevantly provides that 'The jurisdiction conferred on a court ... by this Act shall be exercised in accordance with this Act'.[170] Sub-section 42(2) permits the application of foreign law 'where it would be in accordance with the common law rules of private international law', subject to the Marriage Act.[171] The Marriage Act provides choice of law rules, and restrictions of forum policy, relevant to marriage validity.[172] Otherwise, there are few common law choice of law rules relevant to family law.[173]

166 The federal government's legislative competence is limited to dealing with parties who are or have been married and to matrimonial causes: Constitution of Australia 1901, s 51(xx)–(xxi). The states retain legislative jurisdiction to deal with other matters. The States have recently referred their jurisdiction to deal with issues involving the consequences of relationship breakdowns of de facto spouses to the Commonwealth, so that the Family Law Act now contains provisions dealing with these situations. The States retain jurisdiction over issues relating to child welfare, including adoption and surrogacy.

167 Family Law Act 1975 (Cth) ss 39(3), (4), 69E(1).

168 Most of these provisions give effect to Hague Conventions. For example, the rules relevant to the recognition of foreign decrees of divorce and judicial separation, discussed in this chapter, give effect to the Hague Convention on the Recognition of Divorces and Legal Separations 1970 (Family Law Act 1975 (Cth) s 104(3)).

169 Family Law Act 1975 (Cth) s 42. The Marriage Act 1961 (Cth) contains the choice of law rules relevant to the validity of marriages: ss 22, 88C, 88D, 88EA. The parties also may choose, expressly or impliedly, the law relevant to determining their existing entitlement to marital property: *In the Marriage of Hannema* (1981) 7 Fam LR 542; *Murakami v Wiryadi* (2010) 268 ALR 377.

170 This has been interpreted as a choice of law rule in a range of different situations including parental status: *Brianna v Brianna* (2010) 43 Fam LR 309, [65].

171 There are two other choice of law rules in the Family Law Act, relating to the Hague Convention on Jurisdiction, Applicable Law, Recognition, Enforcement, and Co-operation in Respect of Parental Responsibility and Measures for the Protection of Children 1996. See Family Law Act 1975 (Cth) ss 111CR, 111CS.

172 These rules give effect to the Hague Convention on Celebration and Recognition of the Validity of Marriages 1978. The basic rule is that the law of the place of celebration applies: Marriage Act 1961 (Cth) ss 88C(2), 88D(1). This is subject to Australian requirements of public policy regarding consent, monogamy, age, prohibited relationships and heterosexuality: ibid, s 88D(2).

173 The main exceptions are the rules relating to the determination of the parties' existing entitlement to property and to the legitimation of children.

The governing law is one of the factors that the courts may take into account in determining whether the Australian court should stay proceedings on the basis of *forum non conveniens*.[174] Courts have noted that this factor should be given little weight because the governing law in most family matters is the law of the forum.[175] The governing law is normally an important factor in *forum non conveniens* determinations, and so the identification of more specific factors relevant to international family litigation in *Henry v Henry*[176] was a necessary development.

IV. Review and Reform of Australian Private International Law

As the above discussion suggests, many areas of Australian private international law require improvement. The law should be clearer, simpler, more precise and coherent and better suited to current social and economic conditions. The Australian law should be reviewed and reformed in a carefully planned project, drawing upon international developments.[177] In this Section, I make some suggestions for revision of the Australian law, drawing upon the discussion in Sections II and III.

A. Codification and Internationalisation

There has been no suggestion that private international law ought to be codified in Australia, in the sense of legislation exhaustively comprehending jurisdiction, judgments and choice of law. Any such proposal may meet with the typical common law resistance to codification, and is probably too ambitious. More modestly, it should be possible to refine existing laws, and develop new legislation, to deal with specific elements of private international law—choice of law (for contract, and other civil obligations including tort), jurisdiction and judgments. There are precedents for this even in Australia, including the Family Law Act, which incorporates what is virtually a code for private international law in family matters. Several other statutes include both rules of jurisdiction and of judgments.[178] Reform of the Australian law by means of separate instruments designed to

[174] *Voth v Manildra Flour Mills Pty Ltd* (1990) 171 CLR 538, 564–65.

[175] *In the Marriage of Gilmore* (1993) 16 Fam LR 285, 292.

[176] *Henry v Henry* (1996) 185 CLR 571, 592–93, discussed above at text to nn 72–73.

[177] Some of the better recent Australian developments derive from Hague Conventions; in particular, the Hague Convention on the Recognition of Divorces and Legal Separations 1970 (given effect in the Family Law Act 1975 (Cth) s 104) and the Hague Convention on Choice of Court Agreements 2005 (given effect in the Trans-Tasman Proceedings Act 2010 (Cth) s 20).

[178] The Service and Execution of Process Act 1992 (Cth), the cross-vesting legislation and the Trans-Tasman Proceedings Act 2010 (Cth).

operate coherently is likely to be more achievable and more acceptable than a wholesale reform.[179]

Approaching the improvement of Australian private international law in this way is consistent with recent developments abroad, in which legislation exhaustively covering jurisdiction, judgments and choice of law is unusual.[180] More commonly, these areas are addressed in separate instruments. The legislation referred to in this chapter by way of comparison to the Australian law generally[181] either deals with jurisdiction,[182] sometimes also addressing the related question of judgment recognition;[183] or choice of law, sometimes comprehensively[184] and otherwise in relation to particular areas of law.[185]

B. Jurisdiction

The principles of jurisdiction are severely flawed. Many of the rules of competency are too broad, and the rules relating to the exercise of jurisdiction are inefficient and ineffective in controlling the rules of competency. The overall effect is to permit, if not to encourage, forum shopping. The jurisdictional rules are insufficiently precise in their application to weaker parties, and poorly related to the corresponding rules for choice of law and judgment recognition.

Most of the rules of jurisdictional competency are too wide and too general. In many cases, jurisdiction may be asserted even in cases in which proceedings would certainly subsequently be stayed.[186] Rules which allow service out on the basis of no, or only trivial, connections, with no court supervision before service

[179] This approach (of 'gradual adoption') has been recommended in the admittedly different context of the European Union: European Parliament, Directorate General for Internal Policies, Policy Department C: Citizens' Rights and Constitutional Affairs, Legal Affairs, *A European Framework for Private International law: Current Gaps and Future Perspectives* (Brussels, European Union, 2012) 84–85, 90, 92–93. See A Dickinson, Chapter eight in this volume.

[180] There are several well-regarded comprehensive codes which should inform Australian reforms. The Swiss Federal Private International Law Act of 18 December 1987 is especially noteworthy because of the influence it has had on other codifications: eg Kwang Hyun Suk, 'New Conflict of Laws Act of the Republic of Korea' (2001) 1 *Journal of Korean Law* 197, 203.

[181] The Korean Conflict of Laws Act 2001 principally contains choice of law rules, but it also includes several jurisdictional provisions: arts 2, 27(4)–(6) and 28(3)–(5). These are intentionally incomplete in their coverage of jurisdiction: Suk, ibid, 199.

[182] Eg the Japanese Law to Amend Certain Parts of the Code of Civil Procedure and the Civil Provisional Penalties Act 2011.

[183] Brussels I Regulation.

[184] The Chinese, Japanese and Korean choice of law legislation addresses choice of law for all areas of private law.

[185] The Rome I and Rome II Regulations are examples, providing choice of law rules for contractual and non-contractual obligations respectively. Similarly, the Hague Convention on Choice of Court Agreements 2005 and the Hague Draft Principles on the Choice of Law in International Contracts are relevant only for international commercial contracts: art 2, art 1(1).

[186] *Henry v Henry* (1996) 185 CLR 571 is a good example. The applicant husband satisfied at least two of the three grounds of jurisdiction for a divorce application but the proceedings, brought after the respondent wife had already commenced related proceedings in a foreign court, were stayed.

is effected *ex iuris*, ought to be reviewed. There may be sound reasons for broad assertions of jurisdiction, particularly where weaker parties are concerned, but this should be reviewed carefully. If this is regarded as legitimate, the rules should be clearly articulated so that exorbitant grounds of jurisdiction cannot be used in cases in which they are not justified. It may also be appropriate to recognise limitations on the courts' jurisdiction in cases where vulnerable parties are concerned.[187] The courts which have abolished the requirement of prior leave to serve out of the jurisdiction should consider reinstating it.

In reviewing the rules of jurisdiction, consideration ought to be given to the relationship between jurisdiction and judgments, and to reducing the inconsistency between rules of local and international jurisdiction. Some of the statutory grounds of international jurisdiction, especially in the family jurisdiction, are superior to those of forum jurisdiction, and should be referred to in reviewing the latter.[188]

There was no compelling reason for removing the previous limitations on the service of process *ex iuris* within Australia.[189] The Service and Execution of Process Act is not intended to permit the continuation of litigation which lacks any connection to the forum. The legislation identifies factors relevant to whether proceedings should be stayed,[190] which could be used as factors justifying service within Australia. Consideration should also be given to imposing requirements of nexus or leave to serve out, or both, before service can be made in New Zealand.[191] The factors listed in the Trans-Tasman Proceedings Act, which the courts are directed to consider in deciding whether to stay proceedings, could be used in limiting the circumstances in which service out is permitted.

The total dependence on stay and transfer applications to control inappropriate assertions of jurisdiction in intra-Australian and New Zealand cases[192] and the heavy dependence on stay applications in other international cases is inefficient, ineffective and unfair to defendants. The cross-vesting legislation and the Service and Execution of Process Act do not clearly indicate the status of choice

[187] Brussels I Regulation, sections 4 and 5; Japanese Law to Amend Certain Parts of the Code of Civil Procedure and the Civil Provisional Penalties Act 2011, arts 3–4, 3–7(5), 3–7(6); Korean Conflict of Laws Act 2001, art 27(4)–(6), art 28(3)–(5).

[188] M Keyes, 'Jurisdiction in International Family Litigation' (2004) 27 *University of NSW Law Journal* 42 48–49.

[189] The specific reasons given for recommending the abolition of the nexus requirements in the Service and Execution of Process Act 1901 (Cth) were that nexus requirements may be artificial, too technical or manipulable; that the existing grounds did not 'necessarily establish a significant connection' and were not comprehensive: Australian Law Reform Commission, *Service and Execution of Process* Report, above n 20, [173]–[176]. These criticisms apply equally to the rules of court. It seems strange to regard them as requiring abolition of the requirement of nexus, rather than the need for reform to those rules. More general justifications given for the reforms to the legislation were that it would integrate the State and Territory legal systems as well as simplify and reduce the costs and time involved in interstate litigation: ibid, [152].

[190] Service and Execution of Process Act 1992 (Cth) s 20(4): above at text to n 96.

[191] Reform to the Trans-Tasman Proceedings Act would require a cooperative effort with New Zealand, as the legislation gives effect to a bilateral treaty.

[192] Explanatory Memorandum, Jurisdiction of Courts (Cross-vesting) Bill 1986 (Cth) 3.

of court agreements, and the cases on this point give insufficient weight to such agreements. The Trans-Tasman Proceedings Act provisions on choice of court agreements are preferable.

The *Voth* test is too heavily weighted in favour of claimants, which means that claimants are likely to succeed even if defendants challenge jurisdiction. This test does not on its face take into account the characteristics of disputes in particular areas of law, except in some family cases.[193] The refinement of the *Voth* test in *Henry v Henry*[194] was a substantial improvement. Hopefully, appellate courts will approve its application in non-family cases.[195] The factors identified in *Henry v Henry* should also be referred to in reviewing the legislative stay and transfer provisions.

Although the rules relating to stay of proceedings do not explicitly take into account the parties' characteristics, the courts do seem to be sensitive to the situation of weaker parties.[196] For example, jurisdiction clauses are unlikely to be enforced against consumers,[197] and the courts are extremely unlikely to stay personal injuries proceedings under the *Voth* test.[198] This may well be justified, in which case the law should make existing distinctions clearer.

The different verbal formulae employed in statutory rules relating to stay and transfer of proceedings make the law unnecessarily complex and incoherent, for no apparent reason. This could be simply remedied: the Commonwealth should settle upon a single legislative test for *forum non conveniens* and use it consistently. The Trans-Tasman Proceedings Act provisions are superior to those of the cross-vesting legislation and the Service and Execution of Process Act. Given the High Court's lack of inclination to change the *Voth* test, it has been suggested that this should also be modified by legislation. Unless they have good reasons for preferring different formulae, the States and Territories should consider applying the same test for *forum non conveniens* in primary and delegated legislation.

C. Judgments

The Australian law on the recognition of foreign judgments is also in need of review, particularly taking into account the relationship between jurisdiction and judgments. The lack of reciprocal recognition of the expanded bases of jurisdiction

[193] *Henry v Henry* (1996) 185 CLR 571, 592–93, discussed above at text to nn 72–73.

[194] (1996) 185 CLR 571.

[195] Cases cited above at n 75.

[196] While the courts are generally protective of weaker parties, this is not invariably the case. In *Moldauer v Constellation Brands Inc*, proceedings brought in Australia by an employee were stayed, mainly because of questions of cost and convenience. This was so even though Kourakis CJ acknowledged 'that bringing proceedings in New York would be costly' and noted that unless the plaintiff 'is a man of unusually wealthy means he will find it difficult to maintain an action in New York': [2013] SASC 38, [20].

[197] Above, text to nn 53–54.

[198] Above, text to n 149.

under the rules of court, the lack of development or of acceptance of any other basis of international jurisdiction, and the limited reach of the Foreign Judgments Act together mean that judgments from many countries will only be recognised if the defendant submitted to the jurisdiction of the foreign court or was present in the foreign jurisdiction at the time of service.

There are a number of statutes which contain rules both of jurisdiction and judgments. These rules are more often than not inconsistent, and are insufficiently related. The Service and Execution of Process Act is a striking example. The constitutional imperative to give full faith and credit to sister-State judgments, which is fundamental to the judgments provisions of that Act, makes it essential that the relevant jurisdictional rules are sound and robust. This is not the case, particularly in relation to proceedings in the superior courts.[199] The jurisdictional provisions of the Act should be reviewed in the context of the constitutional requirement of full faith and credit. The Service and Execution of Process was an inapt model for the recognition of judgments in the Trans-Tasman Proceedings Act, because there is no equivalent to the constitutional requirement of full faith and credit for New Zealand judgments. If New Zealand judgments are to be liberally recognised, this should be based on stronger jurisdictional foundations than are found in the Trans-Tasman Proceedings Act.

The inconsistency between the rules of jurisdiction and international jurisdiction requires attention. The statutory grounds of international jurisdiction in the Foreign Judgments Act[200] should be used in reviewing the common law grounds of international jurisdiction generally, as well as the rules of jurisdictional competency. Given the importance of non-money judgments in international civil litigation, consideration should be given to allowing the recognition of foreign non-money judgments. This could easily be done by utilising the authority to make delegated legislation to that effect in the Foreign Judgments Act.[201]

D. Choice of law

The choice of law rules would benefit from revision, drawing on international developments as well as the recommendations of the Australian Law Reform Commission made in 1992.[202] In this section, I identify some possible areas for review of the choice of law rules applicable to contract, tort and family law.

[199] Above, text to nn 83–85.

[200] Foreign Judgments Act 1991 (Cth) s 7(3)(b), (c).

[201] Foreign Judgments Act 1991 (Cth) s 5(6).

[202] The Report proposed that the Commonwealth, the States and Territories enact uniform legislation dealing with choice of law for 'tort-like claims', motor vehicle accidents, workers' compensation, contract, fair trading laws, trusts and succession: Australian Law Reform Commission, *Choice of Law* Report, above n 161. Although aspects of the Report's recommendations in relation to tort choice of law are consistent with subsequent changes to the case law, the High Court does not seem to have been particularly influenced by those recommendations in reforming the law. The Report was cited in argument in all the leading cases: by the applicant in *Pfeiffer v Rogerson* (2000) 203 CLR 503, by the

(i) Contract

The default contract choice of law rule makes prediction of the governing law difficult, and may be likely to lead to the application of forum law. The more precise default rules which have been developed and refined in other legal systems, using the characteristic performance presumption to identify the objective proper law of the contract, should be considered for adoption in Australia.[203] Specific provisions should also be made for weaker parties at the choice of law stage. For example, limitations on express choices of law in consumer and employment contracts should be explicitly articulated in the choice of law rule.[204]

Recent choice of law legislation in other legal systems limits autonomy by reference to the application of mandatory rules,[205] which can be defined. Unlike the current Australian position, the recognition of mandatory rules is usually not limited to those of the forum.[206] This is both clearer and less chauvinistic than the current Australian position.

(ii) Tort

The choice of law rule for tort claim should be reviewed, taking into account criticisms of the Australian rule as well as international developments. A comparative study could consider, for example, whether the law of the place of where the damage occurred should be adopted as the primary rule,[207] whether exceptions to the primary rule (based for example on the existence of a closer connection to another country or its law) should be permitted in particular situations,[208] whether specific choice of law rules for different types of torts should be

respondent in *Renault v Zhang* (2002) 210 CLR 491, and by the respondent in *Neilson v OPCV* (2005) 223 CLR 331. Kirby J was the only member of the High Court who cited the Report in any of these cases. His Honour referred to it in passing in *Renault v Zhang* (2002) 210 CLR 491, 549 and in *Neilson v OPCV* (2005) 223 CLR 331, 388.

[203] Eg Law of the People's Republic of China on the Laws Applicable to Foreign-Related Civil Relations 2010, art 41; Rome I Regulation, art 4.

[204] Eg Law of the People's Republic of China on the Laws Applicable to Foreign-Related Civil Relations 2010, art 42 (consumer contracts), art 43 (employment contracts); Rome I Regulation, art 6 (consumer contracts), art 8 (employment contracts); Japanese Act on the General Rules of Application of Laws, Law No 10 of 1898 (as newly titled and amended 21 June 2006), art 11 (consumer contracts), art 12 (employment contracts); Korean Conflict of Laws Act 2001, art 27(1)–(3) (consumer contracts), art 28(1)–(2) (employment contracts).

[205] Eg Law of the People's Republic of China on the Laws Applicable to Foreign-Related Civil Relations 2010, art 4; Rome I Regulation, art 9; Korean Choice of Law Act 2001, arts 7, 25(4); Hague Principles on the Choice of Law in International Contracts 2012, art 11.

[206] Eg Rome I Regulation, art 9(3).

[207] Rome II Regulation, art 4(1); Japanese Act on the General Rules of Application of Laws, Law No 10 of 1898 (as newly titled and amended 21 June 2006), art 17.

[208] Law of the People's Republic of China on the Laws Applicable to Foreign-Related Civil Relations 2010, art 44; Rome II Regulation, art 4(2) and 4(3); Japanese Act on the General Rules of Application of Laws, Law No 10 of 1898 (as newly titled and amended 21 June 2006), art 20; Korean Conflict of Laws Act 2001, art 32(2).

developed,[209] and what effect should be given to the parties' expressed choices of law in tort claims.[210] Recent foreign legislation typically excludes *renvoi*,[211] sometimes in the context of tort specifically.[212]

As in the area of contract, the interaction between the choice of law rules and statutory claims and defences should be considered in detail.

(iii) Family Law

At common law, forum law was applicable to most family law issues. The application of forum law without any choice of law limitation was justified on the basis of the common law jurisdictional rule, which recognised the exclusive jurisdiction of the courts of the matrimonial domicile.[213] This jurisdictional rule meant that the application of the law of the forum could be justified on the basis that it was necessarily the law of the domicile.[214] Notwithstanding the significant expansion of the jurisdictional rules in the Family Law Act, there has been no corresponding change to the choice of law rules in order to limit the application of forum law. In justifying the recent change to the tort choice of law rule, the High Court emphasised the inappropriateness of applying forum law.[215] This criticism is more cogent in the context of international family law, given the breadth of the rules of jurisdictional competency.

Improving the jurisdictional rules would go some way to rectifying this problem, but given the increasing number of international cases in the family jurisdiction, it remains desirable to consider the development of choice of law rules for family matters. Again, a comparative study could be productive, for example, in considering what effect ought to be given to the parties' express choices of law in areas other than determination of existing rights to property.[216]

[209] For example, in relation to products liability: see Law of the People's Republic of China on the Laws Applicable to Foreign-Related Civil Relations 2010, art 45; Rome II Regulation, art 5; Japanese Act on the General Rules of Application of Laws, Law No 10 of 1898 (as newly titled and amended 21 June 2006), art 18.

[210] Law of the People's Republic of China on the Laws Applicable to Foreign-Related Civil Relations 2010, art 44; Rome II Regulation, art 14; Japanese Act on the General Rules of Application of Laws, Law No 10 of 1898 (as newly titled and amended 21 June 2006), art 21; Korean Conflict of Laws Act 2001, art 33.

[211] Law of the People's Republic of China on the Laws Applicable to Foreign-Related Civil Relations 2010, art 9.

[212] Rome II Regulation, art 24.

[213] *Le Mesurier v Le Mesurier* [1895] AC 517, 540.

[214] The *lex domicilii* is the governing law for most issues that are not governed by the *lex fori*, such as the parties' entitlement to movable property: *In the Marriage of Hannema* (1981) 7 Fam LR 542.

[215] *Renault v Zhang* (2002) 210 CLR 491, 515.

[216] Law of the People's Republic of China on the Laws Applicable to Foreign-Related Civil Relations 2010, art 26; Council Regulation EU 1259/2010 of 20 December 2010 implementing enhanced cooperation in the area of the law applicable to divorce and legal separation OJ L343/10, art 5.

V. Conclusion

As in many other legal systems, private international law in Australia has undergone change during the last 30 years. The changes to Australian law have been haphazard, piecemeal, poorly coordinated and of variable quality. In this chapter, I have identified some of the more obvious problems with the law, and made some suggestions as to how those problems might be rectified, including by reference to international developments. The Standing Council on Law and Justice project indicates the interest of Australian governments in private international law, which by no means should be taken for granted, and offers an opportunity to undertake a comprehensive review of the Australian law. The expert advisory group which has been established as part of this project is ideally placed to guide such a review, drawing on the expertise of judges, civil servants, legal practitioners and academics.

II

First Reactions to the Attorney-General's Consultation

3

Incoherence in Australian Private International Laws

THE HONOURABLE JAMES ALLSOP AND DANIEL WARD

I. Introduction

This chapter identifies some current sources of incoherence in Australian private international laws, the disadvantages stemming from the current disharmony, and the benefits that might come—both for the nation and for litigants—from greater coherence. Something will also be said of the means by which greater coherence might be achieved. The aim here is to address only Australian private international laws as they affect disputes with an overseas element. This paper focuses on two of the three pillars of private international law: jurisdiction, and recognition and enforcement of foreign judgments. It is appropriate, at the outset, to identify two reasons why incoherence in private international law is particularly troublesome. First, private international law is a gatekeeper to the rest of the law. The best substantive laws in the world (of tort, contract or whatever it may be) are of no avail if a court lacks jurisdiction over a party to a dispute. Equally, the justice of those rules is liable to perversion where courts exercise excessive jurisdiction. Moreover, the utility of invoking the law (of Australia or another place) depends upon the enforceability of judgments. It is especially important that the gatekeeper act in a manner conducive to the interests of parties and of the nation as a whole. The second reason is that private international law is a facet of Australia's external affairs. It is of more than mere domestic interest: it affects the way we look at the world, and the way the world looks back.

II. The Present State of Incoherence

A. Establishing Personal Jurisdiction

The sole grounds that found a court's personal jurisdiction over a party at common law are the service of a writ upon that party within the court's territorial jurisdiction, or the party's voluntary appearance. State and Territory courts, as well as the Federal Court, have 'long-arm' rules permitting service of process upon defendants in a broader range of circumstances than at common law.[1] The result of having nine different regimes governing courts' personal jurisdiction over overseas defendants is a bewildering picture.[2] The following paragraphs identify a number of categories of proceeding in which incoherence is most apparent. For the immediate purposes of this discussion, the Trans-Tasman Proceedings Act 2010 (Cth) (TTPA) is briefly put to one side.

(i) A Threshold Issue

In all but three Australian jurisdictions, a party may serve originating process upon an overseas defendant without the court's prior leave, provided the action falls within a relevant ground of long-arm jurisdiction. But a litigant in the Federal Court or Northern Territory Supreme Court requires prior leave.[3] It must satisfy the court that it has a prima facie case for relief.[4] Prior leave is required also in the Western Australian Supreme Court, but there is no requirement to demonstrate a prima facie case.[5] These differences in the rules are of appreciable forensic significance.

(ii) Corporations

Substantively, one of the areas of perhaps most variation across the country concerns overseas service in corporation matters. There are as many as five different regimes across Australia. The first governs Queensland and New South Wales (NSW),[6] where overseas service is permitted in proceedings concerning a person's membership of a corporation incorporated within the State.[7] A second, broader regime covers the ACT and Federal Court.[8] The proceedings may concern not only membership of, but also an office-holding in, a corporation. Further,

[1] The same is true in the United States, following *International Shoe Co v Washington*, 326 US 310 (1945), the difference being that these long-arm rules are all kept within a certain range by the US Constitution's Due Process Clause: Eugene F Scoles et al, *Conflict of Laws*, 4th edn (St Paul, MN, Thomson West, 2004) 321.

[2] See M Davies, A Bell and P Le Gay Brereton, *Nygh's Conflict of Laws in Australia*, 8th edn (Sydney, LexisNexis Butterworths, 2010) xxii. The High Court Rules permit service out of the jurisdiction in the same circumstances as the Federal Court Rules: High Court Rules 2004 (Cth) r 9.07.

[3] Federal Court Rules 2011 (Cth) r 10.43(1)(a); Supreme Court Rules (NT) r 7.02(1).

[4] Federal Court Rules 2011 (Cth) r 10.43(4)(c); Supreme Court Rules (NT) r 7.02(2)(c).

[5] Rules of the Supreme Court 1971 (WA) O 10, r 4.

[6] Uniform Civil Procedure Rules 1999 (Qld) r 124(1)(m); Uniform Civil Procedure Rules 2005 (NSW) Sch 6(q).

[7] Even within this category, though, there may be a divergence. The NSW rule stipulates that the person whose membership is affected must be *the person served*. This may not be a requirement in Queensland, though. The Queensland rule simply refers to the proceeding 'affecting *a person* in relation to the person's membership'.

[8] Court Procedures Rules 2006 (ACT) r 6501(1)(m); Federal Court Rules 2011 (Cth) r 10.42 items 8, 24.

the corporation need not be incorporated within the relevant jurisdiction; it is sufficient that it carry on business there. A third regime exists in Western Australia,[9] where there are two significant points of difference. First, it is not enough that a proceeding *affect* a person's membership of a corporation; the *subject-matter* must be company shares. This appreciably narrows the basis for service. Secondly, the relevant nexus with Western Australia is that the corporation have its principal place of business in the State (as opposed to having been incorporated or merely carrying on business there). In the fourth regime, Tasmania, the equivalent ground of service concerns proceedings affecting the person to be served in respect of his or her membership of a corporation 'in the State'.[10] This seems the broadest possible territorial nexus. Finally, in Victoria, South Australia and the Northern Territory, there are no distinct grounds of overseas service in respect of corporate shareholdings or office-holdings.

(iii) Contract

Rules of service in contract proceedings are obviously of great commercial significance. Yet there are numerous confounding drafting variations in the various Australian rules. One may be noted by way of illustration. In Queensland and the ACT, but nowhere else, the rules allow overseas service in proceedings concerning contracts made by one or more parties carrying on business or residing within the jurisdiction.[11] In those jurisdictions, then, a party to a contract could rely solely upon its residence or business activities in the forum to serve a foreign defendant. All other Australian jurisdictions require some more substantial nexus between the contract and the forum.[12]

(iv) Commonwealth Statutes

There may be some question whether, and in what fora, the fact that proceedings concern the interpretation, effect or enforcement of a Commonwealth statute is sufficient to ground overseas service. The rules of court in NSW, Queensland and Tasmania permit service out where the proceedings concern the interpretation, effect or enforcement of 'an Act'.[13] However, in a broadly familiar provision, the Acts Interpretation Act 1954 (Qld) provides that the word 'Act' means 'an Act of the Queensland Parliament'.[14] Even if it were possible to displace this meaning

[9] Rules of the Supreme Court 1971 (WA) O 10, r 1(1)(a)(ii).

[10] Supreme Court Rules 2000 (Tas) r 147A(1)(r)(i).

[11] Uniform Civil Procedure Rules 1999 (Qld) r 124(1)(g)(ii); Court Procedures Rules 2006 (ACT) r 6501(1)(g)(ii).

[12] Where, however, service out is permitted on the basis that a contract was made within the forum, the relevant nexus may similarly be thought to be insufficiently substantial.

[13] Uniform Civil Procedure Rules 1999 (Qld) r 124(1)(t)(i); Uniform Civil Procedure Rules 2005 (NSW) Sch 6(r); Supreme Court Rules 2000 (Tas) r 147A(1)(k)(i).

[14] Acts Interpretation Act 1954 (Qld) s 6. By virtue of the Statutory Instruments Act 1992 (Qld) ss 14(1) and 14A, that definition of 'Act' holds true for the Uniform Civil Procedure Rules 1999 (Qld).

by contrary intention,[15] the wording of the relevant rule seems, if anything, to confirm it. The rule's first sub-paragraph refers simply to 'an Act', while the second refers to 'an Imperial or Commonwealth Act affecting property in Queensland'.[16] If the term 'an Act' encompassed both State and Commonwealth legislation, what purpose would the second sub-paragraph serve?[17] Similar observations may be made about the equivalent (though not identical) provisions in NSW and Tasmania.[18] The upshot appears to be that in order to rely upon this particular ground of personal jurisdiction in proceedings involving Commonwealth legislation,[19] plaintiffs have two options. They may resort to the Federal Court.[20] Alternatively, and somewhat surprisingly, they may bring proceedings in South Australia, where the rules provide for overseas service if 'the action is brought under a statute of the Commonwealth'.[21] This leads to some particularly odd results when it comes to actions brought under the Civil Aviation (Carriers Liability) Act 1959 (Cth). Some States and Territories have specific grounds of

Cf Interpretation Act 1987 (NSW) s 12(1)(b) (a reference to a locality, jurisdiction or other matter or thing is a reference to such a locality, jurisdiction or other matter or thing in and of NSW); s 65 (an Act passed by Parliament, or by any earlier legislature of NSW, may be referred to by the word 'Act' alone); Acts Interpretation Act 1931 (Tas) s 5 ('the word Act used in relation to a legislative enactment, shall include all Acts and ordinances which have been duly made and passed by the Parliament of Tasmania or by any council or authority empowered to make and pass laws in Tasmania, and to which assent has been duly given by or on behalf of the Sovereign').

[15] It does not appear that this definition could be displaced by contrary intention in the Rules: Statutory Instruments Act 1992 (Qld) s 19; Sch 2.

[16] Uniform Civil Procedure Rules 1999 (Qld) r 124(1)(t)(ii).

[17] This view is supported by the LexisNexis Civil Procedure Practice (Qld). In relation to r 124(t)(i), the author states that the rule 'makes a clear distinction between State and Commonwealth legislation, referring in its first limb to an "Act" (defined by s 6 of the Acts Interpretation Act 1954 to mean "an Act of the Queensland Parliament") and in its second limb to "an Imperial or Commonwealth Act affecting property in Queensland"'.

[18] Interpretation Act 1987 (NSW) s 12(1)(b) (a reference to a locality, jurisdiction or other matter or thing is a reference to such a locality, jurisdiction or other matter or thing in and of NSW); s 65 (an Act passed by Parliament, or by any earlier legislature of NSW, may be referred to by the word 'Act' alone); Acts Interpretation Act 1931 (Tas) s 5 (the word Act used in relation to a legislative enactment, shall include all Acts and ordinances which have been duly made and passed by the Parliament of Tasmania or by any council or authority empowered to make and pass laws in Tasmania, and to which assent has been duly given by or on behalf of the Sovereign.) As to the meaning of 'Act' in the various rules governing service outside the jurisdiction, see Martin Davies, Andrew Bell and Paul Le Gay Brereton, *Nygh's Conflict of Laws in Australia*, 9th edn (Sydney, LexisNexis Butterworths, 2014) 63–64 (Davies, Bell and Brereton, *Nygh's Conflict of Laws in Australia*, 9th edn); cf Martin Davies, Andrew Bell and Paul Le Gay Brereton, *Nygh's Conflict of Laws in Australia*, 8th edn (Sydney, LexisNexis Butterworths, 2010) 53.

[19] As to State legislation operating as 'surrogate' Commonwealth law under the Judiciary Act 1903 (Cth) s 79, it probably goes without saying that the language of the Queensland, NSW and Tasmanian court rules (construed as mandated by the Interpretation Acts) remains wide enough to encompass such legislation.

[20] Federal Court Rules 2011 (Cth) r 10.42 items 14, 15; Judiciary Act 1903 (Cth) s 39B(1A)(c). See James Allsop, 'Federal Jurisdiction and the Jurisdiction of the Federal Court of Australia in 2002' (2002) 23 *Australian Bar Review* 29.

[21] Supreme Court Civil Rules 2006 (SA) r 40(1)(k).

personal jurisdiction related to claims brought under this Act.[22] Others do not. Within the former category, there are at least two possible outcomes. First, if proceedings are brought in Queensland or the ACT, the plaintiff may serve overseas only if he or she resides or has suffered damage in the relevant jurisdiction.[23] Yet, secondly, the same plaintiff could serve overseas in Western Australian, Victorian or the Northern Territory proceedings, irrespective of where he or she resides or suffered damage.[24] Meanwhile, in jurisdictions with no special ground of service in relation to this Act, outcomes are similarly varied. Personal jurisdiction could be established in South Australia by virtue of the aforementioned provision relating to actions 'brought under a statute of the Commonwealth'.[25] The same is true of the Federal Court.[26] However, assuming the above analysis of the meaning of 'Act' in the relevant rules is correct, a plaintiff in NSW or Tasmania might be out of luck.

(v) Property in the Forum

There is a contrast between, on the one hand, jurisdictions where overseas service is allowed if the proceedings 'relate to' property situated within the jurisdiction (South Australia and the ACT[27]) and, on the other hand, other jurisdictions (Western Australia, NSW, Tasmania and the Federal Court) where service out is permitted only where such property is the *subject-matter* of the proceedings.[28] The former is a much broader category, notwithstanding that the phrase 'relates to' has been given a narrow construction in this context.[29] Still another wording is provided in Queensland,[30] where the proceedings must be 'about' property situated in that State. Victoria and the Northern Territory fit within a fourth and more obviously different category; there, land (but not personal property) must be the *whole* subject-matter of the proceedings.[31] The upshot is that the same set of facts might lead to four different outcomes across Australia, depending on

[22] Queensland (Uniform Civil Procedure Rules 1999 (Qld) r 124(1)(q)); Northern Territory (Supreme Court Rules (NT) r 7.01(1)(o)); Victoria (Supreme Court (General Civil Procedure) Rules 2005 (Vic) r 7.01(1)(n)); Western Australia (Rules of the Supreme Court 1971 (WA) O 10, r 1(1)(l)); ACT (Court Procedures Rules 2006 (ACT) r 6501(1)(q)).

[23] Uniform Civil Procedure Rules 1999 (Qld) r 124(1)(q); Court Procedures Rules 2006 (ACT) r 6501(1)(q).

[24] Rules of the Supreme Court 1971 (WA) O 10, r 1(1)(l); Supreme Court (General Civil Procedure) Rules 2005 (Vic) r 7.01(1)(n); Supreme Court Rules (NT) r 7.01(1)(o).

[25] Supreme Court Civil Rules 2006 (SA) r 40(1)(k).

[26] Federal Court Rules 2011 (Cth) r 10.42 item 14.

[27] Supreme Court Civil Rules 2006 (SA) r 40(1)(a)(i); Court Procedures Rules 2006 (ACT) r 6501(1)(b)(i).

[28] Rules of the Supreme Court 1971 (WA) O 10, r 1(1)(a)(i); Uniform Civil Procedure Rules 2005 (NSW) Sch 6(j); Supreme Court Rules 2000 (Tas) r 147A(1)(e); Federal Court Rules 2011 (Cth) r 10.42 item 21.

[29] *Saltram Wine Estates Pty Ltd v Independent Stave Co* (1992) 57 SASR 156.

[30] Uniform Civil Procedure Rules 1999 (Qld) r 124(1)(s).

[31] Supreme Court Rules (NT) r 7.01(1)(a); Supreme Court (General Civil Procedure) Rules 2005 (Vic) r 7.01(1)(a).

the jurisdiction. Similarly, while in most Australian jurisdictions overseas service may occur where proceedings concern the construction, effect or enforcement of deeds and other instruments affecting real or personal property within the jurisdiction,[32] this is not true of Western Australia, Victoria and the Northern Territory. The rules there allow overseas service only where the relevant instrument affects *land* (and, in Western Australia, also hereditaments) within the forum.[33] Those jurisdictions also make special provision for overseas service in proceedings by mortgagors or mortgagees seeking certain remedies in respect of personal property situated within the forum.[34] But such rules are not sufficient to bring these jurisdictions into line with the rest of the country, where overseas service may occur in proceedings concerning a broader range of instruments (not confined to mortgages) affecting personal property.

(vi) Actions to Enforce Foreign Judgments

Some Australian jurisdictions permit overseas service in common law proceedings for enforcement of a foreign judgment.[35] Others do not.[36] As will later be discussed, this disparity remains significant in light of the ongoing relevance of common law enforcement actions, despite enactment of the Foreign Judgments Act 1991 (Cth) (FJA).

(vii) Interaction between the Categories

Further complicating matters are the differing manners in which the grounds of overseas service interact. Broadly speaking, there are two regimes in this country. Under the first (which governs Western Australia, Victoria, South Australia and the Northern Territory), only those claims fitting wholly within a ground of jurisdiction may be served upon an overseas defendant.[37] Additional or related claims in respect of which service is not authorised cannot be brought in the same proceedings.[38] That is because the rules have not displaced the common law precept that long-arm jurisdiction grounds are to be read independently and

[32] Federal Court Rules 2011 (Cth) r 10.42 item 6; Uniform Civil Procedure Rules 1999 (Qld) r 124(1)(c); Uniform Civil Procedure Rules 2005 (NSW) Sch 6(m); Supreme Court Civil Rules 2006 (SA) r 40(1)(a)(ii); Supreme Court Rules 2000 (Tas) r 147A(1)(n); Court Procedures Rules 2006 (ACT) r 6501(1)(c).

[33] Rules of the Supreme Court 1971 (WA) O 10, r 1(1)(b); Supreme Court (General Civil Procedure) Rules 2005 (Vic) r 7.01(1)(b); Supreme Court Rules (NT) r 7.01(1)(b).

[34] Rules of the Supreme Court 1971 (WA) O 10, r 1(1)(j); Supreme Court (General Civil Procedure) Rules 2005 (Vic) r 7.01(1)(m); Supreme Court Rules (NT) r 7.01(1)(m), (n).

[35] Uniform Civil Procedure Rules 2005 (NSW) Sch 6(u); Supreme Court Civil Rules 2006 (SA) r 40(1)(j); Supreme Court Rules 2000 (Tas) r 147A(1)(t); Court Procedures Rules 2006 (ACT) r 6501(1)(w).

[36] In the former category are NSW, South Australia, Tasmania and the ACT. Western Australia, Queensland, Victoria, the Northern Territory and the Federal Court fit within the latter.

[37] *Nygh's Conflict of Laws in Australia*, 9th edn, above n 18, 73.

[38] ibid, 35.

disjunctively.[39] A different regime governs the rest of the country. In Queensland, Tasmania, the ACT and the Federal Court, it is sufficient that proceedings fall only partly within one of the grounds of service.[40] In NSW, meanwhile, if only part of the proceeding falls within one such ground, then it is necessary that the residue fall within one or more of the others.[41] Accordingly, claims not authorised under any ground cannot be added to proceedings.

B. Declining to Exercise Jurisdiction—Staying Proceedings on Discretionary Grounds

Australian courts have a discretion to stay proceedings or, alternatively, to refuse to grant leave to serve or proceed against an overseas defendant.[42] There are three principal applicable tests when it comes to proceedings with an overseas dimension: the 'more appropriate forum', 'clearly inappropriate forum' and 'inappropriate forum' tests. An Australian court may stay proceedings if it is satisfied that a New Zealand court is the more appropriate court.[43] By contrast, the common law test applied in respect of most other overseas courts permits a stay on forum grounds only if the Australian court is a 'clearly inappropriate forum'.[44] This approach has been described as an 'outlier' by comparison to other common law jurisdictions.[45] This is not the place to examine the merits of the *Voth* test. What matters for present purposes is that the common law test differs substantially from that stipulated under the Trans-Tasman Proceedings Act 2010 (Cth). The third relevant test is the 'inappropriate forum' test. The NSW and ACT rules provide expressly that the court may set aside overseas service on the ground that the court is 'an inappropriate forum' for the proceedings.[46] The equivalent Victorian rule uses the phrase, 'not a convenient forum'.[47] Further, the 'inappropriate forum' test applies in the ACT and NSW in respect of proceedings relating to land or immovable property outside the jurisdiction. The common law '*Moçambique* rule' barred jurisdiction in claims concerning title to, possession of, or trespass to, foreign land.[48] In NSW, the rule was totally abolished,[49] while in the ACT it

[39] ibid, 62; *Matthews v Kuwait Bechtel Corp* [1959] 2 QB 57.

[40] Federal Court Rules 2011 (Cth) r 10.42; Uniform Civil Procedure Rules 1999 (Qld) r 124(1)(x); Supreme Court Rules 2000 (Tas) r 147A(1); Court Procedures Rules 2006 (ACT) r 6501(1)(y).

[41] Uniform Civil Procedure Rules 2005 (NSW) Sch 6(w).

[42] *Voth v Manildra Flour Mills Pty Ltd* (1990) 171 CLR 538.

[43] Trans-Tasman Proceedings Act 2010 (Cth) s 19(1).

[44] *Voth v Manildra Flour Mills Pty Ltd*, above n 42.

[45] Attorney-General's Department, 'Reducing Legal Complexity of Cross-Border Transactions and Relationships' (Attorney-General's Consultation Paper) (reprinted in Annex 1 to this collection), [74].

[46] Uniform Civil Procedure Rules 2005 (NSW) r 11.7(2)(b); Court Procedures Rules 2006 (ACT) r 6503(3)(c).

[47] Supreme Court (General Civil Procedure) Rules 2005 (Vic) r 7.05(2)(b).

[48] *British South Africa Co v Companhia de Moçambique* [1893] AC 602.

[49] Jurisdiction of Courts (Foreign Land) Act 1989 (NSW) s 3.

still applies, but only to adjudications upon title or possession.[50] A NSW court may decline to entertain an action in relation to foreign land or immovables if it considers that it is 'not the appropriate court' to hear the proceedings.[51] The ACT provision uses the phrase, 'inappropriate forum'.[52] Is there a difference between an 'inappropriate forum' and a '*clearly* inappropriate forum'? A High Court majority has held that the term 'inappropriate forum' is informed by 'the same concepts and considerations' as is the phrase, 'clearly inappropriate forum'.[53] The majority, however, described the former as 'less emphatic'.[54] As one of the authors of this chapter observed in his judicial capacity in a recent NSW Court of Appeal decision, the adverb 'clearly', at least on its face, imports a difference in quality and emphasis;[55] that is, it is more emphatic. The position is somewhat unclear.

C. Recognition and Execution of Foreign Judgments

There is no coherent Australian regime for the recognition and enforcement of foreign judgments. The FJA seeks to provide such a mechanism, but it does so only in respect of courts prescribed in the regulations. For a court to be prescribed, the foreign jurisdiction in question must agree to assure 'substantial reciprocity' in its courts' treatment of Australian judgments.[56] Though 28 countries are listed in the regulations, the courts of some of Australia's most significant trading partners (such as the United States and China) are excluded.[57] Moreover, even as to prescribed courts, the statutory mechanism currently applies only in respect of monetary judgments.[58] Additionally, although the FJA establishes a simplified procedure for foreign judgment enforcement, the extent to which the procedure functions in a streamlined fashion is at the mercy of the various State and Territory court rules.[59] Those rules are not fully harmonised. The continued

[50] Civil Law (Wrongs) Act 2002 (ACT) s 220.

[51] Jurisdiction of Courts (Foreign Land) Act 1989 (NSW) s 4.

[52] Civil Law (Wrongs) Act 2002 (ACT) s 220(3).

[53] *Regie Nationale des Usines Renault SA v Zhang* (2002) 210 CLR 491, 503 (Gleeson CJ, Gaudron, McHugh, Gummow and Hayne JJ). See also *Nygh's Conflict of Laws in Australia*, 9th edn, above n 18, 196.

[54] *Regie Nationale des Usines Renault SA v Zhang* (2002) 210 CLR 491, 503 (Gleeson CJ, Gaudron, McHugh, Gummow and Hayne JJ).

[55] *Studorp Ltd v Robinson* [2012] NSWCA 382, [5] (Allsop P). See also at [62] (Hoeben JA).

[56] Foreign Judgments Act 1991 (Cth) s 5.

[57] Foreign Judgments Regulations 1992 (Cth) Sch 1.

[58] No regulation enabling enforcement of non-monetary judgments has yet been made although the legislation facilitates this (Foreign Judgments Act 1991 (Cth) s 5(6)).

[59] An example of this is the manner in which s 6(3) of the Act picks up the rules of the various States and Territories. Under that provision, the court's obligation to register a judgment is subject to the applicant proving certain matters set out in the State and Territory rules. These rules are not all the same. Some require evidence of the nature of the claims to which the foreign judgment relates; others do not. Some require that the applicant adduce evidence that there is no stay in force in respect of any part of the foreign judgment; others do not. Though the practical effects of these differences may be minor, the existence of the differences highlights the fact that even the ostensibly streamlined regime enacted by the Commonwealth may not operate uniformly across the nation.

importance of State and Territory rules to the operation of the statutory regime perpetuates one of the flaws of the previous arrangements, under which there was a separate statutory scheme for registration of judgments in each State and Territory. In his Second Reading Speech on the Foreign Judgments Act, the then Attorney-General, Mr Duffy, observed:[60]

> The problem with the current scheme has not been the legislation itself but rather the multiplication of effort involved in implementing and keeping arrangements up to date under the various State and Territory laws. Under the current scheme there is invariably a long delay in implementing arrangements in all jurisdictions.

Where the operation of the scheme depends upon the State and Territory court rules, this problem will still lurk in the background.

(i) Differences Between Common Law and Statutory Enforcement Regimes

If it is sought to enforce a foreign judgment against an overseas party, one key difference between the statutory and common law regimes is the requirement that originating process be served under the latter but not the former. There must therefore be a ground of overseas service in common law but not statutory enforcement proceedings.[61] As previously observed, not all Australian court rules permit overseas service of originating process in a common law enforcement action. Additionally, the grounds upon which judgments may be enforced differ between common law and the FJA. Both put the extent of the foreign court's cognisable jurisdiction in issue. To enforce a foreign judgment at common law, the plaintiff must prove that the foreign court did not exceed the jurisdiction cognisable at common law.[62] The FJA, meanwhile, provides that where a judgment debtor applies to have registration set aside, an Australian court must accede to that application if satisfied that the foreign court lacked jurisdiction, as defined in the Act.[63] In neither case does the term 'jurisdiction' refer to the jurisdictional rules actually applicable to the foreign court.[64] In some instances, also, the common law conception of jurisdiction has been modified in such a way as to harmonise it with the statutory conception. For instance, there are several circumstances in which the common law previously regarded a party as having voluntarily submitted to a foreign court's jurisdiction but which are expressly excluded by the FJA.[65] In this instance, the Act's definition applies to judgment enforcement both under

[60] Commonwealth of Australia, *Parliamentary Debates*, House of Representatives, 29 May 1991, 4218 (Michael Duffy, Attorney-General).

[61] *Hunt v BP Exploration Co (Libya) Ltd* (1979) 144 CLR 565. See also R Mortensen, R Garnett and M Keyes, *Private International Law in Australia*, 2nd edn (Sydney, LexisNexis Butterworths, 2011) 161.

[62] *Nygh's Conflict of Laws in Australia*, 9th edn, above n 18, 896.

[63] Foreign Judgments Act 1991 (Cth) s 7(2)(a)(iv).

[64] The extent of foreign courts' jurisdiction cognisable under Australian law is often, no doubt, much narrower than the jurisdiction authorised by the rules applicable to the foreign court.

[65] *Nygh's Conflict of Laws in Australia*, 9th edn, above n 18, 946; Mortensen, Garnett and Keyes, above n 61, 143.

the FJA and at common law.[66] Beyond this, though, lie significant differences. The statutory definition of 'jurisdiction'[67] is both more and less generous to judgment creditors than the common law. Where it is less generous, it appears the common law cannot be called in aid, as the statutory definition has been treated as exhaustive.[68] For instance, the FJA recognises a foreign court as having jurisdiction over a corporation if its principal place of business was within the country of the court or if the transaction at issue was effected through an office or place of business there, whereas at common law the presence of any office suffices, whether or not it has a connection to the proceedings.[69] Further, it seems mere physical presence of the judgment debtor within the foreign court's jurisdiction is sufficient at common law, whereas the FJA requires not mere presence but rather residence.[70] Again, there is no common law authority for any rule denying the foreign court's jurisdiction where it entertains an action brought in contravention of an exclusive choice of court or arbitration agreement, yet that rule has found its way into the FJA.[71] There are cases, therefore, where the common law, but not the FJA, recognises a foreign court's jurisdiction. In such circumstances, the judgment may be enforced at common law (assuming other criteria are satisfied) but not under the Act.[72] This is surprising. It seems to accord better with the rationale of the FJA that if there are to be discrepancies with the common law, they should favour judgment creditors utilising the statutory scheme. Apparently, the FJA aims to facilitate enforcement of foreign judgments delivered in countries that have reciprocity arrangements with Australia. It seems such enforcement should be easier than in the case of judgments from countries without those arrangements. One would expect, then, that enforcement under the FJA would be possible in a broader, rather than more narrow, range of circumstances than at common law. Of course, the common law may in some respects be considered overly ready to recognise a foreign court's jurisdiction. That may be true, for example, in proceedings brought in contravention of an arbitration or choice of court clause. There are good reasons for modifying the common law in this respect. The FJA introduces a more sensible rule but, surprisingly, that rule applies only to actions brought under the statutory scheme. The Act does not, in this regard, modify the rules applicable in common law actions.[73]

[66] Foreign Judgments Act 1991 (Cth) ss 7(5), 11 (the latter applies to actions at common law).

[67] Foreign Judgments Act 1991 (Cth) s 7(3).

[68] *Sharps Commercials Ltd v Gas Turbines Ltd* [1956] NZLR 819; *Crick v Hennessy* [1973] WAR 74; *Nygh's Conflict of Laws in Australia*, 9th edn, above n 18, 943.

[69] Foreign Judgments Act 1991 (Cth) s 7(3)(a)(iv) and (v); *Nygh's Conflict of Laws in Australia*, 9th edn, above n 18, 946–47; Lord Collins of Mapesbury et al (eds), *Dicey, Morris and Collins on the Conflict of Laws*, 15th edn (London, Sweet & Maxwell, 2012) vol 1, 754.

[70] Foreign Judgments Act 1991 (Cth) s 7(3)(a)(iv); *Dicey, Morris and Collins*, ibid, 754.

[71] Foreign Judgments Act 1991 (Cth) s 7(4)(b). Compare Civil Jurisdiction and Judgments Act 1982 (UK); *Dicey, Morris and Collins*, ibid, 712.

[72] *Nygh's Conflict of Laws in Australia*, 9th edn, above n 18, 943.

[73] In the UK, by contrast, the exclusion of jurisdiction in proceedings breaching arbitration or choice of court clauses applies to all actions for recognition and enforcement, whether under statute

(ii) *Differences with the Trans-Tasman Proceedings Act*

Finally, it should be observed that the Trans-Tasman Proceedings Act enacts another, different set of rules applying only to New Zealand judgments. These may be enforced immediately upon registration under the TTPA, with no requirement to await the elapse of a period within which the judgment debtor could seek to have registration set aside.[74] That is not the position under the FJA.[75] More significantly, too, there are very few grounds upon which registration under the TTPA could be set aside.[76] There is no occasion to inquire into the New Zealand court's jurisdiction. Further, the TTPA regime, unlike the common law and the FJA, is not confined to money judgments.[77]

III. Impacts of the Present State of the Law

A. Impact of the Current Incoherence on Parties and Litigants

(i) *Jurisdiction*

According to the recent Attorney-General's Department Consultation Paper, the current disunity in Australian rules of personal jurisdiction leads to:[78]

1. confusion for parties to litigation with a cross-border element;
2. arbitrariness in the establishment of personal jurisdiction over defendants; and
3. unfair advantage to well-resourced, mobile litigants who are able to engage in forum shopping, thereby exploiting differences between jurisdictions in a way that less well-resourced parties cannot.

Professor Dickinson has labelled the present state of affairs 'deeply unattractive'.[79] It is difficult to gainsay these observations. Consider, for example, a foreign corporation that has entered into identical contracts with two separate Australian companies. The foreign corporation has no other relevant connection with Australia. One of the Australian companies ('Company A') carries on business exclusively in Western Australia. The other ('Company B') carries on almost all

or common law: Civil Jurisdiction and Judgments Act 1982 (UK) s 32; *Dicey, Morris and Collins*, above n 69, 712.

[74] Trans-Tasman Proceedings Act 2010 (Cth) s 74.
[75] Foreign Judgments Act 1991 (Cth) s 6(10).
[76] See Trans-Tasman Proceedings Act 2010 (Cth) s 72.
[77] See Mortensen, Garnett and Keyes, above n 61, 138.
[78] Attorney-General's Consultation Paper, [44].
[79] A Dickinson, 'The Future of Private International Law in Australia' (2012) 19 *Australian International Law Journal* 1.

its business in Western Australia but also happens to have a minor operation in Queensland. The contracts have no other relevant connection to any Australian jurisdiction. Assume the foreign corporation breaches each contract in identical fashion. Company A cannot serve originating process on the corporation. But Company B can, by virtue of the Queensland rule allowing overseas service in actions on a contract to which a person carrying on business in the State is party. This not only offends against the principle that relevantly similar cases ought to be treated similarly, but also makes a foreign party's answerability before Australian courts appear arbitrary. Of course, the Queensland court may, in its discretion, decline to exercise jurisdiction. The important point, though, is that whether forum considerations even enter the picture seems a matter of happenstance. Nor are the effects of this arbitrariness confined to the actual conduct of litigation. Foreign entities must take account of their litigation risk in various Australian jurisdictions when making commercial decisions. As Professor Dickinson has observed, the variation in rules across the nation may make companies in some jurisdictions less competitive than others.[80] Additionally, though, the uncertainty brought by fragmented jurisdictional rules adversely affects the entire country's attractiveness as a venue for investment. The complexity of Australia's fractured jurisdictional regime increases the cost of advice on cross-border transactions. Such increased costs, of course, are also borne if and when litigation is initiated.

(ii) Recognition and Execution of Foreign Judgments

Foreign parties face uncertainty not only as to whether they will be subject to an Australian court's jurisdiction but also as to whether a foreign judgment affecting them will be enforced here. There are at least three reasons for which this is concerning. First, parties' inability to predict whether their assets in Australia will be susceptible to enforcement of a foreign judgment results in doubt as to how cross-border transactions ought to be structured, particularly with respect to the choice of dispute resolution forum. Secondly, dealing with Australian entities becomes a riskier proposition than would otherwise be the case. Such entities might turn out to be enforcement-proof. Thirdly, cross-border transactions and litigation involving Australian parties are more costly than necessary, at least from the perspective of foreign entities. Costs are increased by the de facto requirement that a foreign party, perhaps at considerable expense, resort to Australian courts (rather than its favoured forum) in order to be certain that any favourable judgment will be enforced. They are also increased by the sheer complexity of our various regimes.

[80] ibid.

B. Current Disadvantages for the Nation

Here is how one American commentator has summed up the need, from a national perspective, for coherence in rules governing jurisdiction and enforcement of judgments:[81]

> Effective dispute resolution processes are critical to a well-functioning global economy, and effectiveness for this purpose requires, just as it does for a national or regional economy, generous recognition and enforcement of judgments. Key to such generosity, in turn, are acceptable jurisdiction standards and, experience has demonstrated, reciprocity. Finally, mutual assurance that reciprocity will in fact be forthcoming requires very considerable uniformity and certainty in the governing legal rules.

Australia has an interest in successful negotiation of bilateral and multilateral agreements fostering greater international harmony when it comes to judgment enforcement and jurisdiction. It has been observed that 'simultaneous bargaining on jurisdiction and judgment recognition and enforcement [are] now the norm in treaty making'.[82] As things stand, however, foreign states may reasonably conclude that implementation of any bilateral or multilateral agreement requiring alteration of the Australian jurisdictional rules would be drawn-out and uncertain.[83] In other words, lack of coherence as to jurisdictional matters makes it more difficult to negotiate agreements on judgment enforcement. Of course, we should be careful before jettisoning the precepts of federalism for the sake of accommodating international negotiating counterparts. Yet it is unclear what benefits the present federal fragmentation brings. As Stephen Burbank has put it in the American context:[84]

> Federalism is important in the United States. It is also important that the United States be able to participate effectively in a global economy and that those charged with the conduct of the country's foreign affairs be able to make, and that the country abide by, international agreements that are designed to facilitate transnational commercial activity.

Those remarks are germane also to Australia. That is particularly so where transactions between Australian and foreign-based parties in the resources sector are in many respects the life-blood of the economy. Moreover, it seems contrary to the national interest that the taxpayer should have to fund the elaborate process required each time there is a need to reform the various States' and Territories' rules as to personal jurisdiction. At present, any meaningful change to the law requires the coordinated effort of all State and Territory governments, as well as of the

[81] S Burbank, 'Federalism and Private International Law: Implementing the Hague Choice of Court Convention in the United States' (2006) 2 *Journal of Private International Law* 287, 309.

[82] ibid 295.

[83] The accuracy of this conclusion is perhaps illustrated by the time that elapsed between when Australia and New Zealand signed the Agreement on Trans-Tasman Court Proceedings and Regulatory Enforcement in July 2008 and when the legislation came into effect. The Trans-Tasman Proceedings Act 2010 (Cth) was passed in 2010, but it commenced only in October 2013.

[84] Burbank, above n 81, 308–9.

Commonwealth. Perhaps the words of Alexander Hamilton at the end of the eighteenth century, concerning the place of Admiralty and maritime jurisdiction in the United States Constitution, are apposite. There, the importance of showing a uniform, coherent national face to the outside world was recognised. That great American statesman wrote:[85]

> The most bigotted idolizers of state authority have not thus far shewn a disposition to deny the national judiciary the cognizance of maritime causes. These so generally depend on the laws of nations, and so commonly affect the rights of foreigners, that they fall within the considerations which are relative to the public peace.

Though directed to a specific subject (Admiralty and maritime law), the point is perhaps of force generally in relation to jurisdictional rules affecting foreigners in their legal rights. Yet in today's international commercial environment, and in light of Australia's place in the region, a factor of even greater importance than the elimination of provincialism is a need for the nation to integrate harmoniously with the international community, in particular this region.

IV. How Might Greater Coherence be Achieved?

The call for greater coherence in private international law, whether at a national or transnational level, is not new. Today, however, the call may be made with more urgency than ever. As one commentator has put it, the movement for greater coherence in private international law is driven by[86]

> the growing need for legal certainty in a world where people and corporations have seemingly unfettered mobility. Ensuring legal certainty places enormous responsibility on those in charge of managing justice …

The question, though, is how to overcome the constraints of federalism to provide greater certainty.

A. The Constitutional Position

This is not the place to examine the full extent of the Commonwealth's power over private international law. It suffices to note the importance of domestic private international law rules to Australia's foreign relations. Australian courts' exercise of jurisdiction over overseas defendants and enforcement of foreign judgments seem quintessentially to fall within the ambit of the Commonwealth parliament's

[85] A Hamilton, *The Federalist* No 80. See Alexander Hamilton, James Madison and John Jay, *The Federalist* (New Jersey, Lawbook Exchange, 2005) vol 2, 306–7.

[86] American Law Institute and UNIDROIT, *Principles of Transnational Civil Procedure* (Cambridge, Cambridge University Press, 2006) xxxiv–xxxv.

external affairs power.[87] Jurisdictional rules concern parties physically outside the country, and the recognition and enforcement of foreign judgments appears to be a matter of comity between Australian and foreign governments.[88] As has been observed, the content of our private international laws affects the Commonwealth government's ability to negotiate international agreements.

B. The Options

The Attorney-General's Department has put forward three possible forms that a reform of Australian private international law could take:[89]

1. targeted amendments to existing legislation;
2. 'soft law' options such as model laws or frameworks; and
3. a federal private international law code.

The remainder of this chapter will address the last of these. It will also briefly mention international harmonisation efforts in which Australia is taking part.

C. Federal Codification

Debates over the merits of codes stretch back to the Ancients. It is beyond this chapter's scope to explore the Aristotelian case for flexibility, or Benthamite arguments for legal codification. When it comes to overseas service, each Australian jurisdiction has its own 'long-arm' code. The problem with this system is not so much that it lacks the malleability of a purely common law regime but that the various codes present a fragmented national picture. A benefit of legislative rules is supposed to be legal certainty.[90] Yet the current state of affairs produces the opposite. Equally, as to enforcement of foreign judgments, the problem is neither any undue flexibility of the common law regime nor any rigidity in the statutory framework. The difficulty is the incoherence resulting from placing these side by side. The problem of incoherence may well be solved, it is submitted, by a federal private international law statute. After all, if codification is acceptable at the state, territory and Federal Court levels, why would a uniform code not be acceptable at a national level? The TTPA and FJA provide small-scale models.[91] It is, of course,

[87] *Constitution* s 51(xxix); see also Dickinson, above n 79.

[88] See *Thomas v Mowbray* (2007) 233 CLR 307, 364 (Gummow and Crennan JJ).

[89] Attorney-General's Consultation Paper, [191].

[90] Cf the brilliant refutation of this notion in FA Hayek, *Law, Legislation and Liberty: A New Statement of the Liberal Principles of Justice and Political Economy* (London, Routledge & Kegan Paul, 1973) vol 1, 116–18.

[91] Part 2 of the Trans-Tasman Proceedings Act 2010 (Cth) codifies the rules as to service of process in New Zealand. Part 3 codifies the circumstances in which Australian courts may decline to exercise jurisdiction on the ground that a New Zealand court is a more appropriate forum. Meanwhile Part 7 governs the recognition and enforcement of New Zealand judgments in Australia.

true that the TTPA was enabled by an agreement between the Australian and New Zealand governments. It would be wrong to advocate that the precise TTPA provisions be replicated on a broader scale. The TTPA does stand as proof, though, that federal statutes may iron out private international law inconsistencies.

It might be objected that codification would serve only to petrify what should be a dynamic and responsive area of the law. One advantage of federalism, after all, is that State and Territory governments are able to respond more swiftly than a central government to constituents' concerns. Placing private international law rules entirely within the federal government's hands might, on this view, be a mistake. Yet this argument has diminished force in a world where foreign investors increasingly deal with Australia not as a collection of States and Territories but as a nation. If there was ever a time when private international law rules were of primarily local concern, it is submitted that that time has passed. Certainly, we will need to adapt to rapid technological and other advances that increase the volume and complexity of cross-border transactions. But are the States, Territories and Commonwealth, acting separately, the best agents to ensure that adaptation? Is it of any avail to litigants if a few jurisdictions, acting separately, modernise their rules relating to overseas service, while others lag behind? In this domain, there is a good argument that coherence is more valuable than local responsiveness.

D. The Hague 'Judgments Project'

For some time now, there have been international efforts to streamline rules governing jurisdiction and recognition and enforcement of judgments. At the Hague Conference on Private International Law in the 1990s, the United States proposed a multilateral treaty on the subject. It was an ambitious goal. The move was prompted by the Americans' concern over lack of enforcement of US judgments abroad.[92] Having failed to reach full consensus, the Conference decided in 2003 to narrow its focus to jurisdiction in the context of choice of court agreements. The eventual result was the 2005 Hague Choice of Court Convention, which Australia has neither signed nor ratified. It was a more modest outcome than had originally been anticipated. Nevertheless, the Conference has revived the original project (the 'Judgments Project') of a convention dealing more broadly with jurisdiction and foreign judgments. In February 2013, the Working Group of the Judgments Project met for the first time. Australia was a participant. The Group has been tasked with preparing provisions to be included in a future convention.[93]

[92] Burbank, above n 81, 288. The Hague Convention of 1 February 1971 on the Recognition and Enforcement of Foreign Judgments in Civil and Commercial Matters was already in existence. As was acknowledged at the time of the American proposal, though, that Convention had not been a success: Hague Conference on Private International Law, 'Some reflections of the Permanent Bureau on a general convention on enforcement of judgments' (Preliminary Document No 17, May 1992) [3].

[93] Hague Conference on Private International Law, 'Ongoing Work on International Litigation' (Preliminary Document No 3, March 2013) annex 1.

It reconvened in February 2014. In its March 2013 report on the progress of the 'Judgments Project', the Conference's Permanent Bureau specifically acknowledged the 'significant contribution' of the Australian government.[94] Completion of, and Australian accession to, a viable multilateral instrument in this domain would greatly benefit Australian and international commerce. The difficulty with any general treaty of enforcement of court judgments reflects, at one level, the difficulties faced by sovereign legal systems when compared to arbitration:

1. mistrust of the competence of national political or governmental processes, whether because of corruption or simple provincialism;
2. compounded by the deep procedural suspicion of jury verdicts in the United States and political interference in other countries; and
3. the broad trust in the arbitral system under the New York Convention on the Recognition and Enforcement of Foreign Arbitral Awards and UNCITRAL Model Law on International Commercial Arbitration.

Australia's interests and those of the region may lie in selective bilateral or regional arrangements drawing together major trading partners. Further, consideration might be given to bilateral or regional agreements setting up courts or tribunals administering regional law in law areas with uniform enforcement. This would constitute a transnational or 'a-national' response to the difficulties of enforcement.

V. Conclusion

Australia needs a coherent private international law regime. We need it because our economy depends in large part upon cross-border transactions with overseas parties. Currently, federalism is not serving transnational commerce well. It is to be hoped that Australian law-makers are able to work within the constraints of our federation to produce a more coherent picture, allowing Australia to face the world with greater confidence.

[94] ibid 7.

4

Rationalisation and Rationale: Approaching the Reform of Rules for the Assertion of Jurisdiction over Foreign Defendants

ANDREW BELL SC

I. Introduction[1]

On 12 April 2012, the Australian Standing Council on Law and Justice agreed to the establishment of a Working Group that would commence consultations with key stakeholders to determine whether further reform in the area of harmonisation of jurisdiction, choice of court and choice of law rules would deliver worthwhile micro-economic benefits for the community. Subsequently, the Commonwealth Attorney-General's department issued a Consultation Paper entitled '*Reducing Legal Complexity of Cross Border Transactions and Relationships: Driving Micro-economic Reform through the Establishment of more cohesive and clearer Jurisdictional, Applicable Law and Choice of Court Rules*'.[2] The Attorney-General's Consultation Paper is wide ranging and contemplates, inter alia, the placing of particular choice of law rules on a statutory basis as has occurred in England in many respects. It is important to appreciate, however, that the drivers for this 'reform' in England have largely been externally imposed rather than internally motivated, principally in consequence of participation in the European Union where uniform choice of law rules have been, correctly, seen as an important component of the general harmonisation of law in aid of the goal of facilitating trade and economic interaction.

For my own part, at least with regard to the established choice of law rules in tort and contract, whilst I would not be violently opposed to such a course, I see no pressing need to place those rules on a statutory basis: there is only one common

[1] This chapter is based on a paper delivered on 10 April 2013 at the Sydney Centre for International Law Conference, '*Facing Outwards: Australian Private International Law in the 21st Century*'.

[2] Annex 1 (Attorney-General's Consultation Paper or Consultation Paper).

law in Australia[3] and so the need for harmonisation, which has been so influential in Europe, does not obtain. Furthermore, following *John Pfeiffer Pty Ltd v Rogerson*[4] and *Renault v Zhang*,[5] the choice of law rule in tort has been clearly stated after decades of confusion as Australian courts struggled with *Phillips v Eyre's* notion of double actionability, and has not, in my experience, proved difficult of application since the clarification yielded by those two decisions.

One advantage of retaining the existing common law choice of law rules, particularly in contract, is that they are in line with those applied in New Zealand, Singapore, Malaysia, Hong Kong, Canada and India, with all of which countries Australia enjoys close trading ties. Furthermore, I am not convinced that erecting a statutory foundation for these rules would address any difficulties that arise in practice, for example where the parties have not expressly chosen the law to govern their disputes. One simply cannot legislate to cover all possible factual scenarios. The reality of much of international commerce and international commercial disputation is that there will be conflicting considerations and factors pointing to different applicable laws where no express choice has been made. No amount of legislating will overcome the need for judicial choices to be made.

II. The Case for Reform of Rules of Personal Jurisdiction in Australia

If there is one area that is in pressing need of reform, however, it is with regard to the assertion of personal jurisdiction over foreign defendants. This is currently effected by disparate regimes for the service outside of the jurisdiction on foreign defendants, that is to say those corporations and individuals who do not have a presence in a local jurisdiction and hence are not able physically to be served in that jurisdiction. This topic is dealt with at paragraphs [34]–[45] of the Attorney General's Consultation Paper. That paper comments (at [35]) that:

> [W]hile there is a level of commonality among the court rules that apply to establishing jurisdiction over parties located abroad, some rules differ from jurisdiction to jurisdiction both at state and territory and also at the federal level. Some of the key differences include:
>
> — the grounds for granting or permitting service of process outside Australia
> — whether a court's leave to serve is required, and
> — the information that must be provided to the party being served.

[3] *Lange v Australian Broadcasting Corporation* (1997) 189 CLR 520.
[4] *John Pfeiffer Pty Ltd v Rogerson* (2000) 203 CLR 503.
[5] *Renault v Zhang* (2002) 210 CLR 491.

Embedded in the second of these points of difference is the need in the Federal Court of Australia to establish a prima facie case for the substantive relief sought as a pre-condition of granting leave.[6] This requirement is not, of course, applied to the commencement of proceedings against purely local defendants.

It is difficult to discern a rationale for the existence of differences at least as between the various State and Territory Supreme Courts in relation to the rules for service out of the jurisdiction. Why, for example, do the Western Australian Supreme Court Rules only support jurisdiction over a foreign defendant in respect of claims in tort where the tort is committed in that jurisdiction in circumstances where, in all other States, it is sufficient that damages be sustained in the jurisdiction arising from a tort wherever committed? Why in Western Australia, Victoria and the Northern Territory are there no special rules for service out of statutory claims such that the rules for service out in respect of tort claims appear to be relied upon, not wholly convincingly, to justify service out of claims arising under the Fair Trading Act, Trade Practices Act and Australian Consumer Law?[7] Why are the rules of the Supreme Court of South Australia the only rules of the several Supreme Courts that make explicit that service out of the jurisdiction is authorised when the action is brought under a statute of the Commonwealth or the State? Why, of the various States, do only New South Wales and Tasmania provide for service out of the jurisdiction of proceedings founded on a cause of action arising in those respective States? Why do none of the States expressly make provision for service out of the jurisdiction in respect of restitutionary claims? Why, of all the States, are South Australia and Queensland the only States that appear to permit service out of the jurisdiction (with leave) of claims other than those expressly set out in the rules of court?[8] Why, in some States (for example, New South Wales), is it still necessary that each cause of action sued upon be supported by a particular sub-paragraph of the Rules (with the consequence that service of process with regard to claims based on causes of action not so supported, is not authorised) whereas it is sufficient in the Federal Court of Australia, for example, that only one cause of action be so supported?

All of the disparate sets of rules in relation to the service outside of the jurisdiction of foreign defendants no doubt owe their origins to the rules contained in the first schedule to the Judicature Act 1875 (Imp) and the Rules of the Supreme Court of England and Wales 1883. Their subsequent evolution has, however, been somewhat piecemeal and, in the absence of a uniform approach, no doubt a consequence of the energy of particular Rules Committees and the volume of trans-

[6] Note the same requirement under the Northern Territory Rules 2012. In Western Australia, the other jurisdiction where there is a prior leave requirement, there must be an affidavit stating that in the deponent's belief, the applicant has a good cause of action.

[7] *Mallon and Co Lawyers Pty Ltd v Gam* [2012] WASC 376. Cf *Glendalough Holdings Pty Ltd v Summit Chemicals Pty Ltd* [2003] WASC 183; see also *Williams v The Society of Lloyd's* [1994] 1 VR 274; *Commonwealth Bank of Australia v White* [1999] 2 VR 681.

[8] Supreme Court Rules 2006 (SA), r 40(2); this is permitted also under the Uniform Civil Procedure Rule 1999 (Qld) r 127(a).

national litigation coming before particular jurisdictions. A valuable discussion of the evolution of the relevant rules in New South Wales is contained in the plurality judgment in *Agar v Hyde*,[9] which also noted that different practices historically obtained as between chancery and common law practice.

The Consultation Paper concludes (at [44]) that:

> The differences in the court rules that address the establishment of personal jurisdiction over a party located abroad may:
>
> — cause considerable confusion for Australian and other litigants engaged in cross-border matters
> — lead to a 'luck of the draw' situation where the ability to serve on parties overseas is dependent on the state or territory in which an application is brought, or
> — serve to benefit highly mobile litigants, such as multinational corporations who can 'shop around' (often referred to as 'forum shopping') and litigate in the state or territory whose court rules most benefit their situation, at the expense of smaller companies/individuals.

The Paper also notes (at [45]) the assertion by one commentator that the differences in the relevant rules have effects on (i) the ability of businesses in different States and Territories to compete with each other on equal terms in view of the differing levels of access to local courts in cross-border situations, and (ii) the additional costs and inconvenience involved in litigating disputes abroad when such access is not granted.

Whether or not these claims as to competition and the economic impact of the disparate regimes are or can be supported by empirical evidence is not clear, and I am somewhat dubious as to the ability to gather such evidence in any substantial or statistically significant way. One can certainly say, however, that when looking to commence litigation against a foreign defendant who is likely to take jurisdictional points, very close attention needs to be paid to the particular jurisdictional rules of a particular forum prior to commencement in order to assess the risk and prospects of such attacks in fact being made. Tactical considerations may include whether or not the moving party is in a position to adduce evidence of a prima facie case at the time of commencement, a requirement under the Federal Court Rules. Its ability to do so may in part be a function of the urgency with which it is perceived to be necessary to commence proceedings.

Further and notwithstanding what is said above as to the difficulty of obtaining empirical evidence, some anecdotal support can, however, be provided for the view that the current rules are cumbersome and productive of inefficiency. Thus, in *Perdaman Chemicals and Fertilisers Pty Ltd v ICICI Bank*,[10] Perdaman Fertilizers Pty Ltd (Perdaman), which was the Plaintiff in proceedings in the Supreme Court of Western Australia against various parties associated with the Lanco Group of Companies, wished also to sue ICICI Bank, Lanco's financier, for breach of

[9] *Agar v Hyde* (2000) 201 CLR 552, [42]–[52].
[10] *Perdaman Chemicals and Fertilisers Pty Ltd v ICICI Bank Ltd* [2013] FCA 175.

the statutory unconscionability provisions of the Australian Consumer Law.[11] Perdaman took the view (which is probably correct) that the Rules of Court of the Supreme Court of Western Australia did not expressly permit a claim arising under that Act to be brought against a foreign defendant in the Supreme Court of Western Australia, even though there is, of course, no jurisdictional inhibition (as a matter of subject-matter as opposed to personal jurisdiction) in that Court entertaining such a claim. For that reason, Perdaman sought leave to commence proceedings against ICICI Bank in the Federal Court of Australia with a view to then having those proceedings cross-vested to the Supreme Court of Western Australia, in turn with a view to having such cross-vested proceedings unified with the pending Supreme Court proceedings against the Lanco Group of Companies.

McKerracher J saw nothing objectionable in this course.[12] In the event, leave was not granted to Perdaman to serve outside of the jurisdiction on the basis that it had not established a prima facie case of statutory unconscionability, but the salient point, for present purposes, is that Perdaman was driven, by reason of a perceived lacuna in the Rules of the Supreme Court of Western Australia for service out of the jurisdiction, to commence proceedings in the Federal Court as the first step to seeking to bring ICICI Bank into the Supreme Court proceedings. The inherent inefficiency in such a course is obvious, as this strategy required not only an initial application to the Federal Court for leave to proceed, but would also have required an application in the Federal Court for the subsequent cross-vesting of the proceedings and then an application in the Supreme Court for consolidation. Even if such cross-vesting had occurred by consent, there are obvious actual costs involved as well as costs in terms of potential delay to the resolution of the dispute, not to mention the public costs of the Federal Court's engagement in such procedural steps at the expense of other proceedings pending before it.

As a more general observation, it is obvious that the broader a law area's rules of personal jurisdiction, the more likely there will be multiple law areas capable of exercising jurisdiction in any given matter.[13] Concurrent jurisdiction is what feeds concurrent litigation, and there are obvious 'micro-economic consequences' involved as parties 'litigate about where to litigate'. This was a topic explored

[11] Competition and Consumer Act 2010, Sch 2.

[12] See [2013] FCA 175, [10]–[12]. This view may be contrasted with intimations in the New South Wales Court of Appeal's decision in *Studorp Ltd v Robinson* [2012] NSWCA 382, [6] (Allsop P) and [26] (Meagher JA) that commencement of proceedings against a foreign defendant in the Supreme Court of New South Wales in reliance on Schedule 6 of the Uniform Civil Procedure Rules with a view to having those proceedings transferred to the Dust Diseases Tribunal of New South Wales (the constitutive statute of which makes no provision for service of process abroad on a foreign defendant) may be an abuse of process. Note, however, that the strength of this argument may be more compelling in the case of the Dust Diseases Tribunal (as opposed to what was planned to occur in the *Perdaman* litigation) in light of section 11 of the Dust Diseases Tribunal Act which proscribes the commencement of 'dust litigation' in any court or tribunal other than the Dust Diseases Tribunal of New South Wales.

[13] AS Bell, *Forum Shopping and Venue in Transnational Litigation* (Oxford, Oxford University Press, 2003) [1.19]–[1.29].

extra-judicially on a number of occasions by Chief Justice Spigelman.[14] Thus, his Honour said:[15]

> Jurisdictional disputes are always, and in all circumstances, a waste of money. They are, regrettably, necessary in the current and likely future structure of international institutional arrangements. They represent a transaction cost which is a peculiar imposition on international trade and investment and which, therefore, discourages such trade and investment. We should do whatever we can to minimize the occurrence of such disputation.
>
> The problem of course is that for a growing range of disputes there are at least two, and frequently more, options available for instituting proceedings. Exorbitant or long-arm jurisdiction is a feature of many nations. Australia, in the common law tradition, has rules of court which entitle a court to assume jurisdiction based on service in situations where connection with the jurisdictions is at best tenuous, perhaps amounting no more than residence, or even temporary presence or, in the case of tort, the fact that injury continues after the return of a resident to the jurisdiction.

Whatever the true nature and extent of the micro-economic impact of the disparate regimes for service out of the jurisdiction, it is difficult to understand any particular rationale for the differences which exist between the various State and Territory Supreme Courts and the Federal Court with regard to the applicable rules for the service of proceedings (and therefore the assertion of jurisdiction) over defendants resident abroad. As Professor Martin Davies and I wrote in the preface to the eighth edition of *Nygh's Conflict of Laws in Australia*:[16]

> The lack of uniformity both as between the States and as between the State Supreme Courts and the Federal Court in relation to extended jurisdiction and service upon individuals and corporations resident or present abroad continues to be an undesirable feature of practice in this area and is ripe for coordinated reform by the Rules Committees of the several superior courts of the country.

The remainder of this chapter focuses on the possibility of reform by this means. Coordination of this kind between the Rules Committees of the respective Supreme Courts, it may be noted is, not without precedent. Previous successful harmonisation projects have included the standardisation of procedures for the issue of freezing orders, including freezing orders granted in aid of foreign proceedings where it is anticipated that the foreign judgment may be enforced against assets within Australia.[17]

[14] See, for example, JJ Spigelman, 'Transaction Costs and International Litigation' (2006) 80 *Australian Law Journal* 436.

[15] ibid.

[16] (Sydney, Lexis Nexis, 2010) Preface, xxii.

[17] The regime, at least as implemented in Western Australia, survived a jurisdictional and constitutional challenge in *BCBC Singapore Pte Ltd v Pt Bayan Resources Tbk* [2013] WASC 239. An appeal from this decision has been reserved at the time of writing. The various rules are listed in fn 71 of chapter 4 of M Davies, AS Bell and PLG Brereton, *Nygh's Conflict of Laws in Australia*, 9th edn (Sydney, LexisNexis, 2014).

III. Looking Abroad for Possible Inspiration—The Canadian Approach

Any consideration of reform to the rules for the service outside the jurisdiction should pay some regard to the way these matters have been addressed in Canada. The starting point there is the work of the Uniform Law Conference of Canada which, in 1994, adopted the Court Jurisdiction and Proceedings Transfer Act, which has subsequently been enacted in British Columbia, Saskatchewan and Nova Scotia and has been recommended for enactment in Alberta by the Alberta Law Reform Institute. It can, at once, be observed however that the Act has not been uniformly or universally adopted amongst the Canadian provinces.[18] The approach to jurisdiction taken in the Act, however, is instructive. The structure of the Act is to provide for the existence of jurisdiction where there is a 'real and substantial connection' with the law area in addition to cases of submission, residence, or agreement to jurisdiction. The Act then states that there will presumptively be a real and substantial connection in certain defined circumstances. The list of defined circumstances bears a close similarity to the tables, lists and schedules found in the respective Australian jurisdictions authorising service out.

A very real practical difference between Australia and Canada is that, as Spigelman CJ pointed out in the passage extracted earlier in this chapter, many of the sub-rules in Australia require only a slender or tenuous connection with the jurisdiction, whereas in Canada, the real and substantial connection test appears to mean what it says and is less jurisdictionally aggressive and expansive. The Canadian approach to the grant of stays of proceedings is also more liberal than that available in Australia under *Voth*.[19] The 'real and substantial connection' test, which has a constitutional dimension as well, derives from *Morguard Investments Ltd v De Savoye*[20] (see also *Club Resort Ltd v Van Breda*)[21] and plays a broader role in Canadian conflict of laws jurisprudence, being the touchstone for the enforcement of foreign judgments. Thus in Canada, unlike Australia—whether at common law or pursuant to the Foreign Judgments Act 1991 (Cth)—a foreign judgment will be enforced whether or not the defendant submitted to and participated in the proceedings if there was, in the enforcing court's view, a real and

[18] For a full discussion, see Professor Janet Walker's 2009 paper 'Reforming the Law of Crossborder Litigation: Judicial Jurisdiction', being a Consultation Paper prepared for the Law Commission of Ontario which has not, incidentally, enacted the Court Jurisdiction and Proceedings Transfer Act. The paper is available at: Consultation Paper: Reforming the Law of Crossborder Litigation—Judicial Jurisdiction by Janet Walker: SSRN, last visited 17 March 2014. See also *Club Resorts Ltd v Van Breda* [2012] 1 SCR 572, in which the Supreme Court of Canada modelled the common law of Ontario in the image of the Act.

[19] *Voth v Manildra Flour Mills Pty Ltd* (1990) 171 CLR 538. On one view, the Canadian approach comes very close to eliding technical rules of jurisdiction with *forum non conveniens* applications.

[20] *Morguard Investments Ltd v De Savoye* [1990] 3 SCR 1077.

[21] Above n 18.

substantial connection between the subject-matter of the dispute and the foreign court in which the judgment was given.

Going down the Canadian route would represent a major conceptual and structural departure by Australian courts from both tradition and, if I may so describe it, the more parochial and less internationalist approach to the assertion of transnational jurisdiction that has marked decisions of the High Court, in particular, in this area in recent decades.[22] Given the High Court's refusal to revisit *Voth* in *Puttick v Tenon Ltd*,[23] the prospect of Australian courts following the Canadian lead in this regard is close to non-existent.

IV. The Direction of Reform in Australia

A. Questions and Approach

On the assumption that such a route is not to be taken, where lies the path for more modest reform? If it be accepted, as I think it should be, that uniformity between the Australian jurisdictions, to the extent possible, is desirable in this area, the following questions need to be addressed:

(i) What should be the particular heads of jurisdiction or circumstances in which originating process may be served on a foreign defendant outside of the jurisdiction?

(ii) Should there be included in the various rules of court an omnibus head of jurisdiction authorising service of process where the proceedings have a connection with the particular State or Territory or Australia but are not otherwise covered by a particular rule? A sub-question might be whether any connection is required to be 'real and substantial'.[24]

(iii) Should the rules of the various State and Territory supreme courts continue to be expressed by reference to a nexus to the relevant State or Territory in circumstances where each Supreme Court is invested by the mutual cross-vesting legislation with the jurisdiction of each of the other State and Territory supreme courts?

(iv) Should leave be required prior to the service out of such proceedings?

(v) If leave to serve out is required, should the moving party also be required to establish the existence of prima facie case against the proposed foreign defendant (there being a difference here between the two Australian jurisdictions where leave is still required)?[25] In this context, the related question is why should foreign defendants be treated differently to local defendants?

[22] See, for example, *Renault v Zhang* (2002) 210 CLR 498 and *Puttick v Tenon Ltd* (2008) 238 CLR 265.

[23] *Puttick v Tenon Ltd* (2008) 238 CLR 265.

[24] See above, section III.

[25] Above, text to n 5.

(vi) Should, *and can*, the Rules of the Court also address the criterion or criteria for the *exercise*[26] of jurisdiction over a foreign defendant (ie is this in truth a matter of practice and procedure, within the delegated legislative power of a Rules Committee?) and, if so, what should that criterion or those criteria be?

(vii) Should each jurisdiction's set of rules make clear, as the NSW Uniform Civil Procedure Rules currently do,[27] that a defendant wishing to challenge jurisdiction need not enter an appearance and will not, by making such a challenge or by seeking a stay of proceedings, be taken to have submitted to the jurisdiction of the Court?

Some of these questions admit of easier answers than others. The answer to all of them should, however, be informed by a clear understanding and view of both the conceptual principles underpinning the assertion of jurisdiction over foreign defendants and the policy questions that arise.

In this context, the considerations of principle which originally underpinned the assertion of jurisdiction and therefore sovereignty over foreign defendants in England in the second half of the nineteenth century, when rules for what was then and for many years termed 'exorbitant' jurisdiction were first developed, may not have the same currency at the beginning of the twenty-first century. In terms of policy, the key question that emerges is where on the spectrum between parochialism and internationalism any uniform rules of court should sit. Expressed in this way, nice and important questions arise as to whether or not such rules in truth involve matters merely of practice and procedure, and hence are within the ken of the delegated legislative authority of Court Rules Committees.

In historical terms, the assertion of jurisdiction over a person or corporation not physically present in the law area was regarded as involving the somewhat exceptional and extra-territorial assertion of power, hence the expression 'exorbitant jurisdiction'. As I have written elsewhere:[28]

> Common law courts traditionally exhibited great caution when exercising jurisdiction over foreign defendants under rules of court conferring long arm jurisdiction, Pearson J's dictum in *Société Generale de Paris v Dreyfuss Brothers* perhaps constituting the leading statement in this regard:
>
> > 'It becomes a very serious question, and ought always to be considered a very serious question, whether … this Court ought to put a foreigner, who owes no allegiance here, to the inconvenience and annoyance of being brought to contest his rights in this country, and I for one say, most distinctly that I think this Court ought to be exceedingly careful before it allows a writ to be served out of the jurisdiction'.
>
> Initially, this cautious approach was self-interested, being based on a desire not to encourage the similar treatment of English defendants by foreign courts, but it came ultimately to rest on broad considerations of international comity, premised on the view

[26] Ie *forum non conveniens* considerations.

[27] Uniform Civil Procedure Rules 2005 (NSW) rr 12.11(3) and (4).

[28] AS Bell, above n 13, [4.16]–[4.17].

that such jurisdiction was exceptional and amounted to a derogation from a theory of jurisdiction aligned with notions of territorial sovereignty. In *Seaconsar Far East Ltd v Bank Markazi Jomhouri Islami Iran*, Lord Goff observed that 'it is, of course, true to say that any inconvenience involved has been much reduced by modern methods of communication; *but the point of principle remains*' (emphasis added).

The 'point of principle' of which Lord Goff spoke has manifested itself in a number of ways including (as remains the case in the Federal Court and Western Australia) in the requirement for prior leave and the establishment (in the Federal Court) of a prima facie case, and in the canons of construction said to be applicable to the interpretation of the rules for service out of the jurisdiction. Thus, in *Contender 1 Ltd v LEP International Pty Ltd*,[29] Brennan J (albeit in dissent), observed:

> The asserted jurisdiction is said to arise under Pt 10 r.1 of the Rules of the Supreme Court which authorizes extraterritorial service of process in the cases specified in the sub-rules. The jurisdictions asserted over foreigners under some of the provisions of r.1 are 'exorbitant' jurisdictions which run counter to the normal rules of comity among civilised nations … [and] the sub-rules are to be strictly construed in favour of the foreigner': per Lord Diplock in *Siskina (Cargo Owners) v Distos SA* [1979] AC 210 at 254–5. The jurisdiction asserted in this case is clearly 'exorbitant' in that sense, for a foreigner resident abroad who is served in a foreign place with process commencing an action *in personam* is, in the absence of an overriding local statute, immune from the jurisdiction of a local court: *Sirdar Gurdyal Singh v Rajah of Faridkote* [1894] AC 670 at 684; *Laurie v Carroll* (1958) 98 CLR 310 at 322, 323; *Gosper v Sawyer* (1985) 160 CLR 548 at 564, 565; *Flaherty v Girgis* (1987) 162 CLR 574 at 599, 600.

In an earlier decision of the Supreme Court of New South Wales, *Stanley Kerr Holdings Pty Ltd v Gibor Textile Enterprises Ltd*,[30] Sheppard J made reference to and applied the decision of Megarry J in *GAF Corporation v Amchem Products Inc*[31] to the effect that a foreign defendant should be given the benefit of the doubt not only on matters of construction but 'quite generally'. As recently as 2008, McKerracher J of the Federal Court of Australia appeared to endorse an approach solicitous of the special status of foreign defendants: *Freehills, Re New Tel Ltd*.[32]

A narrow or a pro-foreign defendant approach to questions of construction of the rules relating to service out of the jurisdiction has been expressly eschewed in

[29] *Contender 1 Ltd v LEP International Pty Ltd* (1988) 63 ALJR 26, 82 ALR 394, 398–99.

[30] *Stanley Kerr Holdings Pty Ltd v Gibor Textile Enterprises Ltd* [1978] 2 NSWLR 372.

[31] *GAF Corporation v Amchem Products Inc* [1975] 1 Lloyd's Rep 601, 605.

[32] *Freehills, Re New Tel Ltd* (2008) 66 ACSR 311, [24]: 'Although the scope for granting an order under the current Ord 8 of the Federal Court Rules 1976 (Cth) (the FCR) is expansive, the exercise of the discretion has always been tempered with caution. Speaking of earlier provisions under the English rules, in *GAF Corporation v Amchem Products Inc* [1975] 1 Lloyd's Rep 601, 604–5, Megarry J listed six considerations which have been established by the authorities in relation to service outside the jurisdiction: (1) this discretion should be exercised with great care; (2) the onus lies on the person seeking to serve the originating process; (3) the substance of the matter must be within one of the categories in r 1; (4) if there is a doubt as to whether a case is within one of these categories, then it should be resolved in favour of the foreigner; (5) even where a case is within a category in r 1, it is still a matter of discretion; and (6) there must be a full and fair disclosure where there is an ex parte application'.

a number of decisions subsequent to *Contender 1 Ltd*, most notably in the NSW Court of Appeal in *Hyde v Agar*[33] and in the subsequent decision of the High Court in *Agar v Hyde*.[34] Thus, the Court of Appeal stated that:[35]

> Contemporary developments in communication and transport make the degree of 'inconvenience and annoyance' of a qualitatively different order to that which existed in 1885. It follows that a modern court applying the Rules must be sensitive to the actual degree of 'inconvenience and annoyance' which will be imposed in the circumstances of a particular case, rather than assuming that any person or resident abroad must suffer such consequences in substantial degree …
>
> It also bears remembering that any body, corporate or incorporate, required agents such as legal practitioners to defend proceedings. The ease with which such agents may be contacted by phone, facsimile, e-mail and other modern means of communication do not differ significantly whether the message passes across the city or across the world.

In the High Court, the plurality observed that:[36]

> It is, however, important to notice that rules of court, or local statutes, providing for service outside the jurisdiction are now commonplace—at least in jurisdictions whose legal systems have been formed or influenced by common law traditions. Further, as the Court of Appeal rightly noted in its reasons in these matters, contemporary developments in communications and transport make the degree of 'inconvenience and annoyance' to which a foreign defendant would be put, if brought into the courts of this jurisdiction, 'of a qualitatively different order to that which existed in 1885'.
>
> The considerations of comity and restraint, to which reference has so often been made in cases concerning service out of the jurisdiction, will often be of greatest relevance in considering questions of *forum non conveniens*.
>
> …
>
> It was suggested, in the present matters, that some less demanding test should be adopted in cases where a defendant served overseas seeks to have that service set aside. There are at least two reasons why that should not be done. First, and most fundamentally, what is the criterion which is to be applied? Are proceedings to be terminated upon a prediction (on what almost invariably will be less evidence and argument than would be available at trial) of the 'likely' or 'probable' outcome of the proceeding? That cannot be so. It would be wrong to deny a plaintiff resort to the ordinary processes of a court on the basis of a prediction made at the outset of a proceeding if that prediction is to be made simply on a preponderance of probabilities. And if it is not to be enough to persuade the court that it is more probable than not that the case against a defendant will fail, and some higher test (less than that now applied in applications for summary judgment) is to be applied, how is that test to be described? The attachment of intensifying epithets, such as 'very' or 'highly', offers little useful guidance for those judicial officers who would have to apply the test and who would have to do so, often enough, in a busy practice list. Such a test would be unworkable.

[33] *Hyde v Agar* (1998) 45 NSWLR 487.
[34] *Agar v Hyde* (1998) 201 CLR 552.
[35] Above n 33, 507.
[36] Above n 34, [42]–[43] and [58]–[60].

> Secondly, as the present proceedings show, the application of some different, and lower, test in favour of overseas defendants would lead to unacceptable results. It would mean that proceedings must continue to trial against those defendants who happen to have been served with the originating process within the jurisdiction, but can be brought to a summary end by those who are served overseas even where the claims against the local and overseas defendants are identical.
>
> For these reasons, the same test should be applied in deciding whether originating process served outside Australia makes claims which have such poor prospects of success that the proceeding should not go to trial as is applied in an application for summary judgment by a defendant served locally.

These passages[37] really amount to a rejection of the traditional approach of caution and solicitude to foreign defendants where technical questions of jurisdiction are concerned. The Court's attitude is really manifested in the sub-heading preceding the above passages: 'Service out of the jurisdiction—an exorbitant jurisdiction?' The answer given was in substance and emphatically 'No'.

In this connection, it should also be noted that the traditional narrow construction of Rules of Court concerned with service on foreign defendants runs counter to a well-established line of authority that holds that provisions conferring jurisdiction on courts will be generously construed given that the powers are to be exercised judicially.[38] One can certainly point, in recent decades, to instances of rules of court concerning service out of the jurisdiction being generously construed. Particularly notable examples include the rule relating to damage being suffered in the forum by tortious conduct wherever occurring,[39] as well as the head of jurisdiction allowing for service of a necessary or proper party in circumstances where another party has been or is to be served in the jurisdiction.[40] It may be noted that, as a result, those two heads of jurisdiction may require only a slight or tenuous connection with the jurisdiction. Similarly, in those jurisdictions which authorise service out where there has been a contravention of a statute, the slightest act or conduct in Australia which may comprise the consequences of conduct in fact occurring elsewhere but having its impact in Australia, such as the receipt of an electronic communication in Australia, may be sufficient to attract the operation of a particular Act, and hence the jurisdiction of the Court. In addition to

[37] See also the intervention by a member of the United Kingdom Supreme Court, Lord Sumption JSC, in *Abela v Baadarani* [2013] UKSC 44, [2013] 1 WLR 2043, [53] (noted A Briggs [2013] *Lloyds Maritime & Commercial Law Quarterly* 415; A Dickinson (2014) 130 *Law Quarterly Review* 197).

[38] Where a recipient of a power is a superior court of record, it has been said that it would be contrary to principle for the power to be given anything other than the most liberal and ample construction: see *Re JJT; Ex Parte Victoria Legal Aid* (1998) 195 CLR 184, 201; *Knight v FP Special Assets Ltd* (1992) 174 CLR 178, 205; *PMT Partners Pty Ltd (in liq) v Australian National Parks and Wildlife Service* (1995) 184 CLR 301, 313.

[39] See, for example, *Flaherty v Girgis* (1985) 4 NSWLR 248, 266; *Brix-Neilson v Oceaneering Australia Pty Ltd* [1982] 2 NSWLR 173; *Challenor v Douglas* [1983] 2 NSWLR 405, 409; *Darrell Lea Chocolate Shops Pty Ltd v Spanish-Polish Shipping Co Inc (The 'Katowice II')* (1990) 25 NSWLR 568, 577; *Colosseum Investment Holdings Ltd v Vanguard Logistics Services Pty Ltd* [2005] NSWSC 803, [41]; *Heilbrunn v Lightwood PLC* [2007] FCA 433, [10]; *Sigma Coachair Group Pty Ltd v Bock Australia Pty Ltd* [2009] NSWSC 684, [124].

[40] *In the matter of Mustang Marine Australia Services Pty Ltd (in liquidation)* (2013) 94 ACSR 601.

these examples, the dropping in the Federal Court at least[41] of a requirement that each cause of action be separately underwritten by a head of extended jurisdiction represents a significant and apparently deliberate relaxation of the traditional solicitude shown to foreign defendants over whom it is sought to exercise extended jurisdiction. This reform was probably driven in part at least by the understandable reluctance to split aspects of proceedings between different forums.[42]

When such rules, as interpreted, are juxtaposed with the *Voth* test for a stay proceedings, Australia must be seen as occupying a place at the more aggressive and expansive end of the spectrum of countries in terms of the assertion of jurisdiction over foreign defendants. So long as there is *some* nexus with the jurisdiction, solicitude for foreign defendants has largely evaporated. This is perhaps especially so where those defendants are corporations or perceived to be insured. Certainly, as noted above, there is no requirement, as there is in Canada, for there to be a 'real and substantial connection' between the forum and the claim in order for jurisdiction to be asserted over foreign defendants.

The contemporary Australian approach outlined above to what was formerly known as exorbitant jurisdiction, and which has coincided with a sharp spike in the number of cases involving foreign defendants, does not suggest that a narrow, cautious or overly diffident approach should be taken to any reformulation of the rules relating to the assertion of jurisdiction over foreign defendants.

B. Reshaping the Rules—A Personal Viewpoint

In my opinion, the following practical steps should be taken:

(i) A consolidated list of all of the various sub-heads of jurisdiction should be compiled, noting any variances of language used in relation to similar concepts and seeking to understand the reasons or justifications (if any) for such linguistic differences.

(ii) Obvious gaps in the consolidated list such as, for example, currently exist in relation to restitutionary claims should be identified, and a suitable subparagraph or head of jurisdiction should be drafted.

(iii) The rules of each State Supreme Court should also include, as a separate head of jurisdiction, that proceedings may be served abroad in circumstances where the service abroad of such proceedings was authorised by the Rules of Court of any other Supreme Court of a State or Territory of Australia. Such a rule draws on the logic of the cross-vesting scheme but would need to be constitutionally 'road-tested'.

[41] Federal Court Rules 2011, r 10.42 ('Subject to rule 10.43, an originating application, or an application under Part 7 of these Rules, may be served on a person in a foreign country in a proceeding that consists of, *or includes*, any one or more of the kinds of proceeding mentioned in the following table' (emphasis added).).

[42] Cf *Comandate Marine Corp v Pan Australia Shipping Pty Ltd* (2006) 157 FCR 45.

(iv) The uniform rules should also include a 'catch-all' head of jurisdiction based upon a real and substantial connection with the forum test.[43]

(v) The rules should explicitly state, as do the current Federal Court Rules, that an originating process may be served on a person in a foreign country in a proceeding that consists of, or includes any one or more of the kinds of proceeding mentioned in the following table/list;

(vi) There should be no leave requirement as a pre-requisite to service abroad of proceedings and, consequently, no requirement for the establishment of a prima facie case against the foreign defendant. This would bring the Federal Court and Western Australia into line with other jurisdictions and would seem to be consistent with the High Court's observations in *Agar v Hyde* excerpted above.[44]

(vii) The rules should explicitly state, as do the current New South Wales Uniform Civil Procedure Rules, that a defendant wishing to challenge jurisdiction need not enter an appearance and will not, by making such a challenge or by seeking a stay of proceedings, be taken to have submitted to the jurisdiction of the Court.

(viii) Perhaps most controversially of all, a decision should also be taken as to whether or not there should be a statutory formulation of the test for the *exercise* as opposed to assumption of jurisdiction. Needless to say, variance between jurisdictions as to the content of such a test would be largely destructive of the desired goal of uniformity, and be an inducement to forum shopping.

C. The Exercise of Jurisdiction—From *Forum Non Conveniens* to *Forum Conveniens*?

Of these proposals, the most difficult in many respects is proposal (viii).

There is an attractive case for arguing that broadly-drawn and -interpreted jurisdictional rules in relation to the assertion of jurisdiction over foreign defendants, along the lines described above, should be *tempered* by a more internationalist approach to the exercise of that jurisdiction than is currently manifested in the rule in *Voth v Manildra Flour Mills Pty Ltd*.[45] I have pointed out elsewhere the strong case that can be made for a shift to the 'clearly more appropriate forum'/ *Spiliada* test adopted in most Commonwealth countries.[46]

The word 'clearly', when used in the *Spiliada* formulation, gives the forum court a strong measure of control over the exercise of jurisdiction, as does the residual

[43] Section III above.

[44] Text to n 35.

[45] Above n 19.

[46] AS Bell, 'Transnational Commercial Litigation and the Current State of Australian Law' in KE Lindgren (ed), *International Commercial and Dispute Resolution* (Sydney, University of Sydney, 2010), esp at 55–60.

requirement that any stay must be also satisfy 'the ends of justice', a safety valve that has operated in favour of indigent plaintiffs for whom suing in the natural, foreign forum is a practical impossibility.[47] By way of contrast, the word 'clearly', when used in the *Voth* 'clearly inappropriate forum' formulation, serves an altogether different and more parochial purpose, emphasising that jurisdiction is to be retained and exercised other than in 'clearly inappropriate' cases. Given the requirement in the various jurisdictional rules for a nexus with the forum, the difficultly of satisfying that test is self-evident.

In terms of the economic cost or impact of the *Voth* test, my previously expressed views are as follows:[48]

> *Voth* was a compromise decision,[49] designed to move the Australian approach away from the traditional English 'abuse of process' criterion for a stay of proceedings[50] towards (but not quite as far as) *Spiliada*.[51] Thus it was said that the application of the clearly inappropriate forum test would lead to the same result as the natural forum test in the majority of cases.[52] It was most unfortunate therefore—but was no doubt part of the judicial compromise negotiated—that the court, whilst enunciating the 'clearly inappropriate forum' test, did not choose wholly to discard the language of vexation or oppression in this context. Thus, unnecessarily and confusingly, the Court in the same breath as enunciating the 'clearly inappropriate forum' which was said to be likely to yield the same outcome as in *Spiliada* in most cases, the Court indicated that proceedings would only be stayed if they were vexatious in the sense of '*seriously and unfairly burdensome, prejudicial or damaging*' and oppressive in the sense of '*productive of serious and unjustified trouble and harassment*'.
>
> The continuing employment of these formulae undermine the liberalising and more internationalised approach to the resolution of stay applications that *Voth* intended to introduce, and has certainly ensured that the prediction that the application of the two tests (*Spiliada* and *Voth*) would yield the same result in the majority of cases has simply not been borne out. The current Court has in terms and, in my opinion, contrary to *Voth* itself, relocated this jurisdiction in an abuse of process framework.[53] In this respect, as Sir Anthony Mason said in 2003, *Voth* and its line of authority stand in 'lonely isolation'.[54] Whatever view one takes as to the parochialism or otherwise of the *Voth* test (the alternative view being that, if the Court has jurisdiction, its job is to exercise it save only in cases of pure abuse of process), it certainly has had the consequence that if, in a transnational dispute, a party wishes to commence suit in Australia, it will be difficult to obtain a

[47] See, eg, *Lubbe v Cape plc* [2000] 1 WLR 1545; *Cherney v Deripaska* [2009] EWCA Civ 849; *AK Investment CJSC v Kyrgyz Mobil Tel Ltd* [2011] UKPC 7, [2012] 1 WLR 1804.

[48] A Bell, above n 46, 55–56.

[49] This is made explicit in the judgment: above n 19, (1990) 171 CLR 538, at 552.

[50] *St Pierre v South American Stores (Gath & Chaves) Ltd* [1936] 1 KB 382, 398. The burden of *Voth* was to reject that approach: (1990) 171 CLR 538, 557.

[51] The Court in *Voth* (above n 19) stated (at 558) that the difference between the 'clearly inappropriate forum' test and the English 'more appropriate forum' approach is slight—'the question which the former test presents is *slightly* different' (emphasis added).

[52] Above n 19, 558.

[53] See, for example, *CSR Ltd v Cigna Insurance Australia Ltd* (1997) 189 CLR 345, 391.

[54] AS Bell, above n 13, Foreword.

stay of proceedings. In this respect, Australian courts are more likely to be embroiled in transnational jurisdictional disputes than forums which employ a *Spiliada* style test because, in cases where the Australian forum could not be described as the natural or more appropriate forum, the alternative forum will, by definition, almost always have a closer nexus to the dispute and will be less likely to be inclined to decline to exercise jurisdiction. This is an environment in which anti-suit injunctions come to the fore. For those concerned with the effect on comity of this form of relief, the discarding or modification of *Voth* may be one step in the right direction.

In terms of a micro-economic analysis, the propensity of the *Voth* test to generate duplicative litigation and encourage jurisdictional jockeying is a cogent reason for the adoption of a modified test which could be expressed in terms of either a 'more appropriate' forum test or an 'inappropriate' (as opposed to 'clearly inappropriate') forum test. It should be observed that the NSW Uniform Civil Procedures Rules in fact provide, in rule 11.7, that the Supreme Court may make an order setting aside service on the ground that the Court is 'an inappropriate forum for the trial of the proceedings'. In *Studorp Ltd v Robinson*,[55] Allsop P noted[56] the difference in 'quality and emphasis' which the adverb 'clearly' brought to the analysis. This observation was undoubtedly correct as a matter of language, but its impact may arguably be precluded by observations by the majority of the High Court in *Renault v Zhang*[57] to the effect that the statutory reference to 'inappropriate forum' had the same content as the 'clearly inappropriate forum'.

Defenders of the *Voth* test would argue that it affords a level of protection to injured Australian citizens and corporations who become embroiled in transnational litigation, minimising the prospect of them having to pursue foreign defendants abroad.[58] In this context, the Carriage of Goods by Sea Act 1991 (Cth) has long stood as an example of self-consciously parochial jurisdictional legislation, negating the effect of jurisdiction and arbitration clauses in particular cases which, if enforced, would typically have constrained Australian primary producers to litigate or arbitrate in England.

Whether such a parochial attitude should, in the twenty-first century, underpin our entire body of principles in relation to the assertion and exercise of jurisdiction over foreign defendants is questionable. It may also be a topic upon which members of Supreme Court Rules Committees feel ill-equipped to make such a decision (assuming that the reformulation of the *Voth* test would properly be considered to be a matter of practice and procedure and thus within the scope of the Rules Committees' authority). It might be observed, however, that retention of the *status quo* would be a decision in itself.

[55] [2012] NSWCA 382.

[56] ibid, [5]. See also Hoeben JA, at [62].

[57] (2002) 210 CLR 491, 503.

[58] For a recent example, see *Wilson v Addu Investments Private Ltd; Lee v Addu Investments Private Ltd* [2014] NSWSC 381.

IV. Conclusion

It remains regrettable that as relatively straightforward an initiative as seeking to harmonise the rules for service out of the jurisdiction in respect of foreign defendants served with process remains unfulfilled. There is no rational reason for the retention of diverse sets of rules as currently exist as between the various State and Territory Supreme Courts and the Federal Court of Australia. The current unsatisfactory position will continue to be highlighted as more and more foreign defendants come to be sued in our courts as a result of growth in global economic activity.

5

Uniformity of Outcome in Australian Choice of Law*

RICHARD GARNETT

I. Introduction

The past 30 years have seen dramatic changes in the Australian private international law landscape. In 1987 Australia had a system of choice of law rules inherited largely from England and designed for resolving conflicts between the laws of nation states. Such a system was applied generally without question to both interstate and international conflicts of law before Australian courts. The mantra often repeated in Australian decisions was that 'the States are separate countries in private international law and are to be so regarded in relation to one another'.[1]

While this observation ignored the social, legal and cultural homogeneity within the Australian federation,[2] it did establish a uniformity of *principle* in Australian choice of law in the sense that the same choice of law rules were applied to international and interstate conflicts cases alike. This uniformity of principle was also reinforced by the fact that Australia had inherited a uniform body of common law rules from England and had a final court of appeal (the High Court) on matters of State and federal law. Moreover, not only were the common law choice of law rules essentially identical throughout Australia, there was also substantial uniformity of principle with other Commonwealth countries which had inherited the English common law.

Interruptions to this uniformity of choice of law rules within Australia only arose through statutes passed by individual States and Territories which departed

* An earlier version of this chapter was published in (2013) 37 *Australian Bar Review* 192.

[1] *Pedersen v Young* (1964) 110 CLR 162, 170 (Windeyer J).

[2] As one commentator put it, 'one might reasonably have doubted whether categories derived from Roman law and applied to international conflicts would operate satisfactorily in cases involving modern problems in a federal system': D Kelly, 'Chief Justice Bray and the Conflict of Laws' (1980) 7 *Adelaide Law Review* 17, 31.

from the common law rules. Such statutory choice of law rules have, however, been rare in Australian law.[3]

Yet, despite such uniformity of choice of law *rules*, uniformity of *outcome*, often cited as one of the key objectives of private international law,[4] was neither sought nor accomplished. Uniformity of outcome requires that, as far as possible, a case be decided according to the same substantive law, wherever the matter is heard and that a plaintiff derives no benefit from choice of forum alone. Uniformity in this sense therefore encourages certainty and predictability in the application of laws to a given case and discourages forum shopping, a recognised cardinal sin in private international law.[5] Critics of uniformity of outcome argue however that it pays too little regard to justice in individual cases and ignores important interests that individual countries or States (in a federal system) may have in applying their laws in a given case.

The arguments for and against uniformity of outcome will be examined in this chapter in the context of both international and interstate choice of law rules in Australia. The question is of particular relevance to the Standing Council on Law and Justice (SCLJ) Harmonisation Project as it considers the utility and effectiveness of current Australian principles of private international law. Reference will also be made to developments in the United States and the European Union to assess the extent to which the principle of uniformity of outcome occupies a central place in those legal systems' approaches to choice of law. As will be seen, the US and EU represent polar opposites on the issue.

II. The Pre-1987 Position

Uniformity of outcome was not an articulated objective in the formulation of Australian choice of law rules prior to 1987. If there was a philosophical approach it was largely to replicate the English rules fairly closely without regard to their suitability to the Australian context. This uncritical acceptance of English precedent was all the more surprising since the bulk of Australian choice of law cases concerned conflicts between the laws of Australian States and Territories ('interstate conflicts'), not between Australian law and that of a foreign country ('international conflicts'). In such a context, it might have been thought that a different

[3] R Mortensen, R Garnett and M Keyes, *Private International Law in Australia*, 2nd edn (Sydney, Lexis Nexis, 2011) 315.

[4] E Rabel, *The Conflict of Laws*, 2nd edn (Ann Arbor, MI, University of Michigan Press, 1958) 94; B Opeskin, 'The Price of Forum Shopping: A Reply to Professor Juenger' (1994) 16 *Sydney Law Review* 14. The Australian Law Reform Commission in its 1992 report on choice of law adopted uniformity of result as the main objective in interstate cases: Australian Law Reform Commission, *Choice of Law*, Report No 58 (Sydney, Commonwealth of Australia, 1992) 12.

[5] Sir A Mason, Foreword to R Garnett, *Substance and Procedure in Private International Law* (Oxford, Oxford University Press, 2012) ix.

approach, in particular, one that recognised the close connections between the States and Territories, should have been adopted instead.

A. International Co-operation and Confluence

In any event, the choice of law rules for both interstate and international conflicts prior to 1987 provided only limited scope for uniformity of outcome and this was so for a number of reasons. First, there was almost a complete absence of any treaties to which Australia was a party which harmonised national choice of law rules on the transnational plane. Obviously, harmonisation of choice of law rules by international co-operation and agreement is a valuable method for securing uniformity of outcome since all countries in theory will apply the same rules and so are likely to select the same substantive law to govern the cause of action. Yet the only such treaties on choice of law entered into by Australia in this period were the 1961 Hague Convention on the Conflict of Laws Relating to the Form of Testamentary Dispositions, given effect in statute law of the States and Territories[6] and the 1978 Hague Convention on Celebration and Recognition of the Validity of Marriages, implemented in 1985 amendments to the Marriage Act 1961 (Cth).

B. Forum-Specific Choice of Law Rules

A second reason why uniformity of outcome was difficult to achieve prior to 1987 was the existence of common law choice of law rules, particularly in the areas of tort and the classification of substance/procedure, which excessively favoured the law of the forum. What is interesting to note here is that the mere fact of common or harmonised choice of law rules does not necessarily lead to uniformity of outcome when the rules themselves are forum-biased. So, even though Australian States and Territories before 1987 all applied the same common law choice of law rules on tort and substance and procedure to interstate disputes, because such rules favoured the forum, uniformity of outcome was impossible to achieve. The same point could be made about the Australian position in international conflicts—the fact that all Commonwealth countries applied the same forum-centred rules also meant that uniformity of outcome was elusive, despite the rules themselves being highly similar in content.

The choice of law rule for torts was found in the old English decision in *Phillips v Eyre*,[7] which provided that a plaintiff could recover under the law of the forum in respect of a foreign tort if it could show that the tort was actionable under both the law of the forum and the law of the place of the wrong. In a number of Australian interstate personal injury cases, plaintiffs were allowed to proceed

[6] See eg Succession Act 2006 (NSW) ss 48–50.
[7] *Phillips v Eyre* (1870) LR 6 QB 1.

under forum law despite the action being barred or limited under the law of the place of the wrong.[8] Forum shopping was therefore encouraged by this doctrine.

Choice of law rules also unduly favoured the law of the forum in two other areas before 1987: first, in the context of family law matters such as the dissolution of marriage[9] and the maintenance of wives and children;[10] and secondly in the field of equitable obligations where the application of forum law was justified on the basis that equity protects 'conscience'.[11] Again, uniformity of outcome was impossible to achieve when such issues arose.

C. Substance and Procedure

Another forum-centred rule applicable in both interstate and international cases was found in the Australian classification of substantive and procedural matters. The traditional common law approach was that any matter relating to the 'remedy' or 'the enforcement of a right' was procedural and governed by the law of the forum even if the law of the cause of action was foreign. This rule had the pernicious effect of allowing plaintiffs (especially in tort cases) to bring cases in a forum where the limitation period had not expired on the basis that limitations was a procedural matter, even though the proceeding would have been barred under the law of the cause of action.[12] The rule also allowed plaintiffs to seek out forums in which higher damages were payable than in the place of the wrong or where a statutory 'cap' on damages under such law did not apply on the basis that matters of quantification of damages were procedural.[13]

While such forum-centred choice of law rules applied to both interstate and international conflicts disputes, prior to 1987, it was in the interstate context where the problem arose more frequently. In either case, however, the retention of such rules made the pursuit or achievement of uniformity of outcome impossible.

D. Even-Handed Choice of Law Rules: Contract and Property

By contrast, uniformity of outcome is much more likely to be achieved where choice of law rules are adopted which are widely accepted internationally. In the area of contracts and property, Australian choice of law rules have long been consistent with commonly accepted international standards. Versions of the proper law of the contract doctrine, which defers substantially to the parties' expressly or

[8] See eg, *Breavington v Godleman* [1985] VR 851; *Hartley v Venn* (1967) 10 FLR 151; *Kolsky v Mayne Nickless Ltd* (1970) 72 SR (NSW) 437 and *Kemp v Piper* [1971] SASR 25.

[9] Mortensen, Garnett and Keyes, above n 3, 372.

[10] ibid, 427.

[11] *National Commercial Bank v Wimborne* [1978] 5 BPR 11,958, 11,982.

[12] See eg, *McKain v RW Miller & Co (SA) Pty Ltd* (1991) 174 CLR 1.

[13] See eg, *Stevens v Head* (1992) 176 CLR 433.

impliedly chosen law, exist in almost all legal systems. Similarly, in property cases, the law of the location or *situs* of the property is widely used. Again, it would be plausible to expect that in many cases both a foreign and an Australian court would reach similar outcomes on the law to be applied in these areas if the same facts arose before each court.

E. Public Policy

Apart from the tort choice of law rule and the procedural classification there are also other common law choice of law methods by which an issue may be referred to the law of the forum. One such method is public policy: an Australian court will not apply a foreign law where to do so would offend the fundamental values and principles of the forum State. As one Australian court said, there must be a 'substantial injustice either because … of a repugnant foreign law or a repugnant application of the law in a particular case'.[14]

Although this is a recent statement, it accurately reflects the historically narrow view Australian courts have taken of this exception, both before and after 1987, with very few instances of foreign law being not applied on public policy grounds.[15] In contrast to the procedural classification, and its wide scope of reference to forum law, the narrow confinement of public policy has facilitated the application of foreign law in Australian courts and so assisted uniformity of outcome.

F. Overriding Mandatory Rules

The other major method under Australian choice of law principles of referring a matter to forum law is by use of overriding local mandatory statutes. As mentioned above, litigation involving such statutes has been comparatively rare in Australia with the result being that the applicable foreign law has not often been avoided on this ground. Of course, where statutes are clear in their intention to displace the applicable (foreign) law of the parties' contract then courts must give effect to the terms of the statute, notwithstanding the effect on uniformity of outcome. Examples of such provisions are section 11(1) of the Carriage of Goods by Sea Act 1991 (Cth) (re-enacting section 11(1) of the Sea Carriage of Goods Act 1924 (Cth)), section 67 of the Australian Consumer Law (2010) (Cth) and section 8 of the Insurance Contracts Act 1984 (Cth). Obviously, the accomplishment of uniformity in these contexts has been rendered impossible by the legislature.

The position is different where Parliament does not use clear words to determine the territorial scope of a statute's operation. In this situation, Australian

[14] *Jenton Overseas Investment Pte Ltd v Townsing* (2008) 21 VR 241, [22]; see also *Stern v National Australia Bank* [1999] FCA 1421, [135].

[15] M Pryles, 'Internationalism in Australian Private International Law' (1989) 12 *Sydney Law Review* 96, 104.

courts have generally sought to uphold the parties' chosen law in keeping with the objective of uniformity of result. So, in a number of early decisions, members of the High Court, especially Dixon J, suggested that where a forum statute's territorial scope of operation is uncertain it should be interpreted consistently with the common law choice of law rules.[16] Hence, if the parties have chosen foreign law in their contract, such law should not be displaced by a local mandatory statute unless there are clear words of intent to do so. Most Australian courts have endorsed this view both before and after[17] 1987, although there were occasional suggestions that the 'policy' of the forum statute should be given full effect, even at the expense of the applicable foreign law.[18] The dominant view is consistent with the need to uphold foreign law, especially where it has been chosen by the parties, and also the goal of uniformity of outcome.[19]

One area which has long been uncertain in this regard has been the application of the consumer protection provisions of the old Trade Practices Act 1974 (Cth), especially section 52, now section 18 of the Australian Consumer Law 2010 (Competition and Consumer Act 2010 (Cth), Schedule 2) in the context of an agreement governed by foreign law. Specifically, can parties, by choice of such law, exclude the operation of these provisions? The matter has been discussed in a number of decisions but not conclusively decided.[20] Proponents of uniformity of outcome and party autonomy would suggest that such exclusion is possible,[21] a conclusion which is consistent with the approach of Dixon J above.

G. Constitutional Control of Choice of Law

In the context of interstate choice of law disputes, there was a further impediment to uniformity of outcome prior to 1987: the reluctance of Australian courts to use the Federal Constitution to control the choice of law process. The most significant provision in this regard is section 118, the full faith and credit clause, which relevantly provides that 'full faith and credit shall be given, throughout the Commonwealth to the laws … of every State'.

It has been long accepted that one effect of the full faith and credit clause is to dispense with the need to 'prove' interstate laws and to allow other States' courts to

[16] *Wanganui-Rangitikei Electric Power Board v Australian Mutual Provident Society* (1934) 50 CLR 581, 601; *Barcelo v Electrolytic Zinc Company of Australasia Ltd* (1932) 48 CLR 391 (Dixon and McTiernan JJ).

[17] See eg *Sweedman v Transport Accident Commission* (2006) 226 CLR 362.

[18] See eg *Kay's Leasing Corp Pty Ltd v Fletcher* (1964) 116 CLR 124, 143 (Kitto J).

[19] See M Keyes, 'Statutes, Choice of Law and the Role of Forum Choice' (2008) 4 *Journal of Private International Law* 1.

[20] See eg *Clough Engineering Ltd v Oil and Natural Gas Co of India* (2008) 249 ALR 458, [45].

[21] *Comandate Marine Corp v Pan Australia Shipping Pty Ltd* (2006) 157 FCR 45, [240]–[241] (Allsop J, with whom Finn and Finkelstein JJ agreed); see also M Davies, A Bell and P Brereton, *Nygh's Conflict of Laws in Australia*, 9th edn (Sydney, LexisNexis, 2014) 459.

take judicial notice of them.[22] The only substantive effect, however, of the clause which had been recognised by the High Court prior to 1987 was that the common law exclusionary doctrines may not be applied by a State to deny application of another State's law selected under the common law choice of law rules. Hence a Victorian court could not, for example, refuse to apply a NSW law on the ground of public policy[23] or because it was a penal or revenue law.[24] Prior to 1987, the High Court steadfastly rejected any suggestion that the full faith and credit clause could displace the common law choice of law rules or even influence their content.[25]

III. The Changes After 1987

Major changes have occurred in Australian law since 1987 which have had the effect of installing uniformity of outcome as the dominant objective in choice of law determinations.

A. International Co-operation and Confluence

As was noted above, in the absence of an international court or legislature with the capacity to impose uniform rules on nation states, uniformity of outcome is difficult to achieve in international conflicts. The European Union has a better record on this issue especially recently, and developments there are discussed below.

Harmonisation of choice of law rules by treaty has increased dramatically since 1987, especially in the European Union, although the impact on Australia has been less marked. Australia has adopted the 1991 Hague Convention on the Law Applicable to Trusts, which was given effect in domestic law in the Trusts (Hague Convention) Act 1991 (Cth) and also the United Nations Convention on Contracts for the International Sales of Goods (the Vienna Convention) in 1989, which was given effect in uniform State legislation, for example, the Sale of Goods (Vienna Convention) Act 1989 (Vic). While the Vienna Convention is not a choice of law instrument, it does seek to harmonise the substantive law of international sales and in that way make choice of law rules redundant. The significant scope for evasion of the Convention by the parties under article 6 as well as the wide range of measures excluded from its terms (including matters of essential validity of contracts such as fraud, duress, mistake etc[26]) means, however, that choice of

[22] *Breavington v Godleman* (1988) 169 CLR 41, 148 (Dawson J).

[23] *Merwin Pastoral Co Pty Ltd v Moolpa Pastoral Co Pty Ltd* (1933) 48 CLR 565.

[24] *Permanent Trustee Co (Canberra) Ltd v Finlayson* (1967) 9 FLR 424 (reversed on other grounds (1968) 122 CLR 338).

[25] *Anderson v Eric Anderson Radio & TV Pty Ltd* (1965) 114 CLR 20.

[26] United Nations Convention on Contracts for the International Sale of Goods 1980, art 4.

law remains a live issue in many international sale of goods contracts governed by the Convention and so uniformity of outcome is not guaranteed.

Most recently, there is a current initiative before the Hague Conference on Private International Law: the Draft Hague Principles on the Choice of Law in International Contracts,[27] which, if adopted by Australia, would bring its choice of law rules for contract into even closer alignment with those of the European Union, as expressed in the 1980 Rome Convention on the Law Applicable to Contractual Obligations[28] (now the 2008 Rome I Regulation).[29] Interestingly, the Australian Law Reform Commission had recommended in 1992 that some of the common law choice of law rules be altered in line with the Rome Convention, but no action was taken by State legislatures.[30] The authors of *Nygh*[31] have also advocated this position. The emergence of the Hague Principles provides an opportunity for Australia to revisit this issue and take a further step toward achieving uniformity of outcome in contract choice of law. Importantly, such action may inspire further measures of international cooperation in other areas of choice of law. Yet this method of securing uniformity is likely to be a slow one if past experience is any guide.

B. Constitutional Control and Tort Choice of Law

The first real major step towards uniformity of outcome arose in the area of interstate tort conflicts and appeared in the High Court decision, *Breavington v Godleman* in 1988.[32] In *Breavington*, a majority of the court acknowledged for the first time that the Federal Constitution might have a substantial impact on choice of law questions in interstate disputes within Australia.

Mason CJ noted that a clause existed in the Australian Constitution which confers on the Federal Parliament power to legislate with respect to the 'recognition throughout the Commonwealth of the laws [and] public acts … of the States' (section 51(xxv)) which may be a source of federally enacted choice of law rules. The Australian Law Reform Commission, in its 1992 report on choice of law, supported this view.[33] From the point of view of uniformity of result in interstate choice of law cases, federally enacted choice of law rules would be a major advance, since all courts, State and federal would have to apply the same rules. This conclusion of course assumes that the rules themselves are balanced and do not unduly favour the law of the forum.

[27] www.hcch.net/upload/wop/contracts2012principles_e.pdf. See generally B Marshall, 'Reconsidering the Proper Law of the Contract' (2012) 13 *Melbourne Journal of International Law* 505.

[28] Rome Convention on the Law Applicable to Contractual Obligations [1980] OJ L266/1.

[29] Regulation (EC) No. 593/2008 of the European Parliament and Council of 17 June 2008 on the law applicable to contractual obligations ([2008] OJ L177/6).

[30] Australian Law Reform Commission, above n 4, 97–98.

[31] *Nygh's Conflict of Laws in Australia*, above n 21, 443.

[32] *Breavington v Godleman* (1988) 169 CLR 41.

[33] Australian Law Reform Commission, above n 4, 25; see also Kelly, above n 2, 32.

Yet such federal rules have never been enacted; one explanation may be out of a concern that to do so would curtail State legislative power, since any State legislation (such as overriding mandatory rules) inconsistent with the federal laws would be invalid under section 109 of the Australian Constitution. In other words, the policy of preserving State legislative sovereignty and interests within the federation is regarded as having priority over the accomplishment of uniformity of result. Of course, another explanation for Commonwealth inaction may be simply inertia or uncertainty as to the validity of its constitutional powers. Regardless of the cause, this path to uniformity has not been taken.

Three other judges in *Breavington* suggested that the full faith and credit clause in section 118 of the Constitution (and wider inferences from the Constitution as a whole) had the effect of displacing the common law choice of law rules. According to Wilson and Gaudron JJ, the purpose of the full faith and credit clause is to ensure that 'one set of facts occurring in a State would be adjudged by only one body of law and thus give rise to only one legal consequence, regardless of where in the Commonwealth [of Australia] the matter fell for adjudication'.[34]

In other words, uniformity of outcome is mandated by the Constitution: to achieve this in a tort case an Australian court must apply the law of the place of the wrong as a 'constitutional' rule.

Deane J in *Breavington* similarly found the common law choice of law rules to be ousted by the Constitution which, in his view, required an Australian court to apply the law with the 'predominant territorial nexus' to the facts of the case—which in a tort case will almost always be the law of the place of the wrong.[35]

Perhaps because both of the above views would again have the effect of nullifying State legislative power—specifically the capacity to legislate inconsistently with the 'constitutionalised' choice of law rules—majorities of the High Court in later decisions rejected these approaches. For example, in *McKain v RW Miller & Co (South Australia) Pty Ltd*,[36] Brennan, Dawson, Toohey and McHugh JJ said:[37]

> [A] constitutional imperative that the courts of a State should apply only the substantive law of another part of the Commonwealth [of Australia] in determining a claim for damages for a tort occurring outside the State but within Australia would deny the forum State an important legislative power … The laws of the States, though recognized throughout Australia, are therefore capable of creating disparities in the legal consequences attached in the respective States to the same set of facts unless a valid law of the Commonwealth overrides the relevant State laws and prescribes a uniform legal consequence. That may or may not be thought to be desirable, but it is the hallmark of a federation as distinct from a union.

The above passage suggests that the goal of uniformity of outcome can only be pursued through federally enacted legislation; otherwise, it is subordinate to

[34] (1988) 169 CLR 41, 98.
[35] ibid, 137.
[36] *McKain v RW Miller & Co (South Australia) Pty Ltd* (1992) 174 CLR 1.
[37] ibid, 36.

the protection of State legislative sovereignty within the Australian federation. Obviously much depends upon individual judges' conceptions of the structure of the federal system but nowhere in this passage is there recognition of the problem of plaintiff forum shopping and how such a practice undermines the legislative integrity of States by strategic choice of forum.

If this view on the constitutional issue was not enough of a rebuke to those advocating uniformity of outcome, the above judges in *McKain* then proceeded to hold that the rule in *Phillips v Eyre* should be preserved as the choice of law rule for torts and that the scope of procedure should continue to embrace matters affecting the remedy and the enforcement of any rights, including the applicability of statutes of limitation.

The *McKain* decision was therefore a major setback for the cause of uniformity not only in the context of interstate choice of law but international matters as well. The subsequent decision of the High Court in *Stevens v Head*[38] maintained this position, holding that a NSW statutory limitation on quantum of damages was a matter of procedure, not substance, and so inapplicable to proceedings in the Queensland forum in respect of a tort committed in New South Wales.

Yet uniformity of outcome, at least in interstate choice of law disputes, was not dead and buried. In what has become the leading and authoritative case on interstate choice of law in Australia, *John Pfeiffer Pty Ltd v Rogerson*,[39] a 6:1 majority of the High Court in 2000 recognised a direct role for the Federal Constitution in the formulation of common law choice of law rules. Specifically, the choice of law rule for interstate torts was pronounced to be the law of the place of the wrong (without exception), and adoption of this rule was said to be strongly supported by constitutional principles, such as full faith and credit and the nature of the federal compact including the predominantly territorial concerns of the States and Territories.[40] By contrast, forum-centred principles such as the rule in *Phillips v Eyre* were considered inconsistent with such values, and so rejected. Yet while Wilson, Gaudron and Deane JJ in *Breavington* had considered that the Constitution *ousted* the common law choice of law rules, the majority judges in *Pfeiffer* appeared to state that the Constitution merely determined the *scope and content* of such rules.

Nevertheless, in another passage the Court appeared to suggest that the Constitution may have an even greater effect and that the common law choice of law rules were embedded in the Constitution:[41]

> The matters we have mentioned as arising from the constitutional text and structure may amount collectively to a particular constitutional imperative which dictates the common law choice of law rule which we favour. It may be that those matters operate constitutionally to entrench that rule or aspects of it concerning such matters as 'the

[38] *Stevens v Head* (1992) 176 CLR 433.
[39] *John Pfeiffer Pty Ltd v Rogerson* (2000) 203 CLR 503.
[40] ibid, [67].
[41] ibid, [70].

public policy exception.' If so, the result would be to restrict [State] legislative power to abrogate or vary that common law rule. However we leave those questions open.

Such an 'entrenching' view would produce a result closer to that proposed by Wilson, Gaudron and Deane JJ in *Breavington* in that States' legislative capacity would be confined to enacting laws which were consistent with the common law choice of law rules. The main difference between any entrenchment created by the Court in *Pfeiffer* and the view of those three judges in *Breavington* would be that the common law choice of law rules would be retained although their content would be shaped by the integrated federal structure provided by the Constitution. So, in other words, a choice of law rule which was expressed in favour of the forum would be impermissible.

Interestingly, however, despite some references to the issue in later cases the High Court has refused to confirm whether such 'constitutionalisation' has occurred, and the question remains strictly unresolved. For example, in *Sweedman v Transport Accident Commission*[42] the Court had to consider an action in Victoria for an indemnity by a Victorian insurer under Victorian legislation against a NSW resident in respect of an accident having occurred in New South Wales. It was argued by the defendant that the Victorian statute could not apply because it was inconsistent with a NSW statute. A majority of the Court (Gleeson CJ, Gummow, Kirby and Hayne JJ) found there to be no inconsistency between the statutes on the facts. The majority also held that the Victorian statute applied to allow the claim for indemnity, since such a claim was characterised for choice of law purposes as restitutionary and governed by the law of the State with the closest connection to the obligation to indemnify, which was Victoria. While such a conclusion is consistent with the view that the common law choice of law rules have been constitutionally entrenched, the Court did not reach its decision on that ground and expressed no opinion on the issue.

By contrast, though, when *Sweedman* was before the Victorian Court of Appeal, Nettle JA (with whom Winneke P agreed) commented in *obiter* that a State legislature may have only limited power to change the common law choice of law rules,[43] which suggests some sort of constitutional entrenchment.

Some commentators (predominantly from constitutional law backgrounds) have rejected the view that the common law choice of law rules are constitutionally embedded[44] for the reason that this approach would unduly restrict State legislative power. The same reason has been given for rejecting the view that the principle of uniformity of outcome is constitutionally mandated.[45]

[42] *Sweedman v Transport Accident Commission* (2006) 226 CLR 362.

[43] *Sweedman v Transport Accident Commission* (2004) 210 ALR 140, 154.

[44] G Taylor, 'The Effect of the Constitution on the Common Law as Revealed by *John Pfeiffer v Rogerson*' (2002) 30 *Federal Law Review* 69; G Hill and A Stone, 'The Constitutionalisation of the Common Law' (2004) 25 *Adelaide Law Review* 67, 78–79.

[45] P Herzfeld, 'Constitutional Limitations on State Choice of Law Statutes' (2005) 16 *Public Law Review* 188; J Stellios, 'Choice of Law and the Australian Constitution: Locating the Debate' (2005) 33 *Federal Law Review* 7.

A middle position between full constitutional entrenchment of the common law rules and only 'influence' on such rules is the suggestion that the Constitution operates as a *prohibition* on choice of law rules of a forum-centred nature.[46] In that category would be the rule in *Phillips v Eyre*, the application of the exclusionary doctrines to interstate laws such as the public policy and the penal and revenue exceptions and, possibly, an excessively wide conception of procedure. All such matters could not be the subject of valid State legislation. Certainly this view can be seen to have historical continuity since, as noted above, the High Court as early as 1933[47] suggested that full faith and credit operated to displace the common law public policy exception.[48] In practice, however, this view goes close to entrenchment since it potentially knocks out any State-legislated choice of law rule which favours the forum, which is not so different to saying that the law of the place of the wrong is a constitutionally mandated choice of law rule.

Those scholars championing State legislative sovereignty see a different role for section 118 of the Constitution in resolving interstate conflicts in Australia. The provision should be used to give 'full effect' to State statutes including where they have extraterritorial effect with the result that a statute of State A would prevail over the common law in State B in the event of a conflict. Where a conflict existed *between State statutes* (as was argued but not found in *Sweedman*) principles of statutory interpretation[49] including favouring the State with the closest territorial connection[50] or the most compelling interest[51] would be used to break the deadlock. Although it has been suggested that an analysis based on comparing and evaluating the policies of States is consistent with the objective of uniformity of outcome,[52] the US experience of this type of 'interest analysis' in choice of law has been the opposite; as discussed below, it has often been used to enshrine forum bias[53] and is plagued with uncertainty.

Yet there is no sign that any of these latter approaches, which attempt to shift the focus back to State legislative sovereignty and interests in resolving interstate choice of law disputes, will be adopted by the Court in the near future. After *Pfeiffer* the High Court now seems more concerned with furthering traditionally *private international law* interests in interstate choice of law disputes, namely, providing for certainty, predictability and uniformity of outcome and deterring

[46] Hill and Stone, above n 44, 80, 81, 95.

[47] *Merwin Pastoral Co Pty Ltd v Moolpa Pastoral Co Pty Ltd* (1933) 48 CLR 565.

[48] See also, to the same effect, *Permanent Trustee Co (Canberra) Ltd v Finlayson* (1967) 9 FLR 424 (reversed on other grounds (1968) 122 CLR 338) on the application of penal and revenue laws of other states.

[49] S Gageler, 'Private Intranational Law: Choice or Conflict, Common Law or Constitution' (2003) 23 *Australian Bar Review* 184.

[50] Stellios, above n 45, 54; Justice B Selway, 'The Australian Single Law Area' (2003) 29 *Monash Law Review* 30. See also G Lindell and Sir A Mason, 'The Resolution of Inconsistent State and Territory Legislation' (2010) 38 *Federal Law Review* 391.

[51] J Kirk, 'Conflicts and Choice of Law within the Australian Constitutional Context' (2003) 31 *Federal Law Review* 247.

[52] ibid, 285.

[53] Stellios, above n 45, 53.

forum shopping, rather than preserving State powers. Also, the downplaying of State legislative sovereignty may be seen as consistent with the approach taken by Dixon J in the decisions of *Wanganui*[54] and *Barcelo*[55] that common law choice of law rules should determine the territorial operation and scope of legislation (absent clear statutory wording), not the other way around.

Hence, regardless of whether the common law choice of law rules are only influenced by the Constitution or embedded in it, uniformity of outcome has emerged as a major, guiding principle in interstate choice of law after *Pfeiffer*. For the first time the High Court has established a regime which reflects the cultural, political and legal homogeneity of the Australian federation; this is a significant advance on the earlier position.

C. Substance and Procedure

The High Court in *Pfeiffer* also boosted the cause of uniformity of outcome by redefining the boundaries of substance and procedure, which had been another controversial issue in Australian choice of law. Gone was the distinction between the existence of the right (substantive) and the enforcement of the right or remedy (procedural) which had been a gift to plaintiff forum shoppers, especially in time limitation and quantum of damages cases. After *Pfeiffer* any matter pertaining to the 'mode or conduct of court proceedings' will be classified as procedural and governed by forum law, and any matter directed at the 'existence, extent or enforceability of rights and duties of the parties to the action' will be regarded as substantive and governed by the law of the cause of action.[56] In addition, and to clarify, 'all questions about the kinds of damage or amount of damages that may be recovered' would be regarded as substantive.[57]

In a stroke, much of the previous practice of forum shopping in interstate cases has been extinguished—now the applicable limitation period and all questions relating to the availability and quantum of damages will be governed by the law of the cause of action—regardless of where the matter is heard. This approach provides further support to the cause of uniformity of outcome.

Interestingly, unlike the tort choice of law rule, this change was not said by the Court to be expressly motivated by constitutional concerns. Yet, as noted above, an excessively wide and forum-centred conception of procedure may be precisely

[54] See n 16 above.

[55] ibid.

[56] *John Pfeiffer Pty Ltd v Rogerson* (2000) 203 CLR 503, [99]; the revised definitions of procedure and substance may however come into conflict on occasion, for example, a right of appeal may be both 'procedural' (in that it pertains to court proceedings) and 'substantive' (in that it may affect the rights and duties of the parties) see Garnett, above n 5, 22.

[57] (2000) 203 CLR 503, [100].

the type of common law choice of law rule which the full faith and credit clause should aim to 'prohibit'.[58]

D. International Conflicts

As noted above, similar to interstate conflicts, the main obstacles in international choice of law disputes to uniformity of outcome were in the areas of tort and substance and procedure. As discussed, the choice of law rules for both issues were excessively forum centred and designed to secure the application of Australian law in most cases where an Australian plaintiff was injured abroad.

The highly generous rules for service out of Australia in tort cases—almost all of which have allowed service where some damage was suffered in the Australian forum[59]—when coupled with the plaintiff sympathetic test for *forum non conveniens*[60] also reinforced the opportunities for forum shopping. It was clear that in many cases Australian courts were exercising jurisdiction and applying their own law in circumstances where a foreign court, with a closer connection to the events and the parties, would have applied a different law. Uniformity of outcome was impossible to achieve in this context.

In 2002, following the groundbreaking *Pfeiffer v Rogerson* decision in interstate torts, the High Court took a similar, parallel step towards making Australian choice of law rules for international torts more neutral and even-handed.

In *Regie Nationale Renault SA v Zhang*[61] the Court held, in the context of a tort action based on a personal injury occurring abroad, that the law of the place of the wrong was the applicable law. Such a rule was extolled by the Court for its certainty, predictability and lack of forum bias[62] and also for the fact that it aligned with the position on interstate torts.[63]

Uniformity of outcome between Australian and foreign courts would also be enhanced by such a rule, since it would be expected that most countries would apply their own law to torts occurring within their boundaries in the majority of cases. As Kirby J noted, 'the predominant international principle for the choice of law in respect of wrongs has long been … the … law … of the place where the wrong was committed'.[64] So, on the facts of *Zhang*, if the plaintiff sued in New South Wales, French law would have applied, as French territory was both the place of defective manufacture of the vehicle he was driving and the place where the defect caused him harm. Similarly, if the plaintiff had sued in France,

[58] Compare Hill and Stone, above n 44.

[59] See eg Uniform Civil Procedure Rules 2005 (NSW) Sch 6(e).

[60] *Maritime Insurance Co Ltd v Geelong Harbour Trust Commissioners* (1908) 6 CLR 194; *Oceanic Sun Line Special Shipping Co Inc v Fay* (1988) 165 CLR 197; *Voth v Manildra Flour Mills Pty Ltd* (1990) 171 CLR 538.

[61] *Regie Nationale Renault SA v Zhang* (2002) 210 CLR 491.

[62] ibid, [66], [75] (Gleeson CJ, Gaudron, McHugh, Gummow and Hayne JJ).

[63] ibid, [126] (Kirby J).

[64] ibid, [127].

French law also likely would have applied as the place where the defect caused the plaintiff injury.[65] The result was therefore that the High Court in *Zhang* had introduced a substantial measure in negating the significance of a plaintiff's choice of forum.

Yet, paradoxically, in one respect the Court's refusal to acknowledge any exception to the law of the place of the wrong—for example application of the law of the parties' common domicile– may have limited the scope for uniformity of outcome. Suppose two Australian domiciliaries and nationals were involved in a tort in a foreign country and the plaintiff sued the defendant in New South Wales. In such a case, the New South Wales court would have to apply the law of the foreign country to the tort despite the fact that in many countries, including Canada,[66] the United States,[67] and the European Union[68] the law of the common domicile (or habitual residence) would normally apply. So, even though a flexible exception to the law of the place of the wrong was rejected by the High Court on the ground that it would compromise certainty, adoption of such an approach would in fact have been more consistent with uniformity of outcome since many (if not most) legal systems adopt such a rule.

Indeed, it was precisely the above fact situation—two Australian domiciliaries involved in a tort in a foreign country—which led the High Court to reconsider the rule in the *Zhang* case in *Neilson v OPCV*.[69] This decision is discussed below.

Before considering *Neilson*, the issue of substance and procedure in international conflicts cases should be briefly addressed. It will be recalled that in *Pfeiffer v Rogerson* the High Court redefined the distinction between substantive and procedural matters, declaring that issues relating to the mode or conduct of court proceedings were procedural while those relating to the existence, extent and enforceability of the rights and duties of the parties were substantive. The High Court in *Pfeiffer* also said that all questions relating to damages should be considered substantive.[70]

As noted above, such statements were supportive of uniformity of outcome in the interstate context by decreasing the scope of operation of the law of the forum and giving more coverage to the applicable law of the cause of action. It was assumed by many that these new principles applied to both interstate and international conflicts cases, since there was nothing said in *Pfeiffer* to expressly restrict their operation to the federal context. It therefore came as some surprise when the

[65] See the decision of the French Court of Cassation (1st Civil Chamber) 11 May 1999. For events giving rise to damage after 11 January 2009 the 2007 EU Regulation on the law applicable to non-contractual obligations (Rome II) now applies in France (below n 68) but the applicable law on this issue is likely to be the same (see arts 4(1), 5(1)(c)).

[66] *Tolofson v Jensen* [1994] 3 SCR 1022, 1060, 1078; *Hanlan v Sernesky* (1998) 38 OR (3d) 479; *Wong v Wei* (1999) 65 BCLR (3d) 222.

[67] *Babcock v Jackson* 191 NE 2d 279 (NY Sup Ct 1963).

[68] Regulation (EC) No 864/2007 of the European Parliament and Council of 11 July 2007 on the law applicable to non-contractual obligations (Rome II) ([2007] OJ L199/40, art 4(2)).

[69] *Neilson v Overseas Projects Corporation of Victoria* (2005) 223 CLR 331.

[70] (2000) 203 CLR 503, [100].

High Court in *Zhang* expressly resiled from the above statement on damages in *Pfeiffer* in the context of international tort cases, saying that the position should be left open for future consideration.[71]

From the point of view of uniformity of outcome such an approach is unhelpful, since it opens the way to forum law being expansively applied to questions of damages again at the expense of the foreign law of the cause of action. Fortunately, in the few Australian decisions since *Zhang* which have considered the issue, courts have assumed that the *Pfeiffer* view of damages also applies to international cases.[72] Hopefully on this issue, the interstate policy in favour of uniformity of outcome has carried over to the international context as well, although until the High Court definitively speaks on the issue, the position remains uncertain.

E. Choice of Law and Equity

As was noted above, the traditional view under Australian choice of law principles has been that equitable rights and duties (outside the area of express trusts) are generally governed by the law of the forum. Since 1987, however, there has been an apparent relaxation of this rule. In *Paramasivam v Flynn*[73] the Federal Court had to consider an equitable action for breach of fiduciary duty. The Court suggested that where such an action arose out of a pre-existing relationship between the parties such as a contract, then the law governing the contract should also apply to resolve the claim for breach of fiduciary duty. Where the fiduciary claim, however, had no contractual foundation then forum law should apply in accordance with the traditional principle. This statement was recently referred to with approval by the NSW Court of Appeal in *Murakami v Wiryadi*[74] with the Court noting that where an equitable claim is 'based on a contract', such as where the source of a fiduciary relationship is contractual, the proper law of the contract should be applied to determine such claim.[75]

Such a modification to the law of the forum rule will provide greater scope for achieving uniformity of outcome in international choice of law disputes, particularly since courts in both Singapore[76] and England[77] are now taking similar approaches.

[71] (2002) 210 CLR 491, [76].

[72] See eg *McGregor v Potts* (2005) 68 NSWLR 109, [54].

[73] *Paramasivam v Flynn* (1998) 90 FLR 489, 503.

[74] *Murakami v Wiryadi* (2010) 268 ALR 377.

[75] ibid, [141]–[146]; see also *Nicholls v Michael Wilson & Partners* [2010] NSWCA 222, [342].

[76] See eg *Rickshaw Investments Ltd v Nicolai Baron von Uexhull* [2007] 1 SLR 377 (Sing CA) and generally T Yeo, *Choice of Law for Equitable Doctrines* (Oxford, Oxford University Press, 2004).

[77] See eg *OJSC Oil Yugraneft v Abramovich* [2008] EWHC 2613 (Comm).

F. The Impact of *Neilson*

Yet, it is the next decision of the High Court on choice of law for foreign torts, in 2005, which represents the boldest step so far taken in the direction of uniformity of outcome.

Neilson v OPCV[78] involved a Western Australian domiciled plaintiff who was injured in China while accompanying her husband on a temporary work assignment. The plaintiff sued her husband's Australian employer in Western Australia. Application of the rule in *Zhang* would have led to Chinese law governing the action since there was no scope under the test for excluding the rule where both parties were Australian nationals or domiciliaries. The complication in the case however was that under the *Chinese* choice of law rules for tort, specifically article 146 of the General Principles of Civil Law of the PRC, a Chinese court was given a discretion not to apply Chinese law to a tort occurring within China where both parties were nationals or domiciliaries of the same foreign country. The question for the High Court was whether it should, under the test in *Zhang*, apply not merely the Chinese domestic law of tort but also its choice of law rules. In other words, does Australian law recognise the doctrine of *renvoi* in the case of torts?

The High Court held by a majority of 6:1 (Gleeson CJ, Gummow, Kirby, Hayne, Callinan and Heydon JJ; McHugh J dissenting) that when applying the foreign law of a country under Australian choice of law rules it was necessary also to apply the choice of law rules of the foreign country to determine what law would be selected under those rules. Five judges of the Court went even further (Callinan J disagreeing on this point), stating that it was also necessary to apply any rules of *renvoi* of the foreign country (assuming any existed and were pleaded by the parties). The result of the case was that the High Court applied the Chinese choice of law rule in article 146. The Court then assumed, in the absence of evidence, that the discretion in the Chinese provision would be exercised in favour of applying the law of Western Australia, given the parties' shared Australian domicile, and so this law was applied to the action.

What is significant about this case is the explicit reference by the majority judges[79] to uniformity of outcome and 'no advantage' as the basis for adopting a *renvoi* rule. The Court saw the attainment of the same result as the Chinese tribunal would have reached had it adjudicated the case as the primary objective in the Australian choice of law inquiry. Such an approach represents a truly seismic change from the pre-1987 era where State sovereignty and the interests of the forum were given priority in both international and interstate cases. While *Neilson* was a tort case there is no indication that the Court sought to confine its choice of law approach to torts; indeed in a subsequent decision the Western Australian

[78] *Neilson v OPCV* (2005) 223 CLR 331.

[79] See especially Gummow and Hayne JJ, ibid, [89]–[91]; also Gleeson CJ at [13], Kirby J at [174], Heydon J at [271].

Court of Appeal applied the 'no advantage' test to the realm of contracts, an issue which will be further explored below.[80]

It appears therefore that an entirely new choice of law doctrine based on uniformity of result now exists in Australian law. While it has been suggested in this chapter that this goal is a worthy aspiration in the formulation of choice of law rules, the *Neilson* case shows that an absolutist view of this principle can be very difficult to apply and can lead to absurd results in some cases.

(i) Neilson*: Problem of Double Renvoi*

The first and most obvious problem arises where the law of the foreign country also possesses a *renvoi* doctrine. If the foreign country's approach is based on 'double *renvoi*', then the foreign law will refer the matter back to Australian law including its *renvoi* principle, with the result that the case will become marooned in an inextricable circle. While such a result has not so far been reached, it remains a possible strategy for a litigant who wishes to obstruct proceedings and frustrate resolution of a case.

(ii) Neilson*: Application to Contracts*

It was mentioned above that the High Court did not limit its 'no advantage' test to the area of torts and in *O'Driscoll v J Ray McDermott SA*,[81] the Western Australian Court of Appeal confirmed that it applied to contracts as well. *O'Driscoll* concerned a personal injury claim arising from an alleged breach of an employment contract. The employer was a Paraguayan registered corporation and the employee was Western Australian. The contract of employment was made in Singapore for work to be done in different places in South East Asia. The action was barred by limitation of time under the law of Singapore but not Western Australia.

The question of the applicable statute of limitations in the case is explored later in this chapter but for the moment it is important to focus on the application of *Neilson* to the issue of choice of law in contract. The Western Australian Courtof Appeal first determined that Singapore law would govern the contract under Australian common law principles of choice of law. The Court then, in accordance with the 'no advantage' direction in *Neilson*, examined Singapore choice of law rules and found that Singapore law would also be applied. Hence, on the issue of the applicable law to the contract there was found to be no conflict between the Australian and Singaporean choice of law rules. The result, however, could easily have been different since the elements in this case were widely spread across a number of countries, for example Indonesia. The objective proper law test (applicable in both Singapore and Australian law) seeks the law with which the contract is most closely connected, but this rule is open-ended and flexible enough to yield different outcomes. Had Singapore choice of law rules pointed

[80] *O'Driscoll v J Ray McDermott SA* [2006] WASCA 25.

[81] ibid.

to Indonesian law instead, the Western Australian Court would presumably have applied that law—but what would have happened if the doctrine of *renvoi* existed under Singapore law for contracts? Would it then be necessary for the Australian court to apply Indonesian choice of law rules as well? The task of achieving uniformity of outcome would have been rendered very difficult indeed.

Another unresolved but important issue is whether *Neilson* also applies to a contract where the parties have expressly or implicitly chosen foreign law in their contract. Although there is sound logic in support of the view that when parties make an express choice of law in their contract they are choosing the domestic legal system of that country not its choice of law rules,[82] the court in *O'Driscoll* drew no such distinction and simply assumed that *Neilson* applied to all choice of law questions. While Australian courts since *O'Driscoll* have not addressed the issue, it must remain an open question and another example of uncertainty produced by the *Neilson* case.

(iii) Neilson*: Public Policy and Overriding Mandatory Rules*

Assuming *Neilson* applies to both torts and (at least some) contracts governed by foreign law, another problem arises: can an Australian party still argue that such foreign law offends Australian public policy or that Australian overriding mandatory rules, as expressed in local statute, apply? Arguably such doctrines under Australian law are now rendered nugatory because the *Neilson* 'no advantage' principle requires that an Australian court apply the same law that a foreign country would. Since, in a given case, it is highly unlikely that a foreign court would apply Australian public policy or overriding mandatory rules to displace its own otherwise applicable law, an Australian court would be forced (however reluctantly) to reach the same result.

It is interesting to test this thesis in the context of an important decision of the High Court on choice of law for contract. In *Akai Pty Ltd v People's Insurance Co Ltd*[83] the Court had to consider an action by a NSW insured for indemnity under an insurance policy issued by a Singaporean insurer which was governed by English law. The insured sued in NSW seeking to rely on the Insurance Contracts Act 1984 (Cth). A majority of the Court held that the Act applied as an overriding mandatory rule to displace the English governing law clause. Applying the *Neilson* 'no advantage' principle, such a result could only be reached if an English court—whose law governed the substance of the case—would have reached the same outcome. Once it was shown by the defendant that an English court would likely not apply the Australian statute to override an English governing law clause,[84] the statute then also could not be applied in the Australian proceeding. Such a result severely compromises the legislative sovereignty of the Australian Parliament and

[82] Mortensen, Garnett and Keyes, above n 3, 441.

[83] *Akai Pty Ltd v People's Insurance Co Ltd* (1996) 188 CLR 418.

[84] This result in fact happened in a subsequent hearing of the action in England, see *Akai Pty Ltd v The People's Insurance Co Ltd* [1998] 1 Lloyd's Rep 90.

would seem to be an example of uniformity being taken too far. It remains to be seen how an Australian court will respond when such an argument is put before it.

Can this arguably extreme effect of *Neilson* be avoided? In the context of contract, if parties want to choose a foreign law to govern their agreement they may consider adding a clause which provides for 'the law of country X to govern the agreement, excluding its choice of law rules'. In that way, if a dispute comes before an Australian court, the court will be instructed *not* to apply the choice of law rules of the foreign country to defeat the possible operation of Australian public policy and statutes. It will be interesting to see if an Australian court gives effect to such an 'anti-*Neilson* clause' or whether it regards the principles of no advantage and uniformity of outcome to be so deeply embedded in local public policy that they cannot be excluded by the parties. Of course, if a party wishes to avoid the application of local Australian overriding mandatory rules such as section 8 of the Insurance Contracts Act 1984 (Cth), section 67 of the Australian Consumer Law 2010 (Cth) and section 17 of the Contracts Review Act 1980 (NSW), then *Neilson* now may provide the tools to do so.

(iv) Neilson*: Substance and Procedure*

Application of the common law substance–procedure distinction is also rendered uncertain by the *Neilson* decision. Specifically, does *Neilson* require an Australian court to apply foreign procedures on the basis that such rules would be applied by the foreign court and that a claimant should obtain 'no advantage' from suit in Australia? Such a suggestion is again rather extreme since it would require an Australian court to jettison its own local procedures and practices in favour of those of a foreign court in any case where a party may obtain an advantage from litigating in Australia (for example the existence of more generous costs rules). Fortunately, no Australian court has so far indicated that such an analysis is required by *Neilson*, but again the argument cannot, in principle, be easily dismissed.

Yet, even if this suggestion is rejected, there remains the problem of having to apply the substance and procedure classification of the law of the cause of action which *Neilson* most certainly demands. It will be recalled that in *O'Driscoll v J Ray McDermott SA*,[85] the Western Australian Court of Appeal had to consider a contract claim which was governed by Singapore law and also barred by limitation of time under the law of Singapore but not Western Australia. The court acknowledged that the *Neilson* case required that the court apply the limitation period which would have been applicable in a Singapore court had the case come before it, which necessarily meant employing the Singapore classification of substance and procedure. Although Singapore law considered limitations to be procedural (unlike Australia) it did not matter because, whether procedural or substantive, the limitation would have been applied by the Singapore court on the same facts. Uniformity of outcome was therefore achieved without great difficulty.

[85] *O'Driscoll v J Ray McDermott SA* [2006] WASCA 25.

Once again, however, the matter could have become more complex if, according to Singapore choice of law rules, the law of a third country such as Indonesia had governed the contract. In such a situation, the Western Australian court would have had to apply Indonesian law to the contract, Singapore law to the limitations issue and Western Australian law to everything else, an untidy and awkward result which does not even take into account the possibility of *renvoi* under Singapore law.

It is obvious therefore, that the objective of uniformity of outcome can become extraordinarily complex and lead to absurd results. Urgent review of the status and scope of *Neilson* is required in the SCLJ Harmonisation Project.

G. Cross-Vesting

As a final point on uniformity of outcome and choice of law in Australia, a statutory provision in the interstate choice of law context should be noted. In 1987 the Commonwealth, the States and the Territories enacted cross-vesting legislation[86] the original purpose of which was to overcome the gaps in jurisdiction between Australian superior courts—especially State and federal courts. While the conferral of State jurisdiction on federal courts was subsequently held to be unconstitutional by the High Court,[87] other aspects of the cross-vesting scheme have been highly successful, such as the provision for transfer of actions between Australian superior courts.[88] Of relevance to this chapter is a provision on choice of law in the legislation, which although rarely utilised, has interesting potential effects.

Section 11(1)(b) of the cross-vesting legislation provides that

> [W]hen it appears to a court that the court will … in determining a matter … be exercising [cross-vested] jurisdiction … (b) … if that matter is a right of action arising under a written law of another State and Territory, the Court shall, in determining that matter, apply the written and unwritten law of that other State or Territory.

The Australian Law Reform Commission in its 1992 Report on Choice of Law called for this provision to be repealed on the basis that it was highly uncertain and would lead to increased forum shopping opportunities.[89] Yet the provision appears to have direct relevance to the issue of uniformity of outcome and may in fact have been enacted with that goal in mind.

In interpreting section 11(1)(b), the first step is to consider what is meant by 'cross-vested jurisdiction'. While this issue is not easy to determine, the authors of *Nygh*[90] suggest that such jurisdiction arises (a) where an Australian superior court

[86] See eg Jurisdiction of Courts (Cross-Vesting) Act 1987 (Cth) and Jurisdiction of Courts (Cross-Vesting) Act 1987 (NSW).

[87] *Re Wakim; ex parte McNally* (1999) 198 CLR 511.

[88] Eg Jurisdiction of Courts (Cross-Vesting) Act 1987 (Cth) s 5.

[89] Australian Law Reform Commission, above n 4, 23–24.

[90] *Nygh's Conflict of Laws in Australia*, above n 21, 143.

is exercising jurisdiction after a matter has been transferred to it from another court under section 5 of the cross-vesting legislation or (b) where a claimant raises a right of action under a statute of another Australian State or Territory which would not have been selected by the forum court under the common law choice of law rules.

Assuming that cross-vested jurisdiction exists, section 11(1)(b) would then appear to require the court to apply the statute ('written') law of another State or Territory where the matter arises under such statute.

On its face, this is quite an extraordinary proposition in terms of choice of law. An Australian State or Territory Court must apply the statute law of another State or Territory even where such law would *not* have been selected under the common law choice of law rules. Such a directive is therefore a statutory choice of law rule and would appear to allow an enterprising claimant to select any statute of the States and Territories and commence an action under its provisions, regardless of whether such enactment has any connection with the matter in dispute. As Gummow J astutely pointed out in *David Syme and Co Ltd v Grey*,[91] the effect of section 11(1)(b) is to displace the common law choice of law rules and to provide instead that 'the *lex causae* … be selected by a criterion of uncertain and unspecific application',[92] with the potential of 'anomalous results'.[93]

Some commentators have suggested that a territorial limitation must be implied in section 11(1)(b) to give it a more limited and sensible operation so that, for example, a NSW court could only apply a Queensland statutory right of action if Queensland had a genuine connection with the facts of the case.[94] No specific territorial link is referred to in the legislation however, and since common law choice of law rules generally 'pick up' foreign statutes without regard to their territorial scope of operation[95] it is hard to see why section 11(1)(b), which is itself a choice of law rule, should be interpreted differently.

As to whether section 11(1)(b) aids in the achievement of uniformity of outcome, the answer must be no, since its effect is to create a set of parallel choice of law provisions for interstate cases in Australian law depending upon whether a court is exercising ordinary or cross-vested jurisdiction. Moreover, since a claimant can 'manufacture' cross-vested jurisdiction by the mere expedient of pleading a right of action arising under the statute law of another State or Territory (which would not otherwise be selected under common law choice of law rules[96]), the

[91] *David Syme and Co Ltd v Grey* (1992) 38 FCR 303.

[92] ibid, 330.

[93] ibid, 329.

[94] E Sykes and M Pryles, *Australian Private International Law*, 3rd edn (Sydney, LBC, 1991) 255; P Nygh, 'Choice of Law Rules and Forum Shopping in Australia' (1995) 6 *Public Law Review* 237, 241.

[95] An exception is where the foreign statute itself contains a 'localising' provision which indicates that the statute is not to be applied (a) by foreign courts generally or (b) to events outside the place of enactment; see Mortensen, Garnett and Keyes, above n 3, 322–23.

[96] *Nygh's Conflict of Laws in Australia*, above n 21, 143.

possibilities for forum shopping would seem to be enormous, as both the Law Reform Commission and an early critique of the provision foresaw.[97] Yet curiously, litigants have rarely invoked the provision, probably out of ignorance of its extraordinary possibilities. In the interests of clarity and also to enhance uniformity of outcome, repeal of the provision would be beneficial. Of course, such action would not be needed, however, if the common law choice of law rules were deemed to be embedded in the Constitution as a result of *Pfeiffer*. If that view were correct, section 11(1)(b) would be unconstitutional where it would permit the application of laws other than those selected under the common law choice of law rules.

IV. Comparative Perspectives

The debate on uniformity of outcome in Australian law may be informed by reference to comparative developments in the United States and the European Union which have taken different approaches to the issue.

A. United States

In the US, interestingly and in contrast to Australia, there has been a strong trend *away* from uniformity in the past 50 years. Yet in one sense uniformity of outcome has always been much more difficult to achieve in US choice of law cases since there is no uniform body of common law and no final national appellate court with jurisdiction in both State and federal matters.

Nevertheless, prior to the 1960s, there was an attempt to devise choice of law rules which aimed to achieve uniformity of outcome in most interstate choice of law disputes. US courts almost universally applied the rules of the First Restatement on the Conflict of Laws, which were largely rigid and mechanical, based on a single territorial connection to a jurisdiction and designed to achieve certainty and predictability in choice of law outcomes.[98] So torts questions were resolved by the place of the wrong, contracts were governed by the law of the place where the contract was entered into, and property matters by the law of where the property was situated. Employment of these rules by all US courts meant that the same law generally applied regardless of where the case was litigated—in other words, uniformity of outcome was accomplished.[99] The US Supreme

[97] Australian Law Reform Commission, above n 4, 23–24; D Kelly and J Crawford, 'Choice of Law under the Cross-Vesting Legislation' (1988) 62 *Australian Law Journal* 589.

[98] See generally S Symeonides, 'American Federalism and Private International Law' (2010) 63 *Revue Hellenique de Droit International* 537.

[99] ibid, 548.

Court reinforced this approach by taking a strongly interventionist view of the US Constitution's full faith and credit clause, requiring a US State court to apply the law of another State in any case where the common law choice of law rules pointed to that State's law.[100]

From the 1960s, US courts began to reject this consensus in what was known as the 'conflicts revolution'. Instead of applying narrow, precisely tailored rules, US courts now applied 'approaches' to choice of law based on which state had the greatest interest in having its law applied,[101] which state had the most significant relationship to the issue,[102] which State had the 'better law'[103] or variants of these tests. While some principles that emerged from this revolution, for example, application of the law of the parties' common domicile in a foreign tort case,[104] were balanced and sensible, the overall result was almost total lack of uniformity of outcome and often blatant forum-centredness. At the same time, the Supreme Court dramatically wound back its interpretation of the full faith and credit clause, requiring only that the forum State have 'a significant contact or … aggregation of contacts, creating State interests such that choice of its law is neither arbitrary nor fundamentally unfair' before it could apply its law.[105] The forum favouring, interest-based choice of law rules were now therefore largely preserved by the US Constitution. Consequently, individualised justice, State interests and flexibility rather than uniformity of result and deterrence of forum shopping became the key features of US choice of law;[106] a position which remains largely unaltered today.

It is clear that the US experience with 'interest' or 'connection' approaches has led to a strong forum bias in choice of law decisions and also great uncertainty and unpredictability as to the law to be applied. Gummow and Hayne JJ were therefore surely correct in *Neilson* when they said that the US interest approaches have led to 'a wilderness of single instances'.[107] While, as has been argued in this chapter, absolute pursuit of uniformity of outcome is both undesirable and unachievable, the modern US approaches to choice of law have gone too far in the opposite direction by giving too much weight to individual interests of the forum State.

[100] See eg *New York Life Ins Co v Dodge* 246 US 357 (1918) and E Dodd, 'The Power of the Supreme Court to Review State Decisions in the Field of Conflict of Laws' (1926) 39 *Harvard Law Review* 533, 560 who noted that 'the Supreme Court has quite definitely committed itself to a program of making itself … a tribunal for bringing about uniformity in the field of conflicts'.

[101] The principal exponent of this view was Brainerd Currie, regarded by some as the 'father' of the conflicts revolution: see G Simson, 'Choice of Law after the Currie Revolution: What Role for the Needs of the Interstate and International Systems?' (2012) 63 *Mercer Law Review* 715.

[102] Restatement (Second) on the Conflict of Laws 1971, s 6.

[103] *Clark v Clark* 222 A 2d 205 (Sup Ct NH 1966).

[104] *Babcock v Jackson* 191 NE 2d 279 (NY Sup Ct 1963).

[105] *Allstate Insurance Co v Hague* 449 US 302, 313 (1981).

[106] Symeonides, above n 98, 553–54.

[107] (2005) 223 CLR 331, [93].

B. The European Union

By contrast, in the European Union, ensuring uniformity of outcome has become a major pre-occupation, as it sets out to create a single market to enhance trade and economic interaction. The capacity to make harmonised rules in the EU in the area of private international law has been greatly strengthened by the Treaty of Amsterdam of 1997 which gave new powers to the EU to 'promote the compatibility of the rules applicable in the Member States concerning the conflict of laws'.[108] Accordingly, two important instruments on choice of law, the 2007 Regulation on the law applicable to non-contractual obligations (Rome II)[109] and the 2008 Regulation on the law applicable to contractual obligations[110] (Rome I—which replaced and largely re-enacted the 1980 Rome Convention[111]) have been introduced which will apply to all member states of the EU (excluding Denmark). The choice of law rules in the Regulations, while differing from Australian law in some important respects, confer a wide scope of operation on the applicable law with only limited operation given to the law of the forum. For example, the applicable law covers questions relating to limitation and prescription and all matters concerning damages.[112] There will therefore be relatively few issues which will be considered procedural and so subject to forum law. Secondly, while the applicable law of the obligation may also not be enforced by the forum state where it is 'manifestly incompatible with [the forum's] public policy',[113] the use of the word 'manifestly' was obviously intended to limit the exception's application.

The European rules will obviously provide great scope for uniformity of outcome within the nations of the EU, given both their harmonised content and lack of forum bias. Uniformity of outcome will also be reinforced by the fact that the European Court of Justice is given the power to make binding interpretations of the instruments. The EU regulations may also contribute to uniformity of outcome *outside* the EU as other countries seek to replicate the principles. The Hague Principles on Choice of Law[114] would seem to be an example of this development.

[108] See J Basedow, 'Federal Choice of Law in Europe and the United States: A Comparative Account of Interstate Conflicts' (2008) 82 *Tulane Law Review* 2119, 2143. See now Art 81 of the Treaty on the Functioning of the European Union (consolidated version, [2012] OJ C326/1). See also the contribution of Professor Andrew Dickinson in this collection (Chapter eight).

[109] See above n 68.

[110] See above n 29.

[111] See above n 28.

[112] Rome II art 15(h) and (c); Rome I art 12(1)(d) and (c). See *Wall v Mutuelle de Poitiers Assurances* [2014] EWCA Civ 138 (Court of Appeal, England and Wales).

[113] Rome II art 26; Rome I art 21.

[114] Above, n 27.

V. Conclusion

Australia appears to occupy a position closer to the European Union in terms of the priority given to uniformity of outcome in choice of law, but it has achieved this objective by very different means.

In the interstate context, the High Court has suggested that the Federal Constitution supports uniformity by the elimination of choice of law rules which unduly favour the forum. In the sphere of international conflicts, Australian courts are required, whenever foreign law is chosen under the Australian choice of law rules, to apply the choice of law rules of the foreign country to reach the same result as the foreign court would and so prevent litigants obtaining any advantage from proceeding in Australia. Although the approach taken in interstate cases remains unclear in some respects, the overall direction is to be applauded. The highly integrated and homogenous Australian federation has long required a distinctive approach to Australian interstate choice of law disputes which does not involve treating states as foreign countries with full legislative sovereignty and the High Court has at last recognised this. So, even if uniformity of outcome is not compelled by the Australian Constitution, it is certainly a driving force in the formulation of interstate choice of law rules, which is entirely appropriate. By contrast, the United States approach to interstate choice of law has been to dispense with federal control and leave states with almost complete freedom in the area. Perhaps, not surprisingly, the result has been widespread forum centredness and plaintiff favouritism.

In the international conflicts sphere, the most obvious method of securing uniformity of outcome is by nation States adopting identical or at least substantially harmonised choice of law rules, ideally through the medium of a treaty. Unlike the European Union, which has embarked on a major campaign in this regard, Australia has adopted relatively few treaties on choice of law. Yet, not only does Australia already have a number of even-handed and internationally spirited choice of law rules in the area of contracts and property, a number of common law rules which unduly favoured the forum (in the areas of torts, procedure and equity) have been reformed. Clarification is, however, required of the operation of the consumer protection provisions of the Australian Consumer Law in the context of contracts governed by foreign law. The most significant contribution to uniformity of outcome, however, has been the adoption of the *Neilson* 'no advantage' approach which effectively requires an Australian court to reach the same result as the foreign court whose law governs the substance of the action. While the objective of this approach may be admirable, unfortunately it does impose an onerous burden on Australian courts and also creates the potential for capricious results. This principle is perhaps an example of uniformity of outcome having been taken too far.

III

The Trans-Tasman Treaty—A Model for Engagement with Other Legal Systems?

6

Together Alone: Integrating the Tasman World

REID MORTENSEN

Aneiramaua/e piritahinei/e nohatahinei/komauaanake[1]

I. The Trans-Tasman Judicial Area[2]

The bilateral relationship between Australia and New Zealand achieved a significant legal milestone in 2013: a scheme of civil jurisdiction and judgments that, arguably, exceeds any comparable transnational scheme in efficiency and integration. The Trans-Tasman Proceedings Acts were passed in both countries in 2010, and came into force on 11 October 2013. They create a single trans-Tasman judicial area that parallels the single trans-Tasman economic market.[3] A writ issued out of any court in Australia or New Zealand may be served anywhere in either country and, on service, gives that court an unquestionable competence to

[1] 'Here we are together/in a very close embrace/being together/together alone': N Finn, M Hart, N Wehi, 'Together Alone' from Crowded House, *Together Alone* (Capitol Records, 1993).

[2] In this article—

Australian TTPA = Trans-Tasman Proceedings Act 2010 (Cth), as amended by the Trans-Tasman Proceedings Amendment and Other Measures Act 2011 (Cth).

New Zealand TTPA = Trans-Tasman Proceedings Act 2010 (NZ).

References to the Australian 'States' are taken to include the federal Territories.

[3] For earlier development of this idea, see R Mortensen, 'The Hague and the Ditch: The Trans-Tasman Judicial Area and the Choice of Court Convention' (2009) 5 *Journal of Private International Law* 213 (Mortensen, 'The Hague and the Ditch'); J Davis, 'Closer Economic Relations: A Trans-Tasman Confederation?' (2011) 16 *Canterbury Law Review* 47; R Mortensen, 'A Trans-Tasman Judicial Area: Civil Jurisdiction and Judgments in the Single Economic Market' (2011) 16 *Canterbury Law Review* 61 (Mortensen, 'A Trans-Tasman Judicial Area'); R Mortensen and O Knöfel, 'The Australia and New Zealand Jurisdiction and Judgments Scheme: A Common Law Judicial Area' (2011) 16 *ZeitschriftFürZivilprozess International* 369; R Mortensen, 'Woodhouse Reprised: Accident Compensation and Trans-Tasman Integration' (2013) 9 *Journal of Private International Law* 1 ('Woodhouse Reprised'); D Goddard, 'Trans-Tasman Proceedings and Regulatory Enforcement', Conference Paper, *Facing Outwards: Australian Private International Law in the 21st Century*, University of Sydney, 10 April 2013. Chapter seven in this volume.

judge the proceedings.[4] A judgment of any court in Australia or New Zealand can be enforced anywhere in the market area[5]—unless it is contrary to public policy in the place of enforcement.[6] This means that the Trans-Tasman Proceedings Acts create a 'common Tasman writ' that gives an effective civil jurisdiction over approximately 15 million square kilometres[7]—more than three times the area of the European Union, but with only five per cent of its population. The judicial area means that the national 'border' between Australia and New Zealand has become almost meaningless so far as the enforcement of the civil law is concerned. The Acts also give an unusually exorbitant adjudicative and enforcement jurisdiction to all Australian and New Zealand courts, and so they need new institutions to constrain it, and to avoid *lis pendens* and the potential for different courts to deliver incompatible judgments. Accordingly, the Acts also introduce two structures to guide proceedings into one court, and one court only, in the trans-Tasman judicial area. The first generally applicable structure is a uniform standard of *forum conveniens* to have the most appropriate court in Australia or New Zealand hear and determine civil proceedings.[8] The second is that, where there is an agreement selecting an Australian or New Zealand court as the exclusive place for conducting litigation, the chosen court must deal with the proceedings.[9] Within the trans-Tasman market area, the borders of the different civil law areas are now maintained only by judicial discretion or contractual agreement.

The Trans-Tasman Proceedings Acts 2010 implement the Agreement on Trans-Tasman Court Proceedings and Regulatory Enforcement, which both countries signed at Christchurch in 2008. Together, the Christchurch Agreement and the Acts fulfil a promise made in Darwin in 1988 to improve enforcement jurisdiction in the Tasman market. In course of reviewing their trading relationship, the Australian and New Zealand Governments signed a Memorandum of Understanding on the Harmonisation of Business Laws that aimed, in part, to improve the enforcement of civil judgments between the two countries. It expressly mentioned injunctions, orders for specific performance and revenue judgments[10]—all of which are not usually enforceable internationally. In 1988, there was little expectation that the promise of the Darwin Understanding would eventually find expression in the comprehensive scheme of civil jurisdiction and judgments that the Trans-Tasman Proceedings Acts introduce.

I suggest that the Trans-Tasman Proceedings Acts are now of even greater significance—they have made private international law the source of the central

[4] Australian TTPA, s 9; New Zealand TTPA, s 13; cf *Westpac New Zealand Limited v Boulton* [2014] NZHC 693.

[5] Australian TTPA, s 68; New Zealand TTPA, s 53.

[6] Australian TTPA, s 72(1)(a); New Zealand TTPA, s 61(2)(b). See text to nn 144–160.

[7] Cf W Pengilly, 'On Trans-Tasman Banter and "Things" CER' [1990] *New Zealand Law Journal* 199, 200. The area includes the claims to the Australian Antarctic Territory and Ross Dependency.

[8] Australian TTPA, s 19; New Zealand TTPA, s 24.

[9] Australian TTPA, s 20; New Zealand TTPA, s 25.

[10] Memorandum of Understanding Between the Government of Australia and the Government of New Zealand on the Harmonisation of Business Laws (signed at Darwin, 1 July 1988), art 5(h).

organising institutions of 'the Tasman world'. In doing so, they also suggest directions that will assist in deepening Australia's and New Zealand's legal integration. Accordingly, in the next section of this chapter I examine the nature of the bilateral relationship and how it is structured by the Trans-Tasman Proceedings Acts. The sections after that give thought to improving the inner logic of the Acts, and some potential extension of the bilateral private international law of the Tasman world.

II. The Bilateral Relationship

A. Economic and Political Integration in the Tasman World

New Zealand considers its relationship with Australia its most important international association.[11] The Australian Government does not necessarily reciprocate, and often claims that its relationship with some other country—say, the United States or Indonesia or China—is its most important. While this typifies the imbalance in the Tasman relationship, neither Australia nor New Zealand really has as intimate or as trusting a relationship with any other country as it does with the other.[12]

The bilateral trans-Tasman relationship defies traditional classifications. It quite possibly has no international parallel. The relationship between Canada and Newfoundland (as it was before 1949) has sometimes been drawn as a precedent,[13] but there were greater economic and population disparities between the northern dominions before Confederation in 1949 than have ever been the case for the two southern dominions. Even today, the transnational legal integration of Australia and New Zealand is probably deeper than the internal integration of the Provinces of the Canadian federation. But certainly, for each of Australia and New Zealand the relationship with the other *is* unique, and it *is* more intense than either country enjoys with any other.

The time has come to admit that this relationship is 'confederal'.[14] This has never been a description that has allowed much precision. But as Brian Galligan

[11] New Zealand Ministry of Foreign Affairs and Trade, Diplomatic Missions, New Zealand and Australia: www.nzembassy.com/australia/relationship-between-new-zealand-and-australia/new-zealand-and-australia (accessed 21 October 2013).

[12] Attorney-General's Department (Australia) and Ministry of Justice (New Zealand), *Trans-Tasman Court Proceedings and Regulatory Enforcement—Report by the Trans-Tasman Working Group* (Canberra, Commonwealth of Australia, 2006), 6 ('Working Group Report').

[13] See M Kirby, 'Trans-Tasman Federation—Achievable, Impossible, Unnecessary?' (2011) 16 *Canterbury Law Review* 1, 11.

[14] Davis, above n 3, 47. This is preferable to John Hopkins' description of 'the Tasman federation': 'Trans-Tasman Governance: A Quiet Form of Federalism?' (2010) 16 *Canterbury Law Review* 23, 30. Australians already deal with their own 'federation' and, as much as its institutions have been adapted to the Tasman relationship, the relationships between the Australian states and territories differ

pointed out in 2001, as is the case for many transnational associations, the bilateral Tasman relationship must be understood as transcending ideas of national sovereignty. Instead, we need to recognise that the relationship

> is best understood as an asymmetric pluralist one that has elements of inter-governmental relations between two congenial nations with similar culture and heritage, as well as quasi-federal relations among governments in which New Zealand acts as another regional state.[15]

But Galligan's description serves now as only a point of departure for any attempt at making the Tasman relationship intelligible. His focus in 2001 was on 'functional collaboration rather than jurisdictional consolidation'.[16] 'Functional collaboration' still gives the predominant shape to the relationship, but the advent of a single judicial area in 2013 means that, in an important sense, 'jurisdictional consolidation' has been achieved as well.

The bilateral relationship cannot be understood outside its Imperial origins—Michael Kirby refers to both countries as '"leftovers" from the era of the British Empire'.[17] Strong British contours are given to the two countries' public institutions by predominant Anglo-Celtic populations, the English language, Westminster systems of government, the common law, a shared reliance on United Kingdom statute law models, and an Imperial naval and military tradition. The UK is still the largest source of foreign investment in Australia.[18] However, neither country's Government would now claim that the UK is its most important international partner. Indeed, the point in time at which the UK's policies weakened its own relationship with Australia and New Zealand was also the point that initiated genuine trans-Tasman integration. Once in 1960 the UK began to pursue entry to the European Economic Community, both Australia and New Zealand (with even greater urgency) had to realign their own trade policies. The historical access the two countries had for agricultural exports to English markets would be, and was, denied to them by the EEC Common Agricultural Policy.[19] And so the UK's entry to the EEC, and its simultaneous decolonisation of south-east Asia and the western Pacific, brought Australia and New Zealand to investigate integration of the trans-Tasman market.[20] This came progressively through the New Zealand Australia Free Trade Agreement 1965 and then, most importantly, the Closer Economic Relations Trade Agreement 1983 (CER).

significantly in quality and implications from their relationship, through the national Government, with New Zealand.

[15] B Galligan, 'Closer Political Association: Australia and New Zealand' in A Grimes, L Wevers, and G Sullivan (eds), *States of Mind: Australia and New Zealand 1901–2001* (Wellington, Institute of Policy Studies, Victoria University of Wellington, 2002) 303.

[16] ibid, 304.

[17] Kirby, above n 13 at 8.

[18] Australia is the largest source of foreign investment for New Zealand.

[19] Mortensen and Knöfel, above n 3, 370–71.

[20] ibid, 371.

The bilateral relationship has now moved well beyond the free trade origins of CER. It is now described as a single economic market. This nevertheless amounts to more than economic integration. The Trans-Tasman Travel Arrangement gives citizens of each country free movement between them and unique rights of residence in the other. At least when assessed in terms of Galligan's functional collaboration,[21] there is also a degree of political integration.[22] As will be evident with the legal institutions discussed below, Australia's political clout and its long experience of federalism mean that Australian institutions often provide the actual means, or the model, for confederal cooperation between Australia and New Zealand. So, New Zealand participates as the equivalent of a State in most of the Council of Australian Government's ministerial councils—even when Tasmania does not! According to John Hopkins, New Zealand has 'practical and non-controversial access to the Australian political world' and, as a consequence, this 'allows the Australian government to be Australasian, *without the need to develop institutions*' (emphasis added).[23] Along with the existence of a number of joint national agencies, these reinforce a real and, again, unique political association. There is no prospect in the foreseeable future that any other country will participate in this confederal arrangement.[24] For good reason, the bilateral Tasman relationship could be called 'together, alone'.[25]

Honest admission that the Tasman relationship will remain unique does not necessarily mean that, together, the two countries are xenophobic. Australia's and New Zealand's separate Productivity Commissions have done more than most to articulate the nature of trans-Tasman relations, and continue to emphasise that they 'should remain outward-oriented and not become too narrowly focused on the bilateral relationship'.[26] They should consider the economic relationship within the context of multilateral trade liberalisation and the opportunities of the 'Asian century'.[27] The single market is not a customs union. Although the more intense Tasman relationship has seen some trade diversion,[28] it has not distracted either country from separately entering free trade agreements with others or, in general, promoting internationally competitive and open economies.[29]

[21] Galligan, above n 15, 304.

[22] Hopkins, above n 14, 30.

[23] ibid, 29.

[24] See L Nottage, 'Asia-Pacific Regional Architecture and Consumer Product Safety Regulation for a Post-FTA Era', University of Sydney—Sydney Law School, Legal Studies Research Paper No 09/125, November 2009, 17–20.

[25] Cf H White, 'New Zealand's Strategic Options in the Asian Century: An Australian View' (2011) 7 *Security Challenges* 45, 55. See also Finn, Hart and Wehi, above n 1; Kirby, above n 13, 8.

[26] Australian Productivity Commission and New Zealand Productivity Commission, *Strengthening Trans-Tasman Economic Relations—a Joint Study: Final Report* (Commonwealth of Australia and New Zealand Crown, 2012) 7.

[27] ibid, 7.

[28] ibid, 37–38.

[29] The Association of Southeast Asian Nations (ASEAN) has a bilateral free trade agreement (FTA) with CER as a whole, linking the two free trade areas. Apart from that, each country has a number of

I take it that, when Hopkins claimed that this Tasman confederation did not need institutions,[30] he meant that it did not need political union under a written Constitution. Kirby continues to suggest—perhaps tongue in cheek—that New Zealand could enter the Australian federation through the combined mechanism of clause 6 of the Commonwealth of Australia Constitution Act 1900 (UK) and section 121 of the Australian Constitution. The definition of 'States' in the Constitution Act includes any British colonies admitted to the federation, and New Zealand is mentioned expressly. This option should, however, be immediately dismissed. The 'twelve hundred reasons'[31]—meaning the number of Imperial miles across the Tasman Sea—offered for New Zealand's not planning to join the Australian federation in 1901 have much less weight in 2013. In many respects, the cultural integration of the two countries is much deeper in 2013 than it was in 1901. However, New Zealand identity was distinct from Australian identity in 1901,[32] and is even better established now. It is highly unlikely to be surrendered by New Zealand's political absorption into the Australian federation. Even if some form of constitutionalised Tasman federation were to be contemplated, it is unlikely that New Zealand would settle for a federal model that is as dominated by the central government as Australia has turned out to be. This does not mean, though, that the Australian Constitution has no role to play in the present Tasman confederation or any further development of the trans-Tasman judicial area. As will be seen,[33] it places significant limits on the kind of legal institutions that can have a role in integrating the trans-Tasman market.

The Productivity Commissions have noted the pragmatic and fragmented quality that initiatives for integration of the single Tasman market have taken.[34] The same can be said of the political and legal relationship. 'Kiwi-Aussie pragmatism'[35] reflects the high level of trust in the relationship, and the close historical ties between the two countries. Trans-Tasman institutions can be strikingly casual. The centrepiece of free movement in the market area—the Trans-Tasman Travel Arrangement—is not even reduced to writing, but is simply honoured in a range of immigration, social welfare and education statutes that give detail in both countries to mutual rights of residence. However, the Productivity Commissions also recognise that this causes problems. They have received submissions that there is 'an absence of oversight role, lack of cohesion and cyclical variations in activity'.[36] They add that 'there is no overall design or management'.[37] The

independent bilateral FTAs with others. Australia has FTAs with Chile, Malaysia, Singapore, Thailand and the United States. New Zealand has FTAs with China, Malaysia, Singapore and Thailand.

30 Hopkins, above n 14, 29.
31 R Garran, *Prosper the Commonwealth* (Sydney, Angus & Robertson, 1958) 93.
32 See K Sinclair, *Destiny Apart* (Wellington, Allen & Unwin, 1985) 119.
33 See text to nn 52–53, 76–79, 191–92 below.
34 Productivity Commissions, above n 26, 150.
35 ibid.
36 ibid.
37 ibid.

Commissions' solution is structured cooperation between the two countries' Governments at ministerial level. Similar observations could apply to the question of deeper legal integration. Even leaving efforts at harmonising business and consumer laws to one side, the plans for a common private international law have proceeded at an unacceptably slow rate. It took more than 22 years for the Darwin Understanding's promise of the cross-Tasman enforcement of orders *in specie* to secure unqualified recognition in legislation,[38] and then more than another three years for that legislation to come into force.[39]

Paradoxically, this is one reason why the Trans-Tasman Proceedings Acts are such a significant milestone in the Tasman relationship. They have been a long time coming, but the Acts give a uniform (and not just a harmonised) law of civil jurisdiction and judgments that provides a degree of the legal certainty that markets need for the support of trade and commerce. In general, the national Governments and Productivity Commissions have aimed to secure legal certainty through harmonised substantive laws on consumer protection, competition, insolvency, financial reporting, mutual recognition of occupations, patents, trademarks, insurance, and banking and financial services regulation.[40] Although this has borne some fruit, harmonisation naturally meets resistance while each country and, within Australia, separate States remain entitled to legislate for economy and society in ways they consider best for their own residents. However, while a multistate market might naturally exemplify a high degree of legal diversity, for three reasons the judicial area created by the Trans-Tasman Proceedings Acts provides greater legal certainty than the Tasman world has had to this point.[41] First, the enforceability of a judgment and its recognition as *res judicata* in all parts of the market area with barely any qualification 'sets the one legal relationship at one defined value for every country that is covered by the scheme'.[42] True enough, this gives legal certainty only after the judgment has been rendered in one part of the market area. It is therefore only post-judgment that the parties can predict the consequences of the legal relationship.[43] But, secondly, legal certainty is improved because the conditions for exercising the power to judge are also unified. A prediction can therefore be made as to where a legal relationship is likely to be judicially

[38] See the Foreign Judgments Act 1991 (Cth), s 5(6)–(8) and the Reciprocal Enforcement of Judgments Act 1934 (NZ), which provided for the enforcement of non-money judgments by registration, so long as regulations were made to trigger the provisions. These regulations were never made. The Australian TTPA, s 4 and the New Zealand TTPA, s 4(1) do not require regulations to be promulgated before non-money judgments can be enforced

[39] See text to n 10.

[40] Productivity Commissions, above n 26, 129–31, 143–47; Australian Productivity Commission, *Australian and New Zealand Competition and Consumer Protection Regimes* (Canberra, Productivity Commission, 2004); Memorandum of Understanding between the Government of New Zealand and the Government of Australia on Coordination of Business Law (adopted 31 August 2000); Memorandum of Understanding between the Government of New Zealand and the Government of Australia on Coordination of Business Law (adopted 22 February 2006).

[41] R Mortensen, 'Judgments Extension under CER' [1999] *New Zealand Law Review* 237, 241.

[42] ibid.

[43] ibid.

determined, and therefore which law will be used to turn that legal relationship into a judgment.[44] And thirdly, the Trans-Tasman Proceedings Acts promote a legal certainty that is even greater than a common scheme of civil jurisdiction and judgments would normally give; they strongly direct that agreements relating to choice of court must be enforced.[45] In this connection, the Acts place a higher premium on certainty of contract than the common law does. While the Acts' scheme of civil jurisdiction and judgments does not give the legal certainty that harmonised substantive laws would, they more realistically recognise the legal diversity of the Tasman world and, simultaneously, provide means of improving parties' ability to predict how courts will deal with the legal arrangements they put in place.

Finally, the Trans-Tasman Proceedings Acts mark a confederal relationship between Australia and New Zealand that has a much deeper dimension than the trade and commerce that first triggered closer integration. Almost all private law matters are embraced by the scheme, including commercial matters, personal injuries litigation (where it is permitted), family law, succession, companies matters, competition law, and domestic insolvency matters.[46] As has been the case since 1992, tax collection is also included.[47] A range of regulatory fines can be enforced between the two countries in questions of banking and financial services, food standards, consumer protection, consumer credit, competition law, health and disability, insurance, medicine, veterinary medicine, the securities industry, and takeovers and financial services.[48] Civil penalty orders can also be enforced.[49] As a result, Australia and New Zealand have uniform coordinating laws for determining which country's or State's laws are to apply to a broad range of social and economic relationships. Instead of political union under a Tasman constitutional law, this has been achieved exclusively through the private international law—and through private international law institutions that are used also to coordinate the application of some aspects of each country's public law and regulation in the other. In the provisions for tribunals to be included in this scheme, private international law institutions potentially embrace even more of public law and regulation in the Tasman world. David Goddard has noted that '[i]t seemed sensible to tackle these concerns in a single coherent and principled way, rather than having a number of ad hoc and differing regimes in

[44] ibid.

[45] Australian TTPA, s 20(1); New Zealand TTPA, s 25(1). See text to nn 126–29.

[46] Australian TTPA, ss 80–94; New Zealand TTPA, ss 52–78; cf Trans-Tasman Proceedings Regulations 2012 (Cth) reg 15; Trans-Tasman Proceedings (Specified Australian Judgments Excluded from Recognition or Enforcement in New Zealand and Excluded Matter) Order 2013 (NZ) ss 4–5.

[47] Australian TTPA, s 79(2)(b); New Zealand TTPA, s 68(2)(b); Foreign Judgments Act 1991 (Cth) s 3(1); Reciprocal Enforcement of Judgments Act 1934 (NZ) s 2(1).

[48] Trans-Tasman Proceedings Regulations 2012 (Cth) reg 15; Trans-Tasman Proceedings (Regulatory Regime Criminal Fines) Order 2013 (NZ) ss 3–4.

[49] Australian TTPA, s 66(2)(h); New Zealand TTPA, s 74.

place'.[50] The closer Tasman legal relationship is therefore largely structured by the Trans-Tasman Proceedings Acts.

B. Coordinating Principles for Private Trans-Tasman Law

The structural significance of private international law in trans-Tasman integration also means that it should be shaped by principles that are properly adapted to the conditions of the multistate Tasman world, and to the imperatives of the confederal relationship between Australia and New Zealand. There are at least five normative principles that, I suggest, respond to these conditions and imperatives, and that would help to promote further integration even without substantive harmonisation of the two countries' laws.[51] First, all arrangements are to be cooperative in character, and cannot depend on a unified Tasman judicial system. This must be almost a permanent feature of the trans-Tasman judicial area, and is one of the consequences of constitutional restrictions placed on Australian governance. The Australian Constitution makes it impossible, by uniform legislation, to create any common trans-Tasman court or judicial machinery that could escape the original or appellate jurisdiction of the High Court of Australia.[52] Under the more flexible New Zealand constitutional law, the oversight of the New Zealand courts can probably be excluded from any Tasman institutions. But the relationship is not one in which 'jurisdictional termination'[53] of Tasman institutions could rest only in the Australian High Court. A judicial machinery with exclusive jurisdiction in trans-Tasman law is just not a present possibility, and may not even be needed. The interpretation and application of trans-Tasman law must take place independently in Australia and New Zealand but—happily consistent with the pragmatism and trust of the bilateral relationship—through the cooperation of both countries' judicial systems.

Secondly, local legal resources and institutions should be preferred when developing models for Tasman institutions if the private international law is to respond properly to the legal conditions that prevail in both Australia and New Zealand, and in the single market. Although New Zealand commentators once suggested the adoption of the principles of the European Economic

[50] Goddard, Chapter seven in this volume, pp 148.

[51] This replays and develops the principles first suggested in Mortensen, 'Woodhouse Reprised' above n 3, 3–4.

[52] Ie, a court created or empowered under federal legislation would be subject to an appeal to the High Court of Australia: Australian Constitution, s 73(ii). It may also be subject to the High Court's original jurisdiction to undertake judicial review by prerogative writ: Australian Constitution, s 75(v). For discussion of the possibility of a trans-Tasman commercial court, see M Kirby, 'Closer Economic and Legal Relations Between Australia and New Zealand' (1984) 58 *Australian Law Journal* 383, 395–400; M Kirby, 'Integration of Judicial Systems' in KM Vautier, J Farmer and R Baxt, *CER and Business Competition—Australia and New Zealand in a Global Economy* (Auckland, CCH New Zealand, 1990) 15, 22–30 (Kirby, 'Integration of Judicial Institutions').

[53] Kirby, 'Integration of Judicial Systems', above n 52, 30.

Area's Lugano Convention[54] for cross-border arrangements with Australia (and others),[55] this would import civilian institutions into two common law countries that, for the most part, can more easily structure their relationship with common law institutions. It eases uptake of the new scheme, as the English experience of the Brussels I Regulation[56] and, beforehand, the Brussels Convention[57] (which is the template for the Lugano Convention) suggests that common law courts will resist efforts of a civilian jurisdiction and judgments code to exclude a role for common law principles, and that the resistance will take some time to crush.[58] The Trans-Tasman Working Group, which recommended the scheme that became the Christchurch Agreement and the Trans-Tasman Proceedings Acts, rightly recommended the use of local resources rather than European-style institutions.[59] As Goddard has commented, the Working Group was conscious of 'the limits and complexities' of European institutions and strongly preferred 'a much simpler regime built on our common acceptance of broad service rules coupled with an appropriateness test applied at the request of the defendant'[60]—that is, common law institutions. There are certainly instances in the Tasman relationship where common law institutions are demonstrably insufficient or unworkable,[61] and even where lessons from the Lugano Convention help legal integration in ways that the common law does not.[62] However, reform is much more likely to achieve effective uptake if there is less friction between the legal institutions being adopted and the legal tradition they are to do their work in.

The remaining principles are commonplaces in private international law, but are also informed by Australian constitutional principles relating to the co-existence

[54] Convention on Jurisdiction and the Enforcement of Judgments in Civil and Commercial Matters, Lugano, 16 September 1988, [1988] OJ L319/9, now superseded by the later Convention on Jurisdiction and the Recognition and Enforcement of Judgments in Civil and Commercial Matters between the EU, Iceland, Norway and Switzerland, Lugano, 30 October 2007, [2009] OJ L147/1 ('Lugano Convention').

[55] New Zealand Law Commission, *Electronic Commerce Part One—A Guide for the Legal and Business Community* (Wellington, NZLC, 1998) 106–7; D Goddard, 'Global Disputes—Jurisdiction, Interim Relief and Enforcement of Judgments' (1999) 515 *Law Talk* 29, 30.

[56] Regulation (EC) 44/2001 No 44/2001 on Jurisdiction and the Recognition and Enforcement of Judgments in Civil and Commercial Matters [2001] OJ L12/1, now recast as Regulation (EU) No 1215/2012 [2012] OJ L351/1.

[57] Convention on Jurisdiction and the Enforcement of Judgments in Civil and Commercial Matters, Brussels, 27 September 1968 [1972] OJ L299/32 (consolidated version [1998] OJ C27/1).

[58] Eg, Case C-159/02 *Turner v Grovit* [2004] ECR I-3565; Case C-281/02 *Owusu v Jackson* [2005] ECR I-1383; Case C-185/07 *Allianz SpA (formerly Riunione Adriatica di Sicurta SpA) v West Tankers Inc* [2009] ECR I-663. Further, this kind of resistance would take longer to address in the trans-Tasman scheme, as there is no court that could serve as an equivalent of the European Court of Justice to enforce the exclusion of common law principles.

[59] See Australia (Attorney-General's Department) and New Zealand (Ministry of Justice), *Trans-Tasman Court Proceedings and Regulatory Enforcement—A Public Discussion Paper by the Trans-Tasman Working Group* (Commonwealth of Australia, 2006) 11 ('Discussion Paper'); Working Group Report, above n 12, 7.

[60] Goddard, Chapter seven of this volume, 152.

[61] See text to nn 125–28.

[62] See text to nn 201–3.

of the legal systems established in the Australian States. The third principle is therefore territoriality, the respect given to the claims of different countries and States in the market and judicial area to regulate, or impose liability, for conduct that takes place inside their legal borders.[63] The fourth is the related principle of social policy independence.[64] The legislative and executive institutions of the different countries and States are responsible for the welfare of residents living inside their borders, but have the autonomy to decide how best to provide that welfare. The principle certainly needs greater recognition in trans-Tasman arrangements where, for instance, New Zealand's approach to compensation for injury differs profoundly from the general approach of the Australian States (which still differ between them in detail).[65] The fifth principle is non-discrimination. Inside the market and judicial area, no country or State is to treat the residents of another member country or State differently to its own residents. In the Tasman world, this is an explicit principle of the single economic market,[66] and I suggest that it be a coordinating principle so far as access to justice and general legal entitlements is concerned.[67] It is not without its problems, as non-discrimination on the basis of residence exists in some tension with social policy independence.[68]

III. The Trans-Tasman Judicial Area—Improving its Logic

A. The Foundation

The Trans-Tasman Proceedings Acts are modelled on Australia's Service and Execution of Process Act 1992 (Cth), which itself is ultimately the progeny of a nineteenth-century Australasian experiment in civil jurisdiction and judgments.[69] In what might be roughly called the *travaux préparatoires* for the Christchurch Agreement and the Acts, the Service and Execution of Process Act was claimed to be the best model to adopt because it 'was designed to remove many similar

[63] Mortensen, 'Woodhouse Reprised', above n 3, 3–4.

[64] Productivity Commission (Australia) and New Zealand Productivity Commission, *Strengthening Trans-Tasman Economic Relations*, Discussion Draft (Canberra and Wellington, Productivity Commission and New Zealand Productivity Commission, 2012) 138.

[65] Mortensen, 'Woodhouse Reprised', above n 3, 5–11.

[66] Australian Productivity Commission, *Australian and New Zealand Competition and Consumer Protection Regimes* (Canberra, Productivity Commission, 2004) 7. The New Zealand Government also authorised this report: ibid, 3.

[67] Mortensen, 'Woodhouse Reprised', above n 3, 3–4.

[68] ibid. Non-discrimination on the ground of residence may also be undermined by the reliance on domicile in common law choice of law rules. Residence (*factum*) is an element of domicile and, therefore, the determination of legal rights and capacities by reference to domicile may effectively lead to different treatment on the basis of residence.

[69] See text to nn 205–12.

problems between the Australian States and Territories'.[70] The use of this local resource had considerable advantages, as it secured an alignment between the principles for coordinating interstate civil justice in Australia with those for coordinating trans-Tasman civil justice. Furthermore, the interstate scheme introduced by the Service and Execution of Process Act is already tried and tested, and secures a high degree of legal certainty. Its rules for the service of process and the enforcement of judgments are so simple, and clear, there has been *no* adjudication on their interpretation. And, while embodied in statute, the provisions of the Service and Execution of Process Act for adjudicative jurisdiction rest on deep common law principles. The valid service of process is assumed to establish jurisdiction—though this is not stated in the Act, or in the Trans-Tasman Proceedings Acts.[71] The *exercise* of jurisdiction is restricted by 'appropriate court' criteria learned from the principles of *forum conveniens*,[72] or by contractual agreement. In the Australian setting, this must be read with the cross-vesting scheme, by which any superior State or federal court either transfers proceedings to the most appropriate superior court—or refuses a transfer if it finds that it is itself the more appropriate court.[73] Inferior courts deal with *forum conveniens* questions by statutory principles for the stay of proceedings. Within the Australian scheme, the *forum conveniens* principles are given further effect, in all superior courts, by common law principles for the issue of anti-suit injunctions. Inferior courts usually do not have power to grant injunctions of any kind—including any for restraining proceedings.[74]

The Australian federal scheme for the enforcement of judgments is influenced more by Australian constitutional principles, although these were pre-empted by the earlier Australasian scheme that it grew from.[75] The Australian Constitution's provision for the giving of full faith and credit to the judgments of sister-State courts[76] has been interpreted as, in effect, requiring the recognition of any interstate judgment.[77] There are no grounds for refusing recognition, including the possibility that the interstate court had no jurisdiction to render judgment in the first place.[78] The Service and Execution of Process Act gives effect to the constitutionally-mandated principles for the *recognition* of interstate judgments by securing their *enforcement* in another State just by registration in a suitably similar court—no defences to registration allowed.[79]

[70] Working Group Report, above n 12, 7. For the first proposal to extend the principles of the Service and Execution of Process Act to trans-Tasman arrangements, see Mortensen, 'Judgments Extension under CER', above n 41, 269–73.

[71] Service and Execution of Process Act 1992 (Cth) ss 12, 15.

[72] Service and Execution of Process Act 1992 (Cth) s 20(3).

[73] Jurisdiction of Courts (Cross-vesting) Act 1987 (Cth) s 5; and see Jurisdiction of Courts (Cross-vesting) Act 1987 (NSW) s 5, and identical legislation in all other States.

[74] Cf Service and Execution of Process Act 1992 (Cth) s 21.

[75] See text to nn 204–8.

[76] Australian Constitution, s 118.

[77] *Harris v Harris* [1947] VLR 44; *Re DEF and the Protected Estates Act 1983* (2005) 192 FLR 92.

[78] *Harris v Harris* [1947] VLR 44.

[79] Service and Execution of Process Act 1992 (Cth) s 109.

The Australian federal scheme does have shortcomings, and it may have been followed too slavishly in perpetuating those and in failing to consider whether its language was properly adapted to trans-Tasman conditions. However, it is a robust working scheme, with fewer uncertainties and grounds for disputation than the Brussels I Regulation and the Lugano Convention offer. The suggestions for reform that follow therefore aim only to give more effective force to the structures of the federal-confederal scheme that the joint application of the Service and Execution of Process Act and the Trans-Tasman Proceedings Acts achieve.

B. *Forum Conveniens*

The jurisdictional competence and enforcement jurisdictions granted by the Trans-Tasman Proceedings Acts are, without more, a recipe for legal pandemonium. Every New Zealand and every Australian State and federal court has the power to deal with any person served in Australia and New Zealand, and an almost unlimited ability to enforce its judgments in the same space. The *forum conveniens* and, to a lesser extent, the choice of court provisions of the Acts guard against unrestrained *lis pendens* by guiding proceedings into one court, and one court only, in the Tasman area. The *forum conveniens* provisions also give effect to the principle of territoriality because, in general, they determine where to sue by geographic considerations. And they are supposed to be the centrepiece and most important reform of the scheme.

Section 19(1) of the Australian Act provides:

> On an application … the Australian court may, by order, stay the proceeding if it is satisfied that a New Zealand court—
> (a) has jurisdiction to determine the matters in issue between the parties to the proceeding; and
> (b) is the more appropriate court to determine those matters.

Section 24(1) of the New Zealand Act mirrors this provision. These provisions are codified; resort to the common law of *forum conveniens* in trans-Tasman proceedings is banned.[80] The *forum conveniens* is identified by 'the more appropriate court' standard, which is adapted from 'the more appropriate forum' standard of *Spiliada Maritime Corporation v Cansulex Limited*.[81] In substance, this represents no change for New Zealand courts, which have consistently followed *Spiliada*.[82]

[80] Australian TTPA, s 21; New Zealand TTPA, s 26.

[81] *Spiliada Maritime Corporation v Cansulex Ltd* [1987] AC 460.

[82] *McConnell Dowell Constructors Ltd v Lloyd's Syndicate 396* [1988] 2 NZLR 257, 273, 277, 280–81; *Club Meditérranée NZ v Wendell* [1989] 1 NZLR 216; *Crane Accessories Ltd v Lim Swee Hee* [1989] 1 NZLR 221, 226, 229–30; *Kuwait Asia Bank EC v National Mutual Life Nominees Ltd* [1990] 3 NZLR 513, 526, 528–29; *Biddulph v Wyeth Australia Pty Ltd* [1994] 3 NZLR 49, 58; *Kidd v Van Heeren* [1998] 1 NZLR 324, 342–43; *Jardine Risk Consultants Limited v Beal* [2000] NZCA 106, [26]; *Musashi Pty Ltd v Moore* (2002) 6 NZELC 96,453, [52]–[53]; *Stone v Newman* [2002] NZCA 48, [28]; *Castlelight Maritime SA v China Corporation Register of Shipping* [2005] NZHC 397, [59]–[60]; *Jackson v Henning & Associates* [2006] NZHC 639; *Filter Solutions Limited v Donaldson Australasia Pty Ltd* [2006] NZHC

Rather, as the *travaux préparatoires* make abundantly clear,[83] the reform was intended to correct the Australian approach to *forum conveniens.* In *Voth v Manildra Flour Mills Pty Ltd*,[84] the High Court of Australia held that an Australian court will retain jurisdiction unless it considers itself 'a clearly inappropriate forum' to deal with the litigation. If it is not a clearly inappropriate forum, the Australian court will keep the proceedings even if, under the *Spiliada* standard, another court is a more appropriate forum to deal with them. *Voth* not only represents a greedy and parochial approach to judging cases, the expression of this standard leads to profound distortions in the way that Australian courts sort international litigation. *Voth*'s effect is that, the greater the trust that the relevant Australian law invests in a foreign legal system, the less likely it is that it will let those foreign courts deal with litigation. So, in a *dictum* in *Puttick v Tenon Ltd*,[85] a majority of the High Court held that an Australian court was not likely to be a clearly inappropriate forum to deal with trans-Tasman litigation, given the ease of proving a New Zealand statute, 'geographical proximity' and similar legal systems.[86] That somewhat perverse outcome was confirmed by the Supreme Court of Queensland almost on the eve of the Trans-Tasman Proceedings Acts' commencement. *Robinson v Studorp Ltd*[87] was, typically for trans-Tasman forum shopping, a personal injuries claim for exposure to asbestos in New Zealand. The exposure took place before 1974, when New Zealand's comprehensive no-fault accident compensation scheme began, and so an action at common law was still available in New Zealand.[88] An application for a stay (under the principles of *Voth*) was decided in September 2013, although Jackson J took into account the commencement of the Trans-Tasman Proceedings Act in the coming month and, therefore, that the hearing would have the benefit of all of the procedural advantages brought by the Act. The Act's new procedures for subpoenas and remote appearance of witnesses by video-link, and 'the essential similarity' of the legal systems, were taken into account.[89] Following the *dictum* of *Puttick v Tenon*, Jackson J was led by the new streamlined procedures for trans-Tasman litigation to conclude that they 'significantly strengthen the force of that factor'.[90] He refused to order

762, [117]; *Kidd v Van Heeren* [2006] NZCA 42, [15]; *Dale v Jeffrey* [2008] NZHC 147, [21]; *Igarashi v Pendarves* [2008] NZHC 321, [22]; *Watkins v ANZ National Bank Limited* [2008] NZERA 290, [26]; *Haig v Edgewater Developers Ltd* [2009] NZCA 390, [61]; *Wing Hung Printing Company Limited v Saito Offshore Pty Ltd* [2011] 1 NZLR 754, 765.

83 Working Group Report, above n 12, 16.

84 *Voth v Manildra Flour Mills Pty Ltd* (1990) 171 CLR 538.

85 *Puttick v Tenon Ltd* (2008) 238 CLR 265.

86 ibid, 279.

87 *Robinson v Studorp Ltd* [2013] QSC 238. This decision was confirmed on appeal in *Studorp Ltd v Robinson* [2014] QCA 174. Cf the decision of the New South Wales Supreme Court in earlier proceedings between the same parties ([2012] NSWCA 382).

88 See text to nn 103–10.

89 [2013] QSC 238, [49]–[52], [86].

90 ibid, [83].

a stay. *Voth* plainly could not be used to sort litigation even-handedly between courts in the multistate Tasman world.

Yet, the Trans-Tasman Proceedings Acts do not eliminate *Voth* from trans-Tasman litigation. Nor do they properly address the problem of trans-Tasman forum shopping in personal injuries claims.

First, the Acts make no provision for *forum conveniens* for tribunals.[91] They do enable the national Governments to nominate tribunals that, like the courts, would have jurisdictional competence and enforcement jurisdiction over the whole Tasman area. But the Governments have not yet made this nomination, and fortunately so. As can be seen from the terms of section 19(1) of the Australian Act, an application for a stay may only be made to a 'court'[92] and the Act's provisions for the granting of a stay only give that power to a 'court'.[93] The Acts do not expressly define a 'court', although mutual cross-referencing between them would clarify which Australian forums are to be considered courts.[94] Importantly, they also consistently distinguish a court from a 'tribunal'.[95] There will be some forums called 'tribunals' that are still courts according to law and, therefore, will come under the Act's provisions for venue. For instance, the New South Wales Dust Diseases Tribunal (which has been a focus of trans-Tasman forum shopping) is constituted as a court of record.[96] Putting these to one side, it seems almost impossible to read the Acts as empowering a tribunal to grant a stay on *forum conveniens* grounds under the Acts. They also do not expressly prohibit tribunals from resorting to the common law to decide whether to stay proceedings.[97] The question is just silently passed over.

The problem could have been foreseen, because it is one that had already arisen with State tribunals in the Australian national judicial area. Despite having process that runs throughout the whole nation, tribunals are ignored in the stay provisions in the Service and Execution of Process Act.[98] And the result is that,

[91] See also Mortensen, 'Woodhouse Reprised', above n 3, 29–30.

[92] Australian TTPA, s 17(1); New Zealand TTPA, s 22(1).

[93] Australian TTPA, ss 19(1), 20(1); New Zealand TTPA, ss 24(1), 25(1).

[94] The New Zealand Act does not expressly define an 'Australian court'. However, the Australian Act defines an 'Australian court' as meaning 'a federal court or the court of a State or Territory': Australian TTPA, s 4. The Christchurch Agreement also defines a 'court' for Australia as 'any federal court (including the High Court of Australia) and any court of a State or Territory': art 1. The purpose of both Acts is to implement the Agreement: Australian TTPA, s 3; New Zealand TTPA, s 3(1)(c). Each country's Act recognises that the other implements the Agreement in its own country: Australian TTPA, s 3; New Zealand TTPA, s 3(2).

[95] There are numerous references to 'court or tribunal': see Australian TTPA, ss 4, 7, 9(1)–(2), 12(2), 13(1)–(2), 14, 15(1)–(2), 32(1)–(2), 34, 36(6), 37(4), 38, 39, 40, 43(3), 44(2)–(4), 46, 48(1)–(4), 50(1)–(3), 51, 52, 54, 55, 56(1)–(2), 57, 59, 61(1)–(3), 62(1), 63(1), 63(3), 66(2)–(3), 72(1), 75, 76(2), 76(4), 77(1), 78; New Zealand TTPA, ss 4(1), 9(1), 11(3)–(4), 13(2)-(3), 16(2), 17(1)–(2), 18(2), 20(1)–(3), 34(3), 38(1)–(3), 40, 41, 42(1)–(2), 43, 44(1), 45(1)–(2), 46(1), 48, 50(1)–(4), 51, 61(2), 63(3), 64, 65(2), 65(5), 66(1), 67. See especially, Australian TTPA, s 63(2) where 'an Australian tribunal' is sharply distinguished from 'the Federal Court; the Family Court of Australia; [and] a State or Territory court'.

[96] Dust Diseases Tribunal Act 1989 (NSW) s 4(2).

[97] Cf Australian TTPA, s 21; New Zealand TTPA, s 27;

[98] Service and Execution of Process Act 1992 (Cth) s 20.

even though Australian *courts* are limited by the *Spiliada* standard in interstate litigation, *tribunals* are only limited, if at all, by *Voth*. In tribunal cases that have raised questions of interstate venue, *Voth* has been applied by the Victorian Civil and Administrative Tribunal,[99] the Queensland Civil and Administrative Tribunal[100] and the New South Wales Consumer, Trader and Tenancy Tribunal.[101] The identical language of the Trans-Tasman Proceedings Acts also suggests that, for Australian tribunals, *Voth* would remain the only constraint on tribunals' trans-Tasman jurisdiction. This is not the case for New Zealand, where a tribunal has applied the *Spiliada* standard in a trans-Tasman workplace dispute.[102] The Acts would best be amended to enable tribunals also to apply the provisions for stay of proceedings on *forum conveniens* grounds, and for choice of court.

Secondly, not only do the *forum conveniens* provisions apply only to courts, they only allow a stay when the competing forum is a 'court'. The assumption is that something dealt with by litigation on one side of the Tasman must be dealt with by litigation on the other side. That is patently not the case, and it is patently not the case in the area that has traditionally been, and still is, the source of most trans-Tasman forum shopping—personal injuries.[103] The motivation for this is the New Zealand no-fault accident compensation scheme, which is a unique feature of the New Zealand legal system and, being so profoundly different from anything else in place in any other western country,[104] it challenges the assumption that Australia and New Zealand have 'very similar justice systems'.[105] In force since 1974, the scheme is now implemented through the Accident Compensation Act 2001 (NZ). However, it represents a prime motivation for forum shopping because the sums of administrative compensation that it offers for personal injury are often significantly less than the damages available at common law in Australia, even where States have placed some ceiling on the damages that are recoverable. At times, it is 'miserly'.[106] The source of the problem, however, for New Zealand forum shoppers even in Australia, is that the Accident Compensation Act's administrative scheme is made exclusive by a 'statutory bar': a complete ban on

[99] *Bentley v Cash Resources* [2002] VCAT 1399, [15]; *Carrigans Agricultural Repairs Pty Ltd v Viticulture Technologies (Aust) Pty Ltd* [2003] VCAT 2036, [14]; *Koster v Mike Guiliano Agencies Pty Ltd* [2004] VCAT 1046, [20]–[35]; *Bruce Henderson Architects Pty Ltd v Entertainment Development Group Pty Ltd* [2004] VCAT 1356, [31]–[38]; *Spadaro v Mirvac Victoria PL (Civil Claims)* [2005] VCAT 409, [12]–[21]; cf *Bovalino v Pasquale Crea (Real Property)* [2005] VCAT 1692, [22].

[100] *Perro Colour Render Pty Ltd v Artesian Spa Motor Inn* [2010] QCAT 554, [5]–[7].

[101] *Grayson v Wright Bros House Removers and Renovators (Home Building)* [2009] NSWCTTT 628, 4.

[102] *Watkins v ANZ National Bank Limited* [2008] NZERA 290, [26].

[103] For more detail on this suggested reform, see Mortensen, 'Woodhouse Reprised', above n 3, 29–33.

[104] Ie, through a complete elimination of any element of fault in an assessment of an entitlement to compensation for injury—a development that has profound implications for lateral social relations between citizens. See also ibid, 5–7; A Clayton, 'Some Reflections on Woodhouse and ACC Legacy' (2003) 34 *Victoria University of Wellington Law Review* 449, 449–50.

[105] Working Group Report, above n 12, 6.

[106] S Todd, 'Privatization of Accident Compensation: Policy and Politics in New Zealand' (2000) 39 *Washburn Law Journal* 404, 489.

legal proceedings for compensatory damages for personal injuries (whether in contract or tort).[107] The only exceptions are claims for exemplary damages,[108] or claims relating to accidents that took place before 1974. Compensation must be sought from the Accident Compensation Commission ('the ACC'),[109] which is a Crown corporation.[110]

Section 19(1) of the Australian Act only allows a stay of proceedings when 'a New Zealand court has jurisdiction to determine the matters in issue between the parties to the proceeding'. No other power to consider a stay is available.[111] The difficulty is that, if the personal injuries claim is for compensatory damages, the statutory bar means that there is *no* New Zealand court that has jurisdiction to deal with the claim. And if that is the case, then the Australian court has no power to grant a stay of proceedings. In short, in the most common kind of forum shopping found in the Tasman world, a stay of proceedings cannot be used to guard against the practice.[112] The Acts therefore do not give adequate respect to the principle of territoriality or to New Zealand's social policy independence by allowing courts to force litigants who have raised injuries suffered in New Zealand to go to the ACC.

It is possible that a stay might be granted if the Australian court were to conclude that a New Zealand court had jurisdiction to decide that it could not hear the claim. However, I do not think that 'a jurisdiction-to-declare-no-jurisdiction' is the nature of the condition expressed in section 19(1). It asks for a New Zealand court to have the 'jurisdiction *to determine the matters in issue* between the parties to the proceeding' (emphasis added). A New Zealand court, holding it has no jurisdiction to entertain a personal injuries claim, is just not determining matters in issue.

Assuming that 'a jurisdiction-to-declare-no-jurisdiction' does not satisfy the conditions of section 19(1), the question then is what, if confronted with the Accident Compensation Act as the governing law, the Australian court is to do with the proceedings. There is a line of authority that, if a claim is before an Australian court relating to a personal injury that occurred in New Zealand, the Accident Compensation Act's statutory bar applies to the Australian court as well.[113] If that is so, then the bar has to be honoured in some other way. The proper order would seem to be a strike out or summary dismissal of proceedings.[114] This was apparently endorsed by Kirby J in *John Pfeiffer Pty Ltd v*

[107] Accident Compensation Act 2001 (NZ) s 317.

[108] Accident Compensation Act 2001 (NZ) s 319.

[109] Accident Compensation Act 2001 (NZ) s 48.

[110] Accident Compensation Act 2001 (NZ) s 259.

[111] Australian TTPA, s 21.

[112] A stay would naturally be available in Australia for a claim for exemplary damages, or for an injury in New Zealand that took place before 1974: cf *Robinson v Studorp Ltd* [2013] QSC 238.

[113] *Amaca Pty Ltd v Frost* (2006) 67 NSWLR 635, 652.

[114] There is some slight support for the Australian court dealing with the Accident Compensation Act and calculating (and presumably awarding) compensation in accordance with its terms: Mortensen, 'Woodhouse Reprised', above n 3, 33.

Rogerson[115] for Accident Compensation Act claims in Australia. That might be seen as achieving the same outcome as a stay, and ultimately leaving the plaintiff with no option but to go to the ACC. Ultimately, yes, the plaintiff might, having had the proceedings summarily dismissed, be pushed towards the ACC, but summary dismissal is more costly than the interlocutory proceeding for a stay. The application for a stay largely requires reference only to the geographic considerations applicable to *forum conveniens* applications, and a right to appear remotely by telephone or video-link.[116] The strike out requires proof of the statutory bar in evidence, and there is no right of remote appearance although there is a discretion to allow it.[117] A simple solution would be to revert in the Acts to the use of the common law term of 'forum' instead of 'court'; 'forum' being defined to include tribunals and the ACC.

Thirdly, there is only one legal tool available to get proceedings into the *forum conveniens* in the Tasman judicial area—a stay of proceedings.[118] The common law naturally has another tool for dealing with *forum conveniens*—the anti-suit injunction. However, under the Trans-Tasman Proceedings Acts, anti-suit injunctions are banned where the reason for the injunction is that the other court is a *forum non conveniens*.[119] It would appear that, given Australian authority,[120] this would not prevent any Australian or New Zealand court that has injunctive powers from issuing an anti-suit injunction to restrain trans-Tasman litigation brought in breach of a choice of court agreement or as an abuse of process. So, it is not an objection to anti-suit injunctions per se that leads to this ban. Rather, the reason seems to be a concern that an anti-suit injunction would undermine the central place that *forum conveniens* provisions would have in the trans-Tasman judicial area. The Trans-Tasman Working Group recommended the ban, and stated that this 'will prevent such injunctions being used to circumvent the proposed trans-Tasman regime, including the provisions on staying proceedings on the grounds that another court is the more appropriate forum'.[121]

There are difficulties with this reasoning. The procedure for granting an anti-suit injunction does not circumvent a *forum conveniens* analysis. It actually requires the court that is asked to grant the injunction to undertake that analysis twice—once in assessing its own appropriateness and again in assessing the foreign court's inappropriateness—and then to meet other conditions (including whether the foreign litigation is vexatious or oppressive).[122] Indeed, it is possible to consider that a comprehensive doctrine of *forum conveniens* requires tools both

115 *John Pfeiffer Pty Ltd v Rogerson* (2000) 203 CLR 503, 548 (fn 130); cf *Puttick v Fletcher Challenge Forests Pty Ltd* [2007] VSCA 264, [44].
116 Australian TTPA, s 18(4).
117 Australian TTPA, s 50.
118 Australian TTPA, s 19(1); New Zealand TTPA, s 24(1).
119 Australian TTPA, s 22; New Zealand TTPA, s 28.
120 *Great Southern Loans v Locator Group* [2005] NSWSC 438.
121 Working Group Report, above n 12, 16.
122 *CSR Ltd v Cigna Insurance Australia Ltd* (1997) 189 CLR 345, 395–401. See also *Airbus Industrie GIE v Patel* [1999] 1 AC 119; *Amchem Products Inc v British Columbia (WCB)* [1993] 1 SCR 897.

to exercise self-restraint (by a stay or dismissal) and to compel other-restraint (by injunction). Further, as the language of the Acts mimics something of section 21 of the Service and Execution of Process Act, it may be that the Working Group misread the significance of section 21 in the Australian federal scheme. Section 21 places a limited ban on anti-suit injunctions where the proceedings were commenced by interstate service of a State court writ. This ban is so limited, there is no reported instance of section 21 ever having prevented the issue of an anti-suit injunction. Even in cases commenced by service under the Service and Execution of Process Act, section 21 has been read down so far as to amount to a dead letter.[123]

There is no reported case in New Zealand of a court having been asked to grant an anti-suit injunction.[124] In Australia, they are unremarkable—at least for addressing *lis pendens* in competing interstate litigation, or competing federal-State litigation. The result of the ban on anti-suit injunctions under the Trans-Tasman Proceedings Acts is therefore to compound asymmetry between the trans-Tasman and Australian federal schemes. And the asymmetry is counter-intuitive. In the tight federal Australian scheme, with all courts ultimately accountable to the High Court of Australia, anti-suit injunctions are allowed and granted with some regularity on *forum non conveniens* grounds. In the confederal Tasman scheme under different court hierarchies, they are prohibited. The trans-Tasman scheme therefore gives greater opportunities for *lis pendens* to arise, but it is entirely reliant on both courts' exercise of self-restraint. There is no tie-breaker once each of two courts decides that *it* is the more appropriate court. A repeal of the ban on anti-suit injunctions would, despite the Working Group's fears, bring principles of *forum conveniens* even closer to the centre of the allocation of jurisdiction in the trans-Tasman judicial area.

C. Choice of Court Agreements—Consumer Contracts

The second means by which the Trans-Tasman Proceedings Acts guide litigation into one court only is in the provision they make for exclusive choice of court agreements. The general rules are that, if a choice of court agreement—or 'jurisdiction clause'—requires, for example, litigation to be brought only in a New Zealand court, an Australian court must stay proceedings in favour of the New Zealand court.[125] This implements the *mechanism* of the Hague Convention on Choice of Court Agreements,[126] but it does not implement the Convention's *definition* of an exclusive choice of court agreement. Instead, it uses the common law definition of an exclusive choice of court agreement, requiring the agreement to have a clear expressed

[123] *Great Southern Loans v Locator Group* [2005] NSWSC 438.

[124] Cf *Commissioner of Inland Revenue v Compudigm International Ltd (in rec and in liq)* [2010] NZHC 1832, [17]–[24].

[125] Australian TTPA, s 20(1); New Zealand TTPA, s 25(1).

[126] Convention on Choice of Court Agreements 2005 (signed at The Hague 30 June 2005).

intention that litigation be heard in only one nominated court or court system.[127] Still, the inclusion of the Choice of Court Convention's mechanism for dealing with exclusive choice of court agreements is more respectful of contractual promises than the common law, where courts have a greater discretion to hold on to litigation brought before them, but in breach of an exclusive choice of court agreement. And it was especially important in the Trans-Tasman Proceedings Acts because, through the 1990s and early 2000s, Australian courts had developed (to put it bluntly) an appalling record of holding litigation brought in breach of an agreement to litigate exclusively in a court in some place outside Australia.[128] In effect, it gives businesses involved in trans-Tasman trading and commercial relationships the option of choosing which court in the single Tasman market will deal with any disputes between them, and almost complete certainty that that is where the litigation will be heard. However, consumer disputes are another question.

The Acts expressly provide that an exclusive choice of court agreement does not include 'an agreement the parties to which are or include 1 or more individuals acting primarily for personal, family, or household purposes'.[129] The exclusion is a close approximation of the language of the Choice of Court Convention,[130] and gives rise to questions of consumer protection policy, and of overlap or incompatibility with existing consumer law in Australia and New Zealand.

Even accepting the Convention's policy of ignoring choice of court agreements in consumer contracts,[131] it is still curious that the Acts maintain The Hague's definition of a consumer contract—which is the European Union's definition.[132] Compatibly with the preference for using local legal resources over and above civilian European imports, when developing Tasman institutions the Acts have preferred the common law approach to the definition of an exclusive choice of court agreement. It is anomalous, therefore, when excluding consumer contracts from this definition, to use the European definition of consumer contracts, and particularly when it differs from local definitions.

[127] R Garnett, 'The Enforcement of Exclusive Jurisdiction Clauses in Australia' (1998) 21 *University of New South Wales Law Journal* 1; M Keyes, *Jurisdiction in International Litigation* (Sydney, Federation Press, 2005) 92–94; (Keyes, *International Litigation*); M Keyes, 'Jurisdiction under the Hague Choice of Court Convention: Its Likely Impact on Australian Practice' (2009) 5 *Journal of Private International Law* 181 (Keyes, 'Jurisdiction under the Convention'); Mortensen, 'A Trans-Tasman Judicial Area', above n 3, 82–83; Mortensen, 'The Hague and the Ditch', above n 3, 232–33.

[128] Keyes, *International Litigation*, above n 128, 162–75; Keyes, 'Jurisdiction under the Convention', above n 127, 23; Mortensen, 'A Trans-Tasman Judicial Area', above n 3, 80–81.

[129] Australian TTPA, s 20(3)(b); New Zealand TTPA, s 25(4)(b).

[130] Convention on Choice of Court Agreements 2005, art 2(1)(a): 'This Convention shall not apply to exclusive choice of court agreements … to which a natural person acting primarily for personal, family or household purposes (a consumer) is a party'.

[131] In the United States, choice of court agreements in consumer contracts have been enforced: RA Brand and SR Jablonski, *Forum Non Conveniens: History, Global Practice, and Future Under the Hague Convention on Choice of Court Agreements* (New York, Oxford University Press, 2007) 190–91. In *Carnival Cruise Lines Inc v Shute* 499 US 585, 594 (1991), Blackmun J pointed out that 'passengers who purchase tickets containing a forum clause like that at issue in this case benefit from the reduced fares reflecting the savings that the cruise line enjoys by limiting the fora in which it may be sued'.

[132] J Hill, *Cross-Border Consumer Contracts* (Oxford, Oxford University Press, 2008) 3.

In New Zealand, the Consumer Guarantees Act 1993 defines, for post-sale consumer law, a 'consumer' as:[133]

> a person who—
>
> (a) acquires from a supplier goods or services of a kind ordinarily acquired for personal, domestic, or household use or consumption; and
>
> (b) does not acquire the goods or services, or hold himself or herself out as acquiring the goods or services, for the purpose of—
>
> (i) resupplying them in trade; or
>
> (ii) consuming them in the course of a process of production or manufacture; or
>
> (iii) in the case of goods, repairing or treating in trade other goods or fixtures on land.

Admittedly, this is not too far from the Convention's definition. However, what is more immediately important in trans-Tasman disputes is that the Australian Consumer Law has a different, broader definition of 'consumer' that applies in both the pre-sale and post-sale consumer law. So, as in the Consumer Guarantees Act, a person is taken to be a 'consumer' in Australia if the goods or services 'were of a kind ordinarily acquired for personal, domestic or household use or consumption'.[134] However, a 'consumer' in Australian law is also one who acquires goods or services (of any kind) at a price of no more than AUS$40,000.[135] This means that the Australian Consumer Law will capture *any* gift.[136] Further, anyone who acquires a vehicle or trailer for use principally in the transport of goods on public roads is treated as a 'consumer' for that acquisition.[137] The extended definition of consumer in Australia was introduced in 1986,[138] with the intention that the protection of consumer laws be given to small business transactions in general, and transactions for agricultural businesses in particular.[139] In all cases of the acquisition of goods, the Australian Consumer Law parallels the Consumer Guarantees Act by denying consumer status to a person who acquires the goods—or who holds themselves out as acquiring them—for re-supply; or for consuming or transforming them in the course of production or manufacture, or in the course of repairing or treating other goods or fixtures on land.[140] In proceedings

[133] Consumer Guarantee Act 1993 (NZ), s 2(1).

[134] Australian Consumer Law, found in Competition and Consumer Act 2010 (Cth), Sch 2 and in State and Territory Fair Trading Acts ('Australian Consumer Law'), ss 3(1)(b), 3(3)(b).

[135] Australian Consumer Law, ss 3(1)(a), 3(3)(a). Cf *Atkinson v Hastings Deering (Queensland) Pty Ltd* (1985) 7 ATPR 40-566, 46,572; *Atkinson v Hastings Deering (Queensland) Pty Ltd* (1985) 7 ATPR 40-625, 47,085; *Theo Holdings Pty Ltd v Hockey* (2000) 175 ALR 89, 97–99.

[136] *Clarke v New Concept Import Services Pty Ltd* (1981) 3 ATPR 40-264, 43,348.

[137] Australian Consumer Law, s 3(1)(c).

[138] Trade Practices Revision Act 1986 (Cth) s 5.

[139] J Goldring, L Maher, J McKeough and G Pearson, *Consumer Protection Law*, 5th edn (Sydney, Federation Press, 1998) 27.

[140] Australian Consumer Law, s 3(2). The Australian Consumer Law compounds the complexity of its definition of 'consumer', with provisions dealing with 'mixed supply' of goods and services: ss 3(5), 3(11). The definition resting on acquisitions of goods or services of no more than AUS$40,000 also requires provisions detailing how price is calculated: ss 3(4)–3(9).

under the Australian Consumer Law, there is also a presumption in favour of consumer status. Where one party makes a claim of consumer status, the onus is on the other party to disprove it.[141]

The risk, therefore, is that what are considered consumer contracts under the broader Australian law, in particular, may not be excluded from the Acts' directive to enforce choice of court agreements, and some consumers may be forced into the supplier's preferred court in a standard terms contract. The basic approach taken to choice of court agreements in the Acts is plainly to prefer local understandings of a choice of court agreement to the Convention's understanding. It would give that approach greater coherence if the exclusion were to include any consumer contract classified as such under Australian or New Zealand law.

D. Enforcement Jurisdiction

Although most attention in jurisdiction and judgments schemes is given to the question of the power to judge, the ultimate reason for these schemes is to improve the efficiency of enforcement jurisdiction. This is something that the Australian federal scheme does well, resting as it does on the distinctive Australian approach to the constitutional imperative of full faith and credit. The absence of any defence to the registration and enforcement of a judgment in the Service and Execution of Process Act[142] compels parties to engage with litigation wherever in the federation it is first commenced. Back-end resistance, by ignoring the primary litigation and waiting to defend against proceedings at the enforcement stage, is just not an option for litigants in Australia.

The Trans-Tasman Proceedings Acts extend this efficient scheme of enforcement to the whole Tasman world.[143] That is itself a remarkable development in a transnational judgments scheme, and reinforces the confederal character of the Tasman relationship. However, there is a difference between the trans-Tasman scheme and the Australian scheme. The trans-Tasman scheme allows one defence, and only one, to the enforcement of judgments between Australia and New Zealand: registration of a cross-Tasman judgment can be set aside if enforcement would be contrary to 'public policy' in the country of enforcement.[144]

The public policy defence is an unfortunate inclusion in the Trans-Tasman Proceedings Acts.[145] There may be a need to control the enforcement of specific kinds of judgments, but the use of the language of 'public policy' is truly disproportionate to that purpose.

[141] Australian Consumer Law, s 3(10).

[142] Service and Execution of Process Act 1992 (Cth) s 109.

[143] Australian TTPA, s 79(1); New Zealand TTPA, s 68(1).

[144] Australian TTPA, s 72(2)(b); New Zealand TTPA, s 61(2)(b).

[145] For earlier criticisms, see Mortensen, 'Judgments Extension under CER', above n 41, 270–71; Mortensen, 'The Hague and the Ditch', above n 3, 228–29; Mortensen, 'A Trans-Tasman Judicial Area', above n 3, 93–96; Mortensen and Knöfel, above n 3, 391–92; Mortensen, 'Woodhouse Reprised', above n 3, 34–35.

The preservation of a public policy defence to enforcement of a judgment seems to have worried Wellington more than it did Canberra when striking the Christchurch Agreement. The *travaux préparatoires* indicate two concerns. First, it was suggested that public policy might be used in New Zealand to refuse enforcement of an Australian award of damages for personal injuries for an accident that occurred in New Zealand.[146] Australian courts, however, consistently hold that the Accident Compensation Act applies to New Zealand injuries, and have only claimed to have jurisdiction to award damages when the injuries were suffered before 1974.[147] The second suggestion was that public policy could allow the enforcement of some regulatory regime fines or civil penalty orders to be denied.[148] However, the Trans-Tasman Proceedings Acts expressly provide that a court cannot refuse enforcement of a regulatory regime fine or civil penalty.[149] Further, fines have only become enforceable because the national Governments have made regulations that bring them into the scheme.[150] Civil penalties are enforceable if the Governments have not excluded them from the scheme.[151] Either way, fines and civil penalties are included in the trans-Tasman scheme with the national Governments' express approval. As a question of executive policy, they have been treated as worthy of enforcement. It is unlikely the public policy defence could be invoked in these circumstances.

The best justification for the public policy defence is symbolic.[152] It marks out the Tasman relationship as a confederal association between two sovereignties, and as unlike the relations between States in the Australian federation. It makes perfect sense to recognise this difference, but not through the amorphous catch-all of 'public policy'. Burrough J's famous warning is still worth heeding:[153]

> I, for one, protest … against arguing too strongly upon public policy;—it is a very unruly horse, and when once you get astride it you never know where it will carry you. It may lead you from the sound law. It is never argued at all but when other points fail.

[146] Discussion Paper, above n 59, 16.

[147] *James Hardie and Coy Pty Ltd v Grigor* (1998) 45 NSWLR 20; *Robinson v Studorp Ltd* [2013] QSC 238; *Studorp Ltd v Robinson* [2014] QCA 174. However, all Australian cases dealing with New Zealand injuries have involved plaintiffs who were New Zealand residents at the time the injury was suffered. The Accident Compensation Act denies to a foreign resident *any* compensation, other than New Zealand hospital expenses and a month's attendant care. It would be interesting to see whether an Australian court, dealing with an *Australian* plaintiff injured by wrongdoing in New Zealand, would be prepared to allow the plaintiff to be subject to New Zealand's no compensation law. The use of a public policy exception to the choice of law rule is at least a possibility in a case like this, and then the relevant Australian State personal injuries law would be applied. There may well be a public policy reason for a New Zealand court to deny registration of the Australian judgment in these circumstances. However, the root cause of this problem is New Zealand's discriminatory treatment of non-residents, and its unusual denial of compensation for injuries. A more humane trans-Tasman solution, compatible with the principle of non-discrimination, would be to legislate to allow foreign residents compensation for injuries suffered in New Zealand: Mortensen, 'Woodhouse Reprised', above n 3, 34–38.

[148] Working Group Report, above n 12, 21, 22.

[149] Australian TTPA, s 79(2)(c); New Zealand TTPA, s 68(2)(c).

[150] Australian TTPA, s 66(1)(d); New Zealand TTPA, s 77.

[151] Australian TTPA, s 66(1)(f); New Zealand TTPA, ss 69–72.

[152] Mortensen, 'A Trans-Tasman Judicial Area', above n 3, 93.

[153] *Richardson v Mellish* (1824) 2 Bing 229, 252; 130 ER 294, 303.

The judicial record suggests that there are few prospects that a public policy argument would succeed. In Australia, public policy has only ever been successfully invoked to deny enforcement of a judgment once,[154] and in New Zealand the Court of Appeal has held that the defence needs to have 'a narrow application'.[155] However, the boundless quality of the public policy exception makes it a magnet for back-end litigation designed just to stall the enforcement of judgments, with potential to undermine the efficiency of the trans-Tasman scheme. If the recognition of sovereignty is what is to be secured by a defence to enforcement, then it would be preferable to frame it more directly in terms of setting aside registration of a judgment that would amount to the enforcement of (say for the New Zealand Act) 'an Australian governmental interest'. The High Court of Australia endorsed this as a reason for not applying the usual governing law in choice of law cases when, in *Attorney-General (United Kingdom) v Heinemann Publishers Australia Pty Ltd* (the '*Spycatcher Case*'),[156] Mason CJ and Wilson, Deane, Dawson, Toohey and Gaudron JJ said that:[157]

> It would be more apt to refer to 'public interests' or, even better, 'governmental interests' to signify that the rule applies to claims enforcing the interests of a foreign sovereign which arise from the exercise of certain powers peculiar to government.

Indeed, this formulation was implicitly preferred to Brennan J's concurring view that the enforcement of British national security laws should not be permitted on public policy grounds.[158] The advantage of adapting the *Spycatcher* majority's formulation of the defence to the trans-Tasman enforcement regime is that it expressly protects national sovereignty and, indeed, forbids a New Zealand court, for instance, from allowing judgments giving effect to laws peculiar to the exercise of governmental powers in Australia to be enforced. This naturally extends to 'the relationship between a foreign state and members of its military forces engaged in hostilities against another state in circumstances where this country is not directly involved'[159] and, as in *Spycatcher*, questions of the other country's national security. And, as in *Spycatcher* again, the principle applies despite close international relations between the enforcing country and the country which is attempting to enforce its interests by registration of a judgment.[160] It goes to the heart of the recognition of sovereignty, without opening enforcement jurisdiction to the legal uncertainties of 'public policy'.

A second clarification that would usefully add certainty to the enforcement jurisdiction of the Trans-Tasman Proceedings Acts would be one that addresses

[154] *Marriage of El Ouiek* (1977) 29 FLR 171.

[155] *Reeves v One World Challenge LLC* [2006] 2 NZLR 184, 195–98; *Ross v Ross* [2010] NZCA 447, [28]–[48].

[156] *Attorney-General (United Kingdom) v Heinemann Publishers Australia Pty Ltd* (1988) 165 CLR 30.

[157] ibid, 42.

[158] ibid, 49, 50–51.

[159] ibid, 44.

[160] ibid, 47.

the priority to be given to incompatible judgments. This is another unfortunate consequence of directly adopting the language of the Service and Execution of Process Act, which does not deal with incompatible judgments at all. And it is a step backwards. The scheme that was in place for the registration of judgments between the two countries before the Acts came into force did deal expressly with incompatible judgments.[161] When recommending the legislation that became the Service and Execution of Process Act, the Australian Law Reform Commission thought that the risk of incompatible judgments was low but, if they did arise, courts would probably give priority to the judgment that was made first.[162] It then refused to recommend that the Service and Execution of Process Act should expressly state a rule to that effect. The Trans-Tasman Working Group made the same puzzling recommendation.[163] It is hard to understand why policy-makers, agreeing how to deal with a problem, would then decide not to give certainty to future litigants by including it in the legislation they recommend. This should be corrected, and preferably with a rule that gives priority to the first judgment rendered anywhere in the trans-Tasman area. In short, the first judgment rendered should make the issue in dispute *res judicata* for the whole Tasman world. Any rule that gives priority to a local judgment,[164] even if it is the later in time, will only encourage re-litigation in the place of enforcement and, consequently, undermine the efficiency of the scheme.

IV. Extending Trans-Tasman Law

A. Choice of Law

The exceptional extent to which civil jurisdiction and judgments in the Tasman world have now been integrated gives rise to another question—to what extent might it impel even closer integration of Australia's and New Zealand's civil legal systems? In private international law, the question is almost inevitable. The European experience suggests that an integrated scheme of civil jurisdiction and judgments has potential to motivate uniform choice of law rules and, even, uniform substantive law across the market area. From 1973, the terms of the Brussels Convention (now the Brussels I Regulation)[165] have been extended beyond the European Union into the European Economic Area (through the

[161] Foreign Judgments Act 1991 (Cth) s 7(2)(b); Reciprocal Enforcement of Judgments Act 1934 (NZ) s 6(2).

[162] Australian Law Reform Commission, *Service and Execution of Process, Report No 40* (Canberra, Commonwealth of Australia, 1987) 81; see also Mortensen, 'Judgments Extension under CER', above n 41, 267.

[163] Working Group Report, above n 12, 18.

[164] *Vervaeke v Smith* [1983] 1 AC 145.

[165] Brussels I Regulation (see above n 56).

Lugano Convention).[166] Brussels I has also seen a related regulation developed for insolvency and another for matrimonial and parenting questions.[167] The 'Brussels matrix' in jurisdiction and judgments has been reinforced by a 'Rome matrix' in choice of law: the Rome I Regulation for contractual obligations; the Rome II Regulation for tort, delict and other non-contractual obligations; and the Rome III Regulation for divorce and legal separations (although it is not applicable throughout the whole EU).[168] The Trans-Tasman Proceedings Acts cover the legal ground that the Brussels matrix covers in Europe—and then more. It is therefore worth pondering whether they are likely to stimulate any unification of trans-Tasman choice of law.

There is a significant difference, though, between the underlying European and Tasman legal conditions, and that is the common law. In general, the common law remains the source of Australian and New Zealand choice of law principles, and the respective common laws of the two countries remain deeply indebted to their English origins. That means that there is already a high degree of harmonisation or unification of choice of law in the Tasman world, and little need for legislative reform. However, there are at least two aspects of choice of law where legislative reform is either begging, or where its need is evident because of differences between the two countries: proof of foreign law, and torts.[169]

B. Proof of Foreign Law

The proof that foreign law differs from the local law is the trigger for a choice of law rule to be applied,[170] and that proof must be based on the evidence of experts in the foreign law.[171] If the foreign law does differ from the law of the forum (*lex*

[166] Lugano Convention (see above n 54).

[167] Regulation (EC) No 1346/2000 of 29 May 2000 on Insolvency Proceedings [2000] OJ L160/1; Regulation (EC) No 2201/2003 concerning jurisdiction and the recognition and enforcement of judgments in matrimonial matters and in matters of parental responsibility for joint children [2003] OJ L338/1.

[168] Regulation (EC) No 593/2008 on the Law applicable to contractual obligations (Rome I) [2008] OJ L177/6; Regulation (EC) No 864/2007 of 11 July 2007 on the Law applicable to non-contractual obligations (Rome II) [2007] OJ L199/40; Council Regulation (EC) No 1259/2010 of 20 December 2010 implementing enhanced cooperation in the area of the law applicable to divorce and legal separation [2010] OJ L343/10.

[169] There are more differences between Australian and New Zealand choice of law that could be explored. The scope of procedural law in New Zealand (and so application of the *lex fori*) is probably much wider than in Australia, where the decision in *John Pfeiffer Pty Ltd v Rogerson* (2000) 203 CLR 503 restricted procedural laws to matters relating to the mode or conduct of legal proceedings. Australian principles of international family law are considerably more complex than those in New Zealand, largely because of Australia's extensive adoption of Hague conventions on family law. The complexity of Australia's choice of law rules for marriage and its rules for the recognition of foreign decrees is also compounded by its preserving a role for the common law beside Hague Conventions: eg, Marriage Act 1961 (Cth) ss 22, 88; Family Law Act 1975 (Cth) s 104(5).

[170] *Regie National des Usines Renault SA v Zhang* (2002) 210 CLR 491, 519.

[171] *McKelvey v Meagher* (1906) 4 CLR 265, 284; *Rossano v Manufacturers Life Insurance Company* [1963] 2 QB 352, 367.

fori), the question is whether local choice of law rules require the foreign law to be applied.

There are lingering inefficiencies in trans-Tasman litigation when, in particular, trying to prove the law of New Zealand in Australia. However, as a matter of policy there is really no lack of judicial expertise or capacity that would suggest it was inappropriate for judges in each country to take judicial notice of the law of the other, subject to a discretion to call for expert evidence if the judge considered it necessary.

In general, there are few problems when proving Australian law in New Zealand courts. Lawyers have the right to submit statutes, case-law and textbooks as evidence of foreign law.[172] This extends the means of courts' powers to prove foreign common law. In fact, the similarity of Australian and New Zealand law has meant that New Zealand judges have had no real reluctance in recognising the common law of Australia.[173] In *Dymocks Franchise Systems (NSW) Pty Ltd v Todd*,[174] this power to use case-law and textbooks was used to establish developments in the common law in New South Wales, albeit that, on appeal, these developments were regarded as being more intricate than would justify reliance on the power. It was a case where the complexities of the law required the assistance of experts.[175]

Technically, proof of the common law of New Zealand in Australia is not as straightforward. There is an old power, recognised in both countries, to presume that the common law of a British possession has not been changed by statute.[176] But, as *Dymocks Franchise Systems* had shown for the New Zealand courts, since both countries have been freed from Privy Council supervision it is not as easy to assume the identity of the two countries' common laws. Proof of legislation is simpler; under the Trans-Tasman Proceedings Act, Australian judges can take judicial notice of New Zealand statutes.[177] But they may not, technically, take judicial notice of the common law.

In any case, trial judges on both sides of the Tasman Sea have tried to proceed informally and work out the cross-Tasman law without the benefit of expert witnesses.[178] A New Zealand judge has urged litigants to agree to allow him to read and apply any New South Wales authorities needed to be proved.[179] A New South Wales judge has simply taken counsel's submissions as proof of New Zealand

[172] Evidence Act 2006 (NZ) s 144; Evidence Act 1908 (NZ) s 40.

[173] Eg *Musashi Pty Ltd v Moore* [2002] 1 ERNZ 203, [49]–[50], [60]; *Filter Solutions Ltd v Donaldson Australasia Pty Ltd* [2006] NZHC 762, [119]. See also *Crane Accessories Ltd v Lim Swee Hee* [1989] 1 NZLR 221, 231; *Wing Hung Printing Co Ltd v Saito Offshore Pty Ltd* [2011] 1 NZLR 754, 781.

[174] *Dymocks Franchise Systems (NSW) Pty Ltd v Todd* [2004] 1 NZLR 289, 307–8.

[175] ibid, 305–9; see also *SHC v O'Brien* (1991) 3 PRNZ 1, 15.

[176] *Dryden v Dryden* (1876) 2 VLR (E) 74, 84; *R v Ford* (1913) 32 NZLR 1219, 1225.

[177] Australian TTPA, ss 96–103; *Amaca Pty Ltd v Frost* (2006) 67 NSWLR 635, [62].

[178] *Musashi Pty Ltd v Moore* [2002] 1 ERNZ 203, [60]; *Du Bray v McIlwraith* [2009] NSWSC 888, [37]–[40].

[179] *Filter Solutions Ltd v Donaldson Australasia Pty Ltd* [2006] NZHC 762, [123].

law.[180] In the *Gilmore* litigation,[181] the Full Court of the Australian Family Court more properly accepted affidavits of New Zealand lawyers on New Zealand matrimonial law.[182] It nevertheless had no evidence relating to New Zealand's law on the enforcement of property orders.[183] Instead, the Full Court used its own researches to give a lengthy account of New Zealand's different regimes for enforcing judgments, including New Zealand case-law on the point.[184] The evident frustrations of this position were barely contained in *Robinson v Studorp Ltd*,[185] where Jackson J toyed with the idea of taking judicial notice of the common law of New Zealand on the ground that it was 'notorious'.[186] He still ended up taking evidence of common law that was identical with the Australian law, and that ironically even depended in part on Australian precedents.[187]

The Trans-Tasman Proceedings Acts reinforce the absurdity of this position by giving New Zealand lawyers rights of appearance in applications for stay of proceedings and, with leave, in trials in Australian courts.[188] At present, they are technically required to present their own common law to an Australian court through expert witnesses. Judicial notice is a reform that could be easily made, that could reduce litigation costs and time, and that would simply bring Australian law alongside the position in New Zealand.

C. Torts

After a confusing decade of reworking the double actionability rule of *Phillips v Eyre*,[189] the High Court of Australia decided in 2000 that, in interstate tort litigation, liability would be governed by the law of the State where the wrong occurred (the *lex loci delicti*). No exceptions were permitted. Territoriality was prominent in the development of this rule, and it was held to be demanded by constitutional considerations. As the double actionability rule determined liability for a cross-border tort by reference to the *lex fori* as well as the *lex loci delicti*, it was incompatible with the principle of territoriality.[190] In 2002 this rule was extended to international tort cases,[191] with an exception allowed for the *lex fori* only when the application of the

[180] *Du Bray v McIlwraith* [2009] NSWSC 888, [40].
[181] *Marriage of Gilmore* [1993] FamCA 3.
[182] ibid, [56].
[183] ibid, [73].
[184] ibid, [74]–[117].
[185] *Robinson v Studorp Ltd* [2013] QSC 238.
[186] ibid, [22].
[187] ibid, [55]–[74]. See also *Studorp Ltd v Robinson* [2014] QCA 174, [36]–[38].
[188] Australian TTPA, ss 48, 50.
[189] *Phillips v Eyre* (1870) LR 6 QB 1.
[190] *John Pfeiffer Pty Ltd v Rogerson* (2000) 203 CLR 503, 533–34, 536–37, 541, 551.
[191] *Regie National des Usines Renault SA v Zhang* (2002) 210 CLR 491, 520.

foreign law would be contrary to public policy.[192] Again, a *lex loci delicti* rule was considered the best means of giving effect to the principle of territoriality.[193]

In New Zealand a foreign tort is apparently still dealt with in accordance with the double actionability rule of *Phillips v Eyre*.[194] An action in New Zealand for a tort that occurred in another country can only proceed if it is actionable under the law of New Zealand and, also, actionable under the relevant foreign law—with an exception for one of those places when it has a more significant relationship with the occurrence and the parties.[195] As *Phillips v Eyre* has been progressively abolished across the Commonwealth, New Zealand's choice of law rule has looked increasingly archaic. Still, in contrast to the changes that took place in Canada[196] and Australia, there are fewer prospects for reform of the rule in *Phillips v Eyre* in New Zealand by common law adjudication. As a unitary state it has fewer opportunities for cross-border litigation, and the ban on personal injuries proceedings eliminates the usual source of cases that have motivated reform. Indeed, although it is unlikely to be brought, a personal injuries claim in New Zealand for a foreign tort is likely to fail because *Phillips v Eyre*'s requirement of actionability in New Zealand would not be satisfied. The Accident Compensation Act's ban on proceedings means no claim for compensatory damages is actionable.

In trans-Tasman conditions, there is evident imbalance in choice of law rules that have Australian courts consistently applying New Zealand law to wrongs that occur in New Zealand, but New Zealand courts applying New Zealand law as well as the relevant Australian State law to a wrong that took place in Australia. There are certainly proposals for the statutory reform of New Zealand's choice of law rules for tort. Elsabe Schoeman suggests a *lex loci delicti* rule with a proper law, or 'flexible', exception in favour of the law of the place that has the most significant relationship to the occurrence and the parties.[197] As the proposal includes a proper law exception, it is slightly broader than the Australian rule—for which the proper law exception was rejected.[198] There is ample criticism of the inflexible Australian rule,[199] and a similar statutory reform for Australia is certainly justified. Regardless, the

[192] ibid, 519, 534, 535. This exception is not permitted in interstate tort claims: *John Pfeiffer Pty Ltd v Rogerson* (2000) 203 CLR 503, 533–54.

[193] P St J Smart, 'Foreign Torts and the High Court of Australia' (2002) 118 *Law Quarterly Review* 512, 515.

[194] Cf *Wing Hung Printing Company Limited v Saito Offshore Pty Ltd* [2011] 1 NZLR 754, 781.

[195] *Richards v McLean* [1973] 1 NZLR 521, 526; *Baxter v RMC Group plc* [2003] 1 NZLR 304; *Starlink Navigation Ltd v The Ship 'Seven Pioneer'* (2001) 16 PRNZ 55; *Ocean Towing & Salvage (Vanuatu) Ltd v Custom Fleet (NZ) Ltd* [2006] NZHC 1481, [44].

[196] *Tolofson v Jensen* [1994] SCR 3 SCR 1022.

[197] E Schoeman, 'Tort Choice of Law in New Zealand: Proposals for Reform' [2004] *New Zealand Law Review* 537, 561.

[198] *Regie National des Usines Renault SA v Zhang* (2002) 210 CLR 491, 519–20.

[199] R Anderson, 'International Torts in the High Court of Australia' (2002) 10 *Torts Law Journal* 132, 140–41; G Davis, '*John Pfeiffer Pty Ltd v Rogerson*: Choice of Law in Tort at the Dawning of the 21st Century' (2000) *Melbourne University Law Review* 982, 1014–15; A Gray, 'Flexibility in Conflict of Laws Multistate Tort Cases: The Way Forward in Australia' (2004) 23 *University of Queensland Law Journal* 435, 462–63; E James, '*John Pfeiffer Pty Ltd v Rogerson*: The Certainty of "Federal" Choice of Law Rules for Intranational Torts: Limitations, Implications and a Few Complications' (2001) 23

coordination of civil legal relations in the multistate Tasman world would be better served by a rule that gave a strong preference to the *lex loci delicti* in tort claims.

D. Cooperative Statutory Interpretation

The Trans-Tasman Proceedings Acts are not just harmonised statutes for a private trans-Tasman law; they are statutes with word-for-word identical language. The implicit intention is that they be applied in the same way on each side of the Tasman. This also suggests that it is of the highest joint national policy in the trans-Tasman judicial area that the Acts be interpreted in the same way. However, the first normative principle of the bilateral private international law is that it must function cooperatively, and not through a unified court system.[200] Uniform interpretation therefore has to be achieved cooperatively, and courts in the different Australian or New Zealand hierarchies must make special efforts to interpret the Acts as courts across the Tasman have. This will be especially important for the open-textured provisions for *forum conveniens* or for the public policy defence to the enforcement of judgments.[201] At this point, the Lugano Convention gives some assistance. The courts of the European Economic Area do not answer to a final court of appeal, and structures had to be provided to ensure that interpretation of the Convention was relatively uniform across the EEA and relatively compatible with the interpretation of the Brussels I Regulation. As a result, courts in the EEA are directed to 'pay due account to the principles laid down by any relevant decision delivered by courts of the other Contracting States concerning provisions of the Convention'.[202] It would be worth introducing a similar direction to Australian and New Zealand courts in the Trans-Tasman Proceedings Acts to reinforce the integrity of the scheme.

V. Australasian Confederation Realised

The first attempt at confederal arrangements in the Tasman world was the Federal Council of Australasia, which was established in 1885.[203] Its name shows that the Council was hoped to include New Zealand, as well as all of the Australian colonies and Fiji. In the 15-year history of the Federal Council,[204] though, New Zealand

Sydney Law Review 145, 146, 163; G Lindell, '*Regie National des Usines Renault SA v Zhang*' (2002) 3 *Melbourne Journal of International Law* 362, 372–73.

[200] See text to nn 51–53 above.

[201] See text accompanying nn 80–90, 143–59.

[202] Lugano Convention, Protocol 2, art 1.

[203] Federal Council of Australia Act 1885 (UK).

[204] It was dissolved on the federation of the Australian colonies: Commonwealth of Australia Constitution Act 1900 (UK), s 7.

(as well as New South Wales) never participated. It was a weak, 'quite innocuous body',[205] but the New Zealand Government also thought that the Federal Council would muffle New Zealand's efforts at securing Imperial support for *its* policy in relation to the Pacific.[206]

It is nevertheless that first, nominally Australasian, confederation that developed the jurisdiction and judgments scheme that is ultimately the progenitor of the Trans-Tasman Proceedings Acts. The Council's Australasian Civil Process Act 1886 provided for courts in the participating colonies to have a long-arm jurisdiction based on (the now) traditional heads of jurisdiction that require a defined legal connection between the litigation and the colony.[207] The companion Australasian Judgments Act 1886 (FCA) provided, for the time, a relatively liberal means of enforcing judgments between the participating colonies. It did not allow any of the common law defences to enforcement, other than the need for the rendering court to have exercised an acceptable jurisdiction. That had to be common law jurisdiction, or a jurisdiction assumed under the Australasian Civil Process Act.[208] Already a more efficient jurisdiction and judgments scheme than the common law allowed, the model was gradually revised and simplified after it was adapted in the Australian federation. The first Service and Execution of Process Act 1901 (Cth) maintained the Australasian Civil Process Act's heads of jurisdiction within Australia for State courts,[209] but eliminated all defences to the interstate enforcement of judgments.[210] Then, the Service and Execution of Process Act 1992 (Cth) eliminated the need for the traditional grounds of long-arm jurisdiction to establish competence in interstate proceedings. In effect, as the colonies and States of Australia gradually integrated, the 1886 model was rationalised and extended. Legal certainty was improved for social and economic relationships of growing complexity by progressively simpler rules of adjudicative and enforcement jurisdiction. And, unexpectedly, the rules of jurisdiction, though not of judgments, became even more dependent on common law institutions. Jurisdiction was based at common law on valid service of a writ within the state,[211] but the legislation successively extended the run of the writ to the Australian national border and, now, to the borders of the whole Tasman world. From 1992, *forum conveniens* became the central coordinating principle in the scheme for the exercise of jurisdiction. And in moving into this judicial area with Australia, New Zealand has reinforced its willingness to participate in an

[205] A Ross, *New Zealand Aspirations in the Pacific in Nineteenth Century* (Oxford, Oxford University Press, 1964) 156.

[206] ibid, 155–56.

[207] Australasian Civil Process Act 1886 (FCA) s 8.

[208] Australasian Judgments Act 1886 (FCA) s 3.

[209] Service and Execution of Process Act 1901 (Cth) s 11.

[210] Service and Execution of Process Act 1901 (Cth) s 21.

[211] *Laurie v Carroll* (1958) 98 CLR 310, 322; *Mobil Oil Australia Pty Ltd v State of Victoria* (2002) 211 CLR 1, 23, 36.

Australasian confederation that is more highly integrated, yet more respectful of New Zealand sovereignty, than anything that was contemplated in 1885 or 1901.

It is doubtful that the territorial reach of this scheme could expand any further. A theme of this chapter has been that, as remarkable as this civil jurisdiction and judgments scheme may be, it is only likely to work well in the distinctive conditions of the Tasman relationship. It is too dependent on a high level of mutual national trust that allows a judicial scheme to function just by cooperation but without undermining legal certainty. And it is too dependent on the underlying common law tradition. The countries may be outward looking, but 'together alone'. The trans-Tasman scheme needs fine-tuning, but its basic structures are the best for the judicial area. There is nevertheless ample opportunity, just between Australia and New Zealand, to deepen the countries' integration further under a bilateral private international law.

7

Trans-Tasman Court Proceedings and Regulatory Enforcement

DAVID GODDARD

I. Introduction

The Trans-Tasman Proceedings regime, which came into force in October 2013, has strong claims to be the most innovative and comprehensive regime adopted by any two states to govern cross-border court proceedings, enforcement of judgments and regulatory enforcement. The regime is set out in a Treaty between Australia and New Zealand, and is implemented by parallel legislation in each country.[1] The proposals that led to this legislation were developed by a working group of which I was a member, which was established to review current arrangements concerning trans-Tasman civil proceedings and regulatory enforcement, and to develop proposals for reform.[2]

In this chapter I outline briefly the rationale for these reforms, and their practical significance. I also touch on some of the other methods that might have been adopted to achieve similar outcomes, and why the working group's recommendations took the form that they did.

[1] The Treaty is known as the Agreement Between the Government of Australia and the Government of New Zealand on Trans-Tasman Court Proceedings and Regulatory Enforcement 2008. The implementing legislation is the Trans-Tasman Proceedings Act 2010 (Cth) and the Trans-Tasman Proceedings Act 2010 (NZ).

[2] Trans-Tasman Working Group, *Trans-Tasman Court Proceedings and Regulatory Enforcement: A Report by the Trans-Tasman Working Group* (December 2006), available at: justice.govt.nz/publications/global-publications/t/trans-tasman-court-proceedings-and-regulatory-enforcement-a-report-by-the-trans-tasman-working-group-december-2006/publication (last accessed 19 March 2014).

II. Court Proceedings and Regulatory Enforcement: The Previous Position

Despite the close relationship between Australia and New Zealand, and the many coordination initiatives that have been implemented over the past quarter century, when it comes to trans-Tasman civil proceedings our pre-Trans-Tasman Proceedings Act laws treated each other largely the same as any other foreign country. And there was even less cooperation in the area of regulatory enforcement.

In the context of civil proceedings, the rules on when proceedings could be served on a defendant in the other country were exactly the same as those applied when serving proceedings in—say—Kazakhstan. The rules on enforcement of judgments were also the same as those applied to judgments of any other court, with a few very minor procedural differences.[3] Many judgments of Australian courts were not enforceable in New Zealand—for example, judgments given by default (where the defendant had not contractually submitted to Australian jurisdiction), judgments awarding non-monetary relief—eg an injunction, or specific performance, and interlocutory orders. This could lead to duplication of proceedings, and even in some cases to an inability to obtain effective relief.

Australia and New Zealand also applied the same rules for deciding whether to 'give way' to proceedings in the other country that each applied vis-à-vis proceedings in any other country. And just to complicate the position, these rules differed (and still do differ) in important ways under New Zealand and Australian law,[4] creating a real risk of overlapping proceedings.

[3] The basic regime for recognition of foreign judgments is a common law regime, which provides for unilateral recognition of final money judgments if certain requirements are met. Both countries also have legislation that provides for registration and enforcement of certain foreign judgments, derived from a 1930s UK regime for reciprocal enforcement of final money judgments. This regime applies to judgments from many Commonwealth countries, and also France. The registration regime was extended slightly in the trans-Tasman context in the early 1990s, but these extensions had little or no practical effect: the most ambitious provisions of the 1992 reforms were never brought into force. One significant feature of the 1992 amendments is that they enable tax judgments in one country to be enforced in the other: but this does not assist private litigants.

[4] The New Zealand courts apply a *forum non conveniens* test, seeking to identify the country in which the proceeding can most suitably be tried in the interests of all the parties and for the ends of justice: *Wing Hung Printing Co v Saito Offshore Pty Ltd* [2011] 1 NZLR 754 (CA); *Spiliada Maritime Corp v Cansulex Ltd* [1987] AC 460 (HL). The Australian courts apply the test established in *Voth v Manildra Flour Mills* (1990) 171 CLR 538, which asks whether the Australian court is a clearly inappropriate court to decide the dispute. These different tests created the potential, where parallel proceedings were brought in the two countries, for a finding by the New Zealand court that it was the more appropriate forum, and by the Australian court that it was not a clearly inappropriate forum, with the result that both sets of proceedings would continue in parallel. See eg *In Marriage of Gilmore* (1993) 110 FLR 311 (Family Court of Australia) and *Gilmore v Gilmore* [1993] NZFLR 561 (NZ High Court).

Only in the area of service of subpoenas requiring a person to give evidence, and the taking of evidence by audio- or video-link, had we put in place special rules that reflect the frequency with which disputes have connections with people and assets on both sides of the Tasman.[5]

This means that disputes with a very close connection with one country often had to be litigated in the other, to obtain effective interim or final relief. In some cases, duplicate proceedings in both countries were required.

When it comes to regulatory proceedings—court action to enforce compliance with a regulatory regime, or to seek a penalty or fine for non-compliance—the rules were even more restrictive. Civil penalty and civil enforcement proceedings (eg seeking an injunction to require compliance with the regulatory regime) issued in one country could generally be served on a defendant in the other country. But no resulting order—even a monetary penalty—imposed in the country hearing the proceedings could be enforced in the other.[6]

The position in relation to trans-Tasman service of criminal proceedings was unclear (it may have been possible in some cases, with the assistance of the other country's Government), and resulting orders could not be enforced. Extradition is not much use in the regulatory context, for two reasons: it is only available for the most serious criminal offences, and for obvious reasons it is limited to natural persons.

It was not possible to bring enforcement proceedings (civil or criminal) in one country based on the laws of the other country.

The previous rules led to some significant gaps in regulatory regimes—in particular consumer protection law, securities law, and competition law—where not infrequently the wrongdoer was situated in one country, and those harmed by the breaches were in the other country, even where the two countries' regulatory policy goals (and laws) were very similar.

III. The Impetus for Reform

These issues did not receive much attention in the early stages of the Closer Economic Relations Arrangement between Australia and New Zealand (1983),[7] or even when we began to put in place mutual recognition regimes founded on equivalence of regulatory regimes, such as the Trans-Tasman Mutual Recognition

[5] See the Evidence and Procedure (New Zealand) Act 1994 (Cth), and the Evidence Act 2006 (NZ), Part 4, sub-part 1.

[6] There are some limited exceptions for breach of the competition law prohibitions on abuse of a dominant position in a trans-Tasman market: see Commerce Act 1986 (NZ), s 36A; Competition and Consumer Act 2010 (Cth), s 46A.

[7] The Australia-New Zealand Closer Economic Relations Trade Agreement, a bilateral free trade arrangement covering trade in goods and services, was concluded and entered into force in 1983.

Arrangement which came into force in 1998.[8] They began to attract more attention in the last decade, for two reasons:

— the gaps in enforcement became an issue in their own right, as regulators and Governments became concerned about the potential for firms in one country to exploit enforcement gaps in areas such as consumer protection and securities law;
— other coordination initiatives—the proposed trans-Tasman therapeutic products regulatory regime, mutual recognition of securities offerings, proposals to facilitate cross-border provision of services as an extension to the Trans-Tasman Mutual Recognition Acts—led to concerns being expressed about trans-Tasman enforcement issues, and a number of parallel proposals for enhanced enforcement regimes. It seemed sensible to tackle these concerns in a single coherent and principled way, rather than having a number of ad hoc and differing regimes in place.

These concerns, and a broader desire to ensure that the appropriate legal infrastructure was in place to support continuing coordination, led to the establishment in 2003 by the Prime Ministers of Australia and New Zealand of an officials working group known as the 'Trans-Tasman Working Group on Court Proceedings and Regulatory Enforcement' (the Working Group).

IV. Identifying a Model for Reform

Many of the same concerns had previously arisen in the interstate context in Australia, and became increasingly acute in the second half of the twentieth century. They were addressed in Australia through a number of initiatives, including:

— the Service and Execution of Process Act 1992 (Cth), which resulted from recommendations in an Australian Law Reform Commission report;[9]
— cross-vesting legislation, which enables superior courts in the Australian States and Territories to exercise the jurisdiction and powers of all the other Australian superior courts in certain circumstances.[10]

The Service and Execution of Process Act is widely regarded as an effective, simple and well-functioning regime. Few difficulties or concerns have been

[8] The Arrangement is implemented by the Trans-Tasman Mutual Recognition Act 1997 (Cth) and the Trans-Tasman Mutual Recognition Act 1997 (NZ).

[9] Australian Law Reform Commission, *Service and Execution of Process* Report No 40 (Sydney, Commonwealth of Australia, 1987), available at: www.austlii.edu.au/au/other/alrc/publications/reports/40/ (last accessed 19 March 2014).

[10] Jurisdiction of Courts (Cross-Vesting) Act 1987 (Cth), and legislation of the same name in all the Australian States and Territories.

identified by commentators, and those that have been identified relate mainly to interstate custodial processes.

It is not therefore surprising that one of the possibilities considered by the Working Group (in fact, on the initiative of its New Zealand members) was to adopt a trans-Tasman regime modelled on the Service and Execution of Process Act. Initial research and analysis confirmed that the Service and Execution of Process Act was working effectively—indeed, the Working Group struggled to identify any concerns, theoretical or practical, in the areas in which we were interested.[11]

One key difference between the Australian interstate context and the trans-Tasman context is that there is the potential for differences in public policy to arise in the trans-Tasman context, with separate polities and legislatures, and no over-arching constitutional arrangements to specify the sphere of application of otherwise inconsistent policies and laws. To ensure that neither country is required to give effect to judgments that are inconsistent with its own indigenous public policy, the Working Group considered it essential that a public policy defence be available, as with foreign judgments generally (but not under the Service and Execution of Process Act itself).

Another difference was identified in the context of interim relief, reinforced by the recent European experience with enforcement of interim orders. As the European Court of Justice has observed, a court in the place where assets or persons intended to be affected by an order are situated is often best placed to craft interim orders which are appropriate, and to modify and adapt these as required at the request of the respondent or of affected third parties (eg banks).[12] The Group considered that it was preferable for courts in each country to be given the power to act in aid of each other, and to craft appropriate interim orders for that purpose, rather than to provide for trans-Tasman enforcement of interim orders.

[11] One possible concern was that it might be oppressive for defendants to be sued at a distance and to be forced to apply for a stay, especially in cases involving small sums. It was suggested that lenders might centralise debt collecting of small sums, to the disadvantage of distant debtors. But even anecdotal evidence for this concern was sparse, there were no data to support it, and factors were identified that pointed the other way such as the increased cost of taking two sets of proceedings (to get judgment in one place, and then to enforce it in the debtor's residence). It was also pointed out that lenders were able to do this in the absence of the Service and Execution of Process Act, by including a submission to jurisdiction in lending documents—so this is not a new issue created by SEPA.

[12] *Denilauler v SNC Couchet Frères* [1980] ECR 1553, paras 15–17. In *Denilauler* the ECJ held that orders made ex parte cannot be enforced under the European instruments, but emphasised that this was not a concern, as the instruments expressly contemplate the courts in one Member State acting in aid of another, and generally this will be more appropriate in the context of urgent interim relief. Many European practitioners consider that in general it is quicker and less costly to seek interim relief in the country where the relevant assets or persons are located than to seek the orders in one country, and then apply to enforce them in another.

A discussion paper setting out proposals along these lines was released in August 2005.[13] Submissions were generally supportive of the proposals. A final report to the two Governments was submitted in December 2006.[14]

V. The Working Group's Recommendations

The principal recommendations of the Working Group were that a new regime should be adopted to govern Trans-Tasman court proceedings and regulatory enforcement, under which:

- civil proceedings issued in one country could be served in the other, without the leave of the court;[15]
- a defendant who considers that a court in another jurisdiction would be more appropriate could seek a stay on those grounds, and the test for a stay would be the same in both countries;[16]
- civil judgments from the courts of one country would be enforceable in the other country, using a simple registration procedure. This would extend to money and non-money judgments, and to default judgments where proceedings were served under the trans-Tasman service regime;
- enforcement of judgments from the other country could be refused on public policy grounds, but not on any other grounds. Other grounds that prevent enforcement of a foreign judgment under common law or the Commonwealth reciprocal enforcement regime (eg breach of natural justice) must be raised in the original jurisdiction;
- Australian and New Zealand courts would be able to grant interim relief in support of proceedings in the other country;

[13] Working Group, *Trans-Tasman Court Proceedings and Regulatory Enforcement: A Public Discussion Paper* (August 2005), available at: www.justice.govt.nz/publications/global-publications/t/trans-tasman-court-proceedings-and-regulatory-enforcement-a-public-discussion-paper-by-the-trans-tasman-working-group-published-in-august-2005/trans-tasman-court-proceedings-and-regulatory-enforcement-a-public-discussion-paper-by-the-trans-tasman-working-group-terms-of-reference-for-a-joint-working-group-of-officials-on-trans-tasman-court-proceedings-and-regulatory-enforcement (last visited 18 March 2014).

[14] Working Group, *Trans-Tasman Court Proceedings and Regulatory Enforcement: A Report by the Trans-Tasman Working Group* above n 2.

[15] This is possible in many cases already, under local rules governing service of proceedings abroad. But proceedings served in this manner will not result in a judgment enforceable in other countries, unless there is a submission to jurisdiction by agreement, or by appearance. The proposal would extend this facility to all civil proceedings.

[16] It is possible to seek a stay of proceedings in both countries, on the grounds that the proceedings should be heard elsewhere—but the tests applied differ, as explained in n 4 above. This recommendation effectively adopts the New Zealand *forum non conveniens* test for all trans-Tasman cases.

- civil penalty orders made in one country would be enforceable in the other country, unless the law of the latter provides that a particular penalty regime is to be excluded, or the public policy defence mentioned above applies;
- fines for criminal offences under certain designated regulatory regimes would be enforceable in the other country, in the same way as a civil judgment;
- the availability of trans-Tasman subpoenas would be extended;
- the use of audio- and video-links for trans-Tasman hearings would be facilitated. A party (and their local lawyer) could appear as of right by audio- or video-link in appearances concerning whether proceedings served under the trans-Tasman regime should be stayed. Other audio- and video-link appearances would require the leave of the relevant court.

It is worth pausing to note what was not proposed. There was never any suggestion that there should be a single court system for the two countries, or even a single final court of appeal—that was not necessary to solve these coordination issues (nor, of course, was it within the Working Group's terms of reference).

There was no support within the Working Group or submissions for going further and 'cross-vesting' jurisdiction under regulatory and penal statutes on an across-the-board basis.

Nor was there any suggestion that the whole of the law relating to enforcement of foreign judgments should be made the same, in both countries. And even in the area of civil penalties and enforcement orders, and regulatory fines, the focus was on making two broadly similar regimes with common policy goals work better together—not on trying to adopt a single regulatory regime in one or more areas.

All that was proposed was, in effect, an enhanced mutual recognition regime to replace (in the trans-Tasman context) a mix of common law unilateral recognition rules, statutory provisions which establish a Commonwealth reciprocal enforcement regime for money judgments, and some limited trans-Tasman mutual recognition arrangements developed over the last 15 or so years.

Consideration was given to other models for addressing these concerns. In Europe there is a long-standing regime for service and enforcement of civil judgments. And at the same time that the working group was developing its proposals, work was under way in the Hague under the auspices of the Hague Conference on Private International Law on proposals for a multilateral service and enforcement regime inspired by the European instruments.[17] But the European model had a number of features that made it unattractive in the trans-Tasman context: it is much more complex, and seeks to prescribe where different types of proceedings should

[17] The negotiations towards a broad convention on jurisdiction and enforcement of judgments were unsuccessful, not least because of differences between civilian and common law countries on the interplay between subject-matter-based jurisdiction rules, and 'give way' rules. Participants decided to pursue a more focused, less wide-ranging proposal for a convention on choice of court clauses, which resulted in the adoption in 2005 of a Convention on Choice of Court Agreements: see www.hcch.net/index_en.php?act=conventions.text&cid=98 (last accessed 19 March 2014).

be filed by reference to connecting factors between the court and the parties and/or the dispute, coupled, where there is more than one option, with a 'first to file' rule. The civilian countries that first adopted this regime did not have a *forum conveniens* rule like that of common law countries, which provides for a context-specific assessment of where particular proceedings should most appropriately be heard, and remain unenthusiastic about the introduction into their systems of any such rule.

Study of the European regime, and an awareness of the limits and complexities of that approach which had been identified in the context of the Hague negotiations, led to a strong preference within the Working Group for a much simpler regime built on our common acceptance of broad service rules coupled with an appropriateness test applied at the request of the defendant. With a shared legal culture and heritage, and very similar legal institutions, it was possible to go further, and use simpler tools, than in the more complex and predominantly civilian European context. The difference in volume and complexity of commentary on the European and Australian solutions to these same issues is very striking.

The absence of a single court that can authoritatively determine interpretation issues for both countries also militated against adoption of a regime that depended on a multiplicity of bright-line rules raising difficult interpretation issues, along the lines of the European instruments. The integrity and effectiveness of the proposed regime will not be impaired by occasional divergence in application of—for example—the 'give way' rule, though it is expected that the courts of each country will pay close attention to authorities from the other in developing the law in this area (as they have in the field of competition law, for example).

Some New Zealand observers of the coordination process bridle at proposals such as these which extend an Australian regime to New Zealand. Certainly I am no fan of the idea that Australian law should be adopted uncritically in New Zealand. But this was a case where the same coordination issues had been identified and tackled in Australia more than a decade earlier, and practical experience of the scheme was very positive. The basic structure was sound, and could readily be adapted to our ends. Some changes needed to be made to reflect the difference between the interstate and trans-Tasman context: in particular, retention of a public policy defence; and provision for interim relief to be granted in support of proceedings in the other country, rather than providing for interim orders to be enforced on a trans-Tasman basis. With those changes, the overall package was in our view well suited to the goals that had been identified.

VI. Implementation of the Working Group's Proposals

The Australian and New Zealand Governments accepted the Working Group's recommendations, and the Treaty providing for adoption of a new trans-Tasman proceedings regime was signed in July 2008. As noted earlier, legislation to implement the Trans-Tasman Proceedings Act regime was enacted in both New Zealand and Australia in 2010.

The Trans-Tasman Proceedings Act regime came into force in October 2013, when the necessary rules of court were finalised in all relevant jurisdictions.

VII. Reflections on the TTPA Initiative

In summary, it seems to me that the Trans-Tasman Proceedings Act regime shares a number of attributes of other trans-Tasman initiatives: prompted by specific concerns initially, but developed on the basis of generic principles; pragmatic; relatively simple in structure and content; and based on the concept of mutual recognition rather than on development of common institutions or common legal frameworks.

The TTPA regime is a good example of the context-specific approach to coordination that I described in a 2001 paper on business laws and regulatory institutions. As I said there:[18]

> The debate about business law coordination between Australia and New Zealand is often conducted at an abstract, broad-brush level, with arguments for or against greater coordination put forward based on general economic and legal principles. This paper seeks to develop that debate by exploring in some detail the principal mechanisms for business law coordination.
>
> My basic thesis is that successful coordination depends on developing and implementing models for coordination which are appropriate in a particular context, and that different models will be required depending on the objectives of coordination in that context. The question of whether broader or deeper coordination is desirable cannot be answered in the abstract. It needs to be addressed in relation to a particular sphere of business law, and the answer will depend to a significant degree on whether an appropriate model for coordination in that sphere can be identified and implemented in practice. Well designed coordination models are, at least in principle, capable of achieving the key objectives of coordination—in particular, reducing the costs of differences between business law regimes—without compromising voice for stakeholders in either country, or the accountability of legislators and regulators to those stakeholders.

The goals of the Working Group were to:

- reduce the costs of dispute resolution in the trans-Tasman context for individuals and businesses, and thus enhance access to justice and reduce the costs of cross-border dealings;

[18] David Goddard, 'Business Laws and Regulatory Institutions: Mechanisms for CER Coordination' in A Grimes, L Wevers and G Sullivan (eds), *States of Mind: Australia and New Zealand 1901–2001* (Wellington, Institute of Policy Studies and Stout Research Centre, 2002) 179.

— enhance the effectiveness of existing regulatory regimes such as consumer protection law, securities law and competition law in each country. The issues with which those regimes are concerned now frequently transcend borders, but the reach of the applicable laws does not;
— provide a simple and consistent framework for cross-border enforcement of regulatory regimes, to underpin future coordination initiatives, and reduce the costs and risks associated with such initiatives.

The Trans-Tasman Proceedings Act regime represents the minimum level of coordination required to achieve those objectives. It is based on a mutual recognition regime that has operated effectively within Australia for some 20 years, adapted to reflect differences between the interstate and trans-Tasman contexts. The costs of implementing the new rules are minimal. The Trans-Tasman Proceedings Act regime will give greater effect to shared elements of regulatory policy, without cutting across either country's freedom to pursue its own conception of public policy.

The Trans-Tasman Proceedings Act regime does not solve every cross-border litigation issue that arises in the trans-Tasman context. I am sure that with time and experience, it will be able to be refined and developed. And there are many other issues that need to be addressed to enhance access to justice, remove regulatory barriers to trans-Tasman dealings, and improve the quality and efficacy of regulation on both sides of the Tasman. But it is a useful generic measure that advances those goals in its own right, and provides the legal machinery to underpin other coordination initiatives such as mutual recognition of securities offerings, and the proposed Australia-New Zealand Therapeutic Products Agency.

Nor should the significance of these reforms be underestimated: they represent the furthest reaching proposals of this kind as between any two sovereign states with separate legal systems, so far as I am aware. It is a measure of their clear desirability and appropriateness that despite this, they have produced little excitement or surprise—except, on some occasions, surprise that we are not doing this already!

IV

Drawing from Overseas Perspectives

8

What, if Anything, can Australia Learn from the EU Experience?

ANDREW DICKINSON

I. Introduction[1]

In November 2012, the Attorney-General's Department released, via its consultation website, two consultation papers.[2] These papers are the first public-facing element of the project initiated under the auspices of the Standing Council on Law and Justice (SCLJ) to review the state of private international law in Australia. This review is timely. In the past few years, the increasing number of disputes before Australian courts with an external aspect, and greater competition between legal systems as markets for dispute resolution, have called into question the suitability of Australian private international law rules for modern conditions.[3]

From an economic policy standpoint, it is vital that Australia has a legal environment that encourages beneficial cross-border movements of goods, persons, services and capital, and affords appropriate protection to the natural and legal persons involved. Moreover, cross-border transactions and dispute resolution are sources of economic activity in their own right, commoditising Australian law and the Australian judicial systems as resources capable of legitimate exploitation by economic actors (law and accountancy firms, litigation service providers and financial institutions) in the creation of wealth and jobs. At the same time, there are wider policy interests in play, and which must be taken into account. Most obviously, rapid growth of international litigation in domestic courts may create problems in terms of public funding and longer waiting times for domestic and foreign litigants. Moreover, by engaging, sometimes directly but more often

[1] This chapter is based on a paper given at *Facing Outwards: Australian Private International Law in the 21st Century*, a Conference held at the University of Sydney, 10 April 2013.

[2] See below, Annexes 1 and 2. The first consultation paper, entitled 'Reducing legal complexity of cross-border transactions and relationships: Driving micro-economic reform through the establishment of more cohesive and clearer jurisdictional, applicable law and choice of court rules' (Attorney-General's Consultation Paper) is the focus of this chapter.

[3] See also the contributions in this volume by the Professor Mary Keyes (Chapter two), Hon Chief Justice James Allsop AO and Daniel Ward (Chapter three) and Dr Andrew Bell SC (Chapter four).

indirectly, with foreign legal systems and other external regulatory instrumentalities, private international law has an obvious foreign relations policy aspect, capable of signalling Australia's approval or disapproval of what passes beyond its borders.

In the past 20 years, putting to one side two notable decisions of the High Court[4] and the legislation on personal property security and Trans-Tasman Proceedings[5] (only recently in force and yet to be seriously tested), Australian private international law has been relatively static. The relevant statutory framework remains, in most areas, as it was when the Service and Execution of Process Act (Cth) was enacted in 1992. In the same period, there have been important developments in other jurisdictions. China and Japan have adopted new private international law codifications.[6] The Canadian Supreme Court has continued its purging of the old English common law in favour of rules inspired, in part, by its constitutional structures and, in part, by the concept of 'comity' beloved of the Canadian judiciary.[7] Perhaps most significantly (at least for the present writer, as a frequent visitor to Australian shores from the United Kingdom), the European Union has been a hub of activity ever since the conferral of legislative competence on its institutions by the Treaty of Amsterdam in 1999.[8] Even before this date, Member States of the EU in its former guise as the European Economic Community (an organisation founded by the Treaty of Rome in 1958) had already

[4] *Regie des Usines Renault SA v Zhang* (2010) 210 CLR 491 (stays of proceedings and law applicable to tort); *Neilson v Overseas Projects Corporation of Victoria* (2005) 223 CLR 331 (law applicable to tort), as to which see Section III.B below. The High Court's important decision in *BHP Billiton Ltd v Schultz* (2004) 221 CLR 400 concerned intra-Australian jurisdictional issues, and the later decision in *Puttick v Tenon Ltd* (2008) 238 CLR 265 (stays of proceedings) neither established new principles nor, it is submitted, applied existing principles in a satisfactory fashion. A majority of decisions at the State appellate level during this period have also concerned stays of proceedings.

[5] Personal Property Securities Act 2009 (Cth); Trans-Tasman Proceedings Act 2010 (Cth), as amended. On the latter Act, which entered into force on 11 October 2013, see the contributions in this volume by David Goddard QC (Chapter five) and Professor Reid Mortensen (Chapter six).

[6] See Law of the People's Republic of China on the Laws Applicable to Foreign-related Civil Relations (adopted 28 October 2010, English translation available at conflictoflaws.net/News/2011/01/PIL-China.pdf, last visited 3 March 2014); Act for the Partial Amendment of the Code of Civil Procedure and the Civil Interim Relief Act (Japan, promulgated on 2 May 2011; for commentary and English translation, see K Takahashi, *Japan's New Act on International Jurisdiction*, available at: www.smashwords.com/books/view/81536, last visited 3 March 2014); Act on the General Rules of Application of Laws [*Hō no Tekiyōni Kansuru Tsūsokuhō*], Law No 10 of 1898 (Japan, as newly titled and amended 21 June 2006), English translation available at: blog.hawaii.edu/aplpj/files/2011/11/APLPJ_08.1_anderson.pdf, last visited 3 March 2014).

[7] See, in particular, *Beals v Saldanha* [2003] 3 SCR 416 (enforcement of foreign judgments) and *Club Resorts Ltd v Van Breda* [2012] 1 SCR 572 (personal jurisdiction), with the reasoning in each case being founded on the concept of a 'real and substantial connection' resting in the first case on considerations of comity and in the second on a constitutional imperative. The root of both judgments can be traced to the earlier decision of the Supreme Court in *Morguard v De Savoye* [1990] 3 SCR 1077 (inter-Provincial judgments). The approach in the Canadian cases is open to criticism as engendering considerable uncertainty for litigants, and as exceeding the normal limits of judicial law-making, trespassing into an area more appropriately dealt with by legislative reform.

[8] See EC Treaty (pre-2010), Arts 61 and 65; Treaty on the Functioning of the European Union (post-2010), Art 81.

engaged in important joint ventures in this area. Of these, the most significant were the 1968 Brussels Convention (jurisdiction and the enforcement of judgments in civil and commercial matters[9]) and the 1980 Rome Convention (law applicable to contractual obligations[10]).

Since the turn of the century, and despite a pre-2010 restriction on their competence to measures 'necessary for the proper functioning of the internal market',[11] the legislative organs of the EU[12] have gone into overdrive. In the field of civil justice alone, the Directory of European Union Legislation[13] records the adoption of notable measures with respect to: insolvency (2000);[14] jurisdiction and the recognition and enforcement of judgments in civil and commercial matters (2000, 2008, 2012);[15] jurisdiction and the recognition and enforcement of judgments in matrimonial and parental responsibility matters (2000, 2003);[16] the law applicable to contractual obligations (2008);[17] the law applicable to non-contractual obligations (2007);[18] maintenance (2009);[19] divorce and legal separation (2010);[20] wills

[9] [1998] OJ C27/1 (consolidated version).

[10] [1998] OJ C27/34 (consolidated version).

[11] For the background, discussion and references to other materials, see A Dickinson, 'European Private International Law—Embracing New Horizons or Mourning the Past?' (2005) 1 *Journal of Private International Law* 197.

[12] The EU Council (composed of representatives of the Member State governments, for present purposes mainly justice ministers) and EU Parliament (composed of elected representatives from the Member States).

[13] eur-lex.europa.eu/en/legis/latest/chap1920.htm, last visited 3 March 2014.

[14] Council Regulation (EC) No 1346/2000 on insolvency proceedings ([2000] OJ L160/1).

[15] Council Regulation (EC) No 44/2001 on jurisdiction and the recognition and enforcement of judgments in civil and commercial matters ([2001] OJ L12/1) (Brussels I Regulation); Council Decision concerning the conclusion of the Convention on jurisdiction and the recognition and enforcement of judgments in civil and commercial matters ([2009] OJ L147/1), implementing the second Lugano Convention; Regulation (EU) No 1215/2012 of the European Parliament and of the Council on jurisdiction and the recognition and enforcement of judgments in civil and commercial matters ([2012] OJ L351/1) (Recast Brussels I Regulation).

[16] Council Regulation (EC) No 2201/2003 of 27 November 2003 concerning jurisdiction and the recognition and enforcement of judgments in matrimonial matters and the matters of parental responsibility, repealing Regulation (EC) No 1347/2000 ([2003] OJ L338/1).

[17] Regulation (EC) No 593/2008 of the European Parliament and of the Council on the law applicable to contractual obligations (Rome I) ([2008] OJ L177/6). See also Commission Decision of 22 December 2008 on the request from the United Kingdom to accept Regulation (EC) No 593/2008 ([2009] OJ L10/22) (Rome I Regulation).

[18] Regulation (EC) No 864/2007 of the European Parliament and of the Council on the law applicable to non-contractual obligations (Rome II) ([2007] OJ L199/40) (Rome II Regulation).

[19] Regulation (EC) No 4/2009 of the European Parliament and of the Council on jurisdiction, applicable law, recognition and enforcement of decisions and cooperation in matters relating to maintenance obligations ([2009] OJ L7/1). See also Commission Decision of 8 June 2009 on the intention of the United Kingdom to accept Council Regulation (EC) No 4/2009 ([2009] OJ L149/73); Council Decision on the approval, on behalf of the European Union, of the Hague Convention of 23 November 2007 on the International Recovery of Child Support and Other Forms of Family Maintenance ([2011] OJ L192/39).

[20] Regulation (EU) No 1259/2010 of the European Parliament and of the Council implementing enhanced cooperation in the area of the law applicable to divorce and legal separation ([2010] OJ L343/10). The UK has not participated in the adoption of this instrument.

and succession (2012);[21] service (2000, 2007);[22] the taking of evidence overseas (2001);[23] mediation (2009);[24] the cross-border enforcement of uncontested claims (2004, 2006);[25] small claims (2007);[26] and a myriad of ancillary measures.[27]

These legislative measures, building on the earlier conventions referred to above, have transformed the landscape of private international law in the Member States.[28] In the United Kingdom, the common law and legislation built on common law foundations is now of much reduced significance, prompting Lord Collins of Mapesbury, in his role as the general editor of *Dicey, Morris & Collins, The Conflict of Laws* to comment that:[29]

> Professor Dicey, and even Dr Morris, could not have foreseen the huge impact which a supra-national body of law, namely European law, would have on the subject of the conflict of laws. Since the last edition was published in 2006, the EU has demonstrated its intention to legislate for virtually the whole area.

The authors of *Nygh's Conflict of Laws in Australia*, in turn, suggest that English materials are 'of ever-decreasing utility for Australian lawyers as they understandably focus on the relationship between the United Kingdom and its

[21] Regulation (EU) No 650/2012 of the European Parliament and of the Council on jurisdiction, applicable law, recognition and enforcement of decisions and acceptance and enforcement of authentic instruments in matters of succession and on the creation of a European Certificate of Succession ([2012] OJ L201/107). The UK has not participated in the adoption of this instrument.

[22] Regulation (EC) No 1393/2007 of the European Parliament and of the Council of 13 November 2007 on the service in the Member States of judicial and extrajudicial documents in civil or commercial matters (service of documents), and repealing Council Regulation (EC) No 1348/2000 ([2007] OJ L324/79).

[23] Council Regulation (EC) No 1206/2001 of 28 May 2001 on cooperation between the courts of the Member States in the taking of evidence in civil or commercial matters ([2001] OJ L174/1 [27.6.2001]).

[24] Directive 2008/52/EC of the European Parliament and of the Council of 21 May 2008 on certain aspects of mediation in civil and commercial matters ([2008] OJ L136/5).

[25] Regulation (EC) No 805/2004 of the European Parliament and of the Council creating a European Enforcement Order for uncontested claims ([2004] OJ L143/15 [30 April 2004]); Regulation (EC) No 1896/2006 of the European Parliament and of the Council of 12 December 2006 creating a European order for payment procedure ([2006] OJ L399/1 [30 December 2006]).

[26] Regulation (EC) No 861/2007 of the European Parliament and of the Council of 11 July 2007 establishing a European Small Claims Procedure ([2007] OJ L199/1).

[27] For a detailed list of the legislation in force, see: eur-lex.europa.eu/en/legis/latest/chap1920.htm, last visited 3 March 2014. Further measures in the pipeline include legislation on matrimonial property matters and the attachment of bank accounts. At present, the UK is not participating in the adoption of either of these measures.

[28] Of the 28 current Member States (Croatia acceded on 1 July 2013), Denmark does not participate in civil justice measures, and the UK and Ireland participate only on an opt-in basis. Nevertheless, some of the instruments (notably the Brussels I Regulation) have been extended to Denmark by treaty, and both the UK and Ireland have participated in the three key instruments in the commercial sphere (Brussels I, Rome I, Rome II). Finally, the 2007 Lugano (II) Convention extends the rules on jurisdiction and the recognition and enforcement of judgments to Iceland, Norway and Switzerland as well.

[29] *Dicey, Morris & Collins, The Conflict of Laws*, 15th edn (London, Sweet & Maxwell, 2012) Preface. Professor Briggs has recently described the subject in England as 'a European legal structure of private international law, if one with a residiuum of common law content' (A Briggs, *The Conflict of Laws*, 3rd edn (Oxford, Oxford University Press 2013) Preface).

European neighbours rather than on the traditional common law conflict of laws'.[30]

The title of this chapter asks: 'What, if anything, can Australia learn from the EU experience?'. As someone whose attitudes and approaches to private international law have been shaped largely by experiences of the latter part of what has been described, with just reason, as the European private international law revolution,[31] my own personal view that there is great deal to be learned, in terms both of process and substance. That is not to say that the EU has always got things right, for it quite plainly has not. Nor is it to put forward the EU's legislation as a template to be followed slavishly in drafting future legislation for Australia. Instead, the learning process must necessarily be more selective, taking the best and avoiding the worst of what the European experience has to offer.

By way of an prefatory comment, it is perhaps trite to observe that it is desirable and useful in a reform project such as that currently underway in Australia to look to the practice of other legal systems (as competitors and potential collaborators in the regulation of cross-border transactions and dispute resolution), as well as to the work of international organisations, such as the Hague Conference on Private International Law and the European Union. The sphere of possible influences upon the current review should not be limited to other systems with a common law tradition, particularly as the nation's trade in goods and services directs her towards legal systems with other traditions and approaches. The European Union provides, therefore, a potentially useful avenue of enquiry, albeit by no means the only one.

At the same time, Australia should not shy from retaining or fashioning its own solutions in these areas if it concludes that they meet the needs of those who enter into cross-border transactions and litigants, as well as the wider public interests already alluded to. It is necessary to strike the right balance. In this regard, the EU may be argued to have strayed from individuality into insularity. The EU's private international law *acquis* is driven by the perceived needs of the internal market in persons, goods, services and capital mandated by the EU treaties, and influenced by other EU constitutional imperatives such as the protection of consumers and of the environment. Inevitably, it is also heavily influenced, both in its structure and overall approach and in the content of individual rules, by the legal systems of

[30] M Davies, A Bell and P Brereton (eds), *Nygh's Conflict of Laws in Australia*, 8th edn (Sydney, Lexis Nexis Butterworths, 2010) Preface. Now in its 9th edn, 2013.

[31] R Michaels, 'The New European Choice-of-Law Revolution' (2008) 82 *Tulane Law Review* 1607. Cf J von Hein 'Something Old and Something Borrowed, but Nothing New? Rome II and the European Choice of Law Revolution' (2008) 82 *Tulane Law Review* 1663 and S Symeonides, 'The American Revolution and the European Evolution in Choice of Law: Reciprocal Lessons' (2008) 82 *Tulane Law Review* 1741, preferring the terminology of evolution to that of revolution. In referring to 'European private international law' and 'European experience', the author is conscious that there are many States in Europe that are not part of the EU and have their own rules of private international law. Some, most notably Switzerland, have their own, very detailed private international law codifications (Federal Code of Private International Law of 18 December 1987). It is hoped that, for present purposes, this over-simplification will be forgiven.

the Member States.[32] Although the EU has sometimes looked beyond its borders in seeking solutions to particular problems,[33] its methods and rules are home grown—made in the EU to serve the EU's policies and objectives. In consequence, the EU's legislative instruments display what may appear to be a certain disregard for external legal systems and actors.

This can be seen most clearly in two features of the Brussels I regime governing jurisdiction and the recognition and enforcement of judgments.[34] First, the Regulation applies to all civil and commercial matters falling within its scope, regardless of whether the litigating parties are based or conducting activity in the EU. However, those not domiciled in the EU are significantly disadvantaged in comparison with their EU counterparts. Whereas the latter enjoy the protection of rules that are founded on the cornerstone principle that defendants should, in general, be sued in the place of their domicile,[35] non-EU domiciled parties remain for the most part subject to the Member States' pre-existing 'exorbitant' rules of jurisdiction, without restriction.[36] Both groups, however, are subject to the same set of streamlined rules for the recognition and enforcement of judgments, which in general preclude examination of the jurisdiction of the court of origin, whatever its basis.[37] Although, in 2010, the European Commission advanced proposals

[32] Some would suggest a bias in favour of systems with a civil law tradition, and against those with a common law tradition (see, for example, the discussion in Dickinson, above n 11; T Hartley, 'The European Union and the Systematic Dismantling of the Common Law of Conflict of Laws' (2005) 54 *International Comparative Law Quarterly* 813; A Fiorini, 'The codification of private international law in Europe—could the Community learn from the experience of mixed jurisdictions?' (2008) 23 *Tulane European and Civil Law Forum* 1; and J Harris, 'Understanding the English Response to the Europeanization of Private International Law' (2008) *Journal of Private International Law* 347). The position is undoubtedly more nuanced than this. No doubt, the instruments on jurisdiction and the recognition and enforcement of judgments have a strong civilian influence. That is inevitable, given that the EU had no member with a common law tradition at the time that the Brussels Convention was concluded in 1968. In the case of later instruments (notably the Rome I and Rome II Regulations), the outcomes appear more dependent on negotiating influence, acumen and resources than on a civil/common law divide. As the United Kingdom has engaged actively in negotiations for these instruments, so they have inevitably taken on some of the approaches and priorities of the conflict of laws in the common law world.

[33] For a notable example, see the Commission's Proposal for a Regulation on the law applicable to non-contractual obligations (COM(2003) 427 final) containing several references to the laws of Switzerland and other non-Member States.

[34] Above n 15.

[35] Brussels I Regulation, Art 2; Recast Brussels I Regulation, Art 4.

[36] Brussels I Regulation, Art 4; Recast Brussels I Regulation, Art 6. These rules include those listed in Art 3 of the Regulation (Recast, Art 5), which cannot be applied against persons domiciled in a Member State. They include jurisdiction based on service on a person present in the jurisdiction (England and Wales, common law), and jurisdiction based on the plaintiff's nationality (France, *Code Civil*, Art 14).

[37] Brussels I Regulation, Art 35(1); Recast Brussels I Regulation, Art 45(3). Australian residents are in a rather more favourable position insofar as the enforcement of judgments in the UK is concerned, since a derogation in Art 72 of the two Regulations (referring to Art 59 of the predecessor Brussels Convention) enables the UK to give effect to the terms of Art 3 of the reciprocal enforcement treaty between the two nations (Canberra, 23 August 1990, [1994] ATS 27). The latter provision contains an undertaking by the UK not to recognise or enforce any judgment of another Member State court given against a person domiciled or habitually resident in Australia in the circumstances described in Art 59

to harmonise the rules of jurisdiction over third country defendants,[38] the status quo is maintained in the recast Brussels I Regulation which will enter into force in early 2015.[39] Secondly, the Brussels I Regulation, at least in the form that currently applies, barely acknowledges the existence of legal systems outside the EU.[40] As an instrument concerned with the functioning of the EU's internal market, this comes perhaps as no surprise. However, a difficulty in practice has arisen as a result of more recent jurisprudence of the European Court of Justice, which has (a) denied that Member States have the power to decline Regulation-based jurisdiction on *forum conveniens* grounds, even in favour of a third state,[41] and (b) suggested that the Regulation sets out exclusively the grounds on which Member State courts may decline jurisdiction, thereby precluding (for example) a ruling declining jurisdiction on the grounds of an exclusive choice of court agreement in favour of third country court, pending proceedings (*lis pendens*) in a third country or the existence of a dispute relating to land in a third country.[42] The Recast Brussels I Regulation, which as noted above will enter into force in 2015, does contain new provisions which expressly empower Member State courts to stay proceedings in circumstances where a court in a non-Member State is seised first of proceedings.[43] Nevertheless, the absence of provisions in the recast Regulation dealing with the other situations of connection to a third country mentioned above supports a narrow interpretation of the powers of Member State courts to decline jurisdiction in favour of third country proceedings, and demonstrates in any event the relatively insular approach of the Brussels I regime.[44]

(ie subject to certain limits, where the Member State court giving jurisdiction has relied on a rule of jurisdiction of local, as opposed to EU, origin).

[38] Proposal for a Regulation on jurisdiction and the recognition and enforcement of judgments in civil and commercial matters (Recast) (COM(2010) 748 final), p 8 and Arts 4(2) and 25–26 in particular.

[39] See Recast Brussels I Regulation, Art 6.

[40] Brussels I Regulation, Art 72 makes provision to give effect to agreements between a Member State and a third country for the protection of judgment debtors domiciled or habitually resident in that third country (n 37 above). Recital (5) refers to the 1988 Lugano Convention concluded between certain Member States and EFTA States (Iceland, Norway and Switzerland).

[41] Case C-281/02, *Owusu v Jackson* [2005] ECR I-1383.

[42] See, in particular, Opinion 01/03, *Competence of the Community to conclude the new Lugano Convention on jurisdiction and the recognition and enforcement of judgments in civil and commercial matters* [2006] ECR I-1145, [153]; Case C-420/07, *Apostolides v Orams* [2000] ECR I-3571, Opinion of Advocate General Kokott, [84]–[86]. See also *Goshawk Dedicated Ltd v Life Receivables Ireland Ltd* [2009] IESC 7; *Catalyst Investment Group Ltd v Lewinsohn* [2010] EWHC 1964 (Ch); [2010] 1 Ch 218. Compare *Ferrexpo AG v Gilson Investments Ltd* [2012] EWHC 721, at [128]–[155], [162]–[191], in which an English court reached the conclusion that the Regulation did support a stay in favour of proceedings in a third State in some circumstances. It is doubtful whether the Court of Justice of the European Union would agree with that proposition if questions of this kind were referred to it.

[43] Recast Brussels I Regulation, Arts 33 and 34.

[44] In the case of choice of court agreements, the European Union has for some time been considering accession to the 2005 Hague Convention on Choice of Court Agreements (see below, text to n 126), and the absence of a specific rule for third country choice of court agreements in the Recast Brussels I Regulation has been justified on the basis that it will encourage other states to do likewise to secure reciprocal treatment from the EU. This policy position has attracted criticism from commentators who note that the Hague Convention offers only a limited solution, with important categories of contract being excluded.

The features just described, no doubt, render the EU model for jurisdiction and the recognition and enforcement of judgments less easy to export to other legal systems, which may consider themselves and their citizens ill-treated under its provisions. The failure of efforts at the turn of this century at the Hague Conference to conclude a global convention on civil jurisdiction can, in part, be attributed to a lack of buyers for the European product.[45]

The EU experience also cautions that it is important to build and maintain confidence in the process of reform, and, in particular, to involve stakeholders not only at the beginning of the process but also on an ongoing basis and in particular when detailed legislative proposals are formulated. Too often, the rather secretive legislative processes deployed in Brussels and Strasbourg have resulted in a level of criticism of the end product that is unwarranted by the quality of the texts. Furthermore, on occasions, the legitimacy of the legislative process has rightly been called into question as a result of a failure by EU institutions to consult adequately or at all. The processes leading to the adoption of the Rome II Regulation, in which internal differences within the Commission resulted in a planned Green Paper being shelved, and the Rome I Regulation, in which the Commission refused to undertake an impact assessment despite making a proposal to effect significant changes to the existing regime, did not reflect well on the EU or its institutions. By contrast, the Commission's approach to the recent revision of the Brussels I Regulation, involving the preparation of detailed legal and empirical studies coupled with formal and informal consultations at every stage is to be lauded.[46] In Australia, the Attorney-General's Department has undoubtedly started out on the right track with the launch of its consultation website and the publication of two detailed consultation papers.[47] It is vital that the momentum is maintained.

The EU has also begun to embrace non-legislative solutions to the difficulties resulting from differences between the legal (including procedural) systems of the

See A Layton QC, submission to the European Parliament available at: www.europarl.europa.eu/RegData/etudes/note/join/2011/453203/IPOL-JURI_NT(2011)453203_EN.pdf (last visited 5 March 2014) 12–13; P Rogerson, '*Lis Pendens* and Third States: The Commission's Proposed Changes to the Brussels I Regulation' in E Lein (ed), *The Brussels I Review Proposal Uncovered* (London, British Institute of International and Comparative Law, 2012) 103–24. See further Section III.E below.

[45] For commentary on the Hague Judgments Project, see, for example, Permanent Bureau, 'Some reflections on the present state of negotiations on the judgments project in the context of the future work programme of the Conference' (Preliminary Doc No 16 of February 2002, available at: www.hcch.net/upload/wop/jdgm_bibl.pdf, last visited 5 March 2014); G-P Calliess, 'Value-added Norms, Local Litigation, and Global Enforcement: Why the Brussels-Philosophy failed in The Hague' (2004) 5 *German Law Journal* 1497 and the collected papers in JJ Barcelo and KM Clermont (eds), *A Global Law of Jurisdiction and Judgments: Lessons from The Hague* (The Hague, Kluwer Law International, 2002). A comprehensive bibliography is available at: www.hcch.net/upload/wop/jdgm_bibl.pdf (last visited 5 March 2014).

[46] See A Dickinson, 'Surveying the Proposed Brussels I *Bis* Regulation—Solid Foundations but Renovation Needed' (2010) 12 *Yearbook of Private International Law* 247, 250.

[47] Attorney-General's Consultation Paper, [9] ('The project's central methodology is to conduct a comprehensive public consultation to collect evidence'.).

Member States. A significant body of legal information concerning these matters, as well as the EU private international law instruments, is accessible online via the European eJustice Portal[48] and Judicial Atlas.[49] The provision of information centrally or through insurers has also recently been tabled among the possible solutions to difficulties resulting from the diverse treatment in the Member States' legal systems of limitation periods in traffic accident cases.[50]

Finally, it may be noted that the EU has approached the development of its system of private international law rules incrementally and over time, as and when problems in the functioning of the internal market have been identified, rather than by a single instrument. Although a 'European private international code', consolidating existing instruments and possibly adding gap-filling rules, has been enthusiastically discussed from time to time,[51] and the Legal Affairs Committee (JURI) of the European Parliament has pursued the matter of its own initiative,[52] there appears at present little momentum for the project in the corridors of Brussels. Almost 50 years have passed since the Benelux nations first proposed an extensive codification of private international law rules among the Member States, but the approach of the European private international law experiment has been to proceed step by step, and there remain significant gaps in the *acquis* (for example, in relation to the law applicable to defamation and privacy and the acquisition and transfer of title to tangible movable and immovable property[53]). This incremental approach has served the European Union well. It seems likely to be the right approach for Australia too, enabling the most pressing matters to be given priority while other matters remain under consideration or are left to be developed by the courts.

Against this background, the remainder of this chapter considers the current Australian reform project from an EU perspective. The focus will be on civil and commercial, rather than family law, matters. Rules of personal jurisdiction are considered in Section II, rules of applicable law for contractual and non-contractual obligations in Section III and related topics in Section IV before a brief conclusion (Section V).

[48] e-justice.europa.eu/home.do?action=home, last visited 5 March 2014.

[49] ec.europa.eu/justice_home/judicialatlascivil/html/index_en.htm, last visited 5 March 2014.

[50] ec.europa.eu/justice/newsroom/civil/opinion/121031_en.htm, last visited 5 March 2014.

[51] See, in particular, the papers presented to the European Parliament by Xandra Kramer and the TMC Asser Institute at a Civil Law and Justice workshop held in January 2013: www.europarl.europa.eu/committees/en/juri/events.html?id=workshops, last visited 5 March 2014. Elsewhere, discussions have taken place as to the possibility of a 'Rome 0 Regulation', a general conflicts of law instrument complementing the Rome I, Rome II and other Regulations addressing applicable law issues. See the collected papers in S Leible and H Uberath, *Brauchen wir eine Rom 0-Verordnung?* (Munich, Sellier, 2013); E Rodríguez-Pineau (2013) 9 *Journal of Private International Law* 535.

[52] EP reference 2012/2317(INI) (withdrawn, apparently following a decision of the Conference of Presidents of the European Parliament on 20 November 2012: see European Parliament minutes, 13 June 2013, item 15). The Committee's interest is understood to have revived more recently.

[53] Treaty on the Functioning of the European Union, Art 345: 'The Treaties shall in no way prejudice the rules in Member States governing the system of property ownership'.

II. Personal Jurisdiction

A. The Case for Reform of the Current Australian Rules

As the helpful summary in the consultation paper makes clear,[54] the current position in Australia's several legal systems concerning the assertion of personal jurisdiction over defendants in civil proceedings is far from satisfactory.[55] It is, in the author's view (shared by others[56]), the area of Australian private international law most in need of reform. As matters stand, common law[57] and statutory[58] rules based on the defendant's presence,[59] even temporary, in Australia at the time proceedings are commenced[60] combine with rules governing service outside Australia that are particular to each legal system and which range in their character from the restrained (Western Australia) to the relaxed (Queensland) through various shades of liberality in between.[61] These rules, in combination, share features in common with many English country residences, a historically interesting but outmoded and impractical core attached to later constructions, bolted on higgledy-piggledy without sufficient attention to the overall design or purpose of the building.

Viewed as a whole, the current Australian rules suffer from two principal defects. First, the incoherence and legal uncertainty that results from disparities between the overseas service regimes of the individual States and Territories.[62] Secondly, a propensity to territorial overreach in certain situations, bringing overseas parties within the grasp of Australian court processes in situations hav-

[54] Attorney-General's Consultation Paper, ch 3.

[55] The topic of jurisdiction with respect to internet activities will be addressed separately, and more briefly, below (see below Section IV.C).

[56] See the contributions in this collection by Mary Keyes (Chapter two), The Hon James Allsop AO and Daniel Ward (Chapter three) and Dr Andrew Bell SC (Chapter four).

[57] *Laurie v Carroll* (1956) 98 CLR 310.

[58] Service and Execution of Process Act 1992 (Cth) ss 12, 15, 130.

[59] In the case of corporations, the concept of presence is artificial, requiring resort to a test focusing on the question whether the defendant is carrying on business through an agent, at a fixed place, for a sufficiently substantial period of time (see *National Commercial Bank v Wimborne* (1979) 11 NSWLR 156; *Amalgamated Wireless (Australasia) Ltd v McDonnell Douglas Corporation* [1987] FCA 280; *Commonwealth Bank of Australia v White, ex parte Society of Lloyd's* [1999] VSC 262; [1999] 2 VR 681. Cf *Re Tycoon Holdings* (1992) 34 FCR 31, [24]–[25]).

[60] Ie at the time of service of the originating process or, at least in some cases, at the time of its issue (see *Joye v Sheahan* (1996) 62 FCR 417).

[61] See Federal Court Rules 2011 (Cth) Division 10.4; Rules of the Supreme Court 1971 (WA) Ord 10; Uniform Civil Procedure Rules 1999 (Qld) Part 7; Supreme Court Rules 2000 (Tas) Division 10; Uniform Civil Procedure Rules 2005 (NSW) Part 11 and Sch 6; Supreme Court Civil Rules 2006 (SA) sub-rule 40; Court Procedures Rules 2006 (ACT) rr 6501–6508; Supreme Court Rules 2012 (NT) rule 7; Supreme Court (General Civil Procedure) Rules 2005 (Vic) Ord 7.

[62] For a brief survey, see A Dickinson, 'The Future of Private International Law in Australia' (2012) 19 *Australian International Law Journal* 1, 6–8. For more detailed accounts, see *Nygh's Conflict of Laws in Australia*, 9th edn, above n 30, 35–73; Reid Mortensen, R Garnett and M Keyes, *Private International Law in Australia*, 2nd edn (Sydney, LexisNexis Butterworths, 2011) 52–76.

ing only a negligible connection to the territory and legal systems of Australia.[63] As the Attorney-General's Department's consultation paper correctly notes,[64] the differences between the 'service out' rules are not limited to the specified grounds for summoning an overseas defendant to appear, but extend to the procedural mechanisms and evidential thresholds for doing so. Such disparities create, at least, the potential for distortions in competition between businesses established in different parts of Australia, in that some will have ready access to local courts when a dispute arises with a foreign counterparty whereas others will face additional costs and obstacles to gain such access or may even have no alternative but to pursue a claim abroad. These difficulties may be more apparent than real, and are not as yet (at least to the author's knowledge) substantiated by concrete empirical evidence. Moreover, Australian businesses unable to sue in their 'home' forum because of limitations in the service out regime may be able to proceed in another Australian jurisdiction with more advantageous rules.[65] Even so, the legal costs and deterrents involved, particularly for small and medium-sized businesses, in undertaking a forum shopping expedition of this kind must not be underestimated.

In this connection, it is noteworthy that an argument based on distortions of competition between businesses operating in different parts of the European Union was pressed, unsuccessfully, by the European Commission in support of its proposal that the black letter rules of jurisdiction in the Brussels I Regulation which currently apply principally to defendants domiciled in a Member State should be extended in all cases, albeit in a slightly modified form, to non-domiciled defendants, resulting in a full harmonisation across the EU of the applicable rules of jurisdiction in civil and commercial matters.[66] This proposal was rejected as a step too far (for now, at least) in the Europeanisation of private international law, in the absence of compelling empirical evidence that such

[63] A Dickinson, ibid, 8, pointing to a tendency to interpret the grounds for service out broadly, with particular generosity in relation to tort claims (see further below nn 71–74). See also M Keyes, Chapter two of this volume.

[64] Attorney-General's Consultation Paper, [34]–[47].

[65] See *Perdaman Chemicals and Fertilisers Pty Ltd v ICICI Bank Ltd* [2013] FCA 175, in which the claimant (unsuccessfully) sought leave from the Federal Court to serve a statutory claim abroad, in circumstances where such an order was not apparently available in the Western Australian Supreme Court, where related litigation was on foot. The claimant had also indicated that, if leave were granted, it would seek to transfer the proceedings to the Western Australian Court so that the only purpose of the Federal Court proceedings was to secure advantageous rules of personal jurisdiction. Although McKerracher J (at [12]) did not think this course of action was inappropriate, doubts may be raised as to its legitimacy (cf *Studorp Ltd v Robinson* [2012] NSWCA 382, [6] (Allsop P), [26] (Meagher JA)). The fact that the manoeuvre was attempted highlights, in any case, the unsatisfactory state of current Australian law.

[66] Commission Proposal for a Regulation on jurisdiction and the recognition and enforcement of judgments in civil and commercial matters (COM(2010) 748 final [14 December 2010]) 8, Recitals (16)–(17) and Art 4(2)) and accompanying Impact Assessment (SEC(2010) 1547 [14 December 2010]) 19–27. For a comment on this element of the Proposal, critical of the arguments advanced by the Commission, see Dickinson above n 46, 270–83.

reform was necessary.[67] Constitutional and political considerations, in particular the wish of States and Territories to preserve the autonomy of their legal systems, will inevitably also form part of the Australian debate, and it is vital that these should be addressed from the outset. Nevertheless, it is suggested that the arguments in favour of full (or increased) harmonisation of rules of jurisdiction may be stronger on this continent than in Europe, given that the States and Territories are unified under a single federal structure and share a common legal tradition. In particular, establishing a single set of rules common to the federal, State and Territory courts may make it more straightforward and cost effective for Australian businesses (particularly SMEs) and their foreign trading partners to assess the legal risks involved in cross-border transactions. Consumer confidence could also be increased, especially if particular consumer-protection measures were to be introduced.[68] Further, the hand of Australia's representatives in international discussions, including the continuing discussions in relation to the Hague Judgments project, could be strengthened through domestic uniformity.

If the case for harmonisation/reform of Australian rules of personal jurisdiction is accepted in principle, it will still be necessary to determine the direction of travel, in terms both of the mechanisms and the substance of the rules to be adopted. As to the possible mechanisms, comprehensive legislation at Commonwealth level (assuming that any constitutional objections could be overcome) is not the only option. Significant progress could also be achieved by coordinated action among the rule-making committees,[69] perhaps with the impetus of a 'model rule' developed at the level of the SCLJ.[70] Alternatively, although more controversial from a constitutional and political perspective and requiring greater resources, harmonisation of personal jurisdiction rules could be considered within a wider review of the judicial mechanisms available in international (commercial) cases, which could countenance the creation of a specialist federal

[67] Recast Brussels I Regulation, Art 6(1). See the comments of the European Parliament's Legal Affairs (JURI) committee on Recitals (16)–(17) of the Commission's proposal in its tabled draft report (PE467.046 [28 June 2011]), available at: www.europarl.europa.eu/oeil/popups/ficheprocedure.do?id=589033 (last visited 5 March 2014).

It did not help the Commission's case that the example given (Impact Assessment, above n 66, 20–21) to support its argument that businesses in some Member States were being compromised in their access to justice involved a claimant from Italy, one of the few countries which have already chosen to extend the rules of the Brussels I regime to all cases (see Dickinson, above n 46, 278).

[68] Below nn 87–88.

[69] The approach favoured by the authors of *Nygh's Conflict of Laws in Australia* in the 8th edition of that work, above n 30, Preface, xxii.

[70] The national model for legislation in relation to the cross-border application of workers' compensation legislation, developed by the States and Territories in collaboration with the Workers' Compensation Authorities and the Workplace Relations Ministers' Council, sets a precedent for collaboration of this kind. See Safe Work Australia, *Comparison of workers' compensation arrangements in Australia and New Zealand* (Canberra, Safe Work Australia, April 2012) 88–89, available at: www.safeworkaustralia.gov.au/sites/swa/about/publications/pages/comparison2012 (last visited 5 March 2014), and the *Cross border workers compensation provisions guidelines* (December 2012, Adelaide, Workcover Corporation of South Australia), available at www.workcover.com/documents.ashx?id=1772 (last visited 5 March 2014).

court having (non-exclusive) jurisdiction in such cases involving at least one non-resident party.

B. A Comparison of the Australian and European Approaches

What approach should be taken to reform in this area? Collectively, the current common law and statutory rules described above assert a broad-based jurisdiction in cross-border cases, particularly in tort cases[71] in which the concept of 'damage suffered' within the court's territorial jurisdiction[72] has been stretched to the point where it is highly unlikely that any individual or business connected to Australia[73] will find it difficult to pursue a tort claim in an Australian forum against a foreign party based on an allegation of financial loss paid or accounted for from within the jurisdiction.[74] The current potential for over-reach is tempered principally by the power to grant a permanent stay of proceedings in cases where the Australian forum is held to be clearly inappropriate and in other cases where the Australian proceedings are vexatious or oppressive in the broader, objective senses defined by Deane J in *Oceanic Sun Line v Fay*.[75] These tests were, of course, adopted by the High Court in *Voth v Manildra*[76] in preference to the 'more appropriate' forum test favoured elsewhere in the common law world.[77]

The position in the European Union, so far as defendants domiciled in Member States are concerned, differs in a number of important respects, as follows:[78]

1. Under the common rules of jurisdiction adopted by the Member States, the starting point, subject to a number of qualifications, is that a defendant must

[71] Including, on one view, conduct-based statutory claims such as that for misleading/deceptive conduct under the Australian Consumer Law (set out in the Competition and Consumer Act 2010 (Cth), Sch 2, s 18). See *Commonwealth Bank of Australia v White ex parte Society of Lloyd's* [1999] VSC 262; [1999] 2 VR 681; *Mallon & Co v Gam* [2012] WASC 376. Cf *Williams v Society of Lloyd's* [1994] 1 VR 274.

[72] See, eg, Uniform Civil Procedure Rules 2005 (NSW) Sch 6, para (e); Federal Court Rules 2011 (Cth) r 10.42, item 5.

[73] At least outside Western Australia, where the location of the tort (and not the damage) provides the only basis of jurisdiction specific to tort cases.

[74] *Flaherty v Girgis* (1985) 4 NSWLR 248; *Darrell Lea Chocolate Shops v Spanish Polish Shipping Co Inc* (1990) 25 NSWLR 568; *Sigma Coachair Group Pty Limited v Bock Australia Ltd* [2009] NSWSC 684; *Barach v University of New South Wales* [2011] NSWSC 431; *Heilbrunn v Lightwood plc* [2007] FCA 433; *PCH Offshore v Dunn (No 2)* [2010] FCA 897. A challenge to the constitutional validity of the New South Wales rule was rejected by the Court of Appeal in *Flaherty* (above) and not renewed before the High Court ((1987) 162 CLR 574). Although Kirby J countenanced the prospect in his dissenting judgment in *Renault v Zhang* (n 4 above), [103]–[104], no similar challenge has been raised since then.

[75] *Oceanic Sun Line Special Shipping Co Inc v Fay* (1988) 165 CLR 197.

[76] *Voth v Manildra Flour Mills Pty Ltd* (1990) 171 CLR 538.

[77] *Spiliada Maritime Corp v Cansulex Ltd* [1987] AC 460, an approach currently broadly followed in Canada, Hong Kong, India, Ireland, New Zealand and Singapore.

[78] In the following footnotes, the first reference is to the relevant provision(s) in the currently applicable Brussels I Regulation and the second reference is to the relevant provision(s) in the Recast Brussels I Regulation, which will apply from 10 January 2015. Unless otherwise stated, the relevant provisions in the two instruments are identical.

be sued in the courts of his/her/its domicile.[79] This rule, for the protection of those who do not choose to initiate litigation, is the cornerstone of the Brussels I regime, and exceptions to it should be interpreted narrowly.[80]

2. Unless this domicile-based jurisdiction is excluded (for example, where the parties have agreed to refer disputes to the exclusive jurisdiction of another Member State court[81] or in certain other specified cases[82]), the plaintiff may rely in the alternative on one or more of a number of listed grounds of 'special jurisdiction'.[83] Although these rules bear some similarities to the Australian rules regulating the service of originating process outside the jurisdiction, they are much more narrowly defined and interpreted. For example, although the rule of special jurisdiction for tort cases, like its Australian counterparts (save in Western Australia), enables proceedings to be brought either in the place of the acts or other event giving rise to damage or in the place of damage,[84] the concept of 'damage' has been narrowly defined by the European Court of Justice so as to cover only damage suffered directly in the forum, not reflective or consequential losses.[85] In contract cases, the rule of special jurisdiction focuses on the place of performance of either the principal obligation (for many goods and services contracts) or the obligation sued upon (in other cases), to the exclusion of the place of formation of the contract, the law applicable to the contract and other factors which may be relied on to establish the jurisdiction of Australian courts.[86]
3. Special rules apply in the case of certain insurance, consumer and employment contracts,[87] giving greater protection on the perceived weaker party (the insured, consumer or employee).[88] These rules have in general three features: (a) the protected party is given a wider choice of forum, including the right to sue in the courts of his or her domicile (or, in the case of an employee, the courts of the place where he or she habitually works), (b) the other party's choice of forum is narrowed, the general requirement being that proceedings

[79] Brussels I Regulation, Art 2; Recast Brussels I Regulation, Art 4. In the case of corporate and unincorporated bodies, a common definition of 'domicile' is prescribed (Art 60/Art 63). For individuals, each Member State has its own definition (Art 59/Art 62). For example, domicile in the United Kingdom (or in a part of the United Kingdom) is established by residence indicating a substantial connection to the United Kingdom (or relevant part) (Civil Jurisdiction and Judgments Order 2009, SI 2001/3929 (UK), Art 9).

[80] Case C-533/07, *Falco Privatstiftung v Weller-Lindhorst* [2009] ECR I-3327, [37].

[81] Art 23/Art 25.

[82] Art 22/Art 24, for example in cases having as their object rights *in rem* in immovable property.

[83] Arts 5–6/Arts 7–8.

[84] A principle established in Case 21/76, *Bier v Mines de Potasse d'Alsace* [1976] ECR I-1735, in a notable departure from the approach of narrow construction. The Court of Justice has been drawing back the scope of the rule (Art 5(3)/Art 7(2)) ever since.

[85] Case C-220/88, *Dumez France v Hessische Landesbank* [1990] ECR I-49; Case C-364/93, *Marinari v Lloyd's Bank plc* [1995] ECR I-2719. Compare the Australian authorities referred to above n 74.

[86] Art 5(1)/Art 7(1). Compare eg Uniform Civil Procedure Rules 2005 (NSW) Sch 6, para (d); Uniform Civil Procedure Rules 1999 (Qld) r 124(1)(g). See below, nn 101–105.

[87] Arts 8–21/Arts 10–23.

[88] Recital (13)/Recital (18).

must be brought in the courts of the protected party's domicile, and (c) the parties' ability to contract out of the regime through a choice of court agreement is heavily restricted.

4. As noted, a Member State court cannot (at least on grounds relating to the appropriateness or otherwise of the forum) decline to exercise a jurisdiction conferred by the Regulation's rules.[89] The Regulation does, however, contain rules of *lis pendens* which enable—and in some cases require—a Member State court to stay proceedings in circumstances where another Member State court (and, from 2015, a non-Member State court) has been seised first of connected proceedings.[90] The rules vary depending on whether the proceedings involve both the same parties and the same cause of action, or are simply related in the sense that it is expedient to hear and determine them together to avoid the risk of irreconcilable judgments.[91]

C. Reform of Australian Rules of Personal Jurisdiction—European Foundations

The Brussels I regime (even in the form which it has taken after its recent update[92]) is by no means perfect. It would take a bold commentator to advocate that Australia should adopt rules which closely follow its model or should contemplate accession to the parallel Lugano regime.[93] Nevertheless, it is suggested that a number of features of the European regime could usefully be considered for adoption or adaptation in Australia as part of a common set of jurisdiction rules.

First, it would be preferable for the Australian rules concerning the existence of jurisdiction to be expressly formulated in terms of the court having (or not having) jurisdiction, rather than as following implicitly from steps taken to effect service of originating process on the defendant. Detaching questions of jurisdiction from the procedural rules governing the service of process would promote greater accessibility of Australian private international law to those without access to specialist expertise, and would reduce the procedural complications that have hitherto arisen as a result of their fusion, for example in relation to the exercise of powers to allow substituted or alternative means of service.[94] The current mechanisms for obtaining leave to serve process outside Australia, or leave to

[89] *Owusu v Jackson*, n 41 above.

[90] Arts 27–30/Arts 29–34. The Recast Brussels I Regulation also includes, for the first time, a rule giving priority to a Member State court claimed to have been selected as the exclusive forum for disputes by a choice of court agreement (see Art 31(2); cf Case C-116/02, *Erich Gasser v Misat Srl* [2003] ECR I-14693).

[91] See also Art 31/Art 35, allowing a Member State court to grant provisional measures even if another Member State court has jurisdiction as to the substance of the matter.

[92] Above n 78.

[93] Above n 15.

[94] See, eg, *Laurie v Carroll*, above n 57; *Joye v Sheehan*, above n 60; *Australian Securities and Investments Corporation v Sweeney (No 2)* (2001) 38 ACSR 743; *Building Insurers' Guarantee*

proceed where a defendant does not enter an appearance, could be replaced with a harmonised procedure requiring the claimant to certify that one or more of the stated grounds of jurisdiction exists[95] and a mandatory review of jurisdiction upon application by the defendant or in the event that the claimant wishes to proceed to judgment in circumstances where the defendant has neither made such an application or entered an appearance.[96]

Secondly, although the entry into force of the Trans-Tasman regime (containing provisions extending the current regime based on personal service in Australia to defendants present in New Zealand)[97] presents a complicating factor, a primary ground of jurisdiction based on residence/ordinary residence (in the case of an individual) or the carrying on of business[98] (in the case of a corporate or unincorporated body) at an establishment in any part of Australia would represent a more appropriate and just starting point in defining the jurisdiction of Australian courts than the common law and statutory rules based on the defendant's presence, however temporary. In the case of corporate or unincorporated bodies, consideration could be given to adopting a narrower base, so as to require either the entity's principal place of business or another place of business with which the transaction giving rise to proceedings was connected to be in Australia.[99]

Thirdly, the existing service out grounds should be rationalised and harmonised as grounds of special jurisdiction, and subjected to modest pruning and trimming to ensure the existence in all cases of a genuine, substantial connection between the dispute and Australia.[100] For example, it is submitted that a strong case exists for removing 'special jurisdiction' based on:

— The formation of a contract within the jurisdiction:[101] Attributing a location to the formation of a contract concluded across national borders involves the application of arbitrary tie-break rules promulgated for other purposes (ie to resolve questions as to the timing of contract formation in domestic cases). Moreover, in modern conditions, the place of contracting activity is no longer a factor of any real significance in terms of establishing a connection with the parties' ongoing relationship giving rise to the dispute.[102]

Corporation v Eddie [2008] NSWSC 195; *Howard v Bank of New Zealand* (2002) 121 FCR 366; Service and Execution of Process Act 1992 (Cth) s 8(1).

95 See the mechanism adopted by the English courts in relation to the Brussels I Regulation and other European Conventions—Civil Procedure Rules 1998 (E&W), r 6.34 and Form N510.

96 See the review mechanism in Brussels I Regulation, Art 26; Recast Brussels I Regulation, Art 28.

97 Trans-Tasman Proceedings Act 2010 (Cth) Part 2.

98 Cf *National Commercial Bank v Wimborne* (1979) 11 NSWLR 156; Corporations Act 2001 (Cth) s 21.

99 This would align with the competence model adopted in the Foreign Judgments Act 1991 (Cth) s 7(3)(a)(iv)–(v). See Brussels I Regulation, Arts 5(5), 60; Recast Brussels I Regulation, Arts 7(5), 63.

100 It is suggested that for all courts (and not only the Federal Court) a relevant connection to any part of Australia should suffice.

101 See, eg, Uniform Civil Procedure Rules 2005 (NSW) Sch 6, para (c)(i); Federal Court Rules 2011 (Cth) r 10.42, item 3(a).

102 *Fleming v Marshall* [2011] NSWCA 86, [61]–[66]. Compare Brussels I Regulation, Art 5(1); Recast Brussels I Regulation, Art 7(1), focusing exclusively on the place of performance of a designated obligation.

- The law applicable to a contract:[103] This basis of jurisdiction confuses the distinct questions of jurisdiction and choice of law[104] and requires judges to examine an often complex question of law based on limited materials at an interlocutory stage, without the opportunity of revisiting the question of jurisdiction at trial.[105]
- The commission of a tort causing only limited or only consequential damage within the jurisdiction.[106]
- The tacking of claims not meeting any of the specified jurisdictional criteria to claims that do, without any requirement that the tagged claims be linked to the territory or legal system of the forum.[107]
- The tacking of claims against foreign defendants to claims against defendants served in the jurisdiction, without requiring a significant connection between the two sets of claims such that there would be a risk of irreconcilable judgments or injustice if they were to be tried separately.[108]

Fourthly, and in line with policies reflected in Australian legislation addressing substantive legal issues,[109] special protection could be afforded in cross-border situations to Australian-resident insured parties, consumers and employees, guaranteeing them the right to sue in their home court and controlling the use of foreign choice of court agreements to derogate from that jurisdiction.

It is submitted that these four elements, inspired by the EU model, would provide a firm foundation for the future reform of rules of personal jurisdiction in Australia.

D. Reviewing the Current Approach to Declining Jurisdiction—Horses for Courses

The European model is less instructive when one turns to questions as to whether the court should exercise or decline jurisdiction granted to it under the rules of personal jurisdiction in force. The EU has, in civil and commercial matters

[103] See, eg, Uniform Civil Procedure Rules 2005 (NSW) Sch 6, para (c)(iii); Federal Court Rules 2011 (Cth) r 10.42, item 3(c).

[104] *Renault v Zhang*, above n 4, [106] (Kirby J, in dissent).

[105] See, eg, *Castel Electronics v TCL Air Conditioner (Zhongshan) Co Ltd* [2012] VSC 548; [2013] VSC 92.

[106] See the discussion above, comparing the Australian and EU authorities (text to nn 74–75 and 85); *Renault v Zhang*, above n 4, [201] (Callinan J, in dissent).

[107] See, eg, Federal Court Rules 2011 (Cth) rule 10.42, opening sentence ('or includes'); Uniform Civil Procedure Rules 1999 (Qld) r 124(1)(x). Cf Uniform Civil Procedure Rules 2005 (NSW) Sch 6, para (w), requiring that each claim fit within one or more of the designated grounds.

[108] See, eg, Uniform Civil Procedure Rules 2005 (NSW) Sch 6, para (i); Federal Court Rules 2011 (Cth) r 10.42, item 20. Cf Brussels I Regulation, Art 6(1); Recast Brussels I Regulation, Art 8(1); Case 189/87, *Kalfelis v Bankhaus Schröder* [1988] ECR 5565. See also *AK Investment v Kyrgyz Mobil* [2011] UKPC 10, [2012] 1 WLR 1804, [73] (Lord Collins).

[109] See, eg, the Insurance Contracts Act 1984 (Cth), the Australian Consumer Law (contained in the Competition and Consumer Act 2010 (Cth) Sch 2), Workplace Relations Act 1996 (Cth). See above, text to nn 87–88.

at least,[110] rejected the notion of a *forum conveniens* or *forum non conveniens* as providing a basis for declining jurisdiction, preferring rules based on the existence of situations of *lis pendens* which give priority to the court first seised. This regime has frequently and justifiably been criticised for encouraging a race to court[111] and, against that background, despite modest recent reforms to accommodate Member State (but not third country) choice of court agreements and situations of *lis pendens* involving third countries,[112] the mechanisms for declining jurisdiction in the recast Brussels I Regulation (in particular those in Articles 33 and 34) offer, at most, food for thought or drafting hints in developing an Australian solution to problems resulting from concurrent proceedings in different jurisdictions.

In practice, given the breadth of the service-based rules, the Australian courts' power to decline jurisdiction by granting a stay is the most significant aspect of the current legal environment, and does need to be addressed as part of any reform process, whatever approach is taken to the existence of personal jurisdiction. There is little doubt that the current position in Australia is, from a procedural perspective, unsatisfactory. Notwithstanding the limited nature of the power exercised by Australian courts under *Voth* principles, the very existence of that power and the strategic tactical advantages that it offers to a reluctant defendant drive the parties towards substantial (and expensive) interlocutory applications on questions of the 'appropriateness' or otherwise of the Australian forum.[113] It is suggested that some controls are urgently needed. For example, (a) provision could be made for stay applications to be decided in the ordinary course on the basis of written submissions only,[114] and (b) rights of appeal against a stay decision could be restricted or (subject to the constitutionally guaranteed, exceptional appeal to the High Court on a point of principle) excluded entirely.[115]

[110] Compare Art 15 of Regulation (EC) No 2201/2003 concerning jurisdiction and the recognition and enforcement of judgments in matrimonial matters and matters of personal responsibility ([2003] OJ L338/1 [23 December 2003]).

[111] On this point, see eg U Magnus and P Mankowski (eds), *Brussels I Regulation*, 2nd edn (Munich, Sellier, 2012), Introduction to Arts 27–30, [16-22]; A Dickinson, above n 46, 293–95; C McLachlan, *Lis Pendens in International Litigation* (The Hague, Academy of International Law, 2009) ch 2, Part B and 435.

[112] Recast Brussels I Regulation, Arts 29(1), 31(2)–(4), 33, 34. See above, text to nn 90–91.

[113] See, for example, the thinly veiled criticisms by Rares J in *Atlasnavios Nacegacao v The Ship 'Xin Tai Hai' (No 2)* [2012] FCA 1497, (2012) 301 ALR 357, [107]. The position is, if anything, even less satisfactory in England (and elsewhere in the common law world) where the 'more appropriate' forum test requires an even broader inquiry to be undertaken (see the comments of Lord Collins in *AK Investment CJSC v Kyrgyz Mobil Tel Ltd*, above n 108, [7] and of Lord Neuberger in *VTB Capital plc v Nutritek International Corp* [2013] UKSC 5, [2013] 2 AC 337, [82]–[89]).

[114] Cf *Voth v Manildra*, above n 76, 565 (Mason CJ, Deane, Dawson and Gaudron JJ). See also Trans-Tasman Proceedings Act 2010 (Cth) s 18(1).

[115] A precedent, of course, exists with respect to transfer decisions under the cross-vesting legislation (Jurisdiction of Courts (Cross-Vesting) Act 1987 (Cth) s 13).

As the Attorney-General's Consultation Paper notes,[116] the *Voth* principles have attracted not inconsiderable criticism and several commentators[117] have argued in favour of the 'more appropriate' forum test adopted in other common law jurisdictions, including Canada, England, Hong Kong, India, Ireland, New Zealand and Singapore,[118] and in the Trans-Tasman regime.[119] The present author is much more sceptical of the benefits of adopting such a test, which would not be reciprocated by the large majority of jurisdictions worldwide (including major trading partners in the Asia-Pacific region). It is respectfully submitted that the policy arguments identified by Deane J in *Oceanic Sun Line* and the majority in *Voth* for preferring a 'clearly inappropriate' forum test remain as strong today as when first enumerated. In particular, it is suggested that there is much merit in the submissions that a party should not be deprived, by a rule of a discretionary nature, of a right to bring proceedings before an Australian court without a compelling reason[120] and that the adoption of a clearly inappropriate forum test has the advantage over its competitor that it avoids or at least minimises the need for Australian courts to criticise or to be invited to criticise the judicial systems of other nations.[121]

At the very least, a judgement as to the most appropriate test for declining jurisdiction in cases where personal jurisdiction exists can only be reached once the rules governing the existence of personal jurisdiction are settled. If, as suggested above, the Australian rules of jurisdiction are reformed and put on a narrower footing, the case for a broader discretion to counteract 'exorbitant' rules becomes correspondingly weaker. With respect to other commentators who support the *Spiliada* approach as a more effective brake on a broadly expressed international competence, it is submitted that it is a poor argument for the 'more appropriate' forum test that it is necessary to temper the worst excesses of the common law and statutory rules of jurisdiction.

116 Attorney-General's Consultation Paper 1, [74]–[75].

117 *Nygh's Conflict of Laws in Australia*, above n 30, [8.24]; R Mortensen, R Garnett and M Keyes, above n 62, [4.22]–[4.24].

118 See the cases cited in *Dicey, Morris & Collins*, 15th edn, above n 29, para 12-011. As to the position in Ireland, see *Intermetal Group Ltd v Worslade Trading Ltd* [1998] IR 1. As to the position in New Zealand and Singapore, see the contribution in this volume of Elsabe Schoeman and Adeline Chong (Chapter nine).

119 Trans-Tasman Proceedings Act 2010 (Cth) s 17.

120 *Voth v Manildra*, above n 76, 559–60.

121 *Voth*, above n 76, 559 referring to *Attorney-General (UK) v Heinemann Publishers Australia Pty Ltd* (1988) 165 CLR 30, 40–41. Cf *AK Investment v Kyrgyz Mobil*, above n 108, [97]–[98] (Lord Collins). For notable recent cases, in which the English courts were required to make an enquiry of this kind, see *AK Investment*, above; *Cherney v Deripaska* [2009] EWCA Civ 849.

E. Choice of Court Agreements—Giving Effect to Party Autonomy

The need for intervention is no less pressing in relation to the treatment by Australian courts of exclusive choice of court agreements, given the propensity of Australian courts to find ways of denuding the parties' contractual agreement of force, particularly when faced with statutory claims, such as misleading or deceptive conduct claims under the Australian Consumer Law (formerly under the Trade Practices Act).[122] That is not to say that an Australian court should not be able to investigate for itself whether a choice of court agreement is valid and extends to the subject-matter of the claim before the court, or that it should not have a limited power to override an exclusive choice of court agreement in the public interest. It seems desirable, however, that the court's powers should be more precisely regulated, bringing the treatment of choice of court agreements more closely into line with that of arbitration agreements.[123] In this connection, it is suggested that the provisions of section 20 of the Trans-Tasman Proceedings Act 2010 (Cth), itself modelled on the 2005 Hague Convention on Choice of Court Agreements,[124] should (subject to limited qualifications[125]) be extended to cover all situations involving exclusive choice of court agreements designating a foreign court, without imperilling the public interest. Thus, although section 20(1) of the 2010 Act requires an Australian court to stay proceedings to give effect to an exclusive New Zealand choice of court agreement, section 20(1)(c) (one of five

[122] Attorney-General's Consultation Paper, [51]–[52]; M Keyes, 'Jurisdiction under the Hague Choice of Courts Convention: Its Likely Impact on Australian Practice' (2009) 5 *Journal of Private International Law* 181. See also R Garnett, 'Jurisdiction Clauses Since *Akai*' (2013) 87 *Australian Law Journal* 134; M Keyes, Chapter two of this volume. A good example of 'choice of court hijacking' is *Faxtech Pty Ltd v ITL Optronics Ltd* [2011] FCA 1320 in which Middleton J refused a stay to give effect to an English jurisdiction clauses (even assuming it to be exclusive) because (a) the relief sought under the Australian consumer law could only be determined by an Australian court, and (b) as a result, it was desirable that the Australian court should determine all of the matters in issue between the parties, including claims other than the ACL claim. The reasoning, unsupported by reference to any provision of the ACL, is thin and rather unconvincing. See also *Qantas Airways Limited v Rolls Royce plc* [2010] FCA 1481, in which an anti-anti-suit injunction was used to prevent the issue of proceedings in the contractually chosen forum. In *Society of Lloyd's v White* [2000] HCA Trans 37 (11 February 2009), the arguments surrounding the impact on jurisdictional discretion of a claim under the trade practices legislation were more fully ventilated in the application for special leave, but a majority (McHugh and Kirby JJ, Callinan J disagreeing) denied special leave to appeal from a decision of Byrne J ([1999] 2 VR 681) in the Supreme Court of Victoria in circumstances where the Court of Appeal had already denied leave to appeal. See also the later decision of the Court of Appeal, denying a further application to stay in the same case ([2004] VSCA 101). The issue, which is not resolved by the reasoning in *Akai Pty Ltd v People's Insurance Co Ltd* (1996) 188 CLR 418, is ripe for review by the High Court.

[123] See, in particular, *Comandate Marine v Pan Australia Shipping Pty Ltd* (2006) 157 FCR 45.

[124] See: www.hcch.net/upload/conventions/txt37en.pdf (last visited 5 March 2014), in particular Art 6.

[125] Certain categories of contract for which policy reasons justify greater control on the exercise of party autonomy could be carved out from this regime, for example insurance, consumer and employment contracts involving Australian protected parties (see above, text to n 109) and contracts of carriage from ports in Australia (see Carriage of Goods by Sea Act 1991 (Cth) s 11).

grounds for refusal) excludes that obligation 'if the Australian court is satisfied that … giving effect to it would lead to a manifest injustice or would be manifestly contrary to Australian public policy'. This sets a high threshold, emphasising that the parties' bargain should be upheld in most cases. Nevertheless, at the same time, the public policy exception provides a safety valve which allows the parties' exercise of autonomy to be overridden in the public interest in (and only in) an exceptional case.

If Australia were to adopt this approach and to ratify the 2005 Hague Convention, it may be that the European Union would not be too far behind. In January 2014, the European Commission adopted a proposal for the approval of the Hague Convention, subject to the proposed exclusion of insurance contracts to which the protective rules in the Brussels I Regulation extend.[126] As a result, Australian exclusive choice of court clauses could be recognised and enforced by Member State courts removing the doubt that presently exists as to the power of Member State courts to do so.[127]

F. Conclusion—Personal Jurisdiction

In summary, the Australian law of personal jurisdiction in international cases is in an unsatisfactory state and in urgent need of reform. The European regime, contained in the Brussels I Regulation as extended to other countries by the Lugano Convention, does provide a useful source of inspiration in assessing the current Australian law and in formulating any reform proposals, particularly when viewed from a structural perspective.

III. The Law Applicable to Contractual and Non-Contractual Obligations

A. The Current Position in Australia—Regulation by the Common Law

As noted above,[128] the European Union has adopted general instruments containing rules for ascertaining the law applicable to contractual and non-contractual obligations, the so-called Rome I and Rome II Regulations. By contrast,

[126] COM (2014) 46 final [30 January 2014].

[127] Above, text to nn 40–44.

[128] Above, text to nn 17–18.

and with limited statutory exceptions,[129] Australian choice of law rules in these areas are mostly a product of the common law.[130] There is, however, a vast difference in developmental terms in Australia between the rules governing the law applicable to contractual issues and the rules governing the law applicable to issues in tort. In the former area, the old English common law, now largely superseded in that jurisdiction by European instruments, continues to exert a strong influence on the Australian common law, which has been largely untouched in the modern era by the High Court. A division, albeit rather hazy, is drawn between cases in which the court finds a choice of law by the parties, and cases in which there is no demonstrated choice and the contract will be governed by the law of the system with which it has its closest and most real connection (its natural seat or centre of gravity).[131] By contrast, three decisions of the High Court in the space of five years[132] have re-written the common law rules concerning the law applicable to tort, resulting in a rule that requires the application of the whole of the law of the place of the tort (*lex loci delicti*), being the place where the tort in substance arose.[133] The current position may be summarised as follows:[134]

> If the Australian rules governing the law applicable to tort (*Renault* and *Nielsen*) may be compared to a modernist building, new but not to everyone's taste, the common law rules governing the law applicable to contractual obligations seem more in the nature of a pre-fabricated bungalow, full of character but ripe for renovation or rebuilding.

The following sections consider, in turn, possible reform of the Australian common law rules of applicable law for torts and contract cases.

B. The Law Applicable to Torts

The Attorney-General's Consultation Paper[135] notes justifiable concerns as to the inflexibility and complexity of the newly-formed Australian choice of law rule for torts. The 'whole of the *lex loci delicti*' approach favoured in *Neilson* is particularly problematic, having the consequences that it (a) increases the complexity and the cost of investigating and determining the applicable law,[136] (b) underestimates the difficulties of locating the tort in cross-border cases,[137] (c) gives insufficient

[129] Notably, in relation to intra-Australian cases of defamation, workers' compensation and limitation periods.

[130] As to the law applicable to claims in equity, see *Paramasivam v Flynn* (1998) 90 FCR 489, 501–4; *Nicholls v Michael Wilson & Partners* [2010] NSWCA 222; (2010) 234 FLR 177, [339]–[346] (Lindgren J).

[131] *Akai Pty Limited v The People's Insurance Company Ltd* (1996) 188 CLR 418, 436–42.

[132] *John Pfeiffer Pty Ltd v Rogerson* (2000) 203 CLR 503; *Renault v Zhang*, above n 4; *Neilson v Overseas Projects Corporation of Victoria*, above n 4.

[133] ibid.

[134] Dickinson, above n 62, 5.

[135] Attorney General's Consultation Paper, [122]–[130].

[136] Foreign expertise in private international law being required, in addition to expertise in tort law. The difficulties faced by the High Court in determining the content of Chinese law in *Neilson* illustrate this point.

[137] Cf *Pfeiffer v Rogerson*, above n 132, [81]–[82]; *Dow Jones & Company Inc v Gutnick* (2002) 210 CLR 575, [43]–[44].

recognition to the regulatory claims of legal systems other than that of the *locus delicti* by treating the 'substance of the tort' test, developed for different purposes, as the sole arbiter of regulatory authority,[138] and (d) delegates questions of policy in the formulation of applicable law rules to a foreign sovereign entity.[139]

As *Neilson*'s 'no advantage' principle is itself an instrument (albeit a rather unusual one) targeting forum shopping,[140] it is suggested that it would be sensible to review the rules of applicable law for torts after possible reforms to the current rules on personal jurisdiction have been considered and, if pursued, adopted.[141] Although the current rules of applicable law in cases of tortious wrongdoing are unattractive, for the reasons just given, the case for reform is not as pressing as in the area of jurisdiction.

If reform efforts are to be pursued, the European experience in discussing, adopting and applying the detailed rules in the Rome II Regulation[142] should provide valuable guidance, as the Regulation is the most comprehensive and widely applied international instrument of its kind. In particular, the general rules for tort/delict in Article 4 may provide a useful point of departure in formulating legislative proposals. Article 4 combines a basic rule favouring the law of the country in which damage directly resulted from a harmful event (as opposed to that in which the event giving rise to damage or indirect consequences of that event occurred)[143] with rules of displacement in favour of (i) the law of the common habitual residence of the person suffering damage and the person liable,[144] and (ii) another law with which the tort/delict is in all the circumstances manifestly more closely connected.[145] By contrast, the separate rules (Articles 5–9) for particular kinds of tort (product liability, competition matters, environmental damage, infringements of intellectual property rights, industrial action) are a mixed bag, and perhaps useful only to indicate some of the areas where a departure from the general rule could at least be considered. Other notable features of the Rome II Regulation, for these purposes, include (a) the carving out of certain categories of obligation (including those relating to violations of personality and privacy

[138] *Distillers Co (Biochemicals) v Thompson* [1971]1 NSWLR 83.

[139] For example, if the *lex loci delicti* is in a Member State of the EU bound by the Rome II Regulation, an Australian court would be bound in appropriate cases to give effect to the special rules for product liability, competition matters, environmental liability, intellectual property infringements and industrial action (Arts 5–9), all of which reflect the policies of the European Union (see Recitals (20)–(28)). See *Puttick v Tenon Ltd* [2008] HCA Trans 322 (submissions of Dr AS Bell QC).

[140] *Neilson*, above n 4, [89]–[91] (Gummow and Hayne JJ).

[141] See Section II above.

[142] Above n 18. For the legislative background, see A Dickinson, *The Rome II Regulation: The law applicable to non-contractual obligations* (Oxford, Oxford University Press, 2008) ch 1. The Regulation also contains (Arts 10–12) specific rules concerning the law applicable to non-contractual obligations in the areas of unjust enrichment, *negotiorum gestio* and *culpa in contrahendo*, but these are not addressed here.

[143] Rome II Regulation, Art 4(1).

[144] Art 4(2).

[145] Art 4(3), the so-called 'escape clause'. For comment on these provisions, see A Dickinson, *The Rome II Regulation*, above n 142, ch 4.

rights[146]), (b) the freedom of the parties to choose the law applicable to many contractual obligations,[147] (c) rules governing other kinds of non-contractual obligation (in particular, unjust enrichment),[148] and (d) the express exclusion of the principle of *renvoi*.[149]

C. The Law Applicable to Contracts

Legally, as well as economically, a stronger case can be made for giving priority to possible reform of the rules governing the law applicable to contractual matters.[150] In terms of general principle, the current rules of the common law can be stated concisely. If, upon the proper construction of the contract, the court may properly conclude that the parties have exercised the liberty given by the common law to choose the governing law of the contract, that law will in general be applied by an Australian court to regulate the parties' contractual relationship,[151] subject to (a) any statutory rule to the contrary,[152] (b) the overriding effect of Australian public policy, and (c) (possibly) a requirement that the choice be made bona fide and not for the purpose of circumventing a statutory rule of the law that would otherwise apply.[153] Absent such choice, the law applicable to the contract will be that of the legal system with which the transaction has its closest and most real connection[154] or (to put the same test in different words) its natural seat or centre of gravity.[155]

Although these rules are straightforward in their formulation and by no means unworkable, three reasons suggest that it may be desirable to put the rules on a statutory footing, with appropriate adjustments, for the following reasons. First, to reaffirm the importance in cross-border commercial transactions of the principle of party autonomy in choosing the law applicable to contract, recognised by the EU in the Rome I Regulation[156] and by the Hague Conference in the Hague Principles on the Choice of Law in International Contracts.[157] As noted

[146] Art 1(2)(g), it being impossible to achieve a consensus in relation to any of the proposals for a rule to govern these types of claim.

[147] Art 14.

[148] Art 10.

[149] Art 24.

[150] See also B Marshall, 'Reconsidering the Proper Law of the Contract' (2012) 13 *Melbourne Journal of International Law* 505.

[151] *Akai*, above n 131, 441–42.

[152] ibid.

[153] See, for example, *Golden Acres v Queensland Estates Pty Ltd* [1969] Qd R 378; *BHP Petroleum Pty Ltd v Oil Basins Ltd* [1985] VR 725; *Re Bulong Nickel* (2002) 42 ACSR 52, 66; *Sportsbet Pty Ltd v The State of Victoria* [2011] FCA 961, [46].

[154] *Bonython v Commonwealth of Australia* (1950) 81 CLR 836.

[155] *Akai*, above n 131, 437.

[156] Rome I Regulation, Recital (11) and Art 3(1).

[157] See: www.hcch.net/upload/wop/contracts2012principles_e.pdf, esp Preamble, para 1 and Art 2. The Principles were reviewed and approved by a Special Commission of the Hague Conference organised in November 2012 and were considered by the Conference's Council of General Affairs at its annual meeting on 9–11 April 2013. See also the draft commentary prepared

above, Australian law gives effect to this principle by enabling contracting parties to choose the applicable law, subject to certain restrictions. Nevertheless, the apparent but uncertain requirement of bona fide choice[158] and the approach of the Australian courts in applying the *lex fori* to determine both the validity and existence of a choice[159] tend to undermine it. Adopting legislation on choice of law for contracts in line with the Hague Principles[160] would ensure stability and give parties to cross-border contracts with an Australian connection increased confidence in choosing a foreign law to govern their relationship.

Secondly, in the absence of party choice, the 'closest and most real connection/centre of gravity' test provides courts with no clear guidance as to the identification of the factors which may properly be taken into account and the weight to be given to them.[161] This increases the potential for differences of judicial opinion or errors of the kind that arose in *Fleming v Marshall*,[162] where the trial judge was held to have given too much weight to the finding that the contract was formed in New South Wales. It is submitted that greater predictability and stability could be achieved in determination of the law applicable in the absence of choice by adopting a set of rules such as that contained in Article 4 of the Rome I Regulation, coupling general rules for particular kinds of contracts[163] (Article 4(1)) with a residual rule for other contracts (Article 4(2)) and a limited 'escape clause' where the contract is manifestly more closely connected to a country other than that whose law would apply under the basic rules just described (Article 4(3)). Further guidance could be given as to the factors to be taken into account by an Australian court in determining whether a contract is more closely connected to one country than to another.[164]

by the Hague Conference's Expert Working Group (www.hcch.net/upload/wop/gap2014pd06_en.pdf, last visited 7 March 2014).

For a summary of the principles as drafted, see A Dickinson, 'A principled approach to choice of law in contract? The draft Hague Principles on Choice of Law in International Contracts' [2013] *Journal of International Banking and Financial Law* 151 (March). For further comment on the draft Principles, see the articles cited in the bibliography available on the Hague Conference's website (www.hcch.net/upload/draft_principles_bibl-e.pdf, last visited 7 March 2014).

[158] See the authorities referred to above n 153.

[159] *Oceanic Sun Line Special Shipping Co Inc v Fay* (1988) 165 CLR 197, 224–25 (Brennan J) and 259–61 (Gaudron J). Cf Rome I Regulation, Art 3(5).

[160] The question of whether a choice of non-State law should be allowed would need to be separately examined. In this connection, Art 3 of the Hague Principles seems highly unsatisfactory and should be discarded (see A Dickinson, above n 157, 152).

[161] See, eg, *Mendelson-Zeller Co v T and C Providores* [1981] 1 NSWLR 366.

[162] *Fleming v Marshall* [2011] NSWCA 86, (2011) 279 ALR 737. Compare *Marshall v Fleming* [2010] NSWSC 86. See also *Marshall v Prescott (No 3)* [2013] NSWSC 1949, [103].

[163] Contracts for the sale of goods (including, separately, by auction), provision of services, immovable property contracts, franchise and distribution agreements and certain financial contracts. As noted below, separate provision is made for carriage contracts (Art 5), certain consumer contracts (Art 6), insurance contracts (Art 7) and employment contracts (Art 8).

[164] See eg Rome I Regulation, Recitals (20) and (21) requiring account to be taken of 'whether the contract in question has a very close relationship with another contract or contracts'.

Thirdly, the Australian rules in their current form mainly apply without distinguishing between particular kinds of contract.[165] In particular, in terms of the approach taken in identifying the law applicable, Australian law does not treat consumer, employment and insurance contracts differently from contracts entered into between two parties acting in the course of business. At the same time, the Commonwealth Parliament has enacted statutes which afford substantive protection to consumers, insured parties, and employees in circumstances where contracts have a relevant connection to Australia.[166] Although such legislation is capable of having mandatory effect even if the law applicable to the contract under common law rules is that of a foreign country,[167] the policies served by this legislation could be furthered by adopting special choice of law rules for these categories of contracts, controlling (but not excluding) the principle of party autonomy and favouring (for example) the law of the consumer's country of habitual residence or the law of the place where the employee habitually works. The Rome I Regulation contains rules of this kind in all three categories of contract (as well as contracts for the carriage of goods and persons)[168] and, again, these may provide a useful point of departure in the reform process and in drafting new legislation.

D. Conclusion

In conclusion, although the case for reform in the area of applicable law is not as pressing as that in relation to personal jurisdiction (Section II above), the current legal position in Australia could be strengthened by legislation containing a detailed set of rules for determining the law applicable to contractual and tortious obligations. If a reform of this kind were to be in contemplation, the provisions of the Rome I and Rome II Regulations and the discussions which led to their adoption would—alongside other sources—provide a possible model or source of inspiration in the rule-making process.

IV. Other Topics

It is not possible within this chapter to address every topic raised by the Attorney-General's consultation. Three further topics, however, deserve particular mention.

[165] Cf Carriage of Goods by Sea Act 1991 (Cth) s 11(1), which does contain a special rule for certain carriage of goods contracts.

[166] Above, text to n 109.

[167] See *Akai*, above n 131; *Old UGC Inc v Industrial Relations Commission of New South Wales* (2006) 225 CLR 274; *Insight Vacations Pty Ltd v Young* [2011] HCA 16.

[168] Rome I Regulation, Arts 5–8.

A. The Recognition and Enforcement of Judgments

First, as to the recognition and enforcement of judgments,[169] the EU (Brussels I) Regime seems unlikely to be instructive. The Brussels I Regulation's rules for recognition and enforcement, applicable only between the Member States in a treaty relationship, assuming a high degree of mutual trust and cooperation and tying in with the substantial harmonisation of rules of jurisdiction effected in the same instrument, cannot be carried across to sovereign relationships of a very different kind between Australia and third countries, for the most part unregulated by treaty. For the same reason, the recognition and enforcement provisions for New Zealand judgments in the Trans-Tasman Proceedings Act, founded on a treaty recognising a high degree of trust and cooperation between the legal systems and courts of the two countries, do not provide a reliable template for any future reform.

In terms of overall approach, although there is no necessary relationship or correlation between the rules of personal jurisdiction applied by Australian courts and the limits imposed by Australian law when recognising and enforcing the judgments originating in other legal systems, it seems best to address the topic after any reform in the area of personal jurisdiction (Section II) has been completed. If, for example, jurisdiction based on the presence (even temporary) of the defendant were to be rejected in favour of a more substantial factor such as residence[170] or if a more radical approach were to be taken based on the existence of a 'real and substantial connection' or similar factor,[171] the landscape of private international law in Australia would look very different and the case for adjusting the rules of recognition and enforcement would be correspondingly stronger. If, however, only minor adjustments were made to the rules on personal jurisdiction, the case for reform would appear weaker, particularly as the Foreign Judgments Act 1991 (Cth) reflects (albeit with some infelicities of drafting) principles adopted elsewhere in the common law world and implements Australia's obligations under its mutual recognition treaty with the United Kingdom.[172] If foreign states other than New Zealand wish to secure more favourable treatment in Australia for judgments of their courts, it would be open to them seek to negotiate and enter into a bilateral treaty. Further, Australia has been a longstanding supporter of the efforts within the Hague Conference to secure a global judgments treaty.[173] Unpromising as these negotiations may presently appear, this

[169] Attorney-General's Consultation Paper, [137]–[174].

[170] Above, text to nn 98–99. Compare A Briggs, 'Recognition of Foreign Judgments: A Matter of Obligation' (2013) 129 *Law Quarterly Review* 87.

[171] See the Canadian decisions referred to above n 7.

[172] Signed Canberra, 23 August 1990, and entering into force on 1 September 1994 ([1994] Australian Treaty Series No 27).

[173] See: www.hcch.net/upload/wop/gap2014pd07_en.pdf, last visited 7 March 2014.

is an area where it appears best to proceed by reciprocal agreement rather than unilaterally.[174]

B. The Processes for the Introduction and Ascertainment of Foreign Law

The law and practice in Australia concerning the introduction and ascertainment of foreign law, when applicable by reference to an operative choice of law rule, is in urgent need of review and reform. Statutory measures of limited import[175] combine with ill-defined and frequently misunderstood common law principles, including the notorious 'presumption of identity' to produce a situation which brings the law into discredit, resulting in the excessive costs of instructing and cross-examining foreign law experts and in outcomes which are difficult to predict and, in many cases, to justify.[176] Some notable reforms have been pursued in New South Wales, through the amendment of its procedural rules to impose duties on parties wishing to rely on foreign law to formulate their cases at an early stage, and to enable the Supreme Court to implement bilateral agreements with the judicial systems of Singapore and New York for the ascertainment of issues of foreign law by judges of the foreign system concerned and to appoint referees in other cases.[177] These measures are, on the whole, useful. In most cases, however, the difficulties of proving foreign law by expert evidence, starkly exposed in *Neilson v Overseas Projects Corporation of Victoria*,[178] will remain, and it is suggested that a more radical approach is needed. One possibility, which may deserve closer attention, may be to enhance the role of judges in cross-border cases, requiring them to manage cases actively, to raise with the parties the question of applicable law at an early stage and to secure agreement, if possible, on the procedural approach, and empowering those judges to investigate and make findings as to the content of foreign law of their own motion, using whatever materials they may consider appropriate and proportionate to the matters in dispute. The latter proposal would bring Australian practice more into line with the position in the United States' Federal Courts, and it would be much the better for it.[179]

[174] See Attorney-General's Consultation Paper, [157]–[159].

[175] See, eg, Evidence Act 1995 (NSW) ss 174–176; Evidence and Procedure (New Zealand) Act 1994 (Cth) s 40.

[176] For comment, and criticism, see *Damberg v Damberg* (2001) 52 NSWLR 492 (Heydon JA); J McComish, 'Pleading and Proving Foreign Law in Australia' (2007) 31 *Melbourne University Law Review* 17; A Gray, 'Choice of Law: The Presumption in the Proof of Foreign Law' (2008) 31 *University of NSW Law Journal* 136. For a judicial view, see P Brereton, 'Proof of Foreign Law: Problems and Initiatives' (2011) 85 *Australian Law Journal* 554.

[177] Uniform Civil Procedure Rules 2005 (NSW) Part 6, Division 9. See J Spigelman, 'Proof of Foreign Law by Reference to the Foreign Court' (2011) 127 *LQR* 208; *Marshall v Fleming* [2013] NSWSC 566 and [2014] NSWCA 64.

[178] Above n 4.

[179] See Federal Rules of Civil Procedure, r 44.1 (US), applied by the Court of Appeals (5th Circuit) in *Bodum USA, Inc v La Cafetiere, Inc* (2010) 621 F 3d 624.

The European Union has also yet to grapple satisfactorily with these issues, and differences between the Member States[180] in terms of their approaches to the introduction and ascertainment of foreign law arguably impair the effectiveness of the Rome I and Rome II Regulations in securing consistency of outcome in cases involving contractual and non-contractual obligations. During the passage of the Rome II Regulation, the Justice and Legal Affairs Committee (JURI) of the European Parliament sought to introduce common rules concerning the pleading and proof of an applicable foreign law, but these proposals were rejected and all that remains of them in the final regulation is a requirement that the Commission look again at this matter in its first review of the Regulation.[181] That review is now underway. The topic of access to foreign law is also, it may be noted, on the current agenda of the Hague Conference.[182]

C. The Impact of the Internet and Online Transactions

The Attorney-General's consultation paper asks whether a new approach to personal jurisdiction is required in light of advances in online and mobile technology,[183] and returns to the topic in considering the law applicable to defamation claims.[184] There is no doubt that the internet, and modern social media, have been revolutionary not only in geopolitical terms but also in creating new patterns of business and encouraging individuals and corporations to cross borders in search of new experiences and opportunities. These developments must, of course, be taken into account when considering possible reforms to private international law rules in Australia—the suitability of both existing and proposed new rules must be assessed by reference to the full range of situations to which they are to be applied.

Nevertheless, experience in the EU cautions against adopting new rules of private international law (or rules having equivalent effect) that apply only to an online environment. In particular, the adoption in the eCommerce Directive in 2000 of a so-called 'country of origin' rule prohibiting (subject to certain qualifications[185]) restrictions on the freedom to provide information society services between Member States[186] has proved extremely problematic from a private

[180] For example, the adversarial model in England and Wales, like that in Australia, places control in the hands of the parties, whereas German judges have a duty ex officio to identify and investigate the applicable foreign law. See generally S Geeroms, *Foreign Law in Civil Litigation* (Oxford, Oxford University Press, 2004).

[181] See A Dickinson, *The Rome II Regulation*, above n 142, 600–601.

[182] See: www.hcch.net/upload/wop/gap2012info10en.pdf, last visited 7 March 2014, the outcome of a joint project with the European Commission.

[183] Attorney-General's Consultation Paper, [55]–[66].

[184] ibid, [131]–[133].

[185] See *Dicey, Morris & Collins*, 15th edn, above n 29, paras 35–153 and following for an account of the complex relationship between the country of origin rule, and other provisions within the Directive.

[186] Directive 2000/31/EC on certain legal aspects of information society services ([2000] OJ L178/1 [17 July 2000]), Art 3(2).

international law perspective. Although the Directive disclaimed any intention to create new rules of private international law,[187] some commentators argued that the country of origin rule was in the nature of a choice of law rule requiring application of the law of the online service provider's place of establishment to questions of liability. The European Court of Justice eventually rejected this argument, but at the same apparently favoured an interpretation of the rule which gave it an effect equivalent to a choice of law rule, entitling the service provider to rely on its home law if more favourable than the law otherwise applicable to a non-contractual obligation.[188] In the same case, and possibly in an attempt to balance out the advantage given to the defendant website publisher by the applicable law regime in the eCommerce Directive, the Court adapted the rule of special jurisdiction for tort cases in the Brussels I Regulation (Article 5(3)) so as to confer jurisdiction on the country of the claimant's centre of interests (normally country of habitual residence) in cases of online defamation and privacy violations. Both the Court's reasoning, casting long-established principles of interpretation to one side, and its consequences, creating new categories and problems of delineation and application, are unsatisfactory to say the least.[189]

A more attractive solution has been found in assessing questions of jurisdiction and the law applicable in relation to online consumer contracts. The consumer contract provisions of the international conventions which preceded the Brussels I and Rome I Regulations did not neatly accommodate contracts concluded online.[190] When the Brussels I Regulation was revised, a more suitable—but generally applicable—formula was adopted referring to a contract concluded by the consumer

> with a person who pursues commercial or professional activities in the Member State of the consumer's domicile or, by any means, directs such activities to that Member State or to several States including that Member State, and the contract falls within the scope of such activities.[191]

At the same time, the Council and the Commission published guidance as to how the concept of 'directed activity' was to be interpreted in the case of contracts

[187] ibid, Art 1(4).

[188] Joined Cases C-509/09 and C-161/10, *e-Date Advertising v X* and *Martinez v MGN Ltd* [2011] ECR I-10269.

[189] See the comment by the author of this paper at: conflictoflaws.net/2012/by-royal-appointment-no-closer-to-an-eu-private-international-law-settlement/, last visited 7 March 2014. In a later case, involving allegations of trademark infringements by the use of adverts on Google, the Court of Justice refused to extend its approach in *eDate Advertising*, adopting instead more orthodox analysis resting on the location of the defendant's acts and the country or countries to which they were directed (see Case C-523/10, *Wintersteiger AG v Products 4U Sondermaschinenbau GmbH* [2012] ECLI:EU:C:2012:220). See also Case C-173/11, *Football Dataco Ltd v Sportradar GmbH* [2012] ECLI:EU:C:2012:642.

[190] Both Art 13(3) of the 1968 Brussels Convention (jurisdiction) and Art 5(2) of the 1980 Rome Convention (law applicable to contractual obligations) referred to a 'specific invitation' addressed to the consumer in the Member State of his domicile (Brussels)/his country of habitual residence (Rome) and to the consumer taking the steps necessary for conclusion of the contract in that Member State/country.

[191] Brussels I Regulation, Art 15(1)(c).

concluded online, including by identifying relevant and irrelevant factors.[192] This guidance was expressly referenced in the Recitals to the Rome I Regulation, the consumer contract provisions of which followed the formula in the Brussels I regime.[193] The Court of Justice has also quoted and relied on the guidance in an important 2010 decision concerning the application of the Brussels I Regulation provisions to contracts concluded via, or as a result of information found on, the internet.[194]

In the final analysis, there is no doubt that the internet and mobile telecommunications create problems and challenges for private international law in Australia and elsewhere, just as they create new opportunities and hazards for the world's citizens. Nevertheless, although the internet has the particular quality that it is ubiquitous, in the sense that information uploaded in one place may be immediately available on any other terminal or communication device anywhere in the world,[195] this should not blind us to the fact that the users of the internet (ie natural persons and the corporations that they represent) are present and act in the real world, by typing on a keyboard, swiping a tablet, pressing buttons on a mobile telecom device or reacting to information displayed on a screen. Indeed, the increased mobility of human beings and their gadgets rather than the capacity or inner workings of the internet may represent the greater challenge, but the resulting difficulties are as much evidential as legal.

Private international law has adapted to accommodate revolutionary developments in trade, telecommunications and technology in the past and, if necessary, it can do so again without a radical, separate approach to online transactions

[192] Joint declaration of the Commission and the Council concerning Art 15(1)(c) of the Brussels I Regulation (see ec.europa.eu/civiljustice/homepage/homepage_ec_en_declaration.pdf, last visited 18 March 2014).

[193] Rome I Regulation, Recital (24) and Art 6(1)(c). Recital (24) provides: 'With more specific reference to consumer contracts, the conflict-of-law rule should make it possible to cut the cost of settling disputes concerning what are commonly relatively small claims and to take account of the development of distance-selling techniques. Consistency with Regulation (EC) No 44/2001 requires both that there be a reference to the concept of directed activity as a condition for applying the consumer protection rule and that the concept be interpreted harmoniously in Regulation (EC) No 44/2001 and this Regulation, bearing in mind that a joint declaration by the Council and the Commission on Article 15 of Regulation (EC) No 44/2001 states that "for Article 15(1)(c) to be applicable it is not sufficient for an undertaking to target its activities at the Member State of the consumer's residence, or at a number of Member States including that Member State; a contract must also be concluded within the framework of its activities". The declaration also states that "the mere fact that an Internet site is accessible is not sufficient for Article 15 to be applicable, although a factor will be that this Internet site solicits the conclusion of distance contracts and that a contract has actually been concluded at a distance, by whatever means. In this respect, the language or currency which a website uses does not constitute a relevant factor"'.

[194] Joined Cases C-585/08 and C-144/09, *Pammer v Reederei Karl Schlüter GmbH & Co KG* and *Hotel Alpenhof GmbH v Oliver Heller* [2010] ECR I-12527. See also Case C-190/11, *Mühlleitner v Yusufi*, [2012] ECLI:EU:C:2012:313 (contract not concluded at a distance); Case C-218/12, *Emrek v Sabranovic*, Judgment of 17 October 2013.

[195] See *eDate Advertising*, n 188 above, [45].

being called for. In *Lucasfilm Ltd v Ainsworth*,[196] the English Court of Appeal rejected a submission by the claimant that the common law rules governing the recognition and enforcement of judgments required to be adapted to cope with the demands of the internet age. The Court commented:[197]

> It is true that the internet and its uses take us into a new world, and that its existence as it were in the ether (but based on servers physically located in the real world) has in general presented novel difficulties to the law and to regulators. It is also true that a website can be both wonderfully expressive and can also, subject to change and removal, be found repeatedly at its web address. The question, however, is whether for current purposes the internet or a website are fundamentally different from other matters which have enabled business persons to present themselves and their products where they are not themselves present: such as advertisements, salesmen, the post, telephone, telex and the like. We do not believe so.

Referring to *Dow Jones v Gutnick*,[198] the Court of Appeal noted that the Australian High Court was 'not there driven by the revolutionary omnipresence of the internet to a view of jurisdiction which was other than answerable to well-established principles'. That viewpoint seems correct—special regimes should be contemplated if and only if it proves impossible to apply generally applicable rules to situations involving new technologies. In considering possible reform in this area, careful attention should be given to the problems of characterisation, and practical difficulties, created by the formulation of special rules for particular types of activity.

V. Conclusion

The Attorney-General's Department is justified in its focus on private international law as an important feature of the legal landscape, affecting the willingness of Australian businesses to trade with their foreign counterparts and vice versa. As a first step in the process of reform, the Department's consultation sends the right message. The main consultation paper, and this response to it, have identified a number of areas in which there is a need, more or less pressing, for the rules currently applied by Australian courts to be reconsidered. Of these, the area of personal jurisdiction stands out as that most urgently in need of reform. It is to

[196] *Lucasfilm Ltd v Ainsworth* [2009] EWCA Civ 1328, [2010] Ch 503 (reversed but not on this point [2011] UKSC 39, [2012] 1 AC 208).

[197] ibid, [193].

[198] *Dow Jones v Gutnick* (2002) 210 CLR 575. In conclusion, the English Court of Appeal stated (at [194]) that 'on the contrary, it might be said that the sheer omnipresence of the internet would suggest that it does not easily create, outside the jurisdiction or jurisdictions in which its website owners are on established principle already to be found, that presence, partaking in some sense of allegiance, which has been recognised by our jurisprudence and rules of private international law as a necessary ingredient in the enforceability of foreign judgments'.

be hoped that priority will be given to this when the Department and the SCLJ fix their future course.

There are valuable lessons to be learned, as to both process and substance, from the activity of the European Union in remodelling its Member States' rules of private international law. Not least, the 'European experience' reveals the potential significance of private international law as a tool of economic and social policy, as well as its potential repercussions in the foreign policy sphere. These policy concerns reinforce the call for a root and branch review of Australian law in this area, and targeted legislative reforms which apply across the federation, rather than leaving the future development of Australian private international law to the courts and the individual rules committees of the federal, State and Territory courts.

9

A View from Australia's Regional Partners—Recent Developments in New Zealand and Singapore

ELSABE SCHOEMAN AND ADELINE CHONG

I. Introduction

In considering possible reforms of its rules of private international law, Australia should be alert to developments and trends in the legal systems of important trading partners in the region. Of particular interest, perhaps, are New Zealand and Singapore: two countries with which Australia has close trading ties[1] and which, with Australia, share a common law tradition. This chapter considers a number of recent developments of note which, by no means comprehensive or co-ordinated, may suggest a direction of travel on certain key topics.

II. New Zealand (Elsabe Schoeman)[2]

This review focuses on the most important recent reform, the new High Court Rules, which reaches back in time to address some significant problems and

[1] New Zealand enjoys, of course, particularly close economic and legal ties with Australia. The Australia-New Zealand Closer Economic Relations Trade Agreement (ANZCERTA) (Canberra, 28 March 1982, [1983] Australian Treaty Series 2) is described on the website of the Australian Government's Department of Foreign Affairs and Trade as 'one of the most comprehensive bilateral free trade agreements in existence' (www.dfat.gov.au/fta/anzcerta/, last visited 14 March 2014). The Singapore-Australia Free Trade Agreement (Singapore, 17 February 2003, [2003] Australian Treaty Series 16) was Australia's first bilateral free trade agreement since the ANZCERTA. With Australia, Singapore and New Zealand are parties to the ASEAN-Australia-New Zealand Trade Agreement (Hua Hun, 27 February 2009, [2010] Australian Treaty Series 1).

[2] This section was first published in the *New Zealand Law Review* ('Conflict of laws' [2013] *NZLR* 301) and is reproduced here, in slightly amended form, with the kind permission of the editors of that journal.

uncertainties that had arisen in this area of cross-border litigation in New Zealand over the last couple of decades, while also flagging other recent reforms and developments with a view to the future.[3]

A. Rules of Jurisdiction—The 'New' High Court Rules

The 'new' High Court Rules (Schedule 2 of the Judicature Act 1908) came into operation on 1 February 2009 and replaced the former ('old') High Court Rules that had been in force since 1 January 1986. The most important rules for conflict of laws purposes are those that regulate the existence and exercise of jurisdiction by New Zealand courts in cross-border litigation. In this regard the crucial rules are rule 6.27 (which provides for service abroad without the leave of the court); rule 6.28 (which provides for service abroad with the leave of the court for causes of action falling outside of the rule 6.27 paragraphs/categories); rule 5.49 (under which a defendant served abroad may object to the New Zealand court's jurisdiction); rule 6.29(1) and (2) (under which the court decides a rule 5.49 protest to jurisdiction); and rule 6.29(3) (which deals with the court's discretion to grant a stay on the basis of *forum non conveniens* where service was effected in New Zealand).

These rules have now produced the first batch of cases and, of course, it is in the heat of the battle that the reforms envisaged by the new rules are being put to the test. It did not take long for a rather complicated case to reach the Court of Appeal and the resulting decision, *Wing Hung Printing Co Ltd v Saito Offshore Pty Ltd*,[4] did not disappoint. On the contrary, not only has it clarified a number of issues, which had lingered on from the former rules, but it also set the tone for the future interpretation and application of the new rules in the context of cross-border litigation.

(i) Wing Hung Printing Co Ltd v Saito Offshore Pty Ltd

The case concerned a protest against the jurisdiction of the New Zealand High Court by three overseas defendants (the appellants), who had been served abroad without the leave of the Court pursuant to the former rule 219 (now rule 6.27). It was agreed, by virtue of the transitional provisions (section 9 of the Judicature (High Court Rules) Amendment Act 2008), that the new High Court Rules applied to determine the outcome of the protest to jurisdiction. The appellants' appeal was directed at the finding of Harrison J in the High Court that the plaintiff (the

[3] Note that the jurisdiction cases involving Australian parties (section A below) occurred before the commencement of the Trans-Tasman Proceedings Act 2010 (NZ) in 2013 (section C below). Despite the entry into force of that Act, the interpretation of the relevant High Court Rules in those instances retains its significance in relation to cross-border litigation in general.

[4] *Wing Hung Printing Co Ltd v Saito Offshore Pty Ltd* [2010] NZCA 502, [2011] 1 NZLR 754 (*Wing Hung*).

respondent on appeal) had established a good arguable case in respect of each of its causes of action, and that the New Zealand Court was the appropriate forum for the trial in terms of rule 6.29(1)(a).

The facts were somewhat complicated, but the litigation largely arose out of arrangements between the plaintiff (Saito) and the defendants for the replacement of an IT system (known as W.O.R.L.D.IT) with another one (known as ADAPT IT). The plaintiff used the IT system to provide 'source marked' labels and tags for its customers in New Zealand, Australia and the Pacific Islands. Amongst its customers were well-known retailers, such as The Warehouse, Bendon, Pumpkin Patch, Farmers and Kathmandu. The plaintiff alleged that the defendants, under a Memorandum of Understanding (MOU), had promised a 'seamless transition' from the old to the new IT system, which had not occurred. The status of the MOU was, however, uncertain in respect of who exactly the parties to it were, and whether it constituted a binding agreement at all. Be that as it may, the plaintiff's access to W.O.R.L.D.IT was disabled in May 2007 and access to ADAPT IT was refused by one of the defendants (Adapt). The plaintiff was left without access to a suitable IT system until January 2008. As a result, the plaintiff lost several customers and suffered consequential loss. The plaintiff also alleged that the defendants had wrongfully used its confidential (customer) information, resulting in further consequential loss.

The plaintiff raised seven causes of action against the various defendants: a claim under the Fair Trading Act 1986, a claim based on the misuse of confidential information, a claim based on unlawful conspiracy, two claims for breach of contract and two claims for unlawful interference with contractual relations. The issue before the Court of Appeal was whether the defendants' protest to jurisdiction should have been upheld by the High Court.

While the outcome of the appeal was no doubt of the utmost importance to the parties concerned (this was expensive and potentially intense and prolonged cross-border litigation), it is the substantial and significant guidance offered by the Court (through Randerson J's judgment) in respect of the interpretation and application of the new High Court Rules that will be the focus of this review.

(a) The Relevant High Court Rules—The Legal Framework

The Court of Appeal recognised the significance of the changes brought about by the new High Court Rules. Rule 6.27 (which replaced the old rule 219) contains a number of amendments to existing categories, as well as some additional ones for service abroad without the leave of the court. Provision is now made, for example, for service abroad without leave where interim relief is sought in support of judicial or arbitral proceedings commenced or to be commenced outside New Zealand (rule 6.27(2)(d)(ii)); where a claim is made for restitution or for the remedy of constructive trust (rule 6.27(2)(l)); and where enforcement of any judgment or arbitral award is being sought (rule 6.27(2)(m)). There is also extensive provision for service abroad without leave where a claim arises under a statute (an 'enactment': rule 6.27(2)(j)).

Rule 6.28 (which replaced the old rule 220) provides for service abroad with leave where service cannot be effected under rule 6.27—that is, where the cause of action falls outside of the categories provided for in rule 6.27(2). The important new feature in rule 6.28 is sub-rule (5)(a)–(d), which sets out exactly what the applicant must establish in order to be granted leave to serve abroad.

Rule 5.49 (which replaced the old rule 131) also contains a new feature: it now directs the court specifically (by sub-rule (7)) to decide a protest to jurisdiction in cases where service abroad was effected under rule 6.27 (without the leave of the court) or under rule 6.28 (with the leave of the court) with reference to the criteria set out in rule 6.29(1) and (2).

Rule 6.29 is completely new. It fills a gap that had existed in the old High Court Rules—there were no set criteria against which to determine whether a New Zealand court should assume jurisdiction or not once a protest against jurisdiction had been lodged. The only guidance provided in the old rule 131(4) and (6) was that the court had to be 'satisfied that it has jurisdiction' or 'satisfied that it has no jurisdiction'. Rule 6.29(1) and (2) now set out the requirements to be met in order to defeat a protest to jurisdiction, with the onus being on the party who served proceedings. Importantly, rule 6.29 bridges the gap between service abroad without leave and service abroad with leave by essentially applying the same set of criteria to protests against jurisdiction in respect of rules 6.27 and 6.28 (which corresponds to the requirements for an application to serve abroad with leave under rule 6.28(5)), namely that:

— there is a good arguable case that the claim falls within one of the rule 6.27(2) categories for service without leave (rule 6.29(1)(a)(i)) or the claim has a real and substantial connection with New Zealand for service with leave (rules 6.29(2) and 6.28(5)(a)). In *Wing Hung*, Randerson J confirmed[5] that the criterion of a good arguable case that the claim falls wholly within one or more of the paragraphs of rule 6.27 (rule 6.29(1)(a)(i)) encapsulated the requirement of a real and substantial connection with New Zealand in rule 6.28(5)(a). Moreover, it is only when a claim does not fall into one of the rule 6.27(2) 'without leave' categories that the leave of the court is required to serve abroad (rule 6.28(1));
— there is a serious issue to be tried on the merits;
— the New Zealand court is the appropriate forum for the trial; and
— any other relevant circumstances supporting an assumption of jurisdiction.

Regarding service having been effected without the leave of the court, the party who served proceedings may also establish that leave would have been granted under rule 6.28 had such leave been sought, and that it is in the interests of justice that the failure to apply for leave should be excused (rule 6.29(1)(b)).

[5] *Wing Hung*, [36].

The new High Court Rules present a far more coherent regime for service abroad without and with the leave of the court, joining the dots between protest against the existence of jurisdiction pursuant to service abroad in terms of rule 6.27 and rule 6.28 by essentially requiring the same criteria to be satisfied in each instance (through rule 6.29(1) and (2)). The Court of Appeal also clarified a number of issues in regard to the interpretation and application of key concepts in the new rules.

(b) 'Good Arguable Case' and 'Serious Issue on the Merits'

The Court of Appeal confirmed[6] that there is a difference between the 'good arguable case' and a 'serious issue on the merits' tests, and that these are distinct tests to be applied at different stages of the jurisdictional inquiry. Harrison J's view, expressed in the judgment under appeal, that 'any distinction between the touchstones of good arguable case and a serious issue for trial is moot', was rejected by Randerson J.[7] This should lay to rest the conflation of the 'good arguable case' and 'serious issue on the merits' tests in regard to a protest to jurisdiction pursuant to service abroad without the leave of the court, in the aftermath of Harrison J's decision in *Bomac Laboratories Ltd v F Hoffman-La Roche Ltd*.[8] It is clear that the new High Court Rules follow the distinction between the 'good arguable case' and 'serious issue on the merits' tests, so lucidly explained by Lord Goff in *Seaconsar Far East Ltd v Bank Markazi Jomhouri Islami Iran*.[9]

Randerson J made it clear that the 'good arguable case' test is used to determine if the claim falls within one of the paragraphs or categories set out in rule 6.27(2) (service abroad without leave). It does not relate to the merits of the case—it is by and large a factual inquiry, although in some cases the court may have to consider questions of law, or mixed questions of fact and law, such as whether a contract was made or entered into in New Zealand (rule 6.27(2)(b)(i)), or whether a contract was by its terms or by implication governed by New Zealand law (rule 6.27(2)(b)(iv)). Randerson J emphasised that:[10]

> [T]he good arguable case test does not require the plaintiff to establish a *prima facie* case. This recognises that disputed questions of fact cannot be readily resolved on affidavit evidence. On the other hand, there must be a sufficiently plausible foundation established that the claim falls within one or more of the headings in r 6.27(2). The Court should not engage in speculation.

[6] ibid, [32]–[42].

[7] ibid, [38].

[8] *Bomac Laboratories Ltd v F Hoffman-La Roche Ltd* (2002) 7 NZBLC 103,627 (New Zealand High Court) (see especially at [28]).

[9] *Seaconsar Far East Ltd v Bank Markazi Jomhouri Islami Iran* [1994] 1 AC 438 (House of Lords) (*Seaconsar*) (see E Schoeman, 'Service Abroad Without Leave: Taking Seaconsar Seriously' (2010) 16 *New Zealand Business Law Quarterly* 343).

[10] *Wing Hung*, [41] (footnotes omitted).

Once it has been established that the cause of action falls within one of the categories in rule 6.27(2), the next question is whether there is a serious issue to be tried on the merits: '[T]he Court must be satisfied there is a serious legal issue to be tried and that there is a sufficiently strong factual basis to support the legal right asserted'.[11]

Adopting the *Seaconsar* distinction between the 'good arguable case' and 'serious issue on the merits' tests also means that the New Zealand legal system, in its treatment of jurisdiction issues, now has a clear ranking of the different standards of proof. According to Lord Goff,[12] the 'good arguable case' test represents a lower standard than the normal civil burden of a balance of probabilities, while the 'serious issue on the merits' test represents a lower standard than the 'good arguable case' test. This remains the position under the law of England and Wales[13] and has now been endorsed by the New Zealand Court of Appeal in *Wing Hung*.[14]

The ranking of the different standards of proof also holds implications for deciding a protest to jurisdiction in respect of the different categories of rule 6.27(2), and this was recognised by the Court of Appeal in *Wing Hung* (at [34]). For example, in regard to the breach of contract category (rule 6.27(2)(c)), satisfaction of the 'good arguable case' test will mean that the test of a 'serious issue on the merits' has already been met. This was the case in *Seaconsar* where Lord Goff said[15] that because the claimant would already have demonstrated to the higher standard of a 'good arguable' case that there was a contract and that it had been breached within the jurisdiction, no separate issue arose as to the merits of the plaintiff's case, in respect of which the lesser 'serious issue to be tried' test applied. The higher 'good arguable case' standard would usurp the lesser 'serious issue on the merits' test.

However, in regard to some of the other categories, such as relief being sought 'against any person domiciled or ordinarily resident in New Zealand' (see rule 6.27(2)(g)), a separate issue will arise in regard to the merits of the claim[16]—the relevant category is simply not drafted tightly enough to raise a serious issue on the merits once it has been established to the standard of a good arguable case that the person is domiciled or ordinarily resident in New Zealand.[17] In order to decide whether to assume jurisdiction in terms of rule 6.29(1)(a) the court will have to ask:[18]

> [I]f, at the end of the day, there remains a substantial question of fact or law or both, arising on the facts disclosed by the affidavits, which the plaintiff bona fide desires to try …

[11] ibid, [37].

[12] *Seaconsar*, 448H–449C, 453D–G.

[13] See, eg, *Carvill America Inc v Camperdown UK Ltd* [2005] 1 CLC 845, [45]; *Astrazeneca UK Ltd v Albemarle International Corp* [2010] EWHC 1028 (Comm), [24]. Compare the approach of the High Court of Australia in *Agar v Hyde* (2000) 201 CLR 552, [50]–[52], [56]–[61].

[14] *Wing Hung*, [40].

[15] *Seaconsar*, 454E–F.

[16] ibid, 454B–D.

[17] P Myburgh and E Schoeman, 'Jurisdiction in trans-national cases' [2004] *New Zealand Law Journal* 403, 406.

[18] *Seaconsar*, 452D–E.

> [and] the standard of proof in respect of the cause of action can broadly be stated to be whether, on the affidavit evidence before the court, there is a serious question to be tried.

Of course it must be remembered that *Seaconsar* was decided within the context of the English jurisdictional regime, which requires leave to serve abroad as the norm (there is no equivalent of the New Zealand rule 6.27). Within that context the 'serious issue on the merits' test is directly related to the discretion that the court has to grant leave or not.[19] Therefore, using this test as one of the criteria for granting leave to serve abroad (rule 6.28(5(b)) and to decide protests to jurisdiction in terms of rule 6.29(1) and (2) when a New Zealand court exercises its discretion to decide whether to assume jurisdiction or not, is entirely and absolutely appropriate. This reviewer is delighted that the 'serious issue on the merits' test has been written into rules 6.28 and 6.29 and that Lord Goff's insightful analysis of this test (and how it differs from the 'good arguable case' test) in *Seaconsar* has now been adopted by the Court of Appeal in *Wing Hung* in its rightful context. Apart from simplifying matters for prospective litigants, this places the jurisdictional regime for service abroad (without and with the leave of the court) on a much firmer theoretical footing within the greater private international law context.

(c) Claims, Causes of Action and the 'All or Nothing' Approach

Upon a protest to jurisdiction, rule 6.29(1)(a)(i) requires, amongst other things, the party who served proceedings abroad without the leave of the court (in terms of rule 6.27) to prove that there is 'a good arguable case that the claim falls wholly within 1 or more of the paragraphs of rule 6.27'. What does this mean? The received wisdom from an early case decided in the similar context of service abroad (but well before the 'without leave' regime introduced through rule 219), *Jones v Flower*,[20] was that each and every cause of action should come within the relevant rule in order for service abroad to be permitted. Applied to the old rule 219 and now rule 6.27, it would mean that each cause of action would have to come under one or more of the defined categories in those rules in order to allow for service abroad without the leave of the court. However, during the reign of rule 219, the view developed that this was not necessarily the case; instead, related causes of action, based on the *same operative facts*, could all be allowed in under rule 219 when serving abroad without leave.[21] In other words, one or more causes of action, which did not fall within one of the categories in rule 219, could

[19] *Seaconsar*, 456G–457A. The test in England has now been aligned with the 'reasonable prospects of success' test which applies generally where a party seeks summary judgment on a claim or defence (see *AK Investment CJSC v Kyrgyz Mobil Tel Limited* [2011] UKPC 7, [2012] 1 WLR 1804, [71] (Lord Collins of Mapesbury) (*AK Investment*)).

[20] *Jones v Flower* (1904) 24 NZLR 447 (New Zealand Court of Appeal).

[21] See discussion in *Harris v Commerce Commission* [2009] NZCA 84, (2009) 12 TCLR 379, [70]–[71] (*Harris*).

'piggy-back' on another or other cause(s) of action that did, provided they were related, arising out of 'the same sequence of events'.[22]

In *Wing Hung*, the Court of Appeal rejected this 'operative facts' approach in regard to the application of rule 6.29(1)(a)(i) to a protest against the jurisdiction of the court pursuant to service without leave.[23] In doing so, Randerson J drew a clear distinction between a 'claim' and a 'cause of action'. A 'claim' is a broader concept than a 'cause of action'. A 'claim' is an 'amalgam of the factual and legal basis for the relief sought'.[24] Under rule 5.25 a statement of claim must contain the 'general nature of the plaintiff's claim to the relief sought', as well as sufficient particulars regarding time, place, etc, in support of the plaintiff's cause(s) of action (rule 5.26). As such, a 'claim' may include one or more 'causes of action'. Clearly, the categories in rule 6.27(2)—dealing with claims in tort, contract, etc—are based on causes of action and therefore each cause of action relied on by the plaintiff must fall under one or more of the categories in rule 6.27(2).

This does not mean that the proceeding as a whole will be dismissed for lack of jurisdiction if it is found that one or more of the causes of action relied on do not fall under one of the categories in rule 6.27(2)—rule 6.29(1) does not call for an 'all or nothing' approach. Instead, rule 6.29(1)(b) provides the opportunity for a plaintiff to establish, in regard to those causes of action that do not come under rule 6.27, that, had leave to serve abroad been applied for under rule 6.28, such leave would have been granted, and that it is in the interests of justice that the failure to apply for leave should be excused.[25]

Furthermore, Randerson J confirmed that, if necessary, the Court had inherent jurisdiction (under rule 5.49(8)) to require the party effecting service to file and serve an amended statement of claim, confining the causes of action to those that met the rule 6.29 requirements.[26] This is what happened in *Wing Hung*, where the plaintiff had to abandon two causes of action entirely because they did not meet the 'serious issue on the merits' test and was required to effect some other minor amendments. This is an eminently sensible approach: the advantages gained (in terms of time, cost and procedural efficiency) by having a 'without leave' regime, such as rule 6.27, will not be defeated by the court having to dismiss the entire proceeding, with the result that the plaintiff is sent back to the drawing board to start all over again, which may result in the claim being abandoned altogether.

[22] *Harris*, [71].

[23] *Wing Hung*, [57], [69]–[71].

[24] ibid, [51].

[25] As indeed happened in *Wing Hung* in respect of the wrongful use of confidential information claim, which would have to rely in part on an equitable duty of confidence, a category not provided for in rule 6.27(2): *Wing Hung*, [115].

[26] ibid, [69].

(d) *Forum Conveniens* and *Forum Non Conveniens*

Apart from the 'real and substantial connection'/'good arguable case' and 'serious issue to be tried on the merits' requirements, the party effecting service also has to establish that the New Zealand court is 'the appropriate forum' (as well as any other circumstances supporting the assumption of jurisdiction by the court: rules 6.28(5)(c) and (d) and 6.29). This requirement of *forum conveniens* needs to be established both for obtaining leave to serve abroad (under rule 6.28), as well as on a protest to jurisdiction (under rule 6.29(1) or (2)). In *Wing Hung* Randerson J stated that:[27]

> The party effecting service must also establish that New Zealand is the appropriate forum for the trial. In considering that issue, the court will be guided by existing authority including the matters canvassed by the House of Lords in *Spiliada Maritime Corporation v Cansulex Ltd* (*The Spiliada*). However, an important *difference relates to the onus of proof.*
>
> Prior to the introduction of the new High Court Rules, it was accepted that the burden of proof lay on a defendant seeking a stay of proceedings on the ground that another forum was more appropriate. *It was for the defendant to show there was another available forum which was clearly or distinctly more appropriate. The new rule now places the onus of proof on the party effecting service* (emphasis added).

These two paragraphs are indicative of the New Zealand courts' confusion in regard to *forum conveniens* and *forum non conveniens*, which stems from a failure to distinguish clearly between the 'existence' and the 'exercise' of jurisdiction. Already in 1964–65, the late Dr BD Inglis QC (a New Zealand conflicts scholar and later Family Court Judge) published two excellent articles on the topic.[28] In these articles Inglis distinguished very clearly between *forum conveniens* and *forum non conveniens*. *Forum conveniens* was a requirement that the plaintiff had to meet in order to obtain leave to serve out of the jurisdiction and was therefore concerned with the establishment of the *existence* of jurisdiction—the onus was on the plaintiff to prove that the New Zealand court was the appropriate forum for the trial. *Forum non conveniens*, on the other hand, was concerned with the *exercise* of jurisdiction. Originally pleaded within the context of abuse of process, the defendant was not disputing the existence of jurisdiction; rather the burden was on the defendant to prove that there was another forum, with jurisdiction in the matter, which was clearly or distinctly more appropriate to hear the case. In other words, although the New Zealand court had jurisdiction (jurisdiction *existed*), it should not *exercise* its jurisdiction.

[27] *Wing Hung*, [43]–[44] (footnotes omitted).

[28] BD Inglis, 'Forum Conveniens—Basis of Jurisdiction in the Commonwealth' (1964) 13 *American Journal of Comparative Law* 583 (Inglis, 'Forum Conveniens'), and BD Inglis, 'Jurisdiction, the Doctrine of Forum Conveniens, and Choice of Law in Conflict of Laws' (1965) 81 *LQR* 380 (Inglis, 'Jurisdiction').

This distinction between *forum non conveniens* and *forum conveniens* is also expressed by Lord Goff in the leading English decision, *Spiliada Maritime Corp v Cansulex Ltd*,[29] where he refers) to:[30]

> [C]ases where jurisdiction has been founded as of right by service of proceedings on the defendant within the jurisdiction, but the defendant seeks a stay of the proceedings on the ground of forum non conveniens, and cases where the court is invited to exercise its discretion … to give leave for service on the defendant out of the jurisdiction [*forum conveniens*].

Lord Goff goes on to discuss *forum non conveniens* and *forum conveniens* under separate headings in his speech,[31] and enumerates the distinctions between the *forum non conveniens* and *forum conveniens* inquiries.[32]

So, the burden of proof in respect of *forum conveniens* and *forum non conveniens* has not changed as a result of the new High Court Rules, as suggested in *Wing Hung*.[33] The burden of proof has always been on the plaintiff in respect of *forum conveniens* and on the defendant in respect of *forum non conveniens*. Reference to the correct passages in *The Spiliada*, and Inglis's early scholarly writing on the topic, would have avoided this confusion in the New Zealand courts. Admittedly, the old rule 219 (service abroad without leave) was problematic in the sense that it was difficult to classify it as 'jurisdiction as of right' or otherwise,[34] but the new rule 6.29(1) now subjects a protest to jurisdiction established pursuant to service abroad without leave (under rule 6.27) to the same *forum conveniens* requirement as an application for leave to serve abroad (under rule 6.28). This makes it clear that, in this context, *forum conveniens* is aimed at establishing jurisdiction—the *existence* of jurisdiction—and not the *exercise* of jurisdiction. It is also now clear that rule 6.29(3) deals with *forum non conveniens*, since a defendant, having been served in New Zealand, may apply for a stay of proceedings on the basis that 'New Zealand is not the appropriate forum for the trial'. (One can only hope that this formulation will not obscure the true focus of the *forum non conveniens* inquiry, namely to establish that there is another clearly or distinctly more appropriate forum available to hear the matter;[35] the focus should not be on the inappropriateness of the New Zealand court in the first instance.)

Regarding the application of the *forum conveniens* requirement in respect of a protest to jurisdiction (under rule 6.29(1)(a)) in response to service abroad without leave (in terms of rule 6.27), Randerson J adopted a very sensible approach. While the requirements of a 'good arguable case' and a 'serious issue to be tried

[29] *Spiliada Maritime Corp v Cansulex Ltd* [1987] AC 460 (House of Lords) (*The Spiliada*).

[30] ibid, 473H–474A.

[31] '(6) How the principle is applied in cases of stay of proceedings' (ibid, 475C), and '(7) How the principle is applied in cases where the court exercises its discretionary power under RSC, Ord 11' [leave cases] (at 478F).

[32] ibid, 480G–481E.

[33] *Wing Hung*, [43]–[44].

[34] Myburgh and Schoeman, above n 17.

[35] *The Spiliada*, 477E.

on the merits' are considered with reference to each individual cause of action, in his view:[36] '[I]t will often be appropriate to assess the appropriate forum issue and any other relevant factors supporting the assumption of jurisdiction on a global basis where there are multiple causes of action'.

Since the purpose of the *forum conveniens* (and *forum non conveniens*) inquiry is 'to identify the forum in which the case can be suitably tried for the interests of all the parties and for the ends of justice',[37] the appropriateness of the New Zealand forum should be assessed with reference to all the causes of action and all the circumstances of the case. In *Wing Hung* the factors in favour of a New Zealand or a foreign forum were quite finely balanced, but factors that tipped the scales in New Zealand's favour were that the applicable law was predominantly that of New Zealand (or Victoria, but not China),[38] and the fact that one of the causes of action was based on the Fair Trading Act 1986 (NZ) and that in that respect New Zealand law definitely applied.[39]

The same global approach in respect of *forum conveniens* will no doubt also make sense in the context of a rule 6.28 application for leave to serve abroad.

(ii) Turn and Wave Ltd v Northstar Accounts Pty Ltd

The approach of the New Zealand Court of Appeal in *Wing Hung* has since been followed in a number of cases. One of these cases, *Turn and Wave Ltd v Northstar Accounts Pty Ltd*,[40] which had its origins in investment schemes devised by the Blue Chip group of companies, merits some discussion because of a couple of interesting features.

Briefly, Turn and Wave built apartments in Auckland, which it claimed the defendants had agreed to buy. The units had been marketed in Australia by an Australian Blue Chip company as part of an investment package. When the Australian defendants failed to complete the transactions, Turn and Wave commenced proceedings in the Auckland High Court for specific performance and, against one defendant, damages. All the defendants were from New South Wales or the Australian Capital Territory (ACT). They protested the jurisdiction of the New Zealand Court after having been served abroad without the leave of the Court under rule 6.27. Five of the defendants had also commenced proceedings against Turn and Wave (and the Australian Blue Chip company) in the Supreme Court of the ACT for failure to comply with the contracts, misrepresentation, and several causes of action under Australian investor and consumer protection legislation. A decision on a protest against jurisdiction by Turn and Wave in the ACT proceedings had been reserved by the Supreme Court.

[36] *Wing Hung*, [72].
[37] *The Spiliada*, 480G.
[38] *Wing Hung*, [136].
[39] ibid, [135], [141].
[40] CIV-2010-404-2268, 23 December 2010 (New Zealand High Court) (*Turn and Wave*).

(a) Exclusive Jurisdiction Clause

In regard to the Auckland proceedings, the rule 6.29(1)(a) 'good arguable case' and 'serious issue on the merits' criteria were easily met—apart from other available categories under rule 6.27(2), the alleged contracts had been breached in New Zealand and therefore paragraph 6.27(2)(c) was satisfied. As pointed out in *Wing Hung* (following *Seaconsar*), the breach of contract category does not require the lesser 'serious issue to be tried on the merits' test to be separately satisfied, since the higher standard of a 'good arguable case' has already been met (see discussion at Section II.A.(i).(b). above). It is good to see that this rather sophisticated line of reasoning, which distinguishes between the different categories in rule 6.27(2), has already been applied subsequent to the decision in *Wing Hung*.

The standard form contract used by Turn and Wave contained an exclusive jurisdiction clause in favour of a New Zealand court and an express choice of New Zealand law. The defendants contested the terms of the contract and specifically the exclusive forum clause. According to the defendants, there was a complete mismatch between the agreements they entered into (presented to them by the Australian Blue Chip company), and the agreements relied on by Turn and Wave. Therefore the exclusive jurisdiction clause was disputed. The judge considered the exclusive forum clause as part of the inquiry into the appropriateness of the New Zealand Court to assume jurisdiction in the matter.[41] Regarding the standard of proof for establishing that the exclusive jurisdiction clause bound the defendants, Associate Judge Bell reasoned as follows:[42]

> Under r 6.28(5) the plaintiff has the onus to establish that New Zealand is the appropriate forum for the trial. That requires that the plaintiff must satisfy the Court that New Zealand is more appropriate than any other forum for the trial. It is an onus of persuasion: see *Bankinvest v Seabrook* per Kirby P and *James Hardie Co. Ltd v Valley* per Mason P at 380. If the Court is to be satisfied on balance that New Zealand is the more appropriate forum, then when the Court considers a contractual provision that pre-empts that inquiry, it is appropriate to apply the same standard of requiring the plaintiff to establish on balance that the parties are contractually bound by the exclusive choice of forum clause. Accordingly, I apply the civil standard to this issue, while bearing in mind that any such finding is, in the context of the case, only provisional, given that there will be a later hearing where witnesses will be subject to cross-examination. A decision after a full hearing of evidence may result in different findings on formation of contract.

On the normal civil standard of a balance of probabilities, Turn and Wave did not succeed in proving that the exclusive forum clause was part of the agreement.[43] However, Associate Judge Bell said the evidence regarding the formation of the contract was still strong enough to satisfy the 'good arguable case' requirement for

[41] Although there is no mention of rule 6.29 in *Turn and Wave*, it is clear that this was a protest to jurisdiction in terms of rule 5.49 pursuant to service abroad without leave (rule 6.27) and therefore the rule 6.28(5)(c) *forum conveniens* requirement comes in through rule 6.29(1)(a)(ii).

[42] *Turn and Wave*, [43] (footnotes omitted).

[43] ibid, [73].

the rule 6.27(2) categories.[44] This is correct, because the civil onus of a balance of probabilities is a higher standard than the 'good arguable case' test.[45]

(b) Australian Investor and Consumer Protection Legislation

In considering whether the New Zealand Court was the appropriate forum for the proceedings (with reference to rule 6.28(5)(d) within rule 6.29(1)(a)(ii)), the judge considered the relevance of Australian investor and consumer protection legislation that the defendants wanted to rely on, such as the Corporations Act 2001, the Australian Securities and Investments Commission Act 2001, the Trade Practices Act 1974 and its State and Territorial counterparts. This was a different situation from the one in *Wing Hung*, where one of the plaintiff's claims was made under the New Zealand Fair Trading Act 1986. In *Turn and Wave* the defendants wanted to rely on the protection of foreign (Australian) legislation. Since the other factors relevant to the *forum conveniens* enquiry (witnesses, etc) were quite evenly balanced, the judge considered the defendants' ability to rely on Australian protective legislation to be a significant one. Turn and Wave indicated that they would not object to the defendants raising the relevant Australian investor and consumer protection legislation[46] and this, according to Associate Judge Bell, significantly reduced the risk of injustice to the defendants in having to litigate in New Zealand.[47]

It is interesting to note that there was a strong '*Cambridgeshire* factor'[48] to the proceedings by reason of related pre-existing proceedings in New Zealand: *Hickman v Turn and Wave Ltd*[49] (involving 60 plaintiffs); *Turn and Wave Ltd v Johnson*;[50] and *Turn and Wave Ltd v Bruce Gordon and Others*.[51] Associate Judge Bell said there were clear advantages in hearing all proceedings related to the sale and purchase of the apartments in one country—it would promote 'efficiency in resolution of issues and consistency of decision'.[52] He also pointed out that all the parties had made a significant investment in dealing with the case in New Zealand and that lawyers on both sides had a good grasp of the issues.[53]

However, the key factor that tipped the scales in favour of the New Zealand Court as the appropriate forum was the plaintiff's concession to allow the defendants to invoke Australian investor and consumer protection legislation: 'Without that concession, the balance would be on the other side'.[54] Of course, it would be

[44] ibid, [74].

[45] See above, text to nn 12–13 above.

[46] *Turn and Wave*, [103].

[47] ibid, [104].

[48] See *The Spiliada*, 485F–486B.

[49] CIV-2008-404-5871, 9 December 2009 (New Zealand High Court).

[50] CIV-2009-404-2616, 18 December 2009 (New Zealand High Court).

[51] CIV-2010-404-4372, 13 December 2011 (New Zealand High Court: *Turner and Waverley Ltd v Stannig*); *Turner and Waverley Ltd v Edmonds* [2012] NZHC 288.

[52] *Turn and Wave*, [112], [118].

[53] ibid, [113], [118].

[54] ibid, [119].

interesting to see how these foreign protective statutes would be applied in a New Zealand court, bearing in mind that they are often very territorially focused and not necessarily of a cross-border mandatory nature. In respect of causes of action not governed by Australian law, these statutes would fall into the class of (potentially mandatory) rules of a third significantly connected country (ie, not forming part of either the *lex fori* or the *lex causae*), an area of private international law that has not been explored to any great extent in Anglo-common law countries.

(iii) Exportrade Corporation v Irie Blue New Zealand Ltd

Wing Hung was also followed, in so far as it was relevant, in *Exportrade Corporation v Irie Blue New Zealand Ltd*,[55] the latest instalment in a protracted and complicated litigational battle through the New Zealand courts, dating back to 2008. At the centre of the dispute was the recovery of a debt by the plaintiff, Exportrade (incorporated in Florida), for clothing delivered to the defendants (Mr and Mrs (since deceased) Gribble and their 'alter ego', Irie Blue) in Barbados. Exportrade obtained judgment in Florida against the defendants and commenced proceedings to enforce that judgment in New Zealand. By the time the case reached the Court of Appeal, the plaintiff was advancing five causes of action: enforcement of the Florida judgment (against all defendants); breach of contract (against all defendants); acknowledgement of debt (against Mr Gribble); and two causes of action relating to breach of the Companies Act of Barbados (against Mr and Mrs Gribble). The defendants contested the jurisdiction of the New Zealand Court right from the start.

As the first defendant, Irie Blue, had been served in New Zealand, rule 6.29(3) applied—there could be no protest to the *existence* of jurisdiction, but Irie Blue could object to the *exercise* of jurisdiction on the basis of *forum non conveniens.* The third defendant, Mr Gribble, had been served abroad without leave pursuant to rule 6.27(2) and therefore the *existence* of jurisdiction could be and was contested under rule 5.49. (A further issue regarding substituted service in respect of Mr Gribble is not discussed here; suffice to say it added yet another layer to an already complex procedural saga.)

(a) *Forum Non Conveniens*

In the Court of Appeal White J acknowledged the 'good arguable case' and 'serious issue on the merits' as two distinct tests to be applied at different stages of the jurisdictional inquiry.[56] In respect of Mr Gribble the jurisdictional gateways in rule 6.27(2)(g) and (h) were clearly satisfied on the good arguable case test (with the categories in rule 6.27(2)(b) and (c) being less convincing) and the 'serious issue on the merits' test was also met. White J considered all the requirements of

[55] *Exportrade Corporation v Irie Blue New Zealand Ltd* [2013] NZCA 675 (*Exportrade*).
[56] ibid, [23], following *Wing Hung*.

rule 6.28(5)(b)–(d) (invoked through rule 6.29(1)) to have been met in regard to Mr Gribble, and so jurisdiction *existed*.[57] The issue was whether jurisdiction should be *exercised* and so White J proceeded to a proper *forum non conveniens* inquiry.

Following the approach set out by Lord Goff in *The Spiliada*, White J emphasised that the burden of proof was on the defendant in a *forum non conveniens* inquiry, and that this was different from an application for leave to serve abroad, in which case the burden would be on the applicant (plaintiff) requesting leave.[58] Adopting the two-stage approach set out by Lord Goff in *The Spiliada*,[59] White J first considered factors pointing to Barbados as the clearly more appropriate forum, such as the applicable law, the (lack of) connection of the causes of action with New Zealand, the location of witnesses and the location of documents. He decided that Irie Blue and Mr Gribble[60] had discharged the onus of proving that the 'courts of Barbados rather than New Zealand are prima facie the appropriate forum'[61] for the trial. According to *The Spiliada* a discharge of this first stage onus by the defendant will ordinarily result in the court granting a stay unless the plaintiff can prove that there are 'circumstances by reason of which justice requires that a stay should nevertheless not be granted', for example, 'if established objectively by cogent evidence, that the plaintiff will not obtain justice in the foreign jurisdiction'.[62] In *AK Investment*, Lord Collins of Mapesbury (within the context of a request for leave to serve abroad) discussed at length the threshold for proving that justice will not be obtained in the foreign jurisdiction, concluding that

> the burden can be satisfied by showing that there is a real risk that justice will not be obtained in the foreign court by reason of incompetence or lack of independence or corruption … if it can be shown that justice 'will not' be obtained that will weigh more heavily.[63]

The risk of injustice in the foreign jurisdiction is the prime example of a factor that would be relevant to the second stage of the *forum non conveniens* inquiry. It is clear from *The Spiliada* that general factors relating to the 'appropriateness of forum' are to be considered in the first stage of the *forum non conveniens* inquiry

[57] As regards the requirement in rule 6.28(5)(c), that New Zealand be shown to be the appropriate forum for the trial, White J merely observed (at [28]) that it had not been suggested that, if the court was satisfied that New Zealand was the appropriate forum for trial of the claim against Irie Blue, it was not also the appropriate forum for the trial of the claim against Mr Gribble. The Court proceeded to consider the issue of *forum non conveniens* (below, text to nn 58–67) on the basis that both Irie Blue and Mr Gribble bore the burden of showing another available, more appropriate forum (at [43]). The true position, it is submitted, is that Irie Blue alone had that burden, with the plaintiff, Exportrade, retaining the burden with respect to Mr Gribble under rule 6.28(5)(c), but that if Irie Blue failed to discharge that burden, it would follow as a matter of course that Exportrade would succeed in showing that New Zealand was the appropriate forum for the trial of the claims against Mr Gribble.

[58] ibid, [39], [42].

[59] ibid, [43].

[60] As to the burden of proof in relation to Mr Gribble, see above, n 57.

[61] ibid, [52].

[62] *The Spiliada*, 478C–E.

[63] *AK Investment*, [95].

and that the second stage will not necessarily follow in each and every case. In other words, the second stage, during which the onus is squarely on the plaintiff, is not to be invoked as a matter of course.

In *Exportrade*, White J proceeded to examine the issue of *forum conveniens* in two, apparently distinct stages. Having identified Barbados as the more appropriate forum, White J proceeded to consider in a separate section of his judgment a number of factors which led, in his view, to the conclusion that the plaintiff, Exportrade, had discharged the onus of proving 'special circumstances' requiring that the trial should proceed in New Zealand. The factors addressed during this second stage were the following:[64] the fact that the proceeding had been before the New Zealand courts for five years and that Exportrade would be prejudiced if it had to start afresh in Barbados; the giving of evidence in New Zealand by Mr Gribble (then resident in New Zealand); access to company documents and records in Barbados (which could be done through modern communications); the defendants' assets in New Zealand;the retention of the defendants' New Zealand lawyers of the last five years; the joinder of third parties (though there was no suggestion of that occurring); the enforcement of any judgment obtained by Exportrade against the defendants in New Zealand; the costs of commencing a new proceeding in Barbados; 'well-established procedures available for providing the New Zealand court with evidence of the governing foreign law';[65] the fact that it was the Florida-based plaintiff that had elected to litigate in New Zealand and that it was the defendants who sought to have the proceedings conducted in Barbados in order to avoid judgment, or the enforcement of the Florida judgment, against them in the New Zealand Court. Therefore, the defendants' preference for a Barbadian forum appeared to be for mere tactical advantages, rather than any real benefit in litigating in Barbados. White J also mentioned a possible limitation issue in Barbados, the defendants having indicated that they would not make any concessions in that regard.[66]

It may be questioned why the Court embarked on the second stage of the *forum non conveniens* inquiry at all. None of the factors canvassed during the second stage, except for the possible limitation issue (which had not been established), pointed to any problems specifically related to Barbados. In fact, all the factors considered in the second stage should have been addressed in the first stage of the inquiry, with the plaintiff refuting the defendants' arguments in support of a Barbadian court as the clearly more appropriate forum—those were the same kind of factors considered during the first stage in *The Spiliada*. New Zealand courts will do well to heed Lord Goff's clear instructions in this regard:[67]

> [I]n general the burden of proof rests on the defendant to persuade the court to exercise its discretion to grant a stay. It is however of importance to remember that *each party will*

[64] *Exportrade*, [55].
[65] ibid, [55(g)].
[66] ibid, [56].
[67] *The Spiliada*, 476D–E (footnotes omitted).

> *seek to establish the existence of certain matters which will assist him in persuading the court to exercise its discretion in his favour, and that in respect of any such matter the evidential burden will rest on the party who asserts its existence.* Furthermore, if the court is satisfied that there is another available forum which is prima facie the appropriate forum for the trial of the action, the *burden will then shift to the plaintiff to show that there are special circumstances* by reason of which justice requires that the trial should nevertheless take place in this country (emphasis added).

Clearly, the second stage of the *forum non conveniens* inquiry is reserved for 'special circumstances'; all regular factors related to the appropriateness of the respective fora should be dealt with in the first stage.

(iv) Other Cases of Note

In *Bomac Laboratories Ltd v Life Medicals (MSDN BHD)*,[68] Gilbert J confirmed the decision by Associate Judge Abbott at first instance.[69] The case concerned the supply of medical bags by the defendant (a Malaysian company), to the plaintiff (a New Zealand company), which turned out to be defective (the 'leaky bags' case). The defendant had been served in Malaysia without the leave of the New Zealand court in terms of rule 6.27 and it did not contest the *existence* of jurisdiction. Instead, the defendant contested the *exercise* of jurisdiction in terms of rule 15.1, applying for a stay of proceedings on the basis of *forum non conveniens.*

The defendant argued that a Malaysian court would be clearly more appropriate to decide the matter and Associate Judge Abbot decided the case with reference to the factors and considerations set out in *The Spiliada*. Important for the current discussion is that this was a pure *forum non conveniens* case with the defendant bearing the burden to prove that there was another available forum (in Malaysia) that was clearly more appropriate than the New Zealand one. The defendant's application for a stay did not come under rule 6.29(3), since the defendant had not been served *in New Zealand* and therefore this case illustrates that there is still room for the classic *forum non conveniens* doctrine (rule 15.1, linking up with the doctrine's 'abuse of process' origins[70]).[71]

Finally, another High Court case, *Chevalier Wholesale Produce v Joes Farm Produce Ltd*,[72] presented an issue concerning the place of formation of a contract within the meaning of rule 6.27(2)(b)(i): this category provides for service abroad without leave in cases where a contract being sued upon was 'made or entered into' in New Zealand. It appeared that the parties had conducted their communications by fax. Associate Judge Bell confirmed[73] that in regard to instantaneous

[68] *Bomac Laboratories Ltd v Life Medicals (MSDN BHD)* [2012] NZHC 363, [2012] BCL 254 (an application for review before the New Zealand High Court).

[69] CIV-2010-404-4654, 5 August 2011 (New Zealand High Court).

[70] Inglis, 'Forum Conveniens', above n 28, 592 and Inglis, 'Jurisdiction', above n 28, 387.

[71] See also *Exportrade*, discussed above. See p 204.

[72] CIV-2010-404-4229, 17 November 2011 (New Zealand High Court).

[73] ibid, [11].

communications, such as fax, the postal acceptance rule did not apply. Acceptance of an offer occurs at the place where the offeror receives the fax accepting the offer (and not at the place where the acceptance letter was posted as under the postal acceptance rule when communicating by ordinary mail).

B. Choice of Law—The Limitation Act 2010 (NZ)

The proper classification of limitation rules has always been a challenge for the conflict of laws. If a limitation law was classified as procedural, the *lex fori* governed, whereas the *lex causae* applied if it was classified as substantive. A procedural classification would allow a plaintiff to forum shop for a suitable limitation period and that resulted in uncertainty and unpredictability. (Although a plaintiff could also forum shop for appropriate conflict rules if limitation laws were regarded as substantive, this is less of a problem than a procedural classification.)

There is a definite trend in contemporary conflicts theory and practice favouring the substantive characterisation of a range of matters affecting the outcome of litigation (eg, ceilings on damages, heads of damages, etc), and therefore subjecting as much as possible to the *lex causae*, rather than leaving it to the *lex fori*.[74] Limitation statutes, and the characterisation of these rules, are at the centre of this trend and New Zealand has now caught up with the rest of the world.

The Limitation Act 2010 (New Zealand) makes it clear that foreign limitation laws are to be classified as substantive. Section 55 states that:

> (2) The limitation law of that foreign country is part of the substantive law of that country and must be applied accordingly in that proceeding or arbitration.
> (3) A New Zealand court or tribunal or arbitrator exercising … a discretion under the limitation law of a foreign country must, so far as practicable, exercise it in the manner in which it is exercised in that foreign country.

Two observations must be made in respect of the new legislation. First, it seems, by implication, that New Zealand's own limitation laws should also now be regarded as substantive, and therefore only applying when New Zealand law is the *lex causae* (see also section 15(4)). This may seem like an obvious or even trivial point, but bearing in mind the traditional (mostly procedural) classification of limitation rules in common law jurisdictions on the basis that they merely barred the remedy, rather than extinguishing the right (which would have resulted in a substantive classification), this is a significant shift in conflicts thinking. It brings New Zealand in step with reforms in other common law jurisdictions,

[74] See R Tobin and E Schoeman, 'The New Zealand Accident Compensation Scheme: The Statutory Bar and the Conflict of Laws' (2005) 53 *American Journal of Comparative Law* 493; E Schoeman, 'Rome II and the substance-procedure dichotomy: crossing the Rubicon' [2010] *Lloyds Maritime & Commercial Law Quarterly* 81.

including Australia,[75] as well as the European Union conflicts Regulations.[76] On the international level, this promotes (although of course does not guarantee) certainty, predictability and uniformity of result.

Secondly, no reference is made specifically to the rules relating to the commencement, interruption and suspension of limitation periods in contrast to the Rome II Regulation (Article 15(h)). While the Rome II Regulation makes it clear that everything is to be governed by the applicable law, that may not necessarily be the best solution. In a very insightful judgment in the Novia Scotia Court of Appeal,[77] MacDonald CJNS distinguished very clearly between *when* an action must be commenced (ie, the actual limitation period, which is substantive and governed by the *lex causae*) and *how* an action must be commenced (ie, the method, which is a procedural matter and governed by the *lex fori*) in order to stop the time from running.

Finally, section 56 of the Limitation Act 2010 provides for an 'undue hardship' exception to the application of foreign limitation laws. This is similar to the position in the Foreign Limitation Periods Act 1984 (UK), section 2(2).

C. The Trans-Tasman Proceedings Act 2010 (NZ)

This Act, which entered into force on 11 October 2013, will greatly simplify trans-Tasman litigation.[78] According to section 3(1), the purpose of the Act is to: 'streamline the process for resolving civil proceedings with a trans-Tasman element in order to reduce costs and improve efficiency'; and 'minimise existing impediments to enforcing certain Australian judgments and regulatory sanctions'. Amongst other things, the new regime provides (according to section 3(3)) for:

(a) service in Australia of initiating documents for civil proceedings commenced in New Zealand courts and tribunals;

[75] In Australia, the same outcome has of course been reached principally (but not exclusively) by judicial reform (see *John Pfeiffer Pty Ltd v Rogerson* [2000] HCA 36; (2000) 203 CLR 503, [97]–[100]; *Regie Nationale des Usines Renault SA v Zhang* (2002) 210 CLR 491, [75]–[76]; *Garsec Pty Ltd v His Majesty The Sultan of Brunei* [2008] NSWCA 211, [142], [166]; *Fleming v Marshall* [2011] NSWCA 86, [46]; Limitation Act 1964 (Tas), ss 25A–25E; Limitation Act 1985 (ACT), ss 5–7; Choice of Law Limitation Periods Acts (NSW 1993, NT 1994, Qld 1996, Vic 1993, WA 1994). Legislation was necessary in England (see Foreign Limitation Periods Act 1984 (UK)).

[76] See especially the Rome I Regulation (Regulation (EC) 593/2008 on the law applicable to contractual obligations [2008] OJ L177/6, art 12(1)(d)), and the Rome II Regulation (Regulation (EC) 864/2007 on the law applicable to non-contractual obligations [2007] OJ L199/40, art 15(h)).

[77] *Vogler v Szendroi* 2008 NSCA 18; (2008) 290 DLR (4th) 642, esp at [32], [36]. (See also the Foreign Limitation Periods Act 1984 (UK), under which the commencement of proceedings is governed by the *lex fori* (s 1(3)).

[78] For more detailed commentary on the Trans-Tasman Regime, see the contributions in this volume by Reid Mortensen (Chapter six) and David Goddard QC (Chapter seven). See also Reid Mortensen, 'Judgments Extension under CER' [1999] *New Zealand Law Review* 237; and Reid Mortensen, 'The Hague and the Ditch: The Trans-Tasman Judicial Area and the Choice of Court Convention' (2009) 5 *Journal of Private International Law* 213.

(b) New Zealand courts declining jurisdiction and, by order, staying proceedings in New Zealand on the grounds that an Australian court is the more appropriate forum to determine the proceedings;
(c) New Zealand courts giving interim relief in support of civil proceedings commenced in Australian courts;
(d) recognition and enforcement in New Zealand of specified judgments of Australian courts and tribunals;
(e) recognition and enforcement in New Zealand of judgments (other than those imposing civil pecuniary penalties) given in Australian trans-Tasman market proceedings;
(f) recognition and enforcement in New Zealand of Australian judgments (including those given in an Australian trans-Tasman market proceeding) imposing civil pecuniary penalties;
(g) recognition and enforcement in New Zealand of Australian judgments imposing regulatory regime criminal fines.

Significantly, High Court Rules 6.27 and 6.28[79] will no longer apply to service of proceedings in Australia—parties can be served in Australia as if they were in New Zealand. Furthermore, a judgment may only be refused enforcement on the ground of public policy, and judgments also now include non-money judgments.

D. Intellectual Property

A final development of note is in the area of intellectual property, following on from the earlier decision of the New Zealand High Court in *KK Sony Computer Entertainment v Van Veen*.[80] In *Stewart v Franmara Inc (No 2)*,[81] the plaintiff, who had designed and patented a bottle opener that extracts the cork, wire and foil wrapping from a champagne bottle at the same time, alleged that the defendant had distributed bottle openers based on his design in New Zealand and America. The plaintiff sued the defendant, inter alia, for breach of his New Zealand and American patents for the device. The issue was whether the New Zealand court could entertain a claim for breach of a foreign-registered patent in that country. In rejecting the challenge to the New Zealand court's jurisdiction in *Stewart*, Toogood J referred[82] to *Sony*, where MacKenzie J had endorsed the distinction between claims in respect of the 'validity or existence' of intellectual property rights, and claims in respect of the infringement of 'unchallenged' intellectual property rights (*Sony* was concerned with copyright). This, in the Judge's view, reflected 'an emerging trend towards the international enforcement of intellectual property

[79] See Section A above.
[80] *KK Sony Computer Entertainment v Van Veen* (2007) 71 IPR 179 (HC) (*Sony*).
[81] *Stewart v Franmara Inc (No 2)* [2012] NZHC 1771 (*Stewart*).
[82] ibid, [11].

rights, especially in cases where the validity of those rights is not challenged',[83] and this trend was also demonstrated recently in the United Kingdom Supreme Court's decision in *Lucasfilm Ltd v Ainsworth*.[84] Acknowledging the Supreme Court's observation in *Lucasfilm Ltd v Ainsworth*[85] that 'the rationale of the *Moçambique* rule[86] can be applied to patents, at any rate where questions of validity are involved', Toogood J decided that the New Zealand court had jurisdiction to determine the plaintiff's claim in respect of the infringement of his American patent in America, since no issue arose in regard to the validity of the patent.[87]

E. Conclusion

From the content of this review it is clear that the bulk of cross-border litigation in New Zealand courts still concerns jurisdictional matters. Since the outcome of a conflicts dispute should depend on the *lex causae* governing the substantive matters, rather than on which court assumes jurisdiction, it is hoped that the new High Court Rules will simplify the process of establishing jurisdiction to the extent that disputes can move beyond this initial hurdle and proceed to the choice of law inquiry with increasing frequency. The courts have shown that they are prepared to put the effort into interpreting the new High Court Rules and this is paying off—we see steady trends developing and the Court of Appeal set a good precedent in *Wing Hung*. The focus is on streamlining the process of establishing jurisdiction over foreign defendants while ensuring that the New Zealand court is the appropriate forum. In regard to substantive matters, the courts have adopted a progressive attitude towards the *Moçambique* rule in respect of intellectual property rights, and the Limitation Act 2010 has put New Zealand in step with modern trends in characterising limitation rules. Finally, the Trans-Tasman Proceedings Act 2010 will give New Zealand its first taste of regional cooperation on a conflicts level.

III. Singapore (Adeline Chong)

A. Introduction

This review is divided into two parts. The first part seeks to give a brief explanation of Singapore private international law for the benefit of readers who

[83] ibid, [14].
[84] *Lucasfilm Ltd v Ainsworth* [2011] UKSC 39, [2012] 1 AC 208.
[85] ibid, [106].
[86] *British South Africa Co v Companhia de Moçambique* [1893] AC 602 (House of Lords).
[87] *Stewart*, [18].

may be unfamiliar with it. While there has been no attempt at a comprehensive examination and reform of the whole corpus of private international law along the lines of that currently being undertaken in Australia,[88] Singapore law has deviated in some ways from the English common law. The second part of this review discusses judicial co-operation, which is becoming an increasing necessity in the era of globalisation. Specifically, this review will focus on two issues which are the subject of recent developments, namely, the method of proving foreign law (a topic on which co-operation between one Australian jurisdiction and Singapore is particularly close) and co-operation in cross-border insolvencies.

B. Overview of Singapore Private International Law

This section aims to give readers an overview of the landscape of Singapore private international law by discussing the broad rules on jurisdiction, recognition and enforcement of foreign judgments and choice of law.

As for Australia, Singapore rules on private international law are largely inherited from the English common law. Unlike Australia, however, as a city-state, Singapore avoids having to grapple with the problem of different rules adopted by different States and Territories within a federal unit. Whereas the inconsistency on the rules of service of process inter-State and abroad is currently one of the topics under consideration in the Consultation Paper issued by the Commonwealth Attorney-General's Department,[89] the Singapore rules on jurisdiction are firmly established. The rules on jurisdiction as of right reflect the common law ideas of presence and submission and are put on a statutory basis by section 16 of the Singaporean Supreme Court of Judicature Act.[90] In cases where the defendant is abroad, the Singaporean Rules of Court, Order 11, sets out heads of jurisdiction under which leave to serve out may be granted. While there is room for some modernisation of the Order 11 rules,[91] there has so far been no attempt to do so. On the issue of the exercise of discretion to either hear the claim or decline jurisdiction in favour of a foreign court, the Singapore Court of Appeal[92] has rejected the Australian 'clearly inappropriate forum' test[93] in favour of the English '*forum non conveniens*' test set out in *The Spiliada*.[94]

[88] See the Attorney General's Consultation Paper, Annex 1, and the contributions in this volume by Roger Wilkins AO (Chapter one), His Honour Chief Justice James Allsop AO (Chapter three), Andrew Bell (Chapter four) and Andrew Dickinson (Chapter eight).

[89] Attorney-General's Consultation Paper (Annex 1), [34]–[45].

[90] Cap 322.

[91] For example, it is unclear whether a declaration that a contract is void would fall under the contractual provision set out in O 11 r 1(d); cf the UK Civil Procedure Rule Practice Direction 6B, para 3.1(8).

[92] *JIO Minerals FZC v Mineral Enterprises Ltd* [2011] 1 SLR 391.

[93] *Voth v Manildra Flour Mills Pty Ltd* (1990) 171 CLR 538.

[94] *Spiliada Maritime Corp v Cansulex Ltd* [1987] AC 460 (House of Lords).

There are two statutory registration schemes for the recognition and enforcement of foreign judgments in Singapore. These schemes are based on the English statutory schemes. Australia is one of the gazetted countries under the Reciprocal Enforcement of Commonwealth Judgments Act (Singapore),[95] so an Australian judgment, once registered under that Act, will be treated as a local judgment. The common law rules, again, derived from English common law, cover foreign judgments from countries not gazetted under either statutory scheme.

Of the three primary areas in private international law, it is choice of law in which the Singapore judiciary has made its mark, specifically in relation to choice of law for equitable obligations. In *Rickshaw Investments v Nicolai Baron von Uexkull*,[96] the Singapore Court of Appeal rejected the idea that the *lex fori* will inevitably apply in relation to equitable claims.[97] It held that equitable claims ought to be characterised in accordance with their foundational sources, which would, more often than not, be based on established choice of law categories (such as contract or tort), thereby leading the way to the appropriate choice of law rule. Thus, the breach of fiduciary duty and breach of confidence claims in *Rickshaw* were held to have their root source in an underlying contractual relationship and were governed by the contract choice of law rule. This did lead to the somewhat ironic result that German law, which has no concept of equity, was held to apply to the breach of fiduciary duty and breach of confidence claims in that case, but there is no denying that the Singapore court's approach in relation to choice of law in equitable obligations is internationalist in nature.

The Singapore court has been less innovative in other choice of law areas, in part because it views any reform of the more established choice of law rules to be the domain of Parliament.[98] There was consideration a few years back as to whether Singapore ought to enact legislation akin to that of the 1980 Rome Convention[99] on the law applicable to contractual obligations, but the Singapore Academy of Law Reform Committee ultimately rejected that idea, as it thought that the common law rules were generally adequate.[100] Similarly, a draft tort choice of law bill modelled on the UK Private International Law (Miscellaneous) Provisions Act

[95] Cap 264. The other statutory scheme is the Reciprocal Enforcement of Foreign Judgments Act (Cap 265).

[96] *Rickshaw Investments v Nicolai Baron von Uexkull* [2007] 1 SLR(R) 377 ('*Rickshaw Investments*').

[97] The Singapore Court of Appeal drew heavily on the thesis espoused by TM Yeo, *Choice of Law for Equitable Doctrines* (Oxford, Oxford University Press, 2004). Cf *Paramasivam v Flynn* (1998) 160 ALR 203.

[98] See, eg, *Rickshaw Investments*, [66].

[99] Convention on the Law Applicable to Contractual Obligations 1980 (consolidated version [1998] OJ C27/34). This Convention is now transposed into an EU legislative instrument as Regulation (EC) No 593/2008 on the law applicable to contractual obligations (Rome I) ([2008] OJ L177/6).

[100] Law Reform Committee of the Singapore Academy of Law, *Report on Reform of the Law Concerning Choice of Law in Contract* (2003), available at: www.sal.org.sg/digitallibrary/Lists/Law%20Reform%20Reports/Attachments/19/Report%20on%20Reform%20of%20the%20Law%20Concerning%20Choice%20of%20Law%20in%20Contract.pdf (last accessed 7 April 2014).

1995 was suggested,[101] but the idea did not gain traction in Singapore. Singapore is thus one of the last bastions of the so-called 'double actionability' rule in tort choice of law. However, the Singapore Court of Appeal in *Rickshaw*[102] made two innovations in respect of the double actionability rule (which now, like its English counterpart,[103] embodies a flexible exception). It held that the double actionability rule applies even in relation to torts occurring in Singapore;[104] and that the flexible exception could be used not only to disapply either the *lex fori* or *lex loci delicti* limb, but could also be used to disapply both limbs, to lead to the application of the law of a third country.[105]

C. Recent Advancements in Singapore Private International Law: Judicial Co-operation

The Singapore court has often stressed the importance of preserving comity in its judgments. Comity, at its highest levels, involves active cross-border judicial co-operation. There have been at least two recent developments in Singapore law that have increased the degree of co-operation between the Singapore judiciary and their foreign brethren. This section examines these two developments namely, the method of proving foreign law and judicial co-operation in cross-border insolvencies.

(i) Proving Foreign Law

(a) General

Under Singapore law, the usual common law principle that foreign law must be proved as a matter of fact applies. In the absence of proof, it is presumed that foreign law is identical to forum law. That said, the Singapore court has taken notice, for the purposes of applying the *forum non conveniens* test, that the *lex causae* is not the same as Singapore law despite lack of proof of foreign law.[106] Australian courts have also stated that it may be inappropriate for the court to assume that foreign law is the same as forum law in complex areas of law. Perhaps most notably, in *Damberg v Damberg*, the New South Wales Court of Appeal (Heydon JA, Spigelman CJ and Sheller JA concurring) concluded, after a detailed examination

[101] www.lawnet.com.sg/legal/ln2/comm/PDF/torts_choice_of_law_bill.pdf. Accompanying report available at: lwb.lawnet.com.sg/legal/lgl/html/freeaccess/lrcr/reform_of_choice_of_law.pdf (both last accessed 7 April 2014).

[102] Above n 96.

[103] *Red Sea Insurance Co Ltd v Bouygues SA* [1995] 1 AC 190 (Privy Council).

[104] *Rickshaw Investments*, [63]. Cf the UK position: *Metall und Rohstoff AG v Donaldson Lufkin & Jenrette Inc* [1990] 1 QB 391, 447.

[105] *Rickshaw Investments*, [56].

[106] *Rickshaw Investments*, [43]; *Multi-Code Electronics Industries (M) Bhd v Toh Chun Toh Gordon* [2009] 1 SLR(R) 1000, [49]–[50].

of the authorities, that it should not be assumed that the tax system of the foreign *lex causae* is similar to that of the forum.[107]

Proof of foreign law can be adduced either by directly adducing raw sources of foreign law as evidence or by adducing the opinion of an expert in foreign law. Similarly to the position that is taken under the Australian uniform Evidence Acts, raw sources of foreign law would include books published under the authority of the foreign government which contain authoritative statements of the foreign law, and reports of rulings by foreign courts contained in a book.[108] The court will also take judicial notice of legislation of a Commonwealth country,[109] and appropriate books or documents of reference.[110] Textbooks on foreign law can also be put forward as evidence of foreign law, and unlike the UK position, the author need not give evidence in court if it is not possible or inconvenient for the author to be called as a witness.[111]

The method of proving foreign law through expert opinion in court has attracted stringent criticism.[112] The main criticisms centre on the issue of cost and accuracy of the evidence. There will be inevitable costs in retaining an expert witness, especially a foreign expert witness. However, perhaps the greater concern is whether the forum court would be able to apply an accurate version of the foreign law. The quality of the foreign experts may vary and lead to the misapplication of foreign law. Subtleties may also be lost where the expert evidence has to be translated from a foreign language.[113] Experts may also be partisan, and in most cases each party will often produce their own expert witness with conflicting accounts of the foreign law. In effect, the court may end up applying a version of foreign law that would not be applied by the foreign court itself.

(b) The Memorandum of Understanding between the Singapore and New South Wales Judiciaries

In a bid to circumvent the problems involved in proving foreign law, the Supreme Court of Singapore and the Supreme Court of New South Wales entered into a Memorandum of Understanding (MOU) in September 2010. This provides for

[107] [2001] NSWCA 87, (2001) 52 NSWLR 492, [161]–[164]. See J McComish, 'Pleading and Proving Foreign Law in Australia' (2007) 31 *Melbourne University Law Review* 400.

[108] Evidence Act (Cap 97) (Singapore) s 40.

[109] ibid, s 59(1)(b).

[110] ibid, s 59(2).

[111] ibid, s 62(2): 'if the author is dead or cannot be found or has become incapable of giving evidence or cannot be called as a witness without an amount of delay or expense which the court regards as unreasonable'. See also *Wong Kai Woon v Wong Kong Hom* [2000] SGHC 176.

[112] See, eg, *Bodum v La Cafetiere* (US Court of Appeals, 7th Circuit), 621 F 3d 624, 96 USPQ 2d 1689.

[113] See *Murakami v Wiryadi* [2010] NSWCA 7, (2010) 268 ALR 377, [150] (Spigelman CJ); His Honour Chief Justice James Spigelman AO, 'Law and International Commerce: Between the Parochial and the Cosmopolitan', Address to the New South Wales Bar Association, Sydney, 22 June 2010. (www.lawlink.nsw.gov.au/lawlink/Supreme_Court/ll_sc.nsf/vwFiles/spigelman220610.pdf/$file/spigelman220610.pdf, last accessed 14 March 2014; and same author, 'Proof of Foreign Law by Reference to the Foreign Court' (2011) 127 *Law Quarterly Review* 208.

mutual judicial co-operation in relation to the question of proof of foreign law. In essence, the MOU provides that if an issue relating to a question of New South Wales law arises in Singapore, the parties may seek a direct ruling on that question in the New South Wales court, and vice versa. Each court also undertakes to provide an answer to the referred question of law as quickly as possible.

There are some slight differences in how the MOU has been implemented in each country. For example, rule 6.44(1) of the New South Wales Uniform Civil Procedure Rules 2005 provides for the Supreme Court to order a referral to a foreign court on the application or one or more of the parties, provided all the parties consent.[114] In contrast, the Singapore Rules of Court, Order 101, does not require the consent of both parties; a Singapore court could order that proceedings be commenced in the New South Wales court[115] to determine a question of New South Wales law on the application of only one or more of the parties.[116] Further, the Singapore provision also permits the court to order, on its own motion, the parties to seek a declaration from other foreign courts which are not designated courts under the provision.[117] Given that only New South Wales is currently a specified country under Order 101, the potential reach of the Singapore court's power to ignore party wishes on whether to seek a costly[118] reference overseas is rather wide.[119]

(c) Effect of the Memorandum of Understanding

There is the concern that a foreign court which has been petitioned to answer a question on its own law in circumstances where trial of the substantive claim is taking place in another court may well refuse to do so. When there is no real dispute taking place before it, the court may be of the opinion that it does not fall within its judicial function to act as an advisor.[120] The MOU ensures that the Singapore and New South Wales courts would entertain such requests from each other.

That said, the lack of a similar MOU between the Singapore and English courts has not stopped the latter court from assisting the former. In *Westacre Investments v*

[114] Uniform Civil Procedure Rules 2005, r 6.44(1). In *Marshall v Fleming* [2013] NSWSC 566, a case involving a similar memorandum of understanding between the Chief Justice of New South Wales and the Chief Judge of New York, the application judge (Harrison J) sought to circumvent this requirement of consent by the appointment of a referee under r 6.44(2). His decision was reversed on appeal ([2014] NSWCA 64).

[115] Or any other 'specified foreign country'; to date, only New South Wales is a specified foreign country: Rules of Court (Singapore), Order 101, Rule 6.

[116] Rules of Court, Order 101, Rule 2(1).

[117] Rules of Court, Order 101, Rule 3.

[118] See below, text to nn 125–27.

[119] Rules of Court, Order 101, Rule 3. It is unclear why the court's power to order a referral on its own motion only exists in relation to courts in a non-specified country and does not include a specified country. Yeo hypothesised that it could be a subtle signal to encourage parties to make an application under Order 101 in respect of the latter, but not former, country: TM Yeo, 'Common Law Innovations in Proving Foreign Law' (2010) 12 *Yearbook of Private International Law* 493, 495.

[120] Yeo, ibid, 496.

Yugoimport,[121] the judgment creditor of an English judgment sought the enforcement of that judgment by registering it under one of Singapore's statutory regimes for the recognition and enforcement of foreign judgments by garnishing debts owed to the judgment debtor.[122] One of the pre-requisites for such registration was that the judgment had to be enforceable in the jurisdiction in which it was obtained. The Singapore Court of Appeal directed the parties to apply to the English court to ascertain whether the English court would have given leave to enforce its own judgment, handed down in 1998, by making a third party debt (garnishee) order against a locally-resident debtor on the date in 2004 on which the registration of the English judgment had initially been permitted in Singapore by the ex parte application of the judgment creditor. Tomlinson J (referring to the application as 'unusual although not altogether unprecedented'[123]) noted that he was asked to determine a hypothetical question, that is, to assume that on that date in 2004 there was a third party within the jurisdiction of the English court who owed or held money to the credit of the judgment. However, Tomlinson J held that:

> This court is of course always anxious to respond so far as properly it can to a request for assistance from an overseas court … it is clearly appropriate that the English court should assist the parties and the Singapore court by indicating, so far as it is able, how the discretion of the English court would have been likely to have been exercised in the circumstances posited.[124]

The spirit of judicial co-operation encapsulated by Tomlinson J's willingness to assist the Singapore court is captured on a more formal basis between the New South Wales and Singapore courts in the MOU.

It has been said that the process of referrals would be 'highly cost-effective'.[125] However, former Chief Justice Spigelman, in a speech delivered to the NSW Bar Association in Sydney in June 2010, acknowledged that: 'Often it will prove to be more expensive than expert evidence'.[126] A reference to a foreign court will involve

[121] *Westacre Investments v Yugoimport* [2009] 2 SLR(R) 166.

[122] Reciprocal Enforcement of Commonwealth Judgments Act (Cap 264).

[123] *Westacre Investments v Yugoimport* [2008] EWHC 801 (Comm), [1].

[124] ibid, [2]. Tomlinson J also noted that the judgment creditor would have needed to first ascertain from the English court whether the judgment is enforceable in England before it could be registered under the Singapore statute; hence, on one view he was not dealing with a request for assistance from an overseas court.

[125] See the Singapore and NSW media releases: app.supremecourt.gov.sg/default.aspx?pgid=3401 and www.nswbar.asn.au/circulars/2010/nov/scnswmr.pdf (last accessed 7 April 2014). See also *Marshall v Fleming* [2014] NSWCA 64, [26] describing a similar memorandum of understanding between the Chief Justice of New South Wales and the Chief Judge of New York as providing 'an effective inexpensive method by which questions of foreign law can be determined'.

[126] His Honour Chief Justice James Spigelman, 'Law and International Commerce: Between the Parochial and the Cosmopolitan', above n 113, 23. See also *Fleming v Marshall* [2011] NSWCA 86, (2011) 279 ALR 737, [86] in which Spigelman CJ stated (at [10]): 'It is by no means clear whether the present case is one in which this mechanism for deciding such an issue would be more cost effective than the customary means of determining a question of foreign law by expert evidence. However, the determination of an issue of professional practice is one of the kinds of legal issues for which there

considerable costs: the parties will have to engage foreign counsel, pay court fees, not to mention all the other associated costs of carrying on proceedings. These costs will be in addition to the costs incurred in litigating the substance of the case in the referring court. The alternative traditional method of proving law through the evidence of expert witnesses will also involve additional costs for the parties, but the reality is that it would almost always be cheaper than making a referral to a foreign court, all the more so if evidence through video-link is accepted.[127]

That parties may not always be happy about having to refer a question to a foreign court is borne out by a fairly recent Singapore case. In *Ng Teck Sim v Hat Holdings*,[128] the Singapore High Court considered a breach of contract claim involving an allegation that title to a villa in Thailand had not been properly transferred to the buyers. The Court stayed its proceedings pending the parties obtaining a conclusive ruling from the Thai courts as to whether title had validly been transferred to the buyer.[129] Both parties very obviously did not want to litigate in Thailand, and, in what was described by the Singapore Court of Appeal as an 'extraordinary'[130] situation, both parties appealed to the Singapore Court of Appeal against the High Court's order that an answer had to be obtained from the Thai court. In the end, the Court of Appeal agreed with the parties that a reference to the Thai courts was not warranted.[131] While the reasoning involved need not detain us here, *Hat Holdings* provides a practical example that although the spirit of judicial co-operation encapsulated in the mutual power of referrals is to be lauded, it will often not be in the parties' interests, cost-wise, to take advantage of it. It is suggested that if a question of foreign law is so crucial to the claim, and so difficult that assistance from the foreign court has to be obtained, this will almost always indicate that the forum court is not *forum conveniens* in the first place.

Somewhat paradoxically though, courts' willingness to entertain referrals from and to other courts may well lead the forum to hear a case despite a less than clear case that it is *forum conveniens*. The *lex causae* is a factor to be weighed under both *The Spiliada forum non conveniens* test adopted under Singapore law and the Australian 'clearly inappropriate forum' test. In general, when the foreign *lex causae* is markedly different from Singapore law, this is a factor pointing away from the Singapore court being *forum conveniens*. However, if the foreign court will readily assist in declaring the content and application of its law, a foreign *lex causae* would be a less significant factor in assessing whether Singapore is *forum*

is unlikely to be a single correct answer. Advice from three serving appellate judges of the foreign jurisdiction is much more likely to be accurate than an Australian judge choosing between contesting expert reports'. His Honour's comment concerned the possibility of a reference under the similar New South Wales-New York MOU: see above n 114).

[127] Evidence through live video- or television links may be possible if the Singapore court grants leave: Evidence Act (Cap 97), s 62A.

[128] *Ng Teck Sim v Hat Holdings* [2010] 4 SLR 840.

[129] The High Court was of the opinion that the claim raised the *Moçambique* rule (above n 86), a point overruled by the Court of Appeal: [2011] SGCA 34.

[130] *Ng Teck Sim v Hat Holdings* [2011] SGCA 34, [45].

[131] [2011] SGCA 34.

conveniens. The same line of reasoning also obviously applies under the Australian 'clearly inappropriate forum' test, as demonstrated by the New South Wales Court of Appeal's decision in *Fleming v Marshall*.[132] It is suggested that the court should be mindful of the issue of costs if a referral would later be required when it is deciding whether it is *forum conveniens*.

The true value of judicial co-operation in this area is not in reducing costs for the parties, but in enabling the forum court to apply foreign law accurately.[133] It is clear that the adversarial nature of trial in common law courts creates opportunities for parties to push their own partisan interests. The court, picking over the conflicting evidence of opposing expert witnesses, will rarely end up applying the most accurate version of foreign law. Nevertheless, it has been argued that the purpose of proving foreign law is not to deliver the 'truth', but to reproduce the circumstances in which decisions are made in a foreign court.[134] After all, in local proceedings, counsel for each party will also seek to persuade the court that its particular view of local law is correct. The local court is also faced with conflicting arguments, much as a court, trying to decide the content of foreign law, may also be faced with conflicting expert evidence. One could take the view that it is not necessary for the forum court to arrive at the 'right' answer; indeed, that may be more than can be expected of it given the constraints of the trial process. All that one can expect from the court is that it will do its best on the basis of the material before it.

Bearing this in mind, the parties' concerns about the cost of seeking a declaration from a foreign court should not be subordinated to the court's desire to apply foreign law as it would have been applied in the foreign forum itself. The search for the legal 'truth' will often prove, in practical terms, rather elusive. This is where the Singapore position that the court could make an order under Order 101, without the consent of one of the parties in the case of a potential referral to the New South Wales court, or without the consent of all the parties, in the case of a potential referral to other courts, might create some difficulties. It ought to be the case that the Singapore court should not ordinarily order a referral without unanimous party consent.

(ii) International Co-operation in Cross-border Insolvencies

(a) General

There is increasing awareness that judicial co-operation is important to achieve efficient management of cross-border insolvencies. Instruments such as the EU Regulation on insolvency proceedings[135] and the UNCITRAL Model Law on Cross-Border Insolvency seek to increase court-to-court assistance or increase

[132] *Fleming v Marshall* [2011] NSWCA 86, (2011) 279 ALR 737, [6]–[11] (Spigelman CJ).
[133] Yeo, 'Common Law Innovations in Proving Foreign Law' above n 120, 500.
[134] R Fentiman, *Foreign Law in English Courts* (Oxford, Oxford University Press, 1998) 20.
[135] Council Regulation (EC) No 1346/2000 ([2000] OJ L160/1).

access to court (and the court's assistance) for foreign liquidators and other office-holders.

There are two main competing doctrines in this field. The doctrine of universality provides that insolvency proceedings opened in one country will apply to all of the debtor's assets, wherever situated. Universalism does not necessarily mean just one insolvency proceeding is opened, but could also include the situation where there is one main proceedings in one country and ancillary proceedings in other countries. The assets gathered in the ancillary proceedings will then be remitted to the 'home' country to be distributed to all the debtor's creditors worldwide. The converse doctrine of territoriality provides that insolvency proceedings can be opened in whichever jurisdiction the debtor has assets and that those proceedings only have effect within that particular jurisdiction. Each proceeding will operate more or less independently of the others. Of the two, universalism is generally considered to provide a fairer basis for the distribution of a debtor's assets amongst his creditors as it imposes a single scheme of distribution on all creditors. It is also thought to be more efficient, as costs would be minimised by fewer proceedings being opened. Instruments such as the EU Insolvency Regulation and the UNCITRAL Model Law promote the universalist agenda by encouraging, with varying degrees of success,[136] judicial co-operation in this area. Although Singapore has yet to adopt the UNCITRAL Model Law, the Insolvency Law Reform Committee has recently recommended for it to do so.

The common law too has developed to embrace universalist ideals tentatively. In *Re HIH Casualty and General Insurance Ltd*,[137] Lord Hoffmann, referring to the principle of 'modified' universalism,[138] held that the English court had an inherent common law power to direct the English liquidators to remit the English assets to Australia for distribution in the principal liquidation, notwithstanding that English creditors would have been better off had their claims been decided under English insolvency laws. However, the extent to which Lord Hoffmann's views represent the state of English law is debatable.[139] Only Lord Walker agreed with Lord Hoffmann. Lord Scott, with whom Lord Neuberger agreed,[140] allowed the remittal solely on the basis of section 426 of the UK Insolvency Act, which sets out a statutory scheme of judicial assistance for certain countries. Lord Scott rejected the existence of any common law inherent power to remit assets to Australia in a situation where the Australian and English distribution laws differed. The fifth member of the House, Lord Phillips, refused to be drawn into the issue of whether any common law power of remittal existed, and preferred to base his decision on section 426.

[136] See J Hill and A Chong, *International Commercial Disputes: Commercial Conflict of Laws in English Courts*, 4th edn (Oxford, Hart Publishing, 2010) 750.

[137] *Re HIH Casualty and General Insurance Ltd*, [2008] 1 WLR 852.

[138] ibid, 862.

[139] *In re Alitalia Linee Aeree Italiane SpA* [2011] EWHC 15 (Ch), [2011] 1 WLR 2049, [54].

[140] Lord Neuberger later, extra-judicially, resiled somewhat from the position taken in *Re HIH*: Lord Neuberger, 'The International Dimension of Insolvency' (2010) 23(3) *Insolvency Intelligence* 42.

As far as private international law is concerned, the (temporary) zenith was most probably reached with the Court of Appeal decision in *Rubin v Eurofinance*.[141] The Court of Appeal decided that the normal common law rules of recognition and enforcement of foreign judgments, which in relation to *in personam* judgments require the defendant to be present within the jurisdiction of the judgment-granting court at the time of commencement of proceedings or to have submitted thereto, did not apply to judgments handed down in insolvency proceedings. In reaching its decision, the Court of Appeal relied on the Privy Council decision in *Cambridge Gas Transport Corp v Official Committee of Unsecured Creditors of Navigator Holdings Plc*.[142] In *Cambridge Gas*, their Lordships held that:[143]

> Bankruptcy proceedings do not fall into either category [of judgments *in rem* or judgments *in personam*]. Judgments *in rem* and *in personam* are judicial determinations of the existence of rights: in the one case, rights over property and in the other, rights against a person. When a judgment *in rem* or *in personam* is recognised by a foreign court, it is accepted as establishing the right which it purports to have determined, without further inquiry into the grounds upon which it did so. The judgment itself is treated as a source of the right.
>
> The purpose of bankruptcy proceedings, on the other hand, is not to determine or establish the existence of rights, but to provide a mechanism of collective execution against the property of the debtor by creditors whose rights are admitted or established.

The finding that insolvency proceedings are *sui generis* in nature and subject to different private international law rules excited and dismayed commentators in equal measure.[144] When *Rubin* was heard by the Supreme Court, the majority wasted no time restoring the status quo, with a smaller majority deciding that *Cambridge Gas* was wrong in the process.[145]

(b) The Singapore Approach: Universalism or Territorialism?

Despite the decision of the Supreme Court in *Rubin v Eurofinance* denying any special status to judgments handed down in insolvency proceedings as far as private international law rules are concerned, the need for judicial co-operation in cross-border insolvencies is still acute. In fact, the former Chief Justice of Singapore, Chan Sek Keong, has even stated extra-judicially that the Court of Appeal decision in *Rubin v Eurofinance* 'may receive a sympathetic reception if it

[141] *Rubin v Eurofinance* [2011] Ch 133.

[142] *Cambridge Gas Transport Corp v Official Committee of Unsecured Creditors of Navigator Holdings Plc* [2007] 1 AC 508.

[143] ibid, [13]–[14].

[144] See, eg, A Briggs, 'Recognition: Foreign Judgments or Insolvency Proceedings?' [2010] *LMCLQ* 523 and Look Chan Ho, 'Recognition born of fiction—*Rubin v Eurofinance SA*' (2010) 25 *Journal of International Banking and Financial Law* 579.

[145] *Rubin v Eurofinance* [2012] UKSC 46, [2013] 1 AC 236. See A Chong, 'Recognition of Foreign Judgments and Cross-Border Insolvencies' [2014] *Lloyd's Maritime & Commercial Law Quarterly* 241.

is not contrary to any other law in Singapore'.[146] The comment was made before the Supreme Court in *Rubin* overruled the Court of Appeal decision, but it illustrates the receptive judicial mind-set in Singapore towards greater cross-border co-operation in dealing with insolvencies.

That said, judicial attitudes are sometimes constrained by statute. There is a healthy debate in Singapore as to whether Singapore law ought to adopt universalism or territorialism.[147] Much of that debate centres on section 377(3)(c) of the Singapore Companies Act. It provides:

> A liquidator of a foreign company appointed for Singapore by the Court or a person exercising the powers and functions of such a liquidator–
>
> ...
>
> (c) shall, unless otherwise ordered by the Court, only recover and realise the assets of the foreign company in Singapore and shall, subject to paragraph (b) and subsection (7), pay the net amount so recovered and realised to the liquidator of that foreign company for the place where it was formed or incorporated after paying any debts and satisfying any liabilities incurred in Singapore by the foreign company.

This provision provides for the ring-fencing of the Singapore assets of a foreign company in Singapore in insolvency proceedings. The Singaporean assets of the foreign company have first to be used to pay the debts and liabilities incurred in Singapore by the foreign company before the net amount is remitted to the liquidator of the foreign company of the place where the foreign company was formed or incorporated.

Section 377(3)(c) has been criticised as being 'retrogressive and out of line with internationally-accepted standards of a fair and equitable cross-border insolvency regime'.[148] The Insolvency Law Review Committee has recently recommended that the ring-fencing of assets for the winding up of foreign companies, outside of certain regulated industries, ought to be abolished.[149] The judiciary has also had a recent opportunity to examine section 377(3)(c) and the extent of judicial co-operation in cross-border insolvencies. In *Beluga Chartering GmbH (in liquidation) v Beluga Projects (Singapore) Pte Ltd*,[150] a German incorporated company was undergoing principal insolvency proceedings in Germany. Local insolvency proceedings were also opened. The issue was whether the Singapore liquidators could remit the Singapore assets to the German liquidators to be dealt with in the German proceedings without first satisfying locally-incurred debts. In the

[146] SK Chan CJ, 'Cross-Border Insolvency Issues Affecting Singapore' (2011) 23 *Singapore Academy of Law Journal* 413, 431.

[147] See, eg, Chan CJ, ibid; MS Wee, 'Lessons for the Development of Singapore's International Insolvency Law' (2011) 23 *Singapore Academy of Law Journal* 932.

[148] EB Lee, 'Insolvency Law- Annual Review of Singapore Cases' (2000) 1 *Singapore Academy of Law Annual Review of Singapore Cases* 201, 205 (quoted with apparent approval by Woo Bih Li J in *RBG Resources plc (in liquidation) v Credit Lyonnais* [2006] 1 SLR(R) 240, [65]).

[149] The Singapore Insolvency & Public Trustee's Office (IPTO) is currently working on a reform of Singapore's insolvency laws and preparing an Omnibus Insolvency Bill.

[150] *Beluga Chartering GmbH (in liquidation) v Beluga Projects (Singapore) Pte Ltd* [2014] SGCA 14; [2013] 2 SLR 1035 (SGHC).

High Court, Coomaraswamy JC (as he then was) held that Singapore courts had a discretionary common law power, pursuant to the ancillary liquidation doctrine, to disapply section 377(3)(c) and order the remittal of the Singapore assets directly to the principal liquidation without having first to satisfy locally-incurred debts.[151] This caused a considerable stir as it was directly contrary to generally assumed position under Singapore law.[152] Coomaraswamy JC drew on Lord Hoffmann's principle of 'modified' universalism', articulated in *Re HIH Casualty and General Insurance Ltd*,[153] in reaching his decision. When the case went on appeal, this point was not dealt with by the Court of Appeal as it concluded that the German company was not subject to section 377(3)(c). While the Court of Appeal affirmed that the ancillary liquidation doctrine operated alongside the statutory regime, it reserved its opinion on whether the doctrine allowed the court to remit assets abroad in circumstances where Singapore statute conferred on Singapore creditors a priority which the relevant foreign law did not. In other words, it is still undecided whether Lord Hoffmann's or Lord Scott's views in *Re HIH Casualty and General Insurance Ltd*[154] provide the law in Singapore.

Its other remarks however indicate that the Singapore Court of Appeal is gravitating towards a 'universalist' mind-set, which is more in keeping with Lord Hoffmann's approach. In *Beluga*, the Court was invited to protect Singapore creditors by applying section 377(3)(c) by analogy at common law and refusing remittal of the assets to Germany. However, the Court refused to do so.[155] Essentially the Court held that it had no discretion at common law to ring-fence Singapore assets in favour of Singapore creditors in the absence of any statutory provision giving those creditors a priority under Singapore law. Further, in *obiter* comments, the Court stated its view that in instances where there are no Singapore insolvency proceedings, the court ought in general to recognise the title of a foreign liquidator and assist him in claiming assets belonging to the insolvent entity. This is in line with the recommendation of the Insolvency Law Review Committee for Singapore to adopt the UNCITRAL Model Law.

D. Conclusion

Countries which owe their legal heritage to English common law have not been reticent about forging their own paths in the area of private international law. To do otherwise than to continually examine and develop the law to better fit modern conditions would seem unwise. The Australian Attorney-General's project is therefore timely. Singapore has chosen a more piecemeal approach towards reform

[151] On the facts, Coomaraswamy JC declined to exercise his discretion to disapply the ring-fencing limb of s 377(3)(c) on the basis that this would cause real prejudice to the Singapore creditors.

[152] Chan CJ, above n 146, 424.

[153] *Re HIH Casualty and General Insurance Ltd* [2008] 1 WLR 852.

[154] ibid.

[155] *Beluga* [2014] SGCA 14, [80].

and development of the law in this area. Recent developments have touched on judicial co-operation in particular. On the one hand, Order 101 of the Rules of Court is a welcome development which would enable more accurate application of foreign law in court, but on the other hand, the power to order a referral ought to be one that is ordinarily exercised only when all parties are agreeable, in view of the high costs involved. On co-operation in cross-border insolvencies, former Chief Justice Chan Sek Keong has observed that Singapore judges 'are sympathetic to providing such assistance as is proper to foreign courts and liquidators in the tradition of common law judges'.[156] This is borne out by both the High Court and Court of Appeal judgments in *Beluga Chartering GmbH (in liquidation) v Beluga Projects (Singapore) Pte Ltd*.[157] They paint a largely positive picture of the judicial mind-set towards the principle of universalism and co-operation in cross-border insolvencies. At the very least, the two developments that have been discussed in this paper illustrate the solidarity that the Singapore judiciary share with their brethren elsewhere.

[156] Chan CJ, above n 146, 425.

[157] *Beluga* [2014] SGCA 14; [2013] 2 SLR 1035 (SGHC).

Annex 1

Private International Law Consultation

ATTORNEY-GENERAL'S DEPARTMENT

Reducing Legal Complexity of Cross-Border Transactions and Relationships:

Driving micro-economic reform through the establishment of more cohesive and clearer jurisdictional, applicable law and choice of court rules.

As the international movement of people, property and capital proliferates and intensifies, private international law is a subject of increasing practical importance.

A Mills, *The Confluence of Public and Private International Law* (Cambridge University Press 2009), page 3.

Table of Contents

Chapter 1: Introduction to the Project

History

1. In 2011, the then Standing Committee of Attorneys-General discussed a number of micro-economic reform projects. This discussion included a proposal to develop a project plan to harmonise private international law principles and rules across Australia, such as those governing jurisdiction, choice of court and choice of law, taking account of solutions adopted by other legal systems and internationally.

2. On 12 April 2012, the Proposal was accepted by the Standing Council on Law and Justice (SCLJ). The SCLJ Communiqué stated:

   Ministers today noted the 'Project Plan and Overview: Harmonisation of jurisdictional, choice of court and choice of law rules' and agreed to the establishment of a working group that will commence consultations with key stakeholders to determine whether further reform in this area would deliver worthwhile micro-economic benefits for the community.

Scope

3. Private international law principles and rules are those that govern every civil and commercial—or private—relationship and transaction that has a dimension that crosses borders (state and territory as well as international borders). These rules and principles determine the competence of courts (jurisdiction) and/or the law(s) applicable in a cross-border dispute, as well as whether the judgments of particular courts in one state are capable of being recognised and enforced in other states (domestic or international). Legal subject matters that increasingly attract the application of these principles and rules include contract, tort, property, company, insolvency, family and succession law.

4. The primary focus of this project will be on commercial cross-border relationships and transactions, using examples from the areas of contract law, tort and property.[1]

Purpose and Objectives

5. The increase in cross-border trade, commerce, investment and mobility has resulted in businesses and individuals being more exposed to legal relationships and disputes that extend over state, territory or country borders. This has highlighted the existence of private international law rules and principles in Australia, which may differ between states and territories and may be unclear or confusing. These features can give rise to difficulties, which stand as an impediment to commercial certainty and the efficient resolution of disputes.

[1] This paper and project is not intended to cover arbitration.

6. The project seeks to identify those areas where existing private international law rules and principles may reduce clarity, certainty and predictability of outcome for cross-border trade, commerce, investment and mobility, and to identify options for law reform to overcome these issues.

7. The guiding objectives for identifying options for law reform are to improve:

— the predictability of outcome for parties in cross-border relationships and transactions, and
— clarity, certainty, simplicity and accessibility of the law.

8. In addition, the project seeks to:

— gather evidence on the current legal issues arising in cross-border relationships and transactions—this information will assist in guiding any future law reform in this area
— improve the attractiveness of Australia as a commercial litigation and arbitration centre within the Asia-Pacific region, and
— make the clarity and certainty for cross-border transactions and relationships provided by the Australian legal system a feature that reinforces Australia's status within the region as a leading country in which to conduct business and trade.

Methodology

9. The project's central methodology is to conduct a comprehensive public consultation to collect evidence. To ensure the consultation's broadest possible reach, the project consultation will be run through the online-based Private International Law Consultation Hub (the Hub).[2]

10. The public consultation will be conducted using three different means: this discussion paper, an online-based survey and a series of blogs that invite discussion, promoted through Twitter (@agd_pil), LinkedIn (AGD—Private International Law) and Facebook (Private International Law).[3]

11. This discussion paper will be distributed widely to legal practitioners, in-house counsel, small and large businesses and interest groups. In addition, the discussion paper will be available for download from the Hub.

12. The online-based survey will be distributed to stakeholders and is designed to gather information from businesses and individuals engaged in cross-border transactions and relationships. The survey is not a separate consultation on the reform of private international law but seeks feedback and data from stakeholders who may have no or very little legal knowledge of private

[2] Located at: <http://consult.govspace.gov.au/pil>.
[3] See also below [14].

international law. The survey report will seek to exhibit current attitudes towards private international law principles and rules (in Australia and elsewhere), their practical impact on business and individuals and how much, if any, attention is paid to them at various stages throughout the life of a cross-border transaction or relationship.

13. The blogs on the Hub are intended to encourage those interested in the project to hold conversations, post thoughts, suggestions, comments or experiences in relation to particular issues. There are three blogs, covering the three components of private international law:

    — Jurisdiction[4]
    — applicable law,[5] and
    — the recognition and enforcement of judgments.[6]

14. The first issues for discussion on these blogs will relate to the issues raised in this discussion paper. However, participants are encouraged to add new issues to broaden the discussion. People will be able to subscribe to the site's RSS feed and to follow the project on Twitter, LinkedIn and Facebook so that a continued engagement with the project is possible.[7]

The Discussion Paper

15. This paper is intended to introduce some of the issues that arise in relation to the current private international law rules and principles. It is not an in-depth analysis that considers all aspects of private international law. Rather, the discussion paper provides:

    — brief introductions to each of the three components of private international law and to several related areas, and
    — examples of the issues that may arise for businesses engaged in cross-border transactions or relationships.

16. The discussion paper is made up of six chapters:

    — **Chapter 1** introduces the project.
    — **Chapter 2** offers a brief introduction to private international law.
    — **Chapter 3** discusses issues arising when a court has to determine its jurisdiction in a cross-border matter. Chapter 3 also provides a discussion of current tests that the court applies when determining whether to stay or transfer proceedings. This discussion is short, but it refers to

[4] Located at: <http://consult.govspace.gov.au/pil/comments-on-jurisdiction/>.

[5] Located at: <http://consult.govspace.gov.au/pil/comments-on-applicable-law/>.

[6] The topic recognition and enforcement of judgments is part of a broader blog, which also covers other private international law issues such as the proof of foreign law in domestic proceedings and reform options. The blog is located at: <http://consult.govspace.gov.au/pil/comments-on-other-issues/>.

[7] See also above [10].

a detailed paper prepared by Professor Andrew Dickinson (University of Sydney), which deals with the issues in greater depth. Professor Dickinson's paper will be published at the same time as this discussion paper.[8]

— **Chapter 4** addresses the private international law rules and principles that determine what law should apply to a particular cross-border transaction or relationship.
— **Chapter 5** discusses other private international law issues, and
— **Chapter 6** addresses possible options for reform.

[8] Professor Dickinson's paper on stay and transfer will be published on the Hub under the link 'Consultation Documents', located at: <http://consult.govspace.gov.au/pil/consultation-documents/>.

Chapter 2: What is Private International Law?

17. Private international law is the body of rules and principles directed to addressing legal issues arising out of private relationships or transactions (that is, not relations between countries) with a cross-border element. The need for this body of rules and principles arises because of the interaction between separate legal systems, and differences between the substantive and procedural rules that apply. This includes state and territory legal systems in a federation, such as Australia, as well as different country legal systems.

18. Private international law rules are local rules, which are particular to a single legal system, in the same way as rules of contract or tort law. In Australia, the sources of private international law include: (a) the common law, (b) federal legislation, and (c) state and territory legislation, including rules of court.

The Three Components of Private International Law

19. Although the categorisation is not exhaustive and the categories are not mutually exclusive, private international law is traditionally viewed as being composed of a body of rules addressing three subject areas: jurisdiction, applicable law or choice of law and recognition and enforcement of foreign judgments.

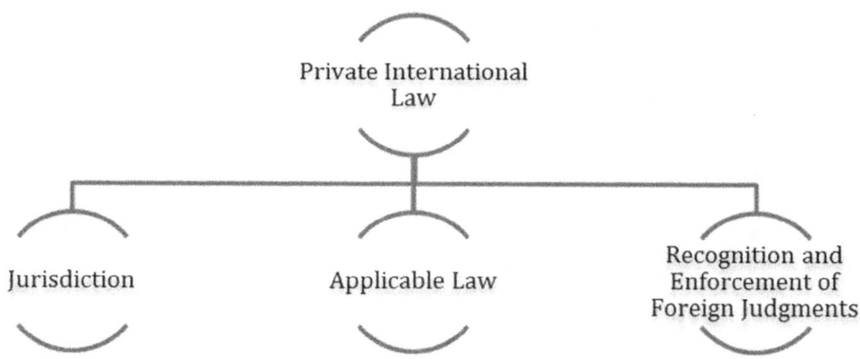

20. This discussion paper will briefly outline each of the three areas in Chapters 3, 4 and 5, respectively, below.

Why is Private International Law Important?

21. For business and individuals alike, private international law provides answers to important questions such as which court can exercise jurisdiction over a dispute or which law will apply. Knowledge of, as well as clarity and certainty around, the rules in this area can therefore enable parties to adequately assess the legal risks involved in particular cross-border transactions

or relationships, and to avoid or minimise those risks where possible. A well-developed private international law regime can:

- reduce regulatory distortions in international trade and commerce
- improve market competitiveness, with flow-on effects for consumers
- serve the policy objectives of the legal system of which they form part [including (but not limited to) trade and foreign policy]
- improve the predictability in the outcomes of disputes
- improve transactional effectiveness, efficiency and accuracy
- improve the resolution of cross-border disputes
- reduce cross-border transaction and litigation risks, and
- reduce risks associated with enforcing awards or judgments, including prohibitive costs associated with the vindication of rights.

Chapter 3: Jurisdiction[9]

22. Mortensen, Garnett and Keyes define the jurisdiction of a court as the 'authority [...] to deal with a particular case, according to its own rules of competency.'[10] Jurisdiction in the context of cross-border issues therefore relates to the competence that a court has to adjudicate a matter, either because the parties chose it as the forum, or because the matter has connections to more than one state, territory or country.

23. This Chapter deals non-exhaustively with three issues relating to jurisdiction. First, the issue of establishing jurisdiction,[11] second, the exercise of jurisdiction by a competent court,[12] and, third, the issues of *lis alibi pendens*, related proceedings and anti-suit injunctions.[13] The Chapter will also discuss the impact that modern technology, including the Internet, has on issues of jurisdiction.

Jurisdiction in Cross-Border Litigation

24. Whether a court can establish its jurisdiction over a dispute will depend on whether the court has 'subject matter jurisdiction' and 'personal jurisdiction'.[14]

Subject Matter Jurisdiction

25. Subject matter jurisdiction relates to whether the court has the authority to hear the kind of dispute that it is being asked to hear, and to grant the remedy that it being asked to give. Where a party applies to a court to have a matter heard, the court will have to determine if the matter falls within one of the subjects it has authority to hear.

[9] Professor Keyes used the term 'adjudicative jurisdiction' to distinguish between jurisdictional questions discussed here and those that arise in the context of the recognition and enforcement of judgments. M Keyes, *Jurisdiction in International Litigation* (The Federation Press, 2005). For that discussion, please see below [137], [165].

[10] R Mortensen, R Garnett and M Keyes, *Private International Law in Australia* (LexisNexis Butterworths, 2nd ed, 2012) 31.

[11] See below [24]-[25] ff.

[12] See below [67] ff.

[13] See below [77] ff.

[14] See for example, the High Court's recent decision in *PT Garuda Indonesia Ltd v Australian Competition & Consumer Commission* [2012] HCA 33 (7 September 2012), [14]-[17]. There, the High Court distinguished between 'jurisdiction in the sense of the subject matter of a particular proceeding' (at [16]) and the 'amenability of a defendant to the process of the Australian courts' (at [17]). Confusingly, the term 'jurisdiction' is also frequently used to describe the territorial limits of a legal system (as in 'within the jurisdiction') (see *Lipohar v R* (1999) 200 CLR 485, 517 [79])

26. Both the common law and legislation provide subject matter jurisdiction to courts as well as the limitations on subject matter jurisdiction in certain circumstances.[15] Common law limitations include a court's lack of jurisdiction over disputes concerning land located in a foreign jurisdiction.[16] Limitations under statute include, for example, the mandatory application of domestic laws.[17]

Personal Jurisdiction

27. Personal jurisdiction relates to whether the court has authority over the parties to the litigation.

28. Under the common law, a court's personal jurisdiction is defined by the court's territorial reach and is asserted by way of personal service of the court's process upon the defendant. This restricts the court's jurisdiction to parties that are present within the territorial boundaries of the legal system of which the court is part[18] (presence) or parties that are willing to voluntarily submit themselves to the court's jurisdiction by appearing before the court and taking part in proceedings without objection (submission by appearance).

29. If a party is located outside the court's jurisdiction and has not voluntarily submitted to the court by appearing in the case, then the court will only be able to establish jurisdiction if legislation permits such an extension.[19]

30. If a court does not have personal jurisdiction and still hears and determines a matter, its orders are unlikely to be capable of enforcement over the party located outside of its jurisdiction.

31. Beyond personal jurisdiction there are other grounds of jurisdiction, such as jurisdiction that is exercised over property. This is particularly relevant in the admiralty and maritime context but will not be covered by this paper.

[15] M Keyes, above n 9, 69-77.

[16] The so-called Moçambique Rule, derived from the decision in *British South Africa Co v Companhia de Moçambique* [1893] AC 602. The Moçambique Rule has been reversed (or partially reversed) by legislation in New South Wales (*Jurisdiction of Courts (Foreign Land) Act 1989* (NSW)) and the ACT (*Law Reform (Miscellaneous Provisions) Act 1955* (ACT)).

[17] Such as the *Insurance Contracts Act 1984* (Cth) or the *Australian Consumer Law*.

[18] That is, the state or territory for a state or territory court; the Commonwealth for federal courts and the High Court.

[19] This includes the case of submission to a court's jurisdiction by a prior (choice of court) agreement. Rules of court presently govern the question whether Australian courts have jurisdiction to hear cases involving foreign parties to an agreement of this kind, although common law principles govern the question whether that power will be exercised or not. On this subject, see below [48] ff.

Establishing Jurisdiction in Cross-Border Litigation

32. Due to the limits of the rules governing personal service of court process, in the context of cross-border litigation, Australian courts are not necessarily able to assert their jurisdiction over parties located outside Australia. For example, the Western Australian Supreme Court may not be able to determine a claim brought against a party located in Brazil even if the claimant is a Western Australian company.

33. However, some legislation, court rules and international arrangements extend the jurisdiction of Australian courts to parties located abroad in certain circumstances.[20]

Serving Process Inter-State and Overseas

34. The rules for establishing a court's personal jurisdiction over matters between states and territories are broadly harmonised by the *Service and Execution of Process Act 1992* (Cth), which permits service of court process anywhere in Australia.[21]

35. However, while there is a level of commonality among the court rules that apply to establishing jurisdiction over parties located abroad, some rules differ from jurisdiction to jurisdiction both at state and territory and also at the federal level. Some of the key differences include:

    — the grounds for granting or permitting service of process outside Australia[22]
    — whether a court's leave to serve is required, and
    — the information that must be provided to the party being served.[23]

[20] For details, see below [36].

[21] When it enters into force, the *Trans-Tasman Proceedings Act 2010* (Cth) will also permit Australian court process to be served in New Zealand, and *vice versa*.

[22] See above, n 21.

[23] M Davies, A Bell and P L G Brereton (eds), *Nygh's Conflict of Laws in Australia* (LexisNexis Butterworths, 8th ed, 2010) 33.

36. The following table highlights some of these inconsistencies.

	WA[24]	QLD[25]	VIC[26]	NSW[27]	SA[28]	TAS[29]	NT[30]	ACT[31]	FC[32]
Is the court's leave required for overseas service?	✓	✗	✗	✗	✗	✗	✗	✗[33]	✓
Is the court's leave required to proceed if an overseas defendant has not entered an appearance?	✗	✗	✓	✓	✓	✓	✓	✓	✗
Do the court rules designate 'categories' of proceedings where service abroad is authorised?	✓	✓	✓	✓	✓	✓	✓	✓	✓
Are the 'categories' to be read 'independently and disjunctively'?[34]	✓	✗	✓	Modified	✓	✗	✓	✗	✗

37. As can be seen from the table, all court rules, except for the Western Australian court rules and the rules of the Federal Court of Australia, authorise service abroad without requiring the court's leave. The table above also indicates that, with one exception, all court rules that do not require the court's leave to serve abroad instead require leave to proceed against a defendant that has not entered an appearance after being served. The exception is Queensland, which does not require leave in this circumstance.

24 Rules of the Supreme Court 1971 (WA), Order 10.
25 Uniform Civil Procedure Rules 1999 (QLD), Chapter 4, Part 7.
26 Supreme Court (General Civil Procedure) Rules 2005 (VIC), Order 7.
27 Uniform Civil Procedure Rules 2005 (NSW), Part 11 and Schedule 6.
28 Supreme Court Civil Rules 2006 (SA), Rule 40.
29 Supreme Court Rules 2000 (TAS), Part 7, Division 10.
30 Supreme Court Rules 2012 (NT), Order 7.
31 Court Procedure Rules 2006 (ACT), Division 6.8.9.
32 Federal Court Rules 2011 (Cth), Part 10, Division 10.4.
33 To the extent permitted under sub-rule 6501(1) of the Court Procedure Rules 2006 (ACT). The service abroad of any other originating process not listed in this sub-rule requires the court's leave.
34 Davies, Bell and Brereton, above n 23, 35. See below at [40] ff.

38. All state, territory and federal court rules provide for certain 'categories' of proceedings where service abroad is authorised. Some categories exist consistently for all Australian courts, such as permitting service abroad for proceedings relating to contracts. This includes, for example, proceedings concerning:

    — a contract made or broken within the state or territory or (in the case of the Federal Court) in Australia, or
    — a contract governed (expressly or otherwise) by the law of the state or territory or (in the case of the Federal Court) by the law of any part of Australia.

39. However, differences remain even in this context, and there is less harmony in the treatment of other 'categories', including those relating to torts or wrongs, property or probate and wills.[35]

40. The present rules also differ in relation to the question of whether each and every part of the claim which is brought before an Australian court must be brought within one of the listed categories, or whether it is sufficient that a single cause of action in the claim document falls within one of the categories. This is the result where the rules do not provide for 'non-connected claims' to be joined to 'connected claims', with the result that each category must be interpreted 'independently and disjunctively'.[36]

41. As indicated in the table above, this rule continues to apply in some jurisdictions. In these jurisdictions, a court would not permit service abroad in relation to a multi-cause matter if one of the causes would not fall within a category's ambit. Similarly, it would not be possible to expand the scope of a matter by adding causes of action that cannot be served abroad.

42. On the other hand, where jurisdictions have allowed for the joinder of causes, service abroad of a multi-cause matter would be possible even if only one cause can be connected to a category. Similarly, the court may permit the adding of causes even though the added cause would not fall within the ambit of a category.

43. The Australian legal systems that allow joinder have significantly expanded the potential range of matters in relation to which service abroad is possible and thus, over which their courts can exercise personal jurisdiction.

44. The differences in the court rules that address the establishment of personal jurisdiction over a party located abroad may:

    — cause considerable confusion for Australian and other litigants engaged in cross-border matters

[35] Mortensen, Garnett and Keyes, above n 10, 57–74.
[36] Davies, Bell and Brereton, above n 23, 35.

— lead to a 'luck of the draw' situation where the ability to serve on parties overseas is dependent on the state or territory in which an application is brought, or
— serve to benefit highly mobile litigants, such as multinational corporations who can 'shop around' (often referred to as 'forum shopping') and litigate in the state or territory whose court rules most benefit their situation, at the expense of smaller companies/individuals.

45. Several commentators criticised these differences as leading to uncertainty and for increasing the legal risks for parties engaged in cross-border relationships or transactions.[37] Specifically, one commentator has noted that the differences have effects on:

— the ability of businesses in different states and territories to compete with each other on equal terms in view of the differing levels of access to local courts in cross-border situations, and
— the additional costs and inconvenience involved in litigating disputes abroad when such access is not granted.[38]

Recalibration of Categories

46. Commentators have noted that some of the categories that allow parties to serve out of the jurisdiction may require recalibration. For example, when the NSW Court of Appeal interpreted the category allowing service out for proceedings where the plaintiff claims damages suffered *within* the jurisdiction, it held that 'physical, financial or social consequences of an injury first received *abroad*' (emphasis added) would constitute 'damages' within the meaning of this category.[39] In response to this development, Garnett observed that the grounds that allow service abroad in relation to tortious claims have been construed 'liberally'.[40]

47. It has also been suggested that the categories relating to contracts may require modernisation considering the increased numbers of contracts that are formed online. For example, it appears that questions can arise in relation to where a contract formed online was 'made', thus creating issues in relation to the service out of jurisdiction based on this category. [41]

[37] A Dickinson, 'The Future of Private International Law in Australia' (*Australian International Law Journal*, 2012, forthcoming).
[38] ibid, 10-11.
[39] *Flaherty v Girgis* [1985] 4 NSWLR 248, 266–7. See also *Darrell Lea Chocolate Shops Pty Ltd v Spanish-Polish Shipping Co Inc (The 'Katowice II')* (1990) 25 NSWLR 568, 577.
[40] R Garnett, '*Dow Jones & Company Inc v Gutnick: An Adequate Response to Transnational Internet Defamation?*' (2003) 4 *Melbourne Journal of International Law* 196, 2003. Available at SSRN: <http://ssrn.com/abstract=473041>. Note the difference in approach in the European Union: *Handelswerkerij GJ Bier BV v Mines de Potasse d'Alsace SA* [1978] QB 708.
[41] See below [55].

Choosing a Court Before a Dispute Arises

48. The previous discussion has focused on establishing personal jurisdiction generally. It is, however, possible for parties to try and ensure that a court will have jurisdiction over any disputes that arise in their relationship or transaction by pre-agreeing to submit to the jurisdiction of the particular court. This is referred to as a choice of court (or jurisdiction) agreement and usually appears as a clause in a contract.[42]

49. The importance of parties being able to make effective choices in cross-border commercial relationships has long been emphasised, including during the recent consultations held in relation to the contract law reform. The ability to make such choices, and have this choice respected, is referred to as the principle of party autonomy, and underpins commercial and other relationships and transactions. This principle is the keystone of the Hague Conference on Private International Law's Choice of Court Convention of 2005.[43]

50. Commentators have frequently observed that Australian courts will not always uphold choice of court agreements. There are two broad reasons for this.

51. The first reason is that Australian courts have held choice of court agreements that deprive Australian mandatory legislation of its application (because the chosen court would not apply it), to be of no effect. Mandatory legislation includes sections in the *Competition and Consumer Act 2010* (Cth) (Competition and Consumer Act),[44] or the *Insurance Contracts Act 1984* (Cth) (Insurance Contracts Act).[45]

52. For example, in the matter of *Akai*,[46] the High Court found that mandatory provisions in the Insurance Contracts Act applied to deprive an express choice of court agreement of its intended effect.

53. The second reason is that Australian courts do not have a consistent approach to determining whether to give effect to a choice of court agreement.[47] In fact, research has shown that between 1991 and 2001, choice of court agreements were only enforced by Australian courts in 11 out of 19 cases. Between 2001 and 2008, such agreements were only enforced in one out of

[42] This choice may be made separate from an express choice that specifies a particular law as the law applicable to their contract. The effectiveness of a choice of law provision of this kind is dealt with below under [89] ff.

[43] This Convention, which affords primacy to exclusive choice of court clauses, is not yet in force.

[44] See Competition and Consumer Act, sch 2, ch 3, pt 3-2, div 1, which provides mandatory consumer guarantees. See in particular Competition and Consumer Act s 64.

[45] See Insurance Contracts Act ss 8, 52.

[46] *Akai Pty Limited v People's Insurance Co Ltd* (1996) 188 CLR 418.

[47] Keyes, above n 9, 122-3.

nine cases.[48] The practice appears no more consistent when the chosen court is another Australian court.[49]

54. The inability of parties to clearly predict whether Australian courts will honour their agreements increases uncertainty and thus unpredictability of outcomes in cross-border transactions. Improving certainty in this area would reduce litigation costs to parties as well as free up court resources.

Questions

— Have you experienced difficulties in determining whether you could serve initiating court process on a person located overseas so as to establish the court's jurisdiction over that person? If so, what kind of difficulty did you experience?
— Have you experienced difficulties as a result of the application of different rules of jurisdiction by different Australian courts? If so, please explain what difficulties you encountered.
— Do you think reform is needed to better harmonise the rules governing jurisdiction?
— Do you think that choice of court agreements should be respected even if this means that Australian mandatory legislation may not be applied?

Jurisdiction and the Internet

55. The Internet and the new digital economy pose new opportunities and challenges for cross-border transactions and relationships. For example, the Internet now reduces the time it takes to conduct cross-border transactions and to enter into cross-border relationships and potentially increases the range of transactions and trade relationships available. Other examples include Internet publications that can be instantaneously accessed in any jurisdiction around the world.[50]

56. In the area of jurisdiction, Hogan-Doran observed as early as 2003, that:

> *From a conflict of laws perspective, parties attempting to assert the jurisdiction of their chosen, territorially limited courts face new technological complexities and need to rely more on the 'long-arm' or 'exorbitant' jurisdiction of national courts.*[51]

[48] M Keyes, 'Jurisdiction Under the Hague Choice of Courts Convention: Its Likely Impact on Australian Practice' (2009) 5(2) *Journal of Private International Law* 181, 203.

[49] Dickinson, above n 37.

[50] See for example the High Court's decision in *Dow Jones & Company Inc v Gutnick* (2002) 210 CLR 575.

[51] J Hogan-Doran, 'Jurisdiction in cyberspace: The when and where of on-line contracts' (2003) 77 *Australian Law Journal* 377, 377.

57. This statement arguably holds true today. However, while posing challenges, the Internet equally opens up opportunities for parties engaging in cross-border litigation. Some of these are set out below.

Challenges

58. Existing 'traditional' jurisdictional principle and rules may need to be adapted for transactions that have occurred over the Internet. There are a variety of reasons for this, most obviously that it can be difficult to determine where these transactions have occurred and that the connection to a particular country or countries may be less obvious than in the case of offline transactions.[52] For example, where two parties in different states contract with one another using mobile devices it may not be clear where the contract was made and therefore which court is characterised as having jurisdiction to hear the matter.[53]

59. Svantesson suggests that the law has not yet picked up these new trends, which are the result of significant technological developments. Rather, it continues to grapple with the application of 'traditional' principles and rules.[54]

Opportunities

60. Information on the jurisdictional or other rules applicable in a state, territory or country unfamiliar to a particular litigant can be made more readily accessible through the Internet.[55] This means that some of the confusion around establishing jurisdiction is potentially minimised due to the accessibility of information on this issue.

61. In addition, well-known social media platforms are increasingly being used by courts in Australia to establish jurisdiction over defendants who could not be located or who attempt to repeatedly evade personal service of court documents.[56]

62. For example, in April 2012, the District Court of New South Wales made orders for substituted service, allowing the Australian music promoter Mothership Music Pty Ltd to serve the US rap musician Flo Rida via

[52] D J B Svantesson, *Private International Law and the Internet* (Wolters Kluwer, 2nd ed, 2011), 8.

[53] The location of offeror and accepting party is also relevant to the question which law governs the contract. Not being able to identify the location with any certainty could thus lead to significant difficulties in determining a contract's proper law.

[54] Svantesson, above n 52, 397.

[55] For examples, blogs dedicated to the subject matter of private international law, such as <www.conflictoflaws.net >, provide a wealth of information, including jurisdictional issues from a number of jurisdictions across the globe.

[56] *MKM Capital Property Limited v Corbo and Poyser*, No. SC 608 of 2008 (ACT, Australia). See also *Axe Market Gardens v Craig Axe*, CIV: 2008-485-2676 (High Court, New Zealand).

Facebook.[57] This decision, which was widely reported in the Australian media,[58] considered that the 'international reach of Facebook is such that it is a matter of notorious fact' and allowed service by posting a comment—which was drafted by the court as part of its orders—on the musician's Facebook wall.

63. English Courts have followed this trend, allowing service of process via Facebook and that of injunctions via Twitter.[59]

A New Approach to Jurisdictional Rules?

64. The opportunities and challenges referred to above demonstrate two things. First, that the Internet has a potentially significant effect on the application of traditional jurisdictional rules. Second, they also show that it is possible to identify first responses to these effects.

65. Whether these responses are the beginning of a changing understanding of personal jurisdiction needs to be seen. As the validity of (substituted) service and personal jurisdiction are two different things, it appears difficult to suggest that these developments are based on notions of a global jurisdiction founded on online personality. Rather, the responses merely seem to have taken into account online activities. However, it may also be conceivable that these responses could be the beginning of a possible future development that may lead to a move away from traditional concepts of personal service, towards accepting a person's online personality.

66. It seems important in undertaking any review of existing jurisdictional rules,[60] to ensure that they meet the opportunities and challenges of the new digital environment.[61]

[57] *Mothership Music Pty Ltd v Darren Ayre (trading as VIP Entertainment & Concepts Pty Ltd) and Flo Rida (also known as Tramar Dillar)* [2012] NSWDC 42.

[58] See for example: *Sydney Morning Herald*, 'Flo Rida served through Facebook', viewed 12 September 2012, <http://www.smh.com.au/entertainment/music/flo-rida-served-through-facebook-20120503-1y08o.html>.

[59] Vertex Law, Court permits service through Twitter, viewed 11 September 2012, <http://www.vertexlaw.co.uk/knowhow/articles/articles_detail.php?id=000118>.

[60] Rules descried by the Canadian Supreme Court in *Morguard Investments v de Savoye* [1990] 3 SCR 1077 as '19th century'.

[61] The importance of better understanding the effect of the internet on jurisdictional principles and rules has recently been acknowledged by the Australian Research Council, awarding the Future Fellows Grant to a project that aims to identify core principles that govern jurisdictional claims over internet conduct [Bond University, 'Bond University researcher recognised as one of Australia's best and brightest' (Media Release, 26 July 2012)].

Questions

- Do you think it is necessary to modernise jurisdictional rules in light of the advances in online and mobile technology and other developments? If so, how should they be modernised?
- Do you think the current law could better harness the opportunities presented by new technologies? If so, in which particular areas relevant to this consultation and in which priority?
- Do you have any other comments on the matters discussed in this paper, or specific reforms that you would propose in relation to jurisdiction?

Exercising Jurisdiction—the Stay and Transfer of Proceedings

67. The second aspect of jurisdiction concerns the question of whether a court, which has established its personal jurisdiction over the defendant, should proceed to exercise this jurisdiction or whether it should decline to do so.

68. In general, Australian courts have the power to decline jurisdiction, although the tests applied in making this decision vary according to the circumstances.

69. A court may decline to exercise its jurisdiction either by way of staying the proceedings or by way of transferring them to another court in a different jurisdiction. The power to transfer is, for the time being, restricted to transfers between state and territory supreme courts and federal courts.[62]

70. Broadly speaking, a decision to stay or transfer proceedings in favour of another court is based on a comparison of a range of circumstances which go to questions of suitability of proceeding in one or another jurisdiction.[63] Slightly misleadingly (as the question is not one of 'convenience'), the test applied, which varies according to the circumstances, is labelled the *forum conveniens* test—or, in the negative, the *forum non conveniens* test.

71. The powers to stay or transfer proceedings are designed to ensure the efficient administration of justice and, in particular, to serve as a tool to minimise the risk of parallel proceedings on the same subject matter, ie the situation in which parties are faced with the prospect of having to litigate the same matter in two different courts. Such parallel litigation may be thought undesirable as it is inefficient and creates the risk of inconsistent judgments.

[62] See the discussion of the state, territory and commonwealth cross-vesting acts below [73].

[63] Issues to be considered in this context include, for example, the applicable law, the convenience to the witnesses or the parties or the closest location to which the suit is connected. See R A Brand and S R Jablonski, *Forum Non Conveniens—History, Global Practice, and Future under the Hague Convention on Choice of Court Agreements* (Oxford University Press, 2007) 33-5, referring to P Beaumont, 'Forum Conveniens/Lis Pendens' (Paper presented at the International Association of Lawyers Seminar, Edinburgh, 20-21 April 2000).

72. It has been said that the existence of powers to stay and transfer would improve parties' certainty and promote procedural efficiency. It has also been suggested that they may also be seen as ameliorating some of the difficulties that arise as a result of the courts' 'exorbitant' jurisdiction, providing a counterbalance to courts 'employing the long arms of the 19th century jurisdiction, increasingly [finding] themselves making inappropriate contact with the jurisdiction of other national courts.'[64]

73. However, the tests in Australia differ significantly according to the circumstances, and the court in which the proceedings have been brought. The following table provides a brief overview:

Test	***Legislation/common law test***	***Applicable in the following proceedings***
Another court is **'the appropriate'** court	*Service and Execution of Process Act 1992* (Cth)[65]	Stay in favour of another state or territory inferior court.
Another court is **'the more appropriate'** court	*Trans-Tasman Proceedings Act 2010* (Cth)[66]	Stay in favour of a New Zealand court.
The Australian court is the **'clearly inappropriate'** court	Common law test[67]	Stay in favour of a court located in a foreign jurisdiction other than New Zealand.
'In the interests of justice' the matter should be transferred to another court	Various Commonwealth, state and territory Jurisdiction of Courts (Cross-Vesting) Acts[68]	Transfer from a state or territory court to a federal court or between state and territory courts.

74. Internationally, in terms of its approach to staying proceedings in favour of foreign jurisdictions, Australia has been described as an 'outlier' when compared to other jurisdictions, including the UK, Canada and the US.[69]

[64] Hogan-Doran, above n 51, 394.
[65] See s 20.
[66] See s 20.
[67] *Voth v Manildra Flour Mills Pty Ltd* (1990) 171 CLR 538.
[68] *Jurisdiction of Courts (Cross-Vesting) Act 1987* (Cth) s 5; *Jurisdiction of Courts (Cross-Vesting) Act 1993 (ACT)* s 5; *Jurisdiction of Courts (Cross-Vesting) Act 1987* (NSW) s 5; *Jurisdiction of Courts (Cross-Vesting) Act 1987 (NT)* s 5; *Jurisdiction of Courts (Cross-Vesting) Act 1987* (QLD) s 5; *Jurisdiction of Courts (Cross-Vesting) Act 1987* (SA) s 5; *Jurisdiction of Courts (Cross-Vesting) Act 1987* (Tas) s 5; *Jurisdiction of Courts (Cross-Vesting) Act 1987* (Vic) s 5.
[69] These jurisdictions have developed broadly the same approach. UK: *Spiliada Maritime Corp v Cansulex Ltd* [1987] AC 460; US: *Piper Aircraft Co v Reyno* (1981) 454 US 135; Canada: *Amchem Products Inc v British Columbia (Workers' Compensation Board)* [1993] 1 SCR 897. This approach has been described as the '*convenience-suitability approach*', whilst the Australian approach was referred to as the '*abuse-of-process approach*' (A T von Mehren, *Theory and Practice of Adjudicatory Authority in Private International Law: A Comparative Study of the Doctrine, Policies and Practices of Common- and Civil-Law Systems*, 295 (2002) *Recueil des Cours/Collected Courses of the Hague Academy of International Law* 326).

75. Some commentators have observed that such lack of uniformity reduces the orderliness and predictability of international litigation.[70] They argue that parties are at an increased risk of facing parallel proceedings because based on their respective tests, both domestic and foreign courts can assert their jurisdiction. Other commentators have, however, defended the Australian approach.[71] In any event, it is suggested that it is 'clearly appropriate' to address the question as to which test to apply in international cases against the background of a wider review of the rules of jurisdiction that are applied in such cases.[72]

76. To aid the discussion regarding this issue, Professor Andrew Dickinson of the University of Sydney, has prepared an in-depth analysis of Australian law, identifying the various inconsistencies that currently exist in the Australian legal system. Professor Dickinson's comprehensive analysis can be accessed on the Hub, which is available at <http://consult.govspace.gov.au/pil/>.

Questions

— Have you ever experienced difficulties that were the result of differing tests for the stay or transfer of proceedings? If so, please explain the nature of these difficulties.
— Do you consider it desirable to amend the *Service and Execution of Process Act 1992* (Cth) (Service and Execution of Process Act) s 20 so as to bring its provisions in line with those in the *Trans-Tasman Proceedings Act 2010* (Cth) (TPPA) Part 3? Please identify your reasons for supporting or opposing this reform measure, and identify any specific amendments that you consider appropriate.
— Do you consider it desirable to make any amendments to the Commonwealth, state and territory Cross-Vesting Acts so as to bring their provisions into line with those in the TPPA, Part 3? Please identify your reasons for supporting or opposing this reform measure, and identify any specific amendments that you consider appropriate.
— What test do you think should be applied to the question of whether an Australian court should stay its proceedings in favour of allowing the matters to be determined by a court outside Australia and New Zealand? Please give you reasons for favouring this test.
— Do you have any other comments on the matters discussed in this paper, or specific reforms to the relevant parts of the Cross-Vesting Acts, the Service and Execution of Process Act or the TPPA that you would propose?

[70] Brand and Jablonski, above n 63, 5.

[71] See for example D Robertson, '*Forum non conveniens* in America and England: "A rather fantastic fiction"' (1987) 103 *Law Quarterly Review* 398.

[72] See for more detail on this discussion Professor Dickinson's paper on this topic. A Dickinson, 'Harmonisation of the *Forum Conveniens* Tests in Australian and Trans-Tasman Proceedings: A Discussion Paper', paper prepared for this consultation, 1 November 2012, available at <http://www.consult.ag.go.au/pil>.

Restraining Jurisdiction: Lis Alibi Pendens, *Related Proceedings and Anti-Suit Injunctions*

77. The third aspect of jurisdiction dealt with in this paper concerns circumstances where proceedings are pending parallel in two or more jurisdictions. In these circumstances, specific questions arise where a party seeks to stay proceedings on the basis that a matter is pending in a foreign jurisdiction. Broadly, it is possible to distinguish two categories of parallel proceedings, including where proceedings are on foot in a foreign jurisdiction which:

— have the same parties and subject matter(s) (*lis alibi pendens*), or
— are related, but deal with different issues and possibly have different parties involved (related proceedings).

78. Specific questions also arise where a domestic court seeks to restrain a party from commencing proceedings in a foreign jurisdiction (anti-suit injunctions). Each of these issues is dealt with below.

Lis Alibi Pendens

79. This issue arises where a party seeks a permanent stay of Australian proceedings because foreign proceedings between the same parties and on the same subject matter are pending. In *Henry v Henry*, the High Court held that Australian courts will consider such applications by applying the 'clearly inappropriate forum' test and that, *prima facie*, the existence of pending foreign proceedings means that the commencement of proceedings in Australia is vexatious and oppressive.[73]

80. However, despite this basic proposition, commentators have noted the *Henry* Court's departure from the *Voth* test, highlighting that the Court failed to explain this departure in any detail.[74] In particular, it was pointed out that unlike *Voth*, which required Australian courts to ascertain their suitability to hear the matter through a 'forum-centric' inquiry conducted in 'isolation',[75] *Henry* considered it appropriate for courts to consider a number of factors, thus requiring a more comparative analysis between the jurisdictions concerned.[76]

[73] See above [73]. The clearly inappropriate forum test was promulgated by the High Court in *Voth v Manildra Flour Mills Pty Ltd* (1990) 171 CLR 538. *Henry v Henry* (1996) 185 CLR 571, 590-1.

[74] Keyes, above n 9, 115.

[75] The term 'forum-centric' has been used by Professor Keyes in this context. See Keyes, above n 9, 114. Professor Garnett noted that the Australian courts' inquiry is conducted in 'isolation', that is, the court does not consider the entitlement of the other jurisdiction to adjudicate the matter. R Garnett, 'Stay of Proceedings in Australia: A "Clearly Inappropriate" Test?' (1999) 23 *Melbourne University Law Review* 30, 51.

[76] Factors the court suggested for consideration included the enforceability of Australian orders in the foreign jurisdiction, the parties' connections to the respective jurisdictions or the stage that each parallel proceeding has reached. See *Henry v Henry* (1996) 185 CLR 571, 592-3.

81. Commentators have also observed that that Court's approach in *Henry* exposed the limited workability of the more rigid *Voth* test.[77] One aspect of this limited workability may include the situation where prospective foreign defendants anticipate litigation in Australian courts and commence proceedings first in the foreign jurisdiction. While Australian courts have traditionally given considerable weight to the fact that foreign proceedings were commenced prior to domestic ones,[78] Garnett pointed to the *Henry* court's particular emphasis on the pre-existence of foreign proceedings.[79]

82. This emphasis may lead to a 'reverse *Voth*' result. In order to ensure that the Australian plaintiff's proceedings will be heard by the Australian court, it is incumbent upon that plaintiff to convince the Australian court that the foreign proceedings have not been brought vexatiously and oppressively. Failing this, the Australian court may stay the matter, a result that resembles the *lis pendens* test under the Brussels I Regulation,[80] and potentially opens the doors for foreign defendants to 'play jurisdictional games' and permanently frustrate a plaintiff's Australian proceedings.

83. In this regard, particular problems may arise where a defendant seeks declarations as to non-liability (negative declarations) in the foreign proceedings. Australian courts remain divided as to whether such proceedings are worthy of deference or simply artificial devices to attract jurisdiction.[81]

Related Proceedings

84. Different issues arise in relation to so-called 'related proceedings'. As noted above, such proceedings exist where matters are pending in different jurisdictions, however (1) the issues dealt with in each jurisdiction are different, and/or (2) different parties are involved in the proceedings.

85. To ascertain whether related proceedings are pending in two or more jurisdictions, the court is required to identify the 'sub-stratum of fact' of the domestic and foreign proceedings. If they are the same, then the proceedings are related. If the proceedings are related, the Australian proceedings may be oppressive or vexatious if they were brought for the dominant purpose of

[77] Garnett, above n 75, 55.

[78] See *The Daeyong Honey* (1993) 120 ALR 109.

[79] Garnett, above n 75, 55.

[80] See the *lis pendens* test in Article 27.1 of the *Council Regulation (EC) No 44/2001 of 22 December 2000 on jurisdiction and the recognition and enforcement of judgments in civil and commercial matters*. As to the application of the *lis pendens* test, see for example *Erich Gasser GmbH v Misat SRL* [2004] 1 Lloyd's Rep 222 (decision in relation to Article 21 of the *Convention of 27 September 1968 on Jurisdiction and the Enforcement of Judgments in Civil and Commercial Matters*, the Council Regulation's predecessor).

[81] Compare *The Daeyang Honey* (1993) 120 ALR 109 and *Armacel v Smurfit Stone Container Corporation* (2008) 248 ALR 537.

preventing the other party from pursuing remedies that would otherwise be available to it in the foreign jurisdiction.[82]

Anti-Suit and Anti-Suit Injunctions

86. Finally, where parallel proceedings are on foot in both an Australian court and another foreign court, a party may apply to an Australian court for an anti-suit injunction. An anti-suit injunction has the effect of restraining a party from proceeding with litigation in a different jurisdiction. Where the party proceeds with litigation in the foreign jurisdiction after an Australian court has issued an anti-suit injunction, the party will be in contempt of that court and the normal consequences for contempt, such as imprisonment, will follow.

87. Some commentators have suggested that alternative ramifications for breach of an anti-suit injunction may be preferable to contempt. These ramifications could include: damages, or an inability to have the foreign judgment recognised and enforced in the jurisdiction that issued the anti-suit injunction.[83] As an anti-suit injunction restrains another court from exercising its jurisdiction over a matter, it is a serious tool that is not issued by courts lightly. In *CSR v Cigna*,[84] the High Court of Australia indicated that a number of steps would need to be taken before a court could consider granting an anti-suit injunction. First, the court would need to consider whether it should restrain the proceedings in its own jurisdiction. Second, where the court decided not to restrain its proceedings, it would need to then consider whether the plaintiff in the local proceedings should apply for a stay or dismissal (or has applied for a stay/dismissal) in the foreign court and whether the anti-suit injunction should be granted.

88. Within Australia, anti-suit injunctions have become less common as a result of the transfer mechanism within the *Jurisdiction of Courts (Cross-Vesting) Act 1987* and the effect of section 21 of the *Service and Execution of Process Act 1992*, which prohibits the making of such orders in respect of initiating process served under the Act.

[82] *CSR Ltd v Cigna Insurance Australia Ltd* (1997) 189 CLR 345, 402.
[83] Mortensen, Garnett and Keyes, above n 10, 131.
[84] *CSR Ltd v Cigna Insurance Australia Ltd* (1997) 189 CLR 345.

Questions

- Have you been involved in parallel proceedings? If so, what kind of difficulties have you experienced? Did this include any of the difficulties referred to above?
- Have you previously applied for an anti-suit injunction and, if so, what were your experiences?
- Do you consider that contempt is an appropriate consequence for breach of an anti-suit injunction? If no, please provide details of which and possible alternatives.

Chapter 4: Principles and Rules Relating to Choice of Law

Choice of Law: a General Overview

89. Questions around what law is to apply to a particular relationship, such as a contractual relationship or transaction, arise even before parties have entered into a dispute. These questions, referred to as choice of law or applicable law questions, are likely to arise where a transaction or relationship extends over state, territory or national borders.

90. In addition, where a dispute between parties arises and a court determines that it has jurisdiction (the power) to hear the matter, questions may still arise as to what law is to govern the matter—with the court possibly called upon to apply a different law to the law applicable where the court is based. For example, in a contractual dispute the New South Wales Supreme Court may determine that it has the jurisdiction to hear the dispute but that, according to the terms of the contract, Singaporean law is to apply.

91. Generally, questions around choice of law in Australia are governed by the common law. This has enabled choice of law principles, in some circumstances, to evolve over the years. However, it is arguable that some of the choice of law principles have not evolved and adapted to respond to the increased incidence of cross-border trade, globalisation and the new digital environment.

92. Acknowledging the need to provide greater certainty to legal matters that cross state and country borders, the Australian Law Reform Commission recommended in its 1992 report, *Choice of Law*,[85] that a complimentary set of federal, state and territory laws should be developed to deal with choice of law in Australia. In 1996, the Australian Law Reform Commission made similar recommendations in its report on Legal Risk in International Transactions.[86] In a speech on 31 January 2011, the Hon J J Spigelman AC, former Chief Justice of the New South Wales Supreme Court, also outlined that reform in this area was needed and was affecting Australia's competitive advantage as a destination for trade.[87]

93. Along this line, several of Australia's major trading partners, including China and Japan, have recently moved to legislate choice of law rules which will assist in guiding companies who wish to trade in their countries.[88]

[85] Australian Law Reform Commission, *Choice of Law*, Report No 58, 1992.

[86] Australian Law Reform Commission, *Legal Risk in International Transactions*, Report No 80, 1996.

[87] The Hon J J Spigelman, 'Global Engagement by Australian Lawyers' (Speech delivered at the Opening of Law Term Dinner 2011, Law Society of New South Wales, 31 January 2011).

[88] For a discussion of legislating private international law principles and rules, see below [195].

94. This chapter will discuss the determination of choice of law in Australia in the context of contract, tort and property law. It is not the intention of this project to address issues surrounding bankruptcy and insolvency as that is currently being considered in the context of other government reforms.

Choice of Law in Contract

> Note
>
> Consultations concerning the reform of Australia's contract law have recently concluded.[89] Several submissions have emphasised the importance of private international law in relation to contract law. The views and opinions put forward as part of that consultation will also inform this Project.

95. In Australia, the law applicable to multi-state contracts (contracts that have aspects to them that are not contained in one state alone) is determined by reference to the common law.

96. The general common law principle is that a multi-state contract is to be governed by its 'proper law'.[90] This includes the formation, validity and operation of the contract. The proper law of a contract can be determined by reference to an express choice made by the parties to the contract, an inferred/implied choice or by an objective determination of where the transaction has its 'closest and most real connection'.[91]

Express Choice of Law

97. A contract governing a relationship or transaction between two or more parties may expressly designate, in a contractual clause, the law that is to govern the contract. Such express choices of law in a contract are generally honoured by Australian courts in the event of a dispute arising under the contract, respecting the parties' freedom to choose, otherwise known as the principle of party autonomy.

[89] The 'Review of Australian Contract Law' project page can be found here: <http://www.ag.gov.au/Consultationsreformsandreviews/Pages/Review-of-Australian-Contract-Law.aspx>.

[90] *Amin Rasheed Shipping Corp v Kuwait Insurance Co* [1984] AC 50. There are legislative exceptions. Note for example the *United Nations Convention on Contracts for the International Sale of Goods* implemented in Australia through various state and territory Sale of Goods Acts. This convention provides for express exceptions that deviate from the applicable law being the proper law of the contract.

[91] See *Bonython v Commonwealth of Australia* [1951] AC 201, 219. This three-step test has been recently applied to identify the proper law of arbitration agreements. *Sulamerica CIA Nacional de Seguros SA and others v Enesa Engenharia SA and others [2012] EWCA Civ 638*. Due to the effects of the doctrine of separability, ascertaining the proper law of an arbitration agreement is a process different to that of ascertaining the proper law of the contract that includes the arbitration agreement. See *Harbour Assurance Co (UK) Ltd v Kansa General International Insurance Co Ltd* [1993] QB 701; see also *C v D* [2007] EWCA Civ 1282 and *Premium Nafta Products Ltd v Fili Shipping Co Ltd* [2007] UKHL 40.

98. However, some Commonwealth as well as state and territory legislation mandatorily requires provisions to apply in particular situations, irrespective of an express choice of law to the contrary by the parties. Such legislation includes provisions in the *Competition and Consumer Act 2010* (Cth),[92] the *Carriage of Goods by Sea Act 1991* (Cth)[93] and the *Insurance Contracts Act 1984* (Cth).[94] In most cases this legislation is prescribed to mandatorily apply to protect parties in unequal bargaining positions, such as consumers and parties to standard insurance contracts.

99. Aside from the effect of mandatory legislation, a court may also disregard the effect of an express choice of law in a contract if application of the chosen law would not be '*bona fide*' or would be contrary to public policy.[95]

100. It is not completely clear what '*bona fide*' means in this context, as courts in practice have arguably not applied it. The requirement that the express choice must not be contrary to public policy generally refers to cases where application of the law would be contrary to another Australian law.

101. The 'public policy' exception generally exists in common law to provide for judicial discretion in multi-state legal matters—whether it is in the context of recognising and enforcing judgments from a foreign country or, in this context, in applying the law of a foreign country.

102. In the context of contracts that cross state and territory borders within Australia, s 118 of the *Constitution* prevents state courts from applying the public policy exception as a reason to avoid the application of an express choice of law of another Australian state or territory.

103. Another exception to an exclusive choice is where that choice is a system or body of rules relating to non-state law. This is often associated with the choice by parties of religiously based rules but can also be associated with the choice by parties of model rules—such as those present in the UNIDROIT Principles of International Commercial Contracts.

104. It should also be noted that Australian courts have determined that unless the choice is made expressly through clear language, a contractual choice of law is promissory only and not declaratory. This means that if one party attempts to avoid the choice by litigating in a foreign court that would not apply the choice of law, this does not amount to a breach of contract.[96]

---

[92] See Sch2, ch 3, Pt3-2, div 1, which provides mandatory consumer guarantees. See in particular ss 64, 67.

[93] See s 11.

[94] See ss 8, 52. The High Court specifically addressed the application of these sections in *Akai Pty Ltd v People's Insurance Co Ltd* (1996) 188 CLR 418 and held that these provisions apply to frustrate any express choice to the contrary.

[95] *Vita Food Products Inc v Unus Shipping Company Ltd* [1939] AC 277.

[96] *Ace Insurance Limited v Moose Enterprise Pty Limited* [2009] NSWSC 724.

105. Therefore, while an Australian court will generally uphold an express choice of law in a contract, there are limited grounds on which the court may disregard such a choice or choose to look behind the choice. These are:

- — because of the effect of a mandatory statute
- — the choice is not *bona fide*
- — the application of the choice would be contrary to public policy
- — the choice relates to a non-state system body of rules, or
- — the choice is not expressly made with clear language.

106. These exceptions can cause difficulties for parties and businesses that are unable to determine whether Australian courts will uphold their contractual agreements.

Inferred Choice of Law

107. Where a contract does not include an express provision indicating the parties' selection of the law that is to govern the contract, Australian courts may infer a choice of law by reference to the other clauses in the contract and the nature of the contract.[97]

108. Factors that a court will take into account when inferring a choice of law by parties in a contract include:

- — express choice of forum clauses—for example, a term stating 'any disputes under the contract are to be heard in the New South Wales Supreme Court' will suggest that the parties intended New South Wales law to apply to the dispute
- — clauses indicating the currency that any money is to be paid in, and
- — the language that the contract is in—for example, the use of English legal terms in a contract.[98]

109. As the inference is made on the basis of the factual circumstances and the clauses in the contract, it can be difficult to determine the inferred choice without the assistance of a court. This can complicate contractual disputes for parties by requiring a court to determine the law applicable to a contract. However, where the choice of law in the contract is expressed in clear language, parties can avoid such future complications.

Objective Assessment

110. Where a contract does not include an express choice and the parties' intended choice cannot be inferred from the other clauses in the contract, a court will need to conduct an objective assessment of what is the 'proper law'

[97] *Akai Pty Ltd v People's Insurance Co Ltd* (1996) 188 CLR 418.
[98] *Amin Rasheed Shipping Corp v Kuwait Insurance Co* [1984] AC 50.

of the contract. The courts have held that this is determined by conducting an assessment of 'the system of law with which the transaction has its closest and most real connection'.[99]

111. This will generally involve a consideration of the place where the contract was formed and performed, the residence or place of business of the parties and the nature and subject matter of the contract. This assessment must be undertaken in light of the circumstances that existed at the time that the contract was entered into.

112. This determination of the place where the contract has its most close and real connection can be complicated in the new digital environment, where, as previously noted, it is often difficult to determine where offer and acceptance of the contract has occurred or where the contract will be performed.

113. In the past, many commentators have criticised the determination of the proper law as the choice of law in multi-state contracts. The major criticism is that the concept can be imprecise and unclear and, in many cases, requires the court to make a determination as to what is the proper law.

114. Additionally, determination of the proper law can result in a circular result. This circularity arises where one party to a multi-state contract argues that the contract was not validly entered into in the first place. In that case a court is called upon to determine and apply the proper law of a contract that arguably never came into existence.

International Developments

115. Work is currently being undertaken in The Hague Conference on Private International Law, to develop a model law on choice of law in international contracts, titled the *Hague Principles of Choice of Law in International Contracts*.[100] As a model law, the instrument will not be binding. It will be a matter for State parties to adopt the model law into their domestic law.

116. Central to this instrument is its adherence to party autonomy, that is, the parties' ability to choose what law will govern the contract in whole or in part. The instrument will not require the chosen law to have any connection to parties or the transaction.

117. Additionally, the *Draft Hague Principles of Choice of Law in International Contracts* currently proposes to allow for parties to choose non-state rules

[99] *Bonython v Commonwealth of Australia* [1951] AC 201, 219.

[100] The most recent text is contained in Hague Conference on Private International Law, *Choice of law in International Contracts: development process of the draft instrument and future planning*, Preliminary Document No 4 (January 2012), available at: <http://www.hcch.net/index_en.php?act=text.display&tid=49>.

of law.[101] This would enable parties to choose non-state rules, such as the *UNIDROIT Principles of International Commercial Contracts*.

118. The European Union has a regulation in place that provides the rules around choice of law in contract. The *Regulation (EC) No 593/2008 of the European Parliament and of the Council of 17 June 2008 on the law applicable to contractual obligations* (also referred to as Rome I Regulation) provides in art 4(2) a rebuttable presumption that the law applicable to a multi-state contract is the law of:

the country where the party who is to effect the performance … has, at the time of the conclusion of the contract, his habitual residence, or in the case of a body corporate or unincorporated, its central administration.

In 1996, the Australian Law Reform Commission has recommended that Australia adopt this presumption relating to habitual residence or central administration for the law applicable to multi-state contracts where the parties' intention is not expressed or cannot be inferred.[102]

Questions

General Questions

— Have you experienced difficulty in determining the law that should apply to a particular multi-state contract? If yes, please provide details.
— Do you think the government should further investigate whether reform is needed around the question of what law is applicable to a multi-state contract?

Specific Questions

— Do you think the common law position with respect to an express choice of law provision in a contract is currently adequate? If not, please provide details.
— Do you think that the application of mandatory legislative rules to multi-state contracts is currently adequate? Do you think that Australia is in need of more or fewer mandatory rules? Please provide details of the areas where you think reform is necessary, if any.
— Would you like to be able to choose non-state bodies of rules to govern your contracts, such as the UNIDROIT Principles of International Commercial Contracts? Why?
— Do you think the common law position with respect to an inferred choice of law is adequate? If not, why not?

[101] See *Draft Hague Principles of Choice of Law in International Commercial Contracts*, art 2.
[102] Australian Law Reform Commission (1996), above n 86.

— Do you think there are issues with respect to the common law objective determination of the proper law? If so, please provide details.
— Do you think Australia should seek to reform the rules relating to the applicable law for contracts to bring it more in line with international developments—for example, those in Europe or the Hague Conference's model law on international contracting when it is finalised?
— Do you think that the government should legislate choice of law rules with respect to contracts? If so, do you think that legislation should be detailed or provide only a high level framework?

Choice of Law in Tort

119. Outside of contract law, such as in the area of tort law, the law applicable to torts is equally important. Following a number of High Court cases, the position with respect to the law that is to govern a tort has been finally determined to be the place where the tort was committed (the *lex loci delicti*).[103]

120. This choice of law rule applies to both interstate torts and international torts. This means that, for example, if you are injured as a result of a person's negligence in Indonesia, Indonesian law will apply to determine liability.

121. The clarification of the general choice of law rule for multi-state torts in these High Court cases has increased certainty and reduced the likelihood of forum shopping occurring. Forum shopping occurs where a plaintiff searches for the court that is likely to apply law that is most generous to their circumstances, and commences litigation in that court—to the detriment of the defendant.

122. As the applicable law for multi-state torts is the law of the place where the tort has occurred, this minimises the likelihood of forum shopping occurring and enables greater access to justice for all parties involved in the litigation. These High Court decisions were therefore praised by a number of commentators at the time for providing final certainty and justice to a complex area.

123. Nevertheless, there have been calls for the introduction of a flexible exception to this choice of law rule in torts to provide courts with discretion where the application of the torts choice of law rule leads to an inequitable result.

[103] See *John Pfeiffer Pty Ltd v Rogerson* (2000) 203 CLR 503; *Regie Nationale des Usines Renault SA v Zhang* (2002) 210 CLR 491.

Recent Issues

124. While the High Court decisions created greater certainty around the common law position with respect to the law that is applicable to torts, questions have since arisen following the High Court's decision in *Neilson v Overseas Projects Corporation of Victoria* (2005) 223 CLR 331 (*Neilson*). Commentators have outlined two residual issues that may require addressing.[104]

125. First, the rigid application of the choice of law rule in tort (the *lex loci delicti*) is far reaching and excludes circumstances in which parties agree to being governed by a law that is different to the law which would ordinarily apply on application of that rule.

126. Second, courts have turned to other devices to avoid the rigid application of the choice of law in tort rule, where such application would lead to an undesirable result. For example, in *Neilson*, the High Court applied the foreign law along with the foreign choice of law rule to the tort in question. This is known as '*renvoi*'.

127. *Renvoi* is a term used to describe a complex process.[105] This process begins with a court deciding to exercise jurisdiction in a multi-state matter. This court then applies a choice of law rule to determine which country or state or territory law is applicable to the matter, such as, in the case of a multi-state tort, the law of the place where the tort was committed. Instead of applying the foreign law on its own, the court then puts itself in the position that the foreign court would be in if faced with the multi-state tort. That is, the court applies the choice of law rule that the foreign court would have applied if it were hearing the matter.

128. This process can lead to a circular result where the local court determines that the overseas court would have determined that the local court's law was applicable, or that a third country or state or territory law was applicable.

129. It is currently not clear whether the judgment in *Neilson* has wider application to, for example, choice of law in contract.

130. Further, questions remain in relation to the characterisation or classification of tortious claims. Particular problems arise when two jurisdictions take different approaches to characterisation, including, for example, where one jurisdiction may characterise a particular matter as tortious, while the other jurisdiction characterises the issue as contractual in nature.

[104] Commentators include Mortensen, Garnett, Keyes, above n 10, 467ff.
[105] This discussion paper does not distinguish between transmission or remission *renvoi*.

Defamation

131. The situation with respect to defamation differs from other cases of multi-state torts. In defamation cases, the High Court has determined that the law where the publication has occurred is the law applicable to the alleged defamation in question.[106] The High Court has previously rejected the argument that a special rule is necessary for Internet publications,[107] potentially opening up liability for defamation in every country in the world where the Internet material has been viewed. Some commentators have criticised this decision as having failed to keep up with technological developments.

132. A matter recently filed in Australia has highlighted some of the potential issues with the choice of law rule applicable to defamation. In early 2012, Joshua Meggitt, a man residing in Melbourne, commenced an action for defamation against Twitter on the basis of its publication of allegedly defamatory material in a tweet by fellow Australian Marieke Hardy.

133. Commentators have suggested that were Australia's existing choice of law rules for defamation to be applied to provide a successful outcome for Mr Meggitt, this could have a significant impact on social media platforms such as Twitter and Facebook, possibly resulting in their removal from Australia due to liability concerns.[108]

Questions

General questions

— Have you experienced difficulty in determining the law that should apply to a particular multi-state tort? If so please provide details.

Specific questions

— Do you think the common law position with respect to the applicable law for a multi-state tort needs review? If so, please provide details.
— Do you think the High Court's apparent application of '*renvoi*' (see explanation above) in the recent *Neilson* decision is cause for concern necessitating further investigation into reform in this area? If so, please provide details.
— Do you think the applicable law rules with respect to defamation are adequate, particularly in the context of the online environment?
— Do you think that the government should look into codifying the common law applicable law rules with respect to torts?

---

[106] *Dow Jones & Co Inc v Gutnick* (2002) 210 CLR 575.

[107] *ibid.*

[108] P Black, 'Will Marieke Hardy's Twitter case change Australian law for ever?', *The Conversation*, 17 February 2012, viewed 11 October 2012, <http://theconversation.edu.au/will-marieke-hardys-twitter-case-change-australian-law-for-ever-5432>.

Choice of Law in Property

134. Where there are multi-state property matters, the choice of law rule traditionally distinguishes between movable and immovable property. This distinction is made on the basis of where the property is situated. The determination of where the property is situated is made in accordance with the law of the forum, that is, the law applicable in the state, territory or country where the dispute is brought.

135. This distinction has been identified as posing some potential problems in the intellectual property area, where property rights may be assessed as immovable and situated in several different countries at the same time, particularly in the new digital environment.

Questions

General questions

- Have you experienced difficulty in determining the law that should apply to property in a multi-state case? If so please provide details.
- Do you think there is a need for the government to reform the choice of law rules in the case of multi-state property?

Specific questions

- Have you experienced difficulty determining the law applicable to immovable property in a multi-state matter? If so, please provide details.
- Do you think there are particular classes of property, for example intellectual property or shares, which require specific attention for reform in this area? Please provide details.

Chapter 5: Other Private International Law Rules and Related Issues

136. The related issues discussed below include:
- the recognition and enforcement of judgments, and
- the pleading and proof of foreign law in domestic courts.

Recognition and Enforcement of Judgments

137. The recognition and enforcement of foreign judgments is the third component of private international law. It addresses whether the judgments of foreign courts are capable of recognition and enforcement in local courts.

138. The primary rule is that a foreign judgment has no inherent force domestically. Thus, the domestic recognition and enforcement of a foreign judgment requires further steps. What these steps are depends on whether special arrangements exist between the foreign country and the country in which the foreign judgment is to be enforced.

139. The intranational recognition and enforcement of domestic state and territory judgments presents little difficulties and the enforcement mechanism is streamlined under the *Service and Execution of Process Act 1992* (Cth). The situation, however, is different in relation to the international recognition and enforcement of foreign judgments.

140. While there exists a well-recognised, multilateral instrument that governs the recognition and enforcement of foreign arbitral awards,[109] there are currently no global, multilateral instruments in place that would facilitate the recognition and enforcement of foreign judgments. In the absence of such instruments, special arrangements exist both regionally, such as those that exist within the European Union,[110] and bilaterally.[111]

[109] The *New York Convention on the Recognition and Enforcement of Foreign Arbitral Awards* of 1958. See for example Professor Van Den Berg's website dedicated to this Convention, located at <http://www.newyorkconvention.org/>. This Convention is implemented in Australia through the *International Arbitration Act 1974* (Cth). It provides for the enforcement of an arbitral award through the courts 'as if' the award is a judgment of the enforcing domestic court. See *Uganda Telecom Ltd v High Tech Telecom Pty Ltd (No 2)* (2011) 277 ALR 441, [12]-[13] and *Traxys Europe SA v Balaji Coke Industry PVT Ltd (No 2)* (2012) 291 ALR 99, [72].

[110] For example, the *Council Regulation (EC) No 44/2001 of 22 December 2000 on jurisdiction and the recognition and enforcement of judgments in civil and commercial matters* (also called Brussels I Regulation). See: <http://europa.eu/legislation_summaries/ justice_freedom_security/judicial_cooperation_in_civil_matters/l33054_en.htm>. This Regulation contains jurisdictional rules and recognition and enforcement mechanisms based on the proposition that judgments given in any member state are to be recognised in another member state without special proceedings (unless they are contested).

[111] Such as included in the *Agreement between the Governments of Australia and New Zealand on Trans-Tasman Court Proceedings and Regulatory Enforcement*. See also below [152] ff, [189].

141. These arrangements usually include jurisdictional rules and enforcement mechanisms that allow for the simplified registration and enforcement of a foreign judgment 'as if it were' a domestic judgment. If no such special arrangements exist, the forum court will enforce a foreign judgment by making its own order in line with the foreign judgment.[112]

142. In Australia, the recognition and enforcement of foreign judgments is possible either at common law or under legislation and it is necessary to distinguish between monetary[113] and non-monetary judgments.[114]

Recognition and Enforcement at Common Law

143. A foreign monetary judgment is *prima facie* evidence that the foreign court created an obligation for a judgment debtor to pay a judgment creditor a certain amount of money.[115]

144. Under common law, Australian courts will recognise and enforce a foreign money judgment if the following four criteria are satisfied:

— the foreign court must have had 'international jurisdiction' (the determination by the local court that the foreign court has exercised a ground of international jurisdiction, such as personal service)
— the judgment must be final and conclusive
— the parties must be identical, and
— the judgment must be for a fixed amount of money.

145. If these criteria are satisfied, and the judgment debtor did not (successfully) raise a defence against the enforcement action,[116] the domestic court will enforce the foreign judgment by rendering its own judgment, which creates an obligation between the judgment debtor, and the judgment creditor, which is equivalent to the obligation contained in the foreign judgment.[117]

[112] K Pham, 'Enforcement of Non-Monetary Foreign Judgments in Australia' (2008) 30 *Sydney Law Review* 663, 665-6.

[113] See below [143]. These judgments can be enforced both at common law and under statute.

[114] Non-monetary judgments include, for example, interlocutory orders such as injunctive relief, but also orders for specific performance. Such judgments cannot be enforced at common law; see below [143]. However, the *Foreign Judgments Act 1991* (Cth) makes provision for the enforcement of non-monetary judgments even though to date, no foreign court has been prescribed for that purpose; see below [150].

[115] Mortensen, Garnett and Keyes observed that '[t]he recognition and enforcement of a foreign judgment at common law depends on the theory of obligations', Mortensen, Garnett and Keyes, above n 10, 139. This discussion paper will primarily consider judgments *in personam*, ie judgments between persons. Where it deals with judgments *in rem*, it will state so expressly.

[116] Defences against the recognition and enforcement of a foreign judgment include that the foreign judgment was obtained by fraud, that a party was denied procedural fairness or that the enforcement would be against Australia's public order.

[117] The recognition and enforcement of a foreign judgment does not rely on reciprocal arrangements between the country in which the foreign judgment originated and the enforcing jurisdiction.

146. However, even if the above criteria are not met by a foreign judgment, a domestic court may still recognise (as opposed to enforce) that judgment. Such recognition of a judgment has important implications. For example, it is possible that the recognised judgment triggers a *res judicata* (a claim preclusion) or issue estoppel in the enforcing jurisdiction.[118]

Recognition and Enforcement Under Statute

147. Australian legislation provides that certain foreign judgments are capable of recognition and enforcement. The legislation offers a streamlined process that assists with having a judgment recognised and enforced, making it faster and more cost efficient. The two main pieces of legislation that provide for simplified recognition and enforcement of foreign judgments are the *Foreign Judgments Act 1991* (Cth) and, upon commencement, the *Trans-Tasman Proceedings Act 2010* (Cth) (not yet in force).

The Foreign Judgments Act 1991 (Cth)

148. The *Foreign Judgments Act 1991* (Cth) (FJA) provides a mechanism for the recognition and enforcement of judgments delivered by foreign courts prescribed in the *Foreign Judgments Regulations 1992* (the Regulations).

149. For a foreign court to be prescribed in the Regulations, the foreign jurisdiction must declare that it will give 'substantial reciprocity' to the treatment of Australian judgments.[119] The scope of the FJA is limited in the sense that it only covers a relatively small range of countries with which Australia has entered into some form of bilateral reciprocity arrangement. Some of Australia's largest trading partners are not included.

150. The FJA allows the registration of both monetary and non-monetary judgments. The latter may include interim relief or orders for specific performance. Non-monetary judgments can only be enforced if they originate in a foreign court that has been prescribed in the Regulations. To date, Australia has not prescribed any foreign courts in that category. In the case of intellectual property, this means that non-monetary judgments relating to foreign intellectual property rights are not currently capable of recognition and enforcement in Australia.

151. The simplified recognition process is based on the registration of the foreign judgment in the states' and territories' supreme courts. Once registered, the judgment has the same force and effect as a judgment of the registering domestic court. To resist enforcement after registration, it is possible to set aside the registration. The grounds upon which a setting aside is possible are

[118] Pham, above n 112, 666.

[119] By necessary implication, this means that Australia, too, must have expressly agreed to extend substantial reciprocity to that country.

listed in s 7 of the FJA. They include the denial of natural justice or where enforcement would be against Australia's public order. In addition, the court must set aside a registration if the judgment has been wholly satisfied or is no longer enforceable in the foreign country.

The Trans-Tasman Proceedings Act 2010 (Cth)

152. The *Trans-Tasman Proceedings Act 2010* (Cth) (TTPA) implements the *Agreement between the Government of Australia and the Government of New Zealand on Trans-Tasman Court Proceedings and Regulatory Enforcement* (Trans-Tasman Agreement) and contains a distinct regime for the recognition and enforcement of certain New Zealand judgments (NZ judgment). The New Zealand legislation, the *Trans-Tasman Proceedings Act 2010* (NZ) contains an identical regime for the recognition and enforcement of certain Australian judgments.

153. A NZ judgment will be enforceable in Australia if it is registered with an Australian court.[120] To be registrable in Australia, a judgment given by a New Zealand court must be characterised as a '*registrable NZ judgment*'.[121] Registrable NZ judgments include, for example:

— final and conclusive judgment given in a civil proceeding by a NZ court
— certain judgments given in criminal and regulatory NZ proceedings, or
— certain cost orders.[122]

154. Applications for the registration of a registrable NZ judgment will lie with superior Australian courts.[123] An application may also be made to an inferior court for the registration of a registrable NZ judgment, as long as the inferior court has the power to grant the relief sought.[124]

155. Upon application the court must register the registrable NZ judgment.[125] The procedure for registration is provided in Division 2 of the TTPA. Upon its registration, the registrable NZ judgment has the same force and effect 'as if' the Australian court in which it was registered had given the judgment.[126]

[120] See TTPA s 65. Registration occurs in accordance with TTPA s 68.

[121] See TTPA s 66.

[122] A registrable NZ judgment also includes NZ market proceedings judgments and judgments registered in an NZ court under the *Reciprocal Enforcement of Judgements Act 1934* (NZ) (see TTPA s 66(1)). The TTPA also expressly specifies certain exclusions, including, for example, proceeds of crimes orders, certain estate instruments or judgments and orders prescribed by regulations (see TTPA s 66(2)).

[123] See TTPA ss 67(1)-(3). A superior Australian court is the Federal Court of Australia, the Family Court of Australia and the state and territory Supreme Courts (TTPA s 4).

[124] See TTPA s 67(1) or (2).

[125] See TTPA s 68.

[126] See TTPA s 74(1). This is, however, subject to TTPA s 74(3). As to the meaning of 'as if' in the arbitration context, see above, n 109.

Also upon registration, the person registering the judgment is required to provide every judgment debtor with notice of the registration.[127]

156. Special provisions contained in the TTPA regulate important issues such as the setting aside of the registration, staying the enforcement subject to pending appeals, currency, interest and cost and expenses.

Multinational Efforts

157. Multinational efforts to ensure greater transportability of judgments across borders are ongoing but are characterised by slow process. Regional instruments that govern recognition and enforcement of judgments include those that govern the recognition and enforcement of judgments in the European Union.[128] The Hague Conference on Private International Law (the Hague Conference) primarily drove global efforts.

158. The Hague Conference's first global recognition and enforcement instrument was the *Convention on the Recognition and Enforcement of Foreign Judgments in Civil and Commercial Matters 1971*. However, it attracted very few signatories,[129] and in 1992, steps were taken to develop a 'wider ranging' convention (the commencement of the so-called 'Judgments Project').[130] Between 1996 and 2002, the Hague Conference progressed work on a global judgments convention. However, while focusing on the international jurisdiction of courts and the mechanisms to recognise and enforce foreign judgments, the Hague Conference member states could not agree on a consensual approach. Finally, negotiations led to the conclusion of the *Convention on Choice of Court Agreements 2005* (Choice of Court Convention) instead.[131] This Convention has been labelled as 'the counterpart for litigation of the

[127] See TTPA s 73(1).

[128] For example, the *Brussels I Regulation*, above n 110. Another instrument is the 1988 *Convention on jurisdiction and the enforcement of judgments in civil and commercial matters* (also called the Lugano Convention) which governs those cases that involve parties located in non-member states. Older multilateral instruments also include general provisions governing the recognition and enforcement of judgments, such as the 1928 *Código de Derecho Internacional Privado* (also called the Bustamante Code). See A T von Mehren, 'Recognition and Enforcement of Foreign Judgments: A new Approach for the Hague Conference' (1994) 55(3) *Law and Contemporary Problems* 271, 273-6.

[129] The 1971 Convention entered into force on 20 August 1979. To date, the parties include Albania, Cyprus, The Netherlands, Portugal and Kuwait. See: <http://www.hcch.net/index_en.php?act=conventions.status&cid=78>.

[130] Reflecting on the poor subscription to the 1971 Convention, the late Justice Peter Nygh explained that '... the near certainty that it will not attract more subscribers was a spur to the attempt to draft a wider ranging convention.' (P Nygh, 'Towards a Global Judgments Convention: The Proposed New Hague Convention on the Recognition and Enforcement of Judgments in Civil and Commercial Matters' (1997) *Australian International Law Journal* 96, 96).

[131] The Choice of Court Convention has been described as '*first and foremost a tool for transaction planning and for subsequent dispute resolution, validating party autonomy through upholding choice of court agreements and enforcing judgments resulting from exclusive choice of court agreements, not all judgments.*' P Winship, L E Teitz, 'Developments in Private International Law: facilitating cross-border transactions and dispute resolution', (2006) 40(2) *The International Lawyer* 505, 507.

New York Convention on the Recognition and Enforcement of Foreign Arbitral Awards' of 1958.[132]

159. In 2011, the Hague Conference resumed work on the Judgments Project. Initially merely mandated to assess the possible merits of resuming this work, the Hague Conference held a first expert meeting in April 2012. Based on the report of this expert group, the Hague Conference decided to re-launch work on the Judgments Project.[133]

Why is the Enforcement of Foreign Judgments Important?

160. The recognition and enforcement of a domestic or foreign judgment ensures that the rights and obligations as confirmed by a court are given effect and are made viable.[134]

161. This viability of judgments depends on how easily judgments can be enforced. As noted above, the cross-border enforcement of domestic state and territory judgments within Australia, is streamlined in the *Service and Execution of Process Act 1992* (Cth).[135]

162. However, the situation changes in the international arena. Here, the enforcement risk can increase significantly. A careful assessment of a variety of factors, including the legal regime governing the enforcement of a foreign judgment, the location of assets or the integrity of the judiciary, becomes necessary. Based on this assessment, parties can then make a decision whether the enforcement is at all possible or at least commercially feasible. As one commentator has observed:

> *... a claimant will not proceed [to trial] at all unless effective enforcement is likely. Nor will a claimant proceed in a given court unless the judgments of that court are likely to be enforced where the defendant's assets are located.*[136]

163. Therefore, a high enforcement risk can be a genuine deterrent for parties that seek to establish their rights through litigation.

Reducing Enforcement Risk

164. Commentators have identified a number of issues that currently increase the risks associated with the recognition and enforcement of foreign judgments.

[132] The Hon Chief Justice J J Spigelman, 'The Hague Choice of Court Convention and International Commercial Litigation' (Address, Commonwealth Law Conference, Hong Kong, 2009).

[133] For more background on the history of the judgments project, see the very informative and comprehensive HCCH website on the Judgments Project located at <http://www.hcch.net/ index_en.php?act=text.display&tid=149>.

[134] R Fentiman, *International Commercial Litigation* (Oxford University Press, 2011), 691.

[135] See above [139].

[136] ibid.

165. The first relates to the interrelationship between the (adjudicative) jurisdiction, that is, the jurisdiction that provides courts with the 'authority [...] to deal with a particular case, according to its own rules of competency',[137] and the (international) jurisdiction that is relevant in relation to the recognition and enforcement of foreign judgments.

166. As noted above,[138] before an Australian forum court can enforce a foreign judgment at common law, it must find that the foreign court had so-called 'international jurisdiction'. The forum court makes this assessment based on its own common law competency rules.[139]

167. For example, in relation to personal jurisdiction, the acknowledged bases for international jurisdiction are, first, the presence of the defendant in the jurisdiction of the foreign court and, second, the defendant's submission to that court. In relation to jurisdiction *in rem*, international jurisdiction is accepted if the *res* was, at the commencement of the proceedings, within the jurisdiction of the foreign court.[140] Other conflict rules, including in relation to movable and immovable property, provide further bases for international jurisdiction.[141]

168. One commentator suggested that any reform to the Australian courts' (adjudicative) jurisdiction should also include a reform of how these courts as forum courts view international jurisdiction. She argues that it would be 'logical to use the forum's entire concept of competence, not just as defined by common law, as the measure of the foreign court's competency.'[142]

169. This suggestion would arguably alleviate some of the issues that arise as a result of the growing schism between the conferral of increasingly broad '19th century'[143] or 'long-arm' jurisdiction of forum courts and the currently accepted grounds of international jurisdiction. The latter have remained largely static and have not kept pace with modern developments, thus presenting a limitation on the forum courts' ability to enforce foreign judgments. This limitation can result in the frustration of a judgment creditor's expectations when seeking to enforce a foreign judgment.

170. In addition, using the forum court's entire concept of jurisdiction would also enable them to consider whether the foreign court should have declined jurisdiction, including on *forum non conveniens* grounds.[144] The applicability of this test, which has been described as 'a later 20th century

[137] Mortensen, Garnett and Keyes, above n 10, 31.
[138] See above [143].
[139] Davies, Bell, Brereton, above n 23, 808. Mortensen, Garnett and Keyes, above n 10, 140.
[140] *Redhead v Admiralty Marshal, WA District Registry* (1988) 87 FCR 229, 242-3.
[141] Davies, Bell, Brereton, above n 23, 817 ff. Mortensen, Garnett and Keyes, above n 10, 143-4.
[142] Keyes, above n 9, 288.
[143] *Morguard Investments v de Savoye* [1990] 3 SCR 1077.
[144] Keyes, above n 9, 288.

"withdrawal" of exorbitant jurisdiction',[145] in this context could further refine the courts' ability to decline, in appropriate circumstances, to enforce a foreign judgment, offsetting any undue consequences that arise from the broadening of the grounds of international jurisdiction.

171. The second issue stems from the list of circumstances according to which the registration of a foreign judgment must be set aside under the Foreign Judgments Act.[146] International jurisdiction plays a role here, too, which is defined in s 7 FJA. Commentators have noted that this definition, which is also incongruous with the common law position, results in a lacuna. As a result, certain foreign judgments must be set aside for want of the adjudicating court's international jurisdiction.[147] The result is the possible frustration of a judgment creditor's expectations when seeking to enforce a foreign judgment.

172. The third issue concerns the availability of streamlined registration processes for the recognition and enforcement of foreign judgments. This availability is currently limited. The FJA's registration processes only cover a relatively small range of countries with which Australia has entered into some form of bilateral reciprocity arrangement. The majority of these countries are jurisdictions of the Commonwealth, plus a number of civil law jurisdictions such as Germany and Italy.[148] At this stage, some of Australia's largest trading partners such as the USA and China are not included in the list. Also, the process under the Trans-Tasman Agreement will only be available for the enforcement of certain New Zealand judgments in Australia.[149]

173. To overcome this limitation, thus offering faster and cheaper enforcement processes for a wider range of foreign judgments, may be achieved either by broadening the current scope of the FJA or by engaging in bilateral negotiations with other countries to establish regimes akin to that established between Australia and New Zealand.[150]

174. However, any such bilateral efforts are resource intensive. Also, any further bilateral agreements are likely to be different from each other, even though they are modelled on the Trans-Tasman Agreement. Any differences would add further complexity because the applicable enforcement process would depend upon the jurisdictional origin of the foreign judgment. Thus, it may be preferable to channel resources and to focus on a genuine global

[145] Hogan-Doran, above n 51. See also above [67] ff. and Professor Dickinson's paper on this issue. Dickinson, above n 72.

[146] See above [151].

[147] Mortensen, Garnett and Keyes, above n 10, 164.

[148] See above [149].

[149] See above [152] ff.

[150] Any such bilateral effort would need to focus on countries that have a similar legal tradition as Australia.

solution such as a convention negotiated under the auspices of the Hague Conference.[151]

Questions

- Have you experienced difficulty in recognising a foreign judgment abroad?
- Have you experienced difficulty in recognising a foreign judgment in Australia?
- Do you think there is a need to reform the current jurisdictional rules that apply in relation to the recognition and enforcement of foreign judgments?
- Do you think there is a need to reform the current jurisdictional rules under s 7 of the Foreign Judgments Act to fill any gaps that currently exist?
- Do you think that the availability of the registration processes under the Foreign Judgments Act should be further expanded by including more foreign courts in the Foreign Judgments Regulations? If so, which countries should be approached?
- Are there any countries with which Australia could negotiate an enforcement process akin to that contained in the Trans-Tasman Agreement? If so, which countries?
- Do you think that Australia should focus on negotiating multilateral agreements concerning the recognition and enforcement of foreign judgments?

Pleading and Proof of Foreign Law

175. In cases where a court is called upon to apply a different law from that which is applicable in it is own jurisdiction, it will be up to the parties to prove the content of that law as a matter of fact. This means that the content of the foreign law is to be pleaded as evidence, usually by relying on foreign experts to provide evidence as expert witnesses. It is then up to the court to finally determine the content of the foreign law on the basis of the expert evidence led by the parties.

176. The exception to this general requirement is where the foreign law is the law of a different state or territory within Australia. In that case, such law does not need to be proved as a matter of fact or pleaded.

177. As it is up to the parties to plead foreign law; if the parties choose not to plead such foreign law, the court will rely on the domestic law. One explanation for a court's reliance on the domestic law is that this is due to the presumption of identity—that is, the court presumes that the local law is the same as the foreign law, in the absence of evidence to the contrary. However,

[151] See above [157].

the presumption of identity has been criticised by some courts in Australia as leading to false results.[152]

178. Therefore, some commentators have suggested that that the better approach to a court's reliance on domestic law is that the court applies its local law as a default, in the absence of pleaded foreign law.

Advantage and Disadvantage to the Current System

179. The approach to reliance on foreign law in Australia, that it must be pleaded as evidence, provides litigants with the option to choose whether or not to plead and rely on foreign law or domestic law and therefore potentially enables greater flexibility. That is, parties are able to choose whether pleading the foreign law will provide them with a more advantageous result than relying on local law.

180. However, given that relying on the testimony of foreign experts can result in considerable expense for litigants, the option to rely on foreign law may only be available to litigants with adequate resources—which may restrict access to justice in that it is more difficult for those affected by the foreign law to understand their legal rights and obligations.

Legislative Responses

181. Evidence legislation in Australia has been amended to enable foreign law to be proved in ways other than through reliance on expert testimony (which, as outlined above, can lead to considerable expense).[153] For example, s 174 *Evidence Act 1995* (Cth) enables parties to tender copies of foreign statutes, treaties, proclamations and Acts of state as proof of that foreign law. Section 175 Evidence Act also enables parties to provide copies of judgments as proof of the common law. New South Wales, Victoria, Tasmania and the Australian Capital Territory have comparable provisions. Queensland, South Australia, Western Australia and Northern Territory evidence laws provide a more restricted approach to the proof of foreign law, allowing legislation to be provided as proof of foreign law, subject to certain restrictions.[154]

182. In addition, Australian and New Zealand reciprocal legislation[155] provides that proof of either country's law is not required in matters before the court and that an Australian or New Zealand judge may inform him or herself of the content of each other's law in any ways the judge thinks fit. This arrangement has been included in the Australian and New Zealand *Trans-Tasman Proceedings Acts 2010*, which will repeal the existing reciprocal legislation on their commencement.

[152] See, for example, *Damberg v Damberg* (2001) 52 NSWLR 492 (Heydon JA).

[153] See above [180].

[154] See, for example, *Evidence Act 1929* (SA) s 63, *Evidence Act 1906* (WA) ss 70-71, *Evidence Act 1977* (Qld) s 68, *Evidence Act 1971* (ACT) s 47(1)(a) and *Evidence Act 1939* (NT) s 63.

[155] See the *Evidence and Procedure (New Zealand) Act 1994* (Cth) and the *Evidence Act 2006* (NZ).

Non-Legislative Responses

183. Recognising the difficulties parties face in proving foreign law and the court resources that are expended when parties do so, the New South Wales Supreme Court developed an innovative approach to proving Singaporean and New York law. Specifically, the court and its former Chief Justice, the Hon J J Spigelman AC, entered into two separate Memoranda of Understanding with a court in Singapore and the Chief Judge of the State of New York on 14 September 2010 and 20 December 2010, respectively.

184. The *Memorandum of Understanding Between the Supreme Court of Singapore and the Supreme Court of New South Wales on References of Questions of Law*[156] (the Singapore Agreement) and the *Memorandum of Understanding Between the Chief Justice of New South Wales and the Chief Justice of the State of New York on References of Questions of Law*[157] (the New York Agreement) allow each party to refer questions of the other party's foreign law to the foreign court.

185. The Agreements were set up following an innovative procedure adopted by the Supreme Court of Singapore, where the court referred a question of foreign law to the High Court of Justice of England and Wales.[158] The Singapore Agreement allows any issue of law to be determined by the courts of the Party of the governing law. The New York Agreement provides a slightly different arrangement where questions of law are to be determined by each Party in accordance with its procedure. This slight difference is to accommodate the inability of the New York courts to exercise non-judicial functions, such as providing an opinion on the content of New York law.

Questions

— Have you experienced issues with proving foreign law in multi-state litigation in Australia? If so, please detail the kinds of issues you have experienced.
— Have you ever chosen not to plead foreign law even though it was open to you and, if so, what were your reasons for not pleading it?
— Do you think the government needs to look at developing a framework to simplify the process for proving foreign law?
— Could the Memoranda of Understanding that the New South Wales Supreme Court entered into with Singapore and New York serve as a viable option for such a framework?

---

156 Available at: <http://www.lawlink.nsw.gov.au/practice_notes/nswsc_pc.nsf/pages/529>.

157 Available at: <http://www.nswbar.asn.au/circulars/2010/nov/mou.pdf>.

158 See *Westacre Investments Inc v The State-Owned Company Yugoimport SDPR* (also known as Yugoimport-SDPR) [2009] 2 SLR(R) 166 and *Westacre Investments Inc v Yugoimport SDPR* [2008] EWHC 801 (Comm).

Chapter 6: A More Coherent Private International Law Regime—Possible Reform Options

186. One of the issues this discussion paper seeks to explore is whether it is necessary to develop a more coherent and more internationalised private international law system in Australia. The subsequent question is then if it is, how should such a system be devised? This question will be discussed in this chapter.

187. Broadly, Australia has two sources of private international law: common law and statute law. Both have undergone significant developments. Two drivers have been particularly responsible for these developments.

188. First, the increase in cross-border trade, commerce, investment and the greater mobility of people across borders has led to more international litigation. This has provided courts with greater opportunities to consider cross-border issues. Examples for the emerging body of common law include the High Court's decisions concerning the *forum* test[159] or the choice of law rule for multi-state torts.[160]

189. Second, there has been increased legislative activity in relation to private international law. Legislation has been used to simplify cumbersome and inefficient common law processes. Legislation has also been used to implement Australia's international obligations, arising under a number of international conventions to which Australia is a party. Examples include the bilateral *Agreement between the Government of Australia and the Government of New Zealand on Trans-Tasman Court Proceedings and Regulatory Enforcement* and several conventions concluded by the Hague Conference on Private International Law, such as the *Convention on the Service Abroad of Judicial and Extrajudicial Documents in Civil or Commercial Matters 1965*.

190. However, as has been noted throughout this discussion paper, these developments have often been fragmented and inconsistent and they have not always reflected international progress. Thus, the question arises whether a more coherent and internationalised Australian private international law regime is needed and, if so, what options there are to achieve such coherence and internationalisation.

[159] See above [73] ff. See also: *Voth v Manildra Flour Mills Pty Ltd* (1990) 171 CLR 538; *Puttick v Tenon Ltd* (2008) 238 CLR 265; *Garsec v His Majesty The Sultan of Brunei* (2008) 250 ALR 682 (a case which was discontinued before it was decided by the High Court).

[160] See above [119]. See also: *Pfeiffer v Rogerson* (2000) 203 CLR 503; *Renault v Zhang* (2002) 210 CLR 491.

191. The choice of options would be broad and could comprise:

— targeted amendments to existing legislation
— 'soft law' options such as a principle-based private international law framework, or
— the development of a Private International Law statute, providing applicable principles for particular areas of the law.

A Private International Law Framework

192. One option could be the development of a principle-based framework that is agreed upon by all jurisdictions and is aimed at harmonising, not at unifying, private international law across Australia.

193. Central to such a framework would be common core principles and definitions that underpin private international law, many of which could be developed, or adopted, from a variety of existing domestic, but also international instruments so that they are developed in line with international developments. A framework of this kind could be used by a variety of actors in a number of ways, including:

— by parties to a contract— as a tool allowing them to shape their contractual and extra-contractual dealings
— by courts—as an aide to interpret international and domestic law, and
— by legislators—as a model or template for domestic legislation.

194. The framework would have a gradual harmonising effect, which over time could lead to greater consistency across Australia. However, it is also possible that such a framework could remain largely unused and thus without any significant effect.

A private International Law Statute

195. Another option to achieve a greater level of coherence may be to develop a private international law statute that legislates key private international law principles.

196. Research suggests that an increasing number of countries have recently legislated private international law principles.[161] Examples include some of

[161] The Rapporteur of the 18th International Congress of Comparative Law, held in Washington in 2010, identified 55 jurisdictions that had legislated private international law in comprehensive, stand-alone legislation, with another seven jurisdictions currently in the process of developing such legislation (S C Symeonides, *Codification and Flexibility in Private International Law*, abbreviated extract of two Chapters in K B Brown and D V Snyder (eds), *General Reports of the XVIIIth Congress of the International Academy of Comparative Law* (2012, Springer Science and Business Media, 2012).

Australia's major trading partners, including China,[162] Japan,[163] Germany,[164] the EU, [165] Switzerland[166] and, most recently, The Netherlands.[167]

197. Of course, legislating private international law rules has been, and remains, controversial in both common law and civil law countries. Opponents regularly argue that private international law rules should remain flexible.[168] They suggest that private international law—and its continued development—should remain a domain for the courts. They have also noted that the development of a private international law statute would be complex, potentially taking considerable time to complete.[169]

198. However, legislation could ensure better coherence and consistency of Australia's private international law rules. Experiences in other jurisdictions have shown that legislation can be drafted to allow flexibility for future changes and emerging areas of private international law. Mechanisms that are currently used include discretionary, escape and specific soft connecting factors that ensure such flexibility. They could also foster the continued

[162] See China's *Law on the Law Applicable to Civil Law Relations with a Foreign Element*, which was adopted on 28 October 2010.

[163] See Japan's *Act for the Partial Amendment of the Code of Civil Procedure and the Civil Provisional Remedies Act* which entered into force on 1 April 2012 and which governs international jurisdiction in civil and commercial matters.

[164] *Einfűhrungsgesetz zum Bűrgerlichen Gesetzbuch* or EGBGB (Introductory Law to the Civil Code). Germany legislated private international principles that underpin a wide range of subject matters, including contract, obligations, tort, family and inheritance law.

[165] Various international instruments including the EU's Brussels I Regulation, see above n 130, or the *Regulation (EC) No 593/2008 of the European Parliament and of the Council of 17 June 2008 on the law applicable to contractual obligations* (the Rome I Regulation).

[166] S.R. 291 *Bundesgesetz űber das Internationale Privatrecht* or IPRG (Federal Statute concerning Conflict of Law). Switzerland passed the stand-alone law that includes detailed chapters on general private international law issues, such as rules concerning determining the applicable law (connectors, *renvoi*, and application of mandatory laws) and the recognition and enforcement of judgments. It also contains specific subject matter-related private international law principles concerning, for example, marriage, divorce and children; natural persons, associations and corporations; the law of obligations, arbitration, succession, property and tort.

[167] Book 10 of the *Dutch Civil Code*. The most recent private international law legislation, the 10th Book of the Dutch Civil Code entered into force on 1 January 2012. It provides a comprehensive compilation of Dutch private international law rules. In order to provide the maximum of certainty, whilst retaining a level of flexibility traditionally inherent in the Dutch approach to private international law, the code contains mechanisms such as discretionary, escape or specific soft connecting factors.

[168] G Letourneau and S A Cohen, 'Codification and Law Reform: Some lessons learned from the Canadian experience' (1989) 10 *Statute Law Review* 183, 183.

[169] Perhaps the Dutch experience may serve here as an example—the decision in favour of a Dutch Private International Law code was taken in the late 1970s and, after what has been described as a step-by-step process, the 10th Book of the *Dutch Civil Code* entered into force on 1 January 2012. For a more detailed history of the development of the Dutch Private International Law code, refer to K Boele-Woelki and D van Iterson 'The Dutch Private International Law Codification: Principles, Objectives and Opportunities' (2010) 14(3) *Electronic Journal of Comparative Law* 1, 1-7 and V van den Eeckhout, 'Private International Law, quo vadis: PIL as a perfect conductor for achieving political objectives? A Tale of Lost Innocence', online opinion published by conflictoflaws.net, available at: <http://conflictoflaws.net/2011/van-den-eeckhout-on-pil-as-a-conductor-for-achieving-political-objectives/>.

internationalisation of Australia's private international law, not only in sync with international obligations, present and future, but also with broader, international developments not driven by bi- or multilateral binding agreements.

199. A private international law statute could possibly fulfil two purposes, including to:

- provide the principles applicable to a range of subject matters
- draw together and consolidate any currently legislated private international law rules, whilst at the same time updating and internationalising them.

200. A statute with such, or similar, features could provide clear, consistent and accessible rules and principles governing this area.[170]

Questions

- Do you think that there is a need to create a more coherent and internationalised private international law system in Australia?
- If so, what could be a mechanism to ensure that in the future, Australian private international law develops coherently and in line with international standards?
- Do you think that the development of an overarching framework could assists with the gradual harmonisation of private international law?
- Do you think that a private international law statute could be a feasible option to achieve a more coherent and international private international law?
- Do you have any other suggestions how a more coherent and international private international law could be achieved?

[170] G Letourneau and S A Cohen, above n 168.

Annex 2

Private International Law Consultation

ATTORNEY-GENERAL'S DEPARTMENT

Harmonisation of the *Forum Conveniens* Tests in Australian and Trans-Tasman Proceedings: A Discussion Paper

PROFESSOR ANDREW DICKINSON[1]

Introduction

1. This discussion paper considers whether the statutory tests[2] applied by Australian courts in deciding whether to decline jurisdiction[3] in favour of another Australian court on what may broadly be described as "appropriate forum" (*forum conveniens*) grounds, should be harmonised with the newly adopted regime in Part 3 of the Trans-Tasman Proceedings Act 2010 (Cth)[4] governing decisions to decline jurisdiction in favour of a court in New Zealand.[5]

2. The creation of a harmonised *forum conveniens* regime for all Australian and Trans-Tasman cases has been put forward as one element of the broader review of rules of jurisdiction, choice of court and choice of law rules mandated

[1] Professor in Private International Law, Law School, University of Sydney. I am grateful to Menaka Vasudevan for research assistance in the preparation of this paper.

[2] Jurisdiction of Courts (Cross-Vesting) Acts 1987 (Cth, ACT, NSW, NT, Qld, SA, Tas, Vic) ("**Cross-Vesting Acts**"), s. 5 (transfer of proceedings); Service and Execution of Process Act 1992 (Cth), s. 20 (stay of proceedings).

[3] Whether by staying or transferring proceedings.

[4] Not yet in force (the "**Trans-Tasman Act**"). References in this paper to the Trans-Tasman Act are to its provisions as amended by the Trans-Tasman Proceedings Amendment and Other Measures Act 2011 (also not yet in force).

[5] The 2010 Act implements in Australian law the Agreement between the Government of Australia and the Government of New Zealand on Trans-Tasman Court Proceedings and Regulatory Enforcement, done at Christchurch on 24 July 2008 (the "Trans-Tasman Agreement") ([2008] ATNIF 12).

by the Standing Committee on Law and Justice in its meeting held on 12–13 April 2012.[6]

3. As there is already a large measure of consistency between the three statutory regimes considered in this discussion paper, all of which apply a test that involves the court considering whether there is a "more appropriate" forum, the issues raised by this proposal would appear to be mostly technical in nature, although not without significance. Accordingly, it may be thought suitable to be considered separately from other elements of the review, which raise broader issues of law and policy.

4. This discussion paper does not consider the test to be applied by Australian courts in deciding whether to decline jurisdiction in international cases, other than those to which the Trans-Tasman regime applies. It does not address, therefore, questions concerning the suitability of the "clearly inappropriate" forum test currently applied by Australian courts in deciding whether to decline jurisdiction in cases of this kind.[7]

5. Although that test has been criticised, both by judges[8] and by some commentators,[9] it is submitted that the case for (and against) legislative reform of this rule is best tackled as part of a wider review of the rules of jurisdiction applied by Australian courts in international cases.[10] For present purposes, it suffices to note that (a) the rules of personal jurisdiction applied by Australian courts *vis-à-vis* defendants outside Australia are non-harmonised[11] and vary greatly between the States and Territories, (b) in the absence of a treaty, there is no guarantee that foreign legal systems would decline jurisdiction in favour of Australian courts in like circumstances, (c) in the absence of the same degree of mutual trust as exists between the legal systems of Australia (and New Zealand), the formulation of the test must take account of the possibility that "substantial justice" may not be afforded by the courts of a foreign legal system,[12] and (d) the source of the "clearly inappropriate" forum test is the common law, not statute. These considerations are very different from those which underlie the subject matter of the present paper.

[6] SCLJ Communiqué, 12–13 April 2012, pp. 2–3. See also SCLJ Communiqué, 21–22 July 2012, p. 2.

[7] *Voth v Manildra Flour Mills Pty Ltd* (1990) 171 CLR 538; *Puttick v Tenon Ltd* (2008) HCA 54.

[8] See, e.g., *BHP Billiton v Schultz* (2004) 221 CLR 400, 462 (Kirby J).

[9] See, e.g., R Garnett (1999) 23 Melb UL Rev 30; P Nygh & M Davies, *Conflict of Laws in Australia* (7th ed., 2002), pp. 129–130 (cf. 8th ed., 2010, pp. 171–172); R Mortensen, R Garnett and M Keyes, *Private International Law in Australia* (2nd ed., 2011), pp. 107–109.

[10] See A Dickinson, *The Future of Private International Law in Australia*, Sydney Law School Research Paper No. 11/30 (http://ssrn.com/abstract=1851047), due to be published in Australian International Law Journal, 2012, forthcoming.

[11] Except, upon the coming into force of the Trans-Tasman Proceedings Act, with regard to defendants in New Zealand.

[12] *Voth v Manildra*, above, 559. Cf. *BHP v Schultz*, above, 465, [164] (Kirby J).

6. Subject to one possible issue, discussed in the next paragraph,[13] there would appear to be no constitutional impediment to the reform of the rules regulating court powers to decline jurisdiction currently contained in the Commonwealth, State and Territory Cross-Vesting Acts and the Service and Execution of Process Act. So far as the transfer of proceedings between courts of competent jurisdiction is concerned, this element of the cross-vesting legislation has not been called into question by the decision of the High Court in *Re Wakim, ex p McNally*[14] striking down the parts of the federal legislation investing State jurisdiction in the Federal Court.[15] Amendments to these legislative provisions would appear to fall clearly within the competence of the adopting Commonwealth, State and Territory legislatures.

7. In considering this proposal, it should be borne in mind that the provisions which regulate Australian courts' powers to decline jurisdiction on "appropriate forum" grounds represent only a relatively small part of legislation which regulates in a much more comprehensive way the relations between the Australian judicial systems, giving rise to "an integrated court system".[16] These provisions provide, however, an important balancing mechanism, tempering the provisions which confer on Australian courts very broad personal and subject matter jurisdiction by requiring or enabling courts to decline jurisdiction in favour of another, equally competent (but more appropriate) Australian court.[17] It would clearly be undesirable to disturb that balance, or to put in jeopardy the broader objectives—supported by the Constitution—which this legislation seeks to attain, or to undermine well-established judicial practice for the sake only of ensuring consistency with the regime now adopted by Trans-Tasman Proceedings.

8. That said, it may be considered that there are at least three potential advantages of introducing reforms aimed at ensuring that a single set of rules is applied by Australian courts in deciding whether to decline jurisdiction in favour of any other Australian or a New Zealand court.

9. First, in terms of promoting legal certainty for litigants, their legal advisers and judges as to the test to be applied in a particular situation, and the considerations to be taken into account, avoiding the current distinctions between inferior and superior State courts and between intra-Australian and Trans-Tasman Proceedings.

[13] See para. [7].

[14] (1999) 198 CLR 511.

[15] *BHP Billiton v Schultz*, above, 431 [47] (Gummow J).

[16] *Bankinvest AG v Seabrook* (1988) 14 NSWLR 711, 713 (Street CJ). See also Rogers A-JA, ibid, 723; *Activate No 1 Pty Ltd v Equuscorp Pty Ltd* [1999] FCA 619, [12] (Tamberlin J); *BHP v Schultz*, above, 463–464, [160], [162] (Kirby J).

[17] *BHP v Schultz*, above, [217] (Callinan J).

10. Secondly, in facilitating the more rapid development of case law refining particular features of the harmonised regime, encouraging a more uniform approach among the different jurisdictions.[18]

11. Thirdly, in furthering the objectives of the Trans-Tasman Agreement, in developing a new, integrated Trans-Tasman judicial co-operation regime, by seeking to ensure that the ultimate allocation of jurisdiction is the same whether (a) proceedings are first brought in an Australian or a New Zealand court, or (b) the subject matter of the proceedings demonstrates links to two or more Australian jurisdictions or to one or more Australian jurisdictions as well as to New Zealand.

12. There may be other good reasons for legislative intervention at this stage.

13. First, there would appear to be a strong case for introducing a comprehensive, uniform regime for giving effect to exclusive choice of court agreements in line with that in the Trans-Tasman regime, itself based on the Hague Convention on Choice of Court Agreements.[19]

14. Secondly, despite the clear emphasis in the leading authorities (and, in particular, the High Court decision in *BHP Billiton v Schultz*[20]) that the test for declining jurisdiction in the Cross-Vesting Acts is to be applied having regard to the interests of both parties, and without regard to the plaintiff's choice of forum, one may detect a tendency in recent State Supreme Court decisions to view matters rather more from the plaintiffs' perspective in evaluating the "interests of justice" and to decline to transfer proceedings to another State Supreme Court on that basis.[21] The introduction of a harmonised test, with appropriate guidance within the adopting legislation, may be thought likely to "reset" this tendency, if it is thought problematic.[22]

15. Thirdly, and subject to the analysis below of the procedural differences between the Trans-Tasman regime and the Cross-Vesting Acts, it may be thought desirable to introduce a single or more uniform procedure for making applications of this kind.

[18] In the case of the Cross-Vesting Acts, that development has been hindered by the legislative prohibition on appeals from a decision to order transfer or to refuse to do so (other than the appeal to the High Court guaranteed by the constitution) (see s. 13(a); *BHP v Schultz*, above, [55] (Gummow J), [127] (Kirby J), [214] (Callinan J)).

[19] See para. [19].

[20] See para. [28].

[21] See, e.g., *Lloyd v Riverland Regional Health Service Inc* [2010] VSC 350; *White v Motor Accidents Insurance Board* [2011] VSC 290; *Irwin v State of Queensland* [2011] VSC 291; *Zmudzinski v Cheapa Campa Pty Limited* [2011] NSWSC 996; *Duncan v State of Western Australia* [2011] NSWSC 1320.

[22] The opportunities for a correction by appellate decision are limited (see above n. 18).

Q1. Do you consider it desirable to introduce a harmonised test for all Australian courts to apply in deciding whether to decline jurisdiction in favour of another Australian court, or a New Zealand court, on "appropriate forum" grounds? Please identify your reasons for supporting or opposing this reform measure.

The Trans-Tasman Regime

16. The relevant provisions of the Trans-Tasman Act are set out in the Annex to this paper. They may be summarised as follows. Under s. 17(1), a defendant in a civil proceeding in an Australian court may apply to the court for an order staying the proceedings on the grounds that the New Zealand court is **the more appropriate court to determine the matters in issue**. Section 17(2) limits the time for bringing that application, and s. 18 regulates procedural aspects of the hearing of the application.

17. Section 19(1) provides that, on an application under s. 17, the Australian court *may* stay the proceeding if satisfied that a New Zealand court (a) has jurisdiction to determine the matters in issue between the parties to the proceeding, and (b) is **the more appropriate court** to determine those matters. Section 19(2) lists specific matters, which the Australian court must take into account in determining whether a New Zealand court is the **more appropriate court.**[23] It is clear that this list is not exhaustive of the factors that may be considered.[24] The Australian court may not, however, take into account the fact that the proceeding was commenced in Australia. Section 19(3) permits the Australian court to impose a stay subject to any conditions, which it considers are appropriate in order to facilitate, without delay, or undue expense, the determination of the matters in issue between the parties to the proceeding.

18. Section 20 addresses, separately, the consequences of an exclusive choice of court agreement,[25] whether in favour of an Australian or New Zealand court. Subject to the exceptions in s. 20(2)-(2A), the court (a) *must* stay the proceeding if satisfied that an exclusive choice of court agreement designates a New Zealand court as competent to determine the matters in issue, and (b) *must not* stay the proceeding if satisfied that an exclusive choice of court agreement designates an Australian court as the court to determine those matters.

[23] See para. [23].

[24] Trans-Tasman Act, s. 19(2)(i) refers to "any other matter that the Australian court considers relevant". See also Trans-Tasman Agreement, Art. 8(4)(b).

[25] As defined in s. 20(3) and requiring a written agreement.

19. Section 21(1) excludes any other power of an Australian court to stay a civil proceeding on forum grounds connected with New Zealand (including on the ground that the Australian forum is "clearly inappropriate"),[26] without prejudice to any power to stay on any other grounds.[27]

20. Finally, s. 22 excludes orders restraining proceedings, or steps in proceedings, in New Zealand (anti-suit injunctions) "on the grounds that the New Zealand court is not the appropriate forum for the proceeding"[28] and s. 23 provides for the operation of limitation periods where proceedings are stayed by a New Zealand court and a claim made in those proceedings is subsequently made before an Australian court.

21. These provisions directly implement Art. 8 of the Trans-Tasman Agreement, as supplemented by mutual agreement between the parties. The reasoning underlying this proposal is to be found in the comment to ***Recommendation 5*** of the December 2006 Report of the Trans-Tasman Working Group.[29] The principal objective was stated to be to remove disparities in the common law rules applied by Australian and New Zealand courts in deciding whether to decline jurisdiction in favour of allowing proceedings to be brought or to continue in a foreign jurisdiction. In summary, whereas Australian courts generally apply a "clearly inappropriate" forum test in international cases (*Voth v Manildra*), New Zealand courts apply the "more appropriate" forum approach also favoured in other common law jurisdictions.[30] It was also suggested to render the two jurisdictions' approach to choice of court agreements consistent with the 2005 Hague Convention on Choice of Court Agreements, a consideration which was thought to be important if either Australia or New Zealand were to become parties to that Convention.[31]

[26] See para. [4]. Although the *Voth* test requires an examination of suitability of the Australian forum, rather than the relative strength of the connections to Australian and foreign forums, "[t]hat is not to deny that considerations relating to the suitability of the alternative forum are relevant to the examination of the appropriateness or inappropriateness of the selected forum" ((1990) 171 CLR 538), It is unclear whether an application, on forum grounds, to stay proceedings with connections to more than one foreign jurisdiction (including New Zealand) is precluded in a case where the New Zealand court is not a more appropriate forum than the Australian court but there is a relatively weak connection to Australia (cf. *Puttick v Tenon Limited* (2008) 238 CLR 265). In these circumstances, it is submitted that there is no reason to exclude application of the *Voth* test.

[27] s. 21(2). This preserves, for example, the power to stay to give effect to an arbitration agreement (International Arbitration Act 1974, s. 7 (Cth)) or on forum grounds not connected to New Zealand.

[28] Cf. *CSR Ltd v Cigna Insurance Australia Limited* (1997) 189 CLR 345, where the test for granting anti-suit injunctions is expressed rather differently. See, in particular, Brennan J, at 372: "Although a domestic court may hold that it is not a clearly inappropriate forum to determine a controversy between parties, it does not follow that it should exercise a jurisdiction to enjoin a party from commencing or prosecuting proceedings in a foreign court which has jurisdiction to determine the same controversy. There must be an equity which entitles one party as against the other to an injunction to restrain the other from proceeding in the foreign court".

[29] See <http://www.ag.gov.au/Documents/5Trans-Tasman%202006.pdf>.

[30] *Club Mediteranée NZ v Wendell* [1989] 1 NZLR 216 (NZCA); *Oilseed Products (NZ) Ltd v H E Burton Ltd* (1987) 1 PRNZ 313 (NZHC); *McConnell Dowell Constructors Ltd v Gardner-Roberts* [1988] 2 NZLR 257 (NZCA); *Wing Hung Printing Company Ltd v Saito Offshore Pty Ltd* [2011] 1 NZLR 754 (NZCA).

[31] As yet, neither has done so and the Convention is not in force.

Relationship between the Trans-Tasman Regime and the Service and Execution of Process Act 1992, and Possible Reform of the 1992 Act

22. As the December 2006 Report of the Trans-Tasman Working Group makes clear, the integrated regime for which the Trans-Tasman Agreement provides is directly modelled on the provisions of the Service and Execution of Process Act 1992 (Cth). The structure of Art. 8, in referring to factors to be taken into account in exercising the jurisdiction to stay proceedings, aligns with that of s. 20 of the 1992 Act, and s. 19 of the Trans-Tasman Bill, as originally drafted, follows very closely the wording of s. 20(3)–(5) of the 1992 Act.

23. Nevertheless, there are important differences between the formulation of the test adopted in the 1992 Act, and that in the Trans-Tasman Act, as follows:

    a. Although the pre-conditions to the exercise of the discretion to stay proceedings in s. 19(1) of the Trans-Tasman Bill followed very closely the wording of s. 20(3) of the 1992 Act ("has jurisdiction to determine all the matters in issue between the parties"; "is the appropriate court to determine those matters"), important amendments were made to this wording by the Trans-Tasman Proceedings Amendment and Other Measures Act 2011. As a consequence, s. 19(1) now requires that a New Zealand court:

        i. has jurisdiction to determine **the matters in issue** between the parties to the proceeding;
        ii. is **the more appropriate court** to determine those matters.

       These amendments align the Trans-Tasman Act with the corresponding provision in s. 20(1) of the New Zealand Trans-Tasman Proceedings Act 2010. As to point (i), the reference to "the matters in issue" rather than "all the matters in dispute" would appear to be designed to reduce the opportunities for a party to adjust its case so as to enable or disable the power to stay. As to point (ii) the reference to "the more appropriate court" rather than "the appropriate court" accords with the wording of Art. 8(1) of the Trans-Tasman Agreement, although the trend in Australian case law applying "the appropriate court" test in the 1992 Act suggests that this particular amendment does not result in any difference in substance as between the two Acts.[32]

    b. The list of matters which the court is required, by s. 19(2), to consider in exercising the power to stay under the Trans-Tasman Act is differently

[32] See Mortensen, Garnett and Keyes, above n. 9, p. 124 referring to *Valkama v Jamieson* (1994) 11 SR (WA) 246; *Workcover Corporation v Pross Chiyoda Pty Limited* [1999] SAWCT 86; *Programmed Maintenance Services Limited v Shell Company of Australia Limited* [2000] QDC 249; *Fertico v Murrat River Corporation* [2002] SADC 89.

formulated from that in s. 20(4) of the 1992 Act, although it seems doubtful whether the differences will be of any significance in practice.[33]

c. More significantly, although both s. 19(2)(d) of the Trans-Tasman Act and s. 20(4)(d) of the 1992 Act refer to "any agreement between the parties about the court or place" in which the matters in issue/proceeding should be instituted, the 1992 Act contains no provision corresponding to that in s. 20 of the Trans-Tasman Act, which enables (indeed requires) effect to be given to an exclusive jurisdiction agreement. The absence of such a provision may be thought to undermine legal certainty, in that parties to a commercial agreement designating an Australian court cannot predict with certainty whether their agreement on jurisdiction will be upheld by another Australian court applying the 1992 Act.

d. The 1992 Act contains no direct equivalent to s. 23 of the Trans-Tasman Act providing for the operation of limitation periods when a claim is made in a civil proceeding stayed by one court, and subsequently brought before another court. However, equivalent protection may be obtained by conditions imposed by the staying court in the exercise of the power conferred on it by s. 20(5) of the 1992 Act.[34]

e. There are some differences between the procedures for determining applications under the Trans-Tasman Act and the 1992 Act. In particular, the Trans-Tasman Act (i) imposes time limits for the making of a stay application (s. 17(2)); and (ii) in certain circumstances, confers a right on the defendant and his lawyer to appear remotely on a hearing of the application.

24. Against this background, it may be thought desirable, for the reasons already discussed,[35] to amend the relevant provisions of the 1992 Act so as to bring them into line with the corresponding provisions of the Trans-Tasman Act. However, it may be doubted this reform measure would be worth pursuing in isolation given that s. 20 of the 1992 Act is of limited significance in practice today due to the overriding effect of the Cross-Vesting Acts.[36] Searches of case law databases suggest that the power to stay under s. 20 is exercised relatively infrequently, and there is no doubt that the power to transfer proceedings in s. 5 of the Cross-Vesting Acts, discussed below, is much more significant. Although the Cross-Vesting Acts do not authorise transfer by

[33] s. 19(2) lists matters under 9 paragraphs, whereas s. 20(4) has only 6. The additional paragraphs are explained as follows: (i) the factors in s. 20(4)(a) (parties' places of residence and witnesses) are divided between s. 19(2)(a) and (b); (ii) s. 19(2)(h) refers to any matter that is prescribed by the regulations (no such matter has been prescribed); (iii) s. 19(2)(i) refers to "any other matter that the Australian court considers relevant".

[34] M Davies, A Bell and P Brereton, *Nygh's Conflict of Laws in Australia* (Sydney, 8th ed., 2010), p. 32, referring to *Seymour-Smith v Electricity Trust of South Australia* (1989) 17 NSWLR 648.

[35] See paras. [8–15].

[36] Service and Execution of Process Act 1992 (Cth), s. 20(10) expressly provides that the section does not affect the operation of the Cross-Vesting Acts.

or to inferior State courts or tribunals, it remains possible for the State and Territory Supreme Courts to order that proceedings before such a court or tribunal be removed to the State or Territory Supreme Court in order that an application be made for their transfer under s. 5.[37] Consequently, it is s. 5 which is the dominant provision.

Q2. Do you consider it desirable to amend s. 20 of the Service and Execution of Process Act 1992 (Cth) so as to bring its provisions into line (or more into line) with those in Part 3 of the Trans-Tasman Act? Please identify your reasons for supporting or opposing this reform measure, and identify any specific amendments which you consider to be appropriate.

The Test for Transferring Proceedings Under the Cross-Vesting Acts

25. As noted above, the power to stay proceedings conferred by s. 20 of the 1992 Act does not extend to situations which fall within the scope of the powers to transfer proceedings in s. 5 of the Cross-Vesting Acts. These provisions impose on the Federal Court, Family Court and State and Territory Supreme Courts the obligation[38] (not merely the power) to transfer proceedings to another Australian court within the same group in the prescribed situations. For example, in the case of transfers between State Supreme Courts, the two most frequently encountered situations are that:[39]

    a. the relevant proceeding arises out of, or is related to, another proceeding pending in the Supreme Court of another State or Territory and it is more appropriate that the relevant proceeding be determined by that other Supreme Court (s. 5(2)(b)(i)); and
    b. it is otherwise in the interests of justice that the relevant proceeding be determined by the Supreme Court of another State or Territory (s. 5(2)(b)(iii)).

26. Although the words "more appropriate" appear only in the first of these two provisions, the High Court has emphasised that the question as to which of two courts is more appropriate as a forum for the proceeding is central to the analysis which the court asked to transfer must undertake: in this connection, the court must ask itself whether "in the interests of justice, the second court is more appropriate".[40] In so doing, it should not give any weight to

[37] Cross-Vesting Acts, s. 8(1).
[38] *BHP v Schultz*, above, 421 [14] (Gleeson CJ, McHugh and Heydon JJ), 434 [61–62] (Gummow J), 481 [222] (Callinan J).
[39] s. 5(2)(b)(ii), concerning the exercise of cross-vested jurisdiction by the court asked to transfer, is omitted here.
[40] *BHP v Schultz*, above, 421 [14].

the plaintiff's choice of forum,[41] and should seek to identify (using factors of the kind identified by Lord Goff in the leading United Kingdom case on *forum conveniens*[42]) the "natural forum" for the dispute,[43] i.e. that with which the dispute has its most real and substantial connection.[44] Normally, but not inevitably, the interests of justice will make it more appropriate that the dispute be determined by the "natural forum".

27. Nevertheless, it is important not to get carried away by similarities between the formulation of the test in the Cross-Vesting Acts, the "more appropriate court" test in the Trans-Tasman Act and the "more appropriate forum" approach applied by courts in the United Kingdom, New Zealand and elsewhere in the Commonwealth to *forum conveniens* applications. As one senior judge has noted, "[g]uidelines offered by the courts in such circumstances may sometimes be useful. But they should not divert judicial attention from the language of the Act".[45] Ultimately, the test prescribed by s. 5 in situations in which there is a proceeding pending in another jurisdiction is the general test of what the "interests of justice" require, and this requires the court to take into account not only the interests of the parties, individually and collectively, but (potentially) interests wider than those of either party.[46] In this last respect, the approach under the Cross-Vesting Acts arguably requires the public interest to be taken into account[47] and, as such, seems broader than the common law *forum conveniens* test both in the United Kingdom and in Australia.[48]

[41] On this point, the position under the Cross-Vesting Acts is aligned to that under the Trans-Tasman Act and the Service and Execution of Process Act (see above, text following n. 18). Contrast, however, the position under the "more appropriate" forum approach adopted for international cases in the United Kingdom, New Zealand and elsewhere in the Commonwealth (*Spiliada Maritime v Cansulex Ltd* [1987] AC 460, 477 (UKHL) emphasising that, by placing an onus on the defendant to show an available, more appropriate forum, "proper regard is paid to the fact that jurisdiction has been founded … as of right)".

[42] *Spiliada Maritime v Cansulex Ltd*, above, 477–478.

[43] *BHP v Schultz*, above, 422 [18] (Gleeson CJ, McHugh and Heydon JJ), 463–467 [161–164], [170–171] (Kirby J), 493 [259] (Callinan J).

[44] See also *Bankinvest v Seabrook*, above; *James Hardie Industries Pty Ltd v Barry* (2000) 50 NSWLR 357.

[45] *Bankinvest v Seabrook*, above, 716 (Street CJ). See also *BHP v Schultz*, above, 466–467 [171] (Kirby J: "Although the language of the NSW Cross-vesting Act is stated in the broadest terms, and should not be glossed by court decisions".

[46] *BHP v Schultz*, above, 421 [14]. In practice, Australian courts have, it is submitted, helpfully provided guidance to litigants and judges in later cases by formulating (non-exhaustive) lists of factors to be taken into account in particular cases (see, e.g., *Irwin v Queensland* [2011] VSC 291, [14(l)]; *Lend Lease Property Management and Construction Pty Limited v National Fire Solutions Pty Ltd* [2011] NSWSC 739, [13]).

[47] See, e.g., *Freier v Australian Postal Corporation* [2012] NSWSC 46, [4].

[48] Cf. *Oceanic Sun Line Special Shipping Co Inc v Fay* (1988) 165 CLR 197, 250–251, 254–255 (Deane J); *James Hardie Industries Pty Ltd v Grigor* (1998) 45 NSWLR 20, 39–40 (Spigelman CJ), 43 (Mason P); *Lubbe v Cape plc* [2000] 1 WLR 1545, 1561, 1566–1567 (Lord Hope) focussing on the private interests of the parties and the ends of justice in the case which is before the court. In *James Hardies Industries Pty Ltd v Barry*, above, 379 [93] referred to these materials and suggested ([94]) that "[t]his approach to *Spiliada* fits comfortably with the more recent case law applying and developing *Bankinvest*". That statement may, however, need to be reconsidered in light of the broader view apparently taken by the

28. Aside from current differences in the wording, and possible application, of the tests applied, there exist more fundamental procedural differences between the Cross-Vesting Acts, on the one hand, and the Trans-Tasman Act and the Service and Execution of Process Act, on the other. Most significantly, of course, an order transferring proceedings from one court to another is quite different in character from an order staying proceedings, leaving the claimant with the choice between letting his claim rest and pursuing proceedings in another forum (most likely but not inevitably, the more appropriate forum).[49]

29. In this connection, s. 11(3) of the Cross-Vesting Acts provides that:

    "Where a proceeding is transferred or removed to a court (in this subsection referred to as the transferee court) from another court (in this subsection referred to as the transferor court), the transferee court shall deal with the proceeding as if, subject to any order of the transferee court, the steps that had been taken for the purposes of the proceeding in the transferor court (including the making of an order), or similar steps, had been taken in the transferee court."

    It will be obvious, therefore, that the key difference as between an order for transfer and an order staying proceedings is that the former order has a direct impact on the transferring court in requiring it to accept and accommodate proceedings. For this reason, a modified test, which requires account to be taken of the consequences of transfer, not only for the parties but also the transferee court, and the administration of justice, may be thought to be desirable.

30. Another difference between the Cross-Vesting Acts regime, and the other regimes discussed here, concerns the procedural and evidential onus. Under s. 5(7) of the Cross-Vesting Acts, a court may transfer a proceeding on the application of a party, of its own motion or on the application of the Attorney-General of the Commonwealth, a State or Territory. It has been said that the consequence of this feature is that the applicant for a transfer does not carry the onus of proving that an order should be made.[50] By contrast under s. 19 of the Trans-Tasman Act, the defendant must make an application within the prescribed time, and would (consistently with the approach to *forum conveniens* applications at common law) have the burden

High Court in *Schultz* (above, text to n. 46). Nevertheless, the objectives of the Cross-Vesting Acts suggest that any wider public interest should be a pan-Australian interest rather than the interests of a single State or Territory (e.g. in affording swifter justice to its own residents by removing cases involving the residents of other States).

[49] See, in this connection, the differences of opinion between the members of the ALRC as to whether the option to transfer proceedings, in addition to the power to stay, should be included in what became the Service and Execution of Process Act 1992 (Cth) (Law Reform Commission, *Service and Execution of Process* (Report No. 40, 1987), pp. 91–95).

[50] *Bankinvest v Seabrook*, above, 727 (Rogers AJA); *BHP v Schultz*, above, 437 [71] (Gummow J).

of persuading the court of the existence of a "more appropriate" forum.[51] Nevertheless, the significance of this difference should not be overstated. In the large majority of cases under the Cross-Vesting Acts, the application will be made by a defendant and, as Mason P noted in *James Hardie & Co v Barry*, it is somewhat elusive to speak of a lack of onus in the context of a contested court application and the question of onus will seldom if ever be determinative at the end of the day.[52]

31. Two other differences between the Cross-Vesting Acts and the Trans-Tasman Acts, one procedural and one going to the substance of the test may be noted.

32. First, it has already been noted that the Cross-Vesting Acts contain restrictions on the right of an unsuccessful party to appeal against a decision to transfer, or not to transfer.[53] There is no such restriction in the Trans-Tasman Act: general restrictions on rights of appeal will apply.

33. Secondly, and importantly from a commercial perspective, the Cross-Vesting Acts do not contain a provision corresponding to that in s. 20 of the Trans-Tasman Act and giving effect to an exclusive choice of court agreement in favour of another Australian court. In consequence, agreements of this kind have been seen as only one factor (albeit sometimes a decisive factor) in deciding in which forum the "interests of justice" may best be served. In a Queensland Supreme Court decision, *World Firefighters Games Brisbane v World Firefighters Games Western Australia*, Philippides J rejected the submission that the common law approach to exclusive jurisdiction clauses (exhibiting a "strong bias" in favour of giving effect to them[54]) should be followed under the Cross-Vesting Acts: an exclusive jurisdiction clause was a "relevant consideration, on the basis that the 'interests of justice' require that due acknowledgment be accorded to such a clause as representing the bargain between the parties and that proper regard be given to the need to hold parties to their bargain", but "[t]he weight to be given to such clauses will vary depending on the other surrounding and countervailing circumstances".[55]

[51] *Spiliada Maritime v Cansulex*, above, 476 (Lord Goff); *Voth v Manildra*, above, 556 (Mason CJ, Deane, Dawson and Toohey JJ). A different approach prevails in England in cases where the claimant had sought to serve the initiating process (*Spiliada*, at 480). The same distinction was drawn by the majority in *Voth* (at 564), but is now relevant only in those Australian jurisdictions where prior leave to serve out is required (*Agar v Hyde* (2000) 201 CLR 552; *Nygh's Conflict of Laws in Australia*, pp. 36–37). In other cases, the burden of demonstrating that the Australian forum is "clearly inappropriate" lies on the defendant.

[52] *James Hardie & Co v Barry*, above, [100].

[53] See above, n. [10], footnote 18.

[54] *Huddart Parker Ltd v The Ship "Mill Hill"* (1950) 81 CLR 502, 509 (Dixon J); *Akai Pty Ltd v Peoples Insurance Ltd* (1996) 118 CLR 418, 428 (Dawson and McHugh J), 445 (Toohey, Gaudron and Gummow J).

[55] [2001] QSC 164; (2001) 161 FLR 355, [38]. See also *River Gum Homes Pty Ltd v Meridian Pty Ltd* [2010] QCA 293, [20].

34. By contrast, in *Slater & Gordon Ltd v Porteous*, in the Supreme Court of Victoria, Whelan J considered the existence of an exclusive choice of court agreement to be an "overwhelming factor".[56]

35. Neither the divergence in approach between Australian jurisdictions, nor the lack of clear criteria for upholding the parties' choice of court agreement, contribute to legal and commercial certainty. Despite the apparent view of Philippides J and others to the contrary, it seems no less desirable to encourage the parties to agree in advance as to a binding method of dispute resolution in an intra-Australian case than in a Trans-Tasman or an international case.[57]

36. In conclusion, and although one may disagree with the reasoning or outcome of individual decisions, the transfer regime in the Cross-Vesting Acts would appear on the whole to have worked well. Against this background, it may be thought undesirable for significant changes to be made, in particular to the procedural aspects, in order to bring it into line with the Trans-Tasman Act and the Service and Execution of Process Act.

37. Nevertheless, with a view to encouraging greater harmony between the regimes, at least some modifications to the test to be applied could be contemplated, as follows:

    a. the residual "interests of justice" test[58] could be amended so as to introduce a reference to the concept of a "more appropriate" forum, in line with the High Court's decision in *BHP v Schultz*;[59]
    b. a non-exhaustive list of factors to be taken into account in deciding whether to transfer, modelled on that in the Trans-Tasman Act,[60] could be introduced;
    c. specific provision could be made, along the lines of s. 20 of the Trans-Tasman Act, for giving effect to exclusive choice of court agreements in favour of another Australian court.

[56] [2006] VSC 398, [39]. To the same effect, see *Asciano Services Pty Ltd v Australian Rail Track Corp Ltd* [2008] NSWSC 652, [18] (Palmer J). See also *Safe Effect Technologies Ltd v Hood Group Holdings Ltd* [2006] FCA 758. [25] (Besanko J); *Re Huntingdale Village Pty Ltd* [2009] FCA 1323, [23] (Gordon J); *PaperlinX Australia Pty Ltd v Canty* [2011] VSC 127, [25–28] (Habersberger J).

[57] *World Firefighters*, above, [14], referring to *Aldred v Australian Building Industries Pty Ltd* (1987) 48 NTR 59 at 64, 65; *Nilsen Electric (WA) Pty Ltd v Jovista Pty Ltd* (unreported Byrne J, SupCt Vic, 8 March 1995); P Nygh, Conflicts of Laws in Australia (6th ed, 1995), p. 110; R Garnett (1998) UNSW Law Jo 1, 22.

[58] ss. 5(1)(b)(iii), 5(2)(b)(iii), 5(3)(b)(iii), 5(4)(b)(iii), 5(5)(b)(ii), 5(6)(b)(ii).

[59] E.g. "it is otherwise more appropriate in the interests of justice that the relevant proceeding be determined by the Supreme Court of another State or Territory". See *BHP v Schultz*, above, 421 [14] (Gleeson CJ, McHugh and Heydon JJ) ("It is both necessary and sufficient that, in the interests of justice, the second court is more appropriate.").

[60] s. 19(2).

Q3. Do you consider it desirable to make any amendments to the Commonwealth and State Cross-Vesting Acts so as to bring their provisions into line (or more in line) with those in Part 3 of the Trans-Tasman Act? Please identify your reasons for supporting or opposing this reform measure, and identify any specific amendments which you consider to be appropriate.

Q4. Do you have any other comments on the matters discussed in this paper, or specific reforms to the relevant parts of the Cross-Vesting Acts, the Service and Execution of Process Act or the Trans-Tasman Act that you would propose?

Annex

Extract from the Trans-Tasman Proceedings Act 2010 (as amended by the Trans-Tasman Proceedings and Other Measures Act 2011)

Part 3—Australian courts declining jurisdiction on the grounds that a New Zealand court is a more appropriate forum

Division 1—Introduction

16 Guide to this Part

This Part is about when an Australian court may stay a proceeding on the grounds that a New Zealand court is the more ~~appropriate court to determine the matters in dispute~~ [**appropriate court to determine the matters in issue**].

The Australian court may only stay the proceeding if the defendant applies for the proceeding to be stayed. The defendant must make the application within 30 working days after being served with the initiating document for the proceeding, or such shorter or longer period that the court considers appropriate.

The Australian court may only stay the proceeding if it is satisfied that a New Zealand court has jurisdiction to determine ~~all the matters in dispute~~ [**the matters in issue**] and that it is the more appropriate court to determine those matters. In determining whether the New Zealand court is the more appropriate court, the Australian court must take certain matters into account. They are set out in section 19.

However, if the parties have made an exclusive choice of court agreement that designates either an Australian court or a New Zealand court as ~~the court to determine the matters in dispute~~ [**the court to determine the matters in issue**], the Australian court's order as to whether or not to stay the proceeding must be consistent with that agreement (see section 20).

Division 2—Australian courts declining jurisdiction on the grounds that a New Zealand court is a more appropriate forum

17 Application to stay Australian proceeding on forum grounds

(1) A defendant in a civil proceeding in an Australian court may apply to the court for an order staying the proceeding on the grounds that a New Zealand court is the more appropriate court to determine the ~~matters in dispute~~ [**matters in issue**].

(2) The application must be made within:

- (a) 30 working days of the Australian court after the day on which the defendant was served with the initiating document for the proceeding; or
- (b) if, before or after the end of that period, the plaintiff or defendant applies to the Australian court for a shorter or longer period—any shorter or longer period the Australian court considers appropriate.

18 Hearing on the application

(1) The Australian court may determine the defendant's application under section 17 without a hearing.

(2) However, the Australian court must determine the defendant's application with a hearing if any of the following requests the court to do so:

- (a) the plaintiff;
- (b) the defendant;
- (c) any other person who is required or permitted, by the regulations or the Australian court's procedural rules, to be served with the defendant's application.

(3) The request must be made within:

- (a) 10 working days of the Australian court after the day the defendant made the application; or
- (b) if, before or after the end of that period, a person referred to in subsection (2) applies to the Australian court for a shorter or longer period—any shorter or longer period the Australian court considers appropriate.

(4) The defendant and the defendant's lawyer may appear remotely in a hearing in the Australian court about the application for an order to stay the proceeding if:

- (a) the defendant was served, or purportedly served, with the initiating document for the proceeding in New Zealand under section 9; and

(b) within the period (if any) prescribed by the regulations, the defendant made a request to the Australian court for that remote appearance; and
(c) a remote appearance medium is, or can reasonably be made, available.
This subsection applies despite Subdivisions A and B of Part 6, but is subject to the rest of Part 6.

> Note
> Ordinarily, for a person to appear remotely from New Zealand in a proceeding in an Australian court, the person needs the leave of the Australian court (see sections 48 and 50).

19 Order of stay of proceeding

(1) On application under section 17, the Australian court may, by order, stay the proceeding if it is satisfied that a New Zealand court:

(a) has jurisdiction to determine ~~all the matters in dispute~~ [**the matters in issue**] between the parties to the proceeding; and
(b) is the more appropriate court to determine those matters.

(2) In determining whether a New Zealand court is the more appropriate court to determine those matters, the Australian court must take into account the following matters:

(a) the places of residence of the parties or, if a party is not an individual, its principal place of business;
(b) the places of residence of the witnesses likely to be called in the proceeding;
(c) the place where the subject matter of the proceeding is situated;
(d) any agreement between the parties about the court or place in which those matters should be determined or the proceeding should be commenced (other than an exclusive choice of court agreement to which subsection 20(1) applies);
(e) the law that it would be most appropriate to apply in the proceeding;
(f) whether a related or similar proceeding has been commenced against the defendant or another person in a court in New Zealand;
(g) the financial circumstances of the parties, so far as the Australian court is aware of them;
(h) any matter that is prescribed by the regulations;

(i) any other matter that the Australian court considers relevant; and must not take into account the fact that the proceeding was commenced in Australia.

(3) An order under subsection (1) may be made subject to any conditions the Australian court considers are appropriate in order to facilitate, without delay or undue expense, the determination of ~~all the matters in dispute~~ [**the matters in issue**] between the parties to the proceeding.

20 Exclusive choice of court agreements

(1) On application under section 17 (and despite section 19), the Australian court:

(a) must, by order, stay the proceeding, if satisfied that an exclusive choice of court agreement designates a New Zealand court as the court to determine the ~~matters in dispute~~ [**matters in issue**]; and
(b) must not, by order, stay the proceeding, if satisfied that an exclusive choice of court agreement designates an Australian court as the court to determine those matters.

(2) ~~However, subsection (1)~~ [**Paragraph (1(a)**] does not apply to an exclusive choice of court agreement if the Australian court is satisfied that:

(a) it is null and void under New Zealand law (including the rules of private international law); or
(b) a party to it lacked the capacity to conclude it under Australian law; or
(c) giving effect to it would lead to a manifest injustice or would be manifestly contrary to Australian public policy; or
(d) for exceptional reasons beyond the control of the parties to it, it cannot reasonably be performed; or
(e) the court designated by it as the court to determine the ~~matters in dispute~~ [**matters in issue**] between the parties to the proceeding has decided not to determine those matters.

[**(2A) Paragraph (1)(b) does not apply to an exclusive choice of court agreement if the Australian court is satisfied that it is null and void under Australian law (including the rules of private international law).**]

(3) ***Exclusive choice of court agreement***, in relation to ~~matters in dispute~~ [**matters in issue**] between parties to a proceeding, means a written agreement between those parties that:

(a) designates the courts, or a specified court or courts, of a specified country, to the exclusion of any other courts, as the court or courts to determine disputes between those parties that are or include those matters; and
(b) is not an agreement the parties to which are or include an individual acting primarily for personal, family, or household purposes; and
(c) is not a contract of employment.

21 How this Part affects powers of the court to stay proceeding

(1) An Australian court cannot stay a civil proceeding on forum grounds connected with New Zealand otherwise than in accordance with this Part.

(2) However, this Part does not affect any power of the Australian court to stay the proceeding on any other grounds.

22 No restraint of proceedings

(1) An Australian court must not restrain a person from commencing a civil proceeding in a New Zealand court on the grounds that the New Zealand court is not the appropriate forum for the proceeding.

(2) Also, an Australian court must not restrain a party to a civil proceeding before a New Zealand court from taking a step in that proceeding on the grounds that the New Zealand court is not the appropriate forum for the proceeding.

23 Suspension of limitation periods

(1) This section applies if:

- (a) a claim is made in a civil proceeding (the ***NZ proceeding***) in a New Zealand court that is later stayed by an order of the New Zealand court made under the NZ Act on the grounds that an Australian court is the more appropriate court; and
- (b) the claim is to be made again in a civil proceeding (the ***Australian proceeding***) in an Australian court after the staying of (and, if applicable, before any deadline stated in the condition of that order staying) the New Zealand proceeding.

(2) For the purposes of every applicable limitation period or defence under Australian law, the Australian proceeding is to be treated as commencing at the time the New Zealand proceeding commenced.

INDEX

All references to case law, policy documents, official publications and legislation refer to Australian items unless otherwise indicated.

www.ingramcontent.com/pod-product-compliance
Lightning Source LLC
LaVergne TN
LVHW052243200926
848481LV00002B/251